# HESPERUS

OR

# *Forty-Five Dog-Post-Days*

## A BIOGRAPHY

FROM THE GERMAN OF

*JEAN PAUL FRIEDRICH RICHTER*

TRANSLATED BY

CHARLES T. BROOKS

"The Earth is the *cul-de-sac* in the great city of God, — the camera obscura full of inverted and contracted images from a fairer world, — the coast of God's creation, — a vaporous halo around a better sun, — the numerator to a still invisible denominator, — in fact, it is almost nothing at all."

*Selections from the Papers of the Devil.*

IN TWO VOLUMES.

VOL. II.

BOSTON:
TICKNOR AND FIELDS.
1865.

UNIVERSITY PRESS:
WELCH, BIGELOW, AND COMPANY,
CAMBRIDGE.

# CONTENTS OF VOL. II.

## 25. DOG-POST-DAY.



## 26. DOG-POST-DAY.



## 27. DOG-POST-DAY.



## 28. DOG-POST-DAY.



## 29. DOG-POST-DAY.

## 30. DOG-POST-DAY.



## 31. DOG-POST-DAY.



## 32. DOG-POST-DAY.



## 33. DOG-POST-DAY.



## 34. DOG-POST-DAY.



## 35. DOG-POST-DAY.



## 36. DOG-POST-DAY.



## 37. DOG-POST-DAY.

## 38. DOG-POST-DAY.



## 39. DOG-POST-DAY.



## 40. DOG-POST-DAY.



## 41. DOG-POST-DAY.



## 42. DOG-POST-DAY.



## 43. DOG-POST-DAY.



## 44. DOG-POST-DAY.



## 45. OR LAST CHAPTER.



---

## APPENDIX.

# HESPERUS,

OR

# 45 DOG-POST-DAYS.

## 25. DOG-POST-DAY.

FEIGNED AND REAL SWOONS OF CLOTILDA. — JULIUS. — EMANUEL'S LETTER CONCERNING GOD.

OOD, beautiful sex! Sometimes, when I see a diamond heart hanging above thy warm one, I ask: Is it for some such reason as *this* thou wearest a copied heart on thy bosom, in order to indicate to Love, Fate, and Slander a common mark for their different arrows, as the poor soldier who is shot kneeling points out to the balls of his comrades, by a heart cut out of paper, the place of the beating one?

— When this chapter is ended, the reader will no longer ask me, why I begin it thus. . . .

Once Victor came back from a day's walk, when Marie ran breathless to meet him with a letter from Matthieu. It contained the question whether he would not accompany him and his sister to-day to Kussewitz via St. Luna. Marie's running had arisen merely from a rich messenger's-fee and gratuity on the part of Mat, who often treated poor people at once with generosity and with persiflage, just as he thought his sister at once amiable and absurd. To people who knew him, he therefore appeared comic when he must have been serious. But Victor said "No" to the request for his company; which was very well, for in fact the two had already started. I cannot determine whether it was after two or after three days that they came back, the sister with the coldest face towards him and the brother with the warmest. This double temperature could not be wholly explained, but only about half, on the ground of discoveries which the couple might have made at Tostato's and Count O.'s concerning his disguise and his shop-drama. Heretofore Joachime's anger had always been a consequence of his: now it was the reverse; but this vexed him exceedingly.

Some days after he was standing with the Princess and Joachime in a window of the Ministerial *Louvre*. The conversation was lively enough; the Princess counted over the shops in the market, Joachime was following with her eye the swift zigzag of a swallow, Victor was standing secretly on one leg (the other he set, only apparently and without resting on it, on the floor), to try how long he could hold out. All at once the Princess said, "Holy Mary! how can one carry round a poor child shut up so in a box!" They all peered out into the street. Victor took the liberty to remark that the poor child was "made of wax." A woman was carrying a little glass case hanging before her, wherein there slept a swaddled waxen angel; she begged, like the rest, as if for this child, and the little one supported her better than if it had been alive. The Princess called up the new apparition. The woman came in trembling with her mummy-chest, and drew back the little curtain.

The Princess bent an artistically enchanted eye on the sweet slumbering form, which (like its wax material) seemed to have been born of flowers and reared in spring-times. All beauty penetrated deeply into her heart; hence she loved Clotilda so exceedingly and many Germans so little. Joachime was fond of only *one* child and *one* beauty, — and each was *herself*. Victor said, "This waxen mimic and copy of life had always made him sad, and that he could not even see his own wax counterfeit in St. Luna without shuddering."

"Does n't it stand in a frock-coat at the window of the parsonage?" asked Joachime, becoming much more pleasant.

"Is n't it true," he asked in return, "that you thought, some days ago, it was I myself?" He guessed from her look her former error, which perhaps had contributed to excite her against him.

The father confessor of the Princess now came up and added, — after his custom of being complimentary, — that, in order to save him the trouble of a sitting, he would draw him the next time merely from his wax image. The Pater was well known to be a good draughtsman.

I let circumstances which are less important lie unrelated, and gayly proceed.

It was as early as March, when the higher classes, on account of their sedentary winter sleep, are more full-blooded than cold-blooded, — any one who does not understand the matter takes for granted that their overflow of blood proceeds more from their sucking that of others, — when sicknesses leave their visiting-cards in the form of recipes with the whole court, — when the eyes of the Princess, the *embonpoint* of the princely ether, and the gouty hands of the court apothecary continued the storms of winter; it was even then, I say, that Clotilda also experienced every day more intensely the influence of the winter, and of her double withdrawal from relaxations and of her intercourse with her fancies. . . . If I must speak sincerely, I attribute little to her seclusion, but all to the necessity which propriety imposes on her of intercourse with the noble Mat, with the Schleuneses and with other cold-blooded Amphibia;* an innocent heart must, in moral frosty weather, like alabaster garden statues in the physical, when the former and the latter have soft, absorbing veins, get cracks, and break.

Thus matters stood with her on a weighty day, when he found with her little Julia. This beloved name she affixed to the child of the Senior, Flamin's landlord, in order to keep alive her sad yearning after her dead Giulia by a similarity of sound, by the relic of an echo. "This funereal tone," said Victor to himself, "is indeed to her the welcome distant roll of the hearse which shall come to take her to the friend of her youth; and her expectation of a like fate is truly the most mournful evidence of a like grief." If anything further was needed to purify his friendship from all love, it was this swift falling-off of the leaves of so fair a passion-flower; — towards the suffering, one is ashamed of the least selfishness. During the conversation, from which the jealous Julia was excluded by not understanding it, the child in a pet twitched at the servants' bell; for girls make claims to attention eight years earlier than boys. Clotilda forbade this ringing by a too late interdict; the little one, delighted that she had set in motion the chambermaid, who came hastening up, tried again to twitch at the cord. Clotilda said in French to the Doctor, "One must

* See Titan, Vol. I. p. 38. — Tr.

not give her any command too monarchically; now she will not rest till I have tried my extremest method." "Julia!" said she once more, her large eye overflowing with love; but in vain. "Well, now I am going to die!" said she, already dying away, and leaned her fair head, inhabited by a departing genius, back against the chair, and closed her pure eyes, which deserved to open again only in a heaven. — While Victor stood in silent emotion before the still-tranced one, and thought to himself: "If now she should never wake again, and thou shouldst vainly snatch her stiff hand, and her last word on this dreary earth should have been, 'Now I am going to die,'— O God! would there be any other remedy for the inconsolableness of her friend than a sword and the last wound? And I should clasp with a cold hand her hand, and say, I go with thee!" As he thought thus, and as the little one, weeping, lifted the sinking right hand, her countenance really grew paler, and the left hand glided down from her lap; — here was that sword's sharp edge drawn across his heart; — but soon she opened her wandering eyes again, coming out of the drowsiness of the death-sleep to herself and to a sense of shame. She excused the transient swoon with the remark, "I have done as that player * did with the urn of his child: I imagined myself in the place of my Giulia in her last moments, but a little too successfully."

He was just on the point of drawing up medical pastoral letters against this consuming enthusiasm, — so much does an unhappy love translate every female heart from the *major* tone into the *minor*, even that of a Clotilda,

* The Greek Polus (in Aulus Gellius, Book VII. Chap. V.), who, having to enact Electra with the bones of Orestes, took instead the ashes of his own son, who had just died, and uttered *real* sorrow. — Tr.

whose forehead had a manly elevation, and whose chin expressed almost more courage than beauty,—when quite other pastoral letters arrived. The bearer of them was Victor's *happier* friend Agatha. Send back with thy laugh, thou untroubled one, life into two hearts on which death has flung his flying cloud-shadows! She fell confidingly into two friendly arms; but towards her doctor brother, who so long, instead of his whole person, had let only his hand, i. e. his handwriting, go to St. Luna, she was still shy. But this fault of his, when he had avoided a house one quarter of a year *for* reasons, of absenting himself from it another quarter of a year *without* reason, —this fault I cannot wholly condemn, because I—have it myself. She could not satisfy her eyes with looking at him; her blooming country face showed him, instead of his present passion-week of grief, a red chalk drawing of his and her vanished days of joy in the parsonage-garden. He solemnly promised her to be her Easter guest with her brother, and, instead of heads and windows, to break nothing but eggs; he rested not till he was the same old Sebastian and she the same old Agatha again. As she delivered to the two court-people, smiling only from love, the long duodecimo history of the village and her father, not at all as a compiler or epitomist, or in a mutilated edition, but in volumes as long as her heel-ligaments; then did Clotilda and Victor feel how soothing to them was this descent from the glittering, sharp court-glaciers into the soft vales of the middling stations of life, and they both yearned to exchange polished hearts for warm ones. Among men and Borsdorf apples the best are not the smooth ones, but the rough ones that have some warts. This longing for sincere souls, too, it may well have been which wrung from Clotilda the assertion, that there were mismatches only between souls, not between ranks. Hence came her growing love for this Agatha, who bloomed outside of the forcing-box of a genealogical tree only in the common pasture, — a love which the reader and I in the first volume, from sharp-sightedness, explained as the hiding-cloak of another love toward Flamin, and which ought to wean us both from bringing a reproach upon a heroine, who in the sequel continually refutes it.

The superscription of the thick letter-packet which Agatha brought was in the handwriting of Emanuel, whom Clotilda got to superscribe everything to the parson's wife, in order to save her stepmother the trouble of — closing her letters. Madame Le Baut had learned this *insight* into documents, this Socratic art of midwifery, in the ministry, which possesses the right of search into the letters of all subjects, because it can hold them either as infected or arrested, if it please. While the step-daughter, in the adjoining chamber, broke open the outer packet, because from its thickness she prophesied an enclosed communication for the Doctor: the latter breathed, by chance — or design, for he had, this long time, established everywhere his deciphering offices of women, in the narrowest corner, in every fold of a dress, in the marks of books which had been read, — he breathed, I said, accidentally on the window-panes, on which one can then at once read what a warm finger has written thereon. There came out, after the involuntary breathing, nothing but French initial S's, sketched with the finger-nail. "S!" thought he, "that is singular; that is the beginning of my own name."

His conjectures were interrupted by Clotilda's returning with a face blissfully cleared of all its clouds, and, handing to the thoughtful Medicus a great letter from

Emanuel. Upon the heels of this second pleasure followed, in the place of the third, a piece of news; she now disclosed to him, "that Emanuel had at last enabled her to be an obedient, though not believing patient." She had, namely, hitherto suppressed the purpose of her obedience and her spring cure, until her friend in Maienthal had secured her for some spring months a sick-chamber at the Abbess's, — the very one Giulia had had, — that the fanning of spring might there lift her drooping pinions, the incense of flowers heal her torn heart, and the great friend enable *his* great friend to stand upright.

Victor slipped away hastily, not only from hunger and thirst after what he held in his hand, but because a new flood of thought broke through his old trains of ideas. "Bastian!" said Bastian to himself on the way, "I have often held thee to be stupid, but so stupid as that — no, never. It is sinful that a man, a court-medicus, a thinker, should ruminate for months, often half-evenings together, and yet not bring the matter out, till he hears it, now for the first time. Verily, even the 'S' on the window fits!" The reader and I will take out of his hands the thing with which he is stoning himself before our faces; for he throws at both of us as well, because we failed to guess at anything just as much as he did. In short, the unknown happy one who makes the fair Clotilda unhappy, and for whom she sighs out her dumb, shy soul, and who for most of her charms has no eye at all, is the blind— Julius in Maienthal. Hence her desire to go thither.

I should like to fill a folio volume with the proofs of this: Victor counted them off on his five fingers. On his thumb he said, "For Julius's sake she seeks little Julia; so, too, is it with Giulia." At the forefinger he said, "The French initial *I* looks like an *S* without the cross-stroke." At the middle finger, "Minerva has furnished him, indeed, not merely the flute, but also Minerva's fair face, and in this blind Cupid's-face Clotilda could lose herself without blushing; even from love for his friend Emanuel, she might have loved him." At the ring-finger, "Hence her justification of mis-matches, since his citizenly ring-finger is to be joined to her noble one." At the little finger, "By Heaven! all this proves not the least."

For now, for the first time, all the proofs came upon him in a flood: in the first volume of this book there came often an unknown angel to Julius and said: "Be good, I will hover round thee, I will guard thy veiled soul, — I go back into heaven." —

Secondly, this angel once gave Julius a paper, and said, "Conceal it, and after a year, when the birches grow green in the temple, let Clotilda read it to thee; I take my flight, and thou wilt not hear me sooner than a year hence." — —

All this fitted Clotilda as if it were moulded on her: she could never unfold to the blind one her dying heart, — she was going just now to Maienthal (how long is it still to Whitsuntide?) to read to him herself the leaf which she had handed to him in the character and mask of an angel, — finally, she was going off precisely then to St. Luna; — — in short, everything hits to a hair.

If the Biographer might venture to put in a word, it would be this: The Mining-Superintendent, the Biographer, for his part, believes it all with great pleasure; but as to Clotilda, who hitherto has come forth whitely radiant from every pitchy cloud, and on whom, as on the sun, one has so often confounded *clouds* with *sun-spots*, he cannot blame her, until she herself sets the example.

Victor, as I myself did in the first edition, has even forgotten many proofs of Clotilda's love for Julius: e. g. her warm interest in his blindness, and her desire of his recovery (in her letter to Emanuel), Flamin's obsolete jealousy in Maienthal, even the rapture with which, in the playhouse, she calls the vale an Eden, and rejects the Lethe.

Victor tore open the packet, and two leaves fell out of a large sheet. One of the notes and the large sheet were from Emanuel, the other from his Lordship. He studied the last, written in double cipher, first; it was as follows:—

"I come in autumn, when the *apples* ripen, — the Trinity [his Lordship means the Prince's three sons] is found; but the fourth Person [the fourth, merry son] is wanting. — Flee from the Palace of the Empress of all the Russias [with this cipher the two had concerted to designate the Minister Schleunes], but the grand duchess [Joachime] avoid still more: she wants no heart, but a princely hat. — In Rome [he means Agnola] beware of the crucifix, out of which a stiletto springs! Think of the *Island*, ere thou makest a misstep."

Victor was astonished at first at the accidental appropriateness of these prohibitions; but when he bethought himself that he would have given them to him even on the Island, if they had not referred to his more recent circumstances, then he was still more astonished at the channels through which the espionage-despatches of his present relations might have reached his father, — (as if my correspondent and spy might not have been the father's also!) — and most of all at the warning against Joachime. "Oh! if she were false to me!" he said, sighing, and would not complete the dark picture nor the sigh. —— But he drove both away by the little leaf from Emanuel, which read thus: —

"My Son: —

"The dawn of the new year shone on my face across the snow, as I placed before me the paper [Emanuel's second immediately following letter], upon which I sought to impress for the last time my soul with all its images reaching out beyond this globe. But the flames of my soul dart even to the body, and singe the frail thread of life; I was obliged often to turn away my too easily bleeding breast from the paper and from my rapture.

"I have, my son, written to thee with my blood. — Julius has now the thought of God. — The spring glows under the snow, and will soon lift itself up out of the green, and bloom even to the clouds. — My daughter [Clotilda] takes spring by the hand and comes to me, — let her take my son with the other hand, and lay him on my breast, wherein is a failing breath and an everlasting heart. . . . O how melodiously sound around me the evening bells of life! — Ay, when thou and thy Clotilda and our Julius, when we all, we who love each other, stand together, when I hear your voices, then shall I look to Heaven and say, The evening bells of life sound around me too mournfully; I shall for ecstasy die still earlier than the eve of the longest day, and ere my sainted father has appeared to me.

"Emanuel."

* * * * * *

Dear Emanuel, that, alas! thou wilt do! The heaven of joy presses downward to thy lips, and amidst breezes, amidst tones, amidst kisses, it drinks up thy flickering breath; for the earthly body which will only *graze*, not *pluck*, digests only *lowly* joys, and chills under the beam of a higher sun! —

With emotion I draw aside from Victor's distracted, irrecognizable face the veil which covers his sorrows. Let us look upon thee, disconsolate man, who art going to meet a spring where thy heart is to lose everything: Emanuel by death, Clotilda by love, Flamin by jealousy, even Joachime by suspicion! Let us look upon thee, impoverished one; I know why thy eye is still dry, and why thou sayst brokenly and with a shake of the head, "No, my dear Emanuel, I shall not come, for indeed I cannot." — What ate most deeply into thy heart was, that thy true Emanuel should be the very one who still believed thou wert loved by his friend. — An undeveloped sorrow is without tears or signs; but when man through fancy draws out of his own bosom a heart full of confluent wounds, and counts the gashes, and then forgets that it is his own, then does he weep sympathetically at that which beats so painfully in his hands, and then he bethinks himself and weeps still more. Victor would fain release as it were by warming his stiff soul from frozen tears, and went to the balcony window and pictured to himself, while the suppressed evening-glow of March burned out of the clouds over the hills of Maienthal, Clotilda's marriage to Julius. — O, in order to make himself right sad, he drew a spring day over the vale, the genius of love flung open, above the nuptial altar, the blue heaven, and bore the sun as bridal torch without cloud-smoke through the pure immensity. — There walked, on that day, Emanuel transfigured, Julius blind, but blissful, Clotilda blushing and long since well again, and every one was happy. Only one unhappy one he saw there standing among the flowers, namely, himself; he saw there, how this afflicted one, chary of words for sorrow, joyous from virtue, more familiar and confidential with the bride from coldness, went round among the rest, so unknown, properly so superfluous; how the guiltless pair, with every sign of love, reckoned up before him all that he had lost, or indeed concealed those signs from forbearance, because they guessed his grief; — this thought darted at him like a blaze; — and how at last, as the heavy-laden past brought all his slain hopes and his withered wishes before him, he turned round, when the beloved pair went from him to the altar and to the eternal covenant, how he turned round inconsolably toward the still, empty fields, to weep infinitely, and how he then remained so alone and dark in the fair region, and said to himself: "In thee, no human being takes an interest to-day, — none presses thy hand, and says, 'Victor, why weepest thou so?' — Oh! this heart is as full of unspeakable love as any other, but it fades unloved and unknown, and its dying and its weeping disturb no one. Nevertheless, nevertheless, O Julius! O Clotilda! I wish you eternal happiness, and only contented days." . . . Then he could do no more; he pressed his eyes to his hands and to the window-frame, and gave free play to them, and thought of nothing more; the sorrow, which, like a rattlesnake, had watched with distended jaws him and his charmed and writhing approaches, now seized and swallowed him and crushed him to pieces. . . .

Soft hearts, ye torment yourselves as much on this flinty earth as hard ones do *others*, — the spark which only makes a burn, ye swing round till it becomes a wheel of fire, and under the blossoms a sharp leaf becomes to you a thorn! . . . But why, I say to myself, dost thou show that of thy friend and open afresh remote similar wounds in men who have been healed? — O, answer for me, ye who resemble him, could you do without a single tear? And since the woes of fantasy are to be reckoned among the joys of fantasy, — a moist eye and a heavily drawn breath are the least with which we buy a fair hour. . . .

— Pride — the best counterpoise to effeminate tears — wiped away my hero's, and said to him: "Thou art worth as much as they who are more fortunate; and if unhappy love has hitherto made thee bad, how good might not a happy love make thee!" There was stillness in and around him; night stood in heaven; he read Emanuel's letter.

"MY HORION!

"Within a few hours Time has reversed its hour-glass, and now the sands of a new year are trickling down. — Uranus strikes for our little earth the centuries, the sun strikes the years, the moon the months; and on this concert clock, constructed out of worlds, human beings come forth as images, that utter cries and tones of joy, when it strikes.

"I too come out gladly under the fair new-year's dawn, which gleams through all the clouds, and flames up the high hemisphere of heaven. In a year I shall look into the sun from another world: O how my heart, for this last time, under the earthly cloud, overflows with love toward the Father of this fair earth, toward his children and my brothers and sisters, toward this flowery cradle, wherein we only once awake, and amidst its rocking in the sun only once fall asleep!

"I shall never live to see another summer-day, therefore will I describe the fairest one, on which, with thy Julius * I for the first time tremblingly penetrated through

* Julius did not become blind till his twelfth year, and had therefore conceptions of the face.

luminous clouds, and through harmonies, and fell down with him before a thundering throne, and said to him, 'Overhead, in the immeasurable cloud which they call eternity, He dwells, who has made us and loves us.' This day will I to-day repeat in my soul; and never, too, may it be extinguished in my Julius or my Horion!

"I have often said to my Julius, 'I have not yet given thee the greatest thought of man, which bows down his soul and yet erects it again forever; but I will name it to thee on the day when thy spirit and mine are the purest, or when I die.' Hence he often begged me, when *his angel* had been with him, or when the flute and the awe-inspiring night or a tempest had exalted him, 'Name to me, Emanuel, the greatest thought of man!'

"It was a sweet July evening, when my beloved one lay on my bosom, weeping, under the birch-tree on the mountain, and said: 'Tell me why I weep so very much this evening? Dost thou, then, never do it, Emanuel? But there fall also warm drops from the clouds on my cheeks.' I answered: 'There are little warm clouds that float round in heaven, and shake out a few dew-drops; but does not the angel walk up and down in thy soul? For thou stretchest out thy hand to touch him.' Julius said: 'Yes, he stands before my thoughts; but it was only thou that I wanted to touch: for the angel indeed is gone from the earth, and I long right earnestly for his voice. Dreamy shapes undulate into each other within me, but they have no such bright colors as in sleep,— gracious, smiling faces look upon me, and come up to me with outspread, shadowy arms, and beckon to my soul, and melt away, ere I can press them to my heart.* My

* See the blind girl's song in Bulwer's "Last Days of Pompeii." — Tr.

Emanuel, is not thy face, then, one among my shadowy forms?' Here he pressed his wet face glowingly to mine, which seemed to hover before him in shadowy outline; a cloud sprinkled the consecrating water of heaven upon our embrace, and I said: 'We are softened so to-day only by that which encircles us, and which I now see.'—He answered: 'O, tell me what thou seest, and leave not off till the sun is gone down.'

"My heart swam in love and trembled in rapture at my words: 'Beloved, the earth is to-day so beautiful! that indeed makes man more tender: heaven rests with a caress and kiss of love on the earth, as a father on a mother and her children,—the flowers and beating hearts fall into the embrace and nestle around the mother. The twig gently rocks its singer up and down, the flower cradles its bee, the leaf its fly and its drop of honey: in the open flower-cups hang the warm tears, into which the clouds dissolve themselves, as if in eyes, and my flower-beds bear the rainbow, which is built up on them, without sinking. The woods lie nursing themselves at the breast of heaven, and having drunken deeply of the clouds, all summits stand fixed in silent bliss. A zephyr, not stronger than a warm sigh of love, breathes along by our cheeks among the steaming corn-blossoms, and lifts clouds of seed-dust, and one little breeze after another plays its antics with the flying harvests of the lands; but it lays them at our feet when it has done playing. O beloved, when all is love, all harmony, all loves and is loved, all meadows *one* intoxicating blossom-chalice, then indeed in man also does the lofty spirit stretch out its arms, and long to embrace with them a spirit, and then, when it folds its arms only around shadows, then it grows very sad for infinite, inexpressible longing after love.'

"'Emanuel, I am sad too,' said my Julius.

"'Lo, the sun goes down, the earth veils itself: let me still see all and tell it to thee. Now a white dove flies dazzling, like a great snow-flake, across the deep blue. . . . Now she sails round the gold-spark of the lightning-rod, as if around a glistening star hung out in the day-sky. O, how she floats and floats, and sinks and vanishes in the tall flowers of the churchyard! . . . Julius, didst thou feel nothing, while I spoke? Ah, the white dove was perhaps thy angel, and therefore thy heart melted when he was so near thee to-day. The dove does not fly up, but clouds of dew, with a silver border, like fragments torn from summer-nights, glide across the church-yard, and overspread the blooming graves with colored shadows. . . . Now, one such shadow falling from heaven swims towards us and bathes our mountain. Melt, melt, fleeting night, emblem of life, and hide not long from me the sinking sun! . . . Our little cloud moves on into the flames of the sun. . . . O thou gracious sun, looking back so softly from behind the shore of earth, thou maternal eye of the world, truly thou sheddest thy evening light from thee as warmly and slowly as trickling blood, and palest as thou sinkest, but the earth, hung up and laid upon thee in fruit-festoons and flower-chains, reddens as if new-created, and with swelling energy. . . . Hark! Julius, now the gardens resound, — the air hums, — the birds with their calls wheel across each other's tracks, — the storm-wind lifts its mighty wing, and flaps against the woods; hark! they give the sign that our good sun is departed.

"'O Julius, Julius!' said I, and embraced his breast, 'the earth is great; but the heart which rests upon it is still greater than the earth, and greater than the sun. . . . For it alone thinks the *greatest thought!*'

"Suddenly there came forth a coolness from the death-bed of the sun, as from a grave. The high sea of the air undulated, and a broad stream, in whose bed woods lay prostrate, came roaring back through the heaven along the path by which the sun had departed. The altars of Nature, the mountains, were veiled in black as at a great mourning. Man was fastened down to the earth by the mist-cloud and separated from heaven. Transparent lightnings licked at the foot of the cloud, and the thunder smote three times at the black arch. But the storm upreared itself and rent it asunder; it drove the flying ruins of the shattered prison through the blue, and flung the dismembered masses of vapor down below the sky, — and for a long time it still continued to roar alone over the open earth, through the bright and cleansed plain. . . . But above it, behind the curtain which it had torn aside, glistened the all-holiest, the starry night. —

"Like a sun, the greatest thought of man rose in heaven, — my soul was borne down when I looked toward heaven, it was lifted up when I looked upon the earth. —

"For the Infinite has sowed his name in the heavens in burning stars, but on the earth He has sowed his name in tender flowers.

"'O Julius,' said I, 'hast thou been good to-day?' He answered: 'I have done nothing but weep.'

"'Julius, kneel down and put away every evil thought, — hear my voice quiver, feel my hand tremble; — I kneel beside thee.

"'We kneel here on this little earth before immensity, before the immeasurable world floating over us, before the radiant circumference of space. Raise thy spirit and conceive what I see. Thou hearest the storm-wind which drives the clouds around the earth, — but thou hearest not the storm-wind which drives the earth around the sun, nor yet the greatest, which blows beyond the suns and carries them around a veiled All which lies with sun-flames in the abyss. — Step from the earth into the void ether, here float and see it dwindle to a flying mountain, and with six other particles of sun-dust play around the sun, — moving *mountains*, after which *hills* * flutter, whirl along before thee, and go up and down before the sunshine, — then gaze about thee in the round, flashing, high vault, built up of crystallized suns, through whose chinks looks the immeasurable night in which hangs the sparkling arch. — Thou fliest for thousands of years, but thou wilt never set foot on the last sun, nor step out into the great night. — Thou shuttest thine eyes and throwest thyself with a thought over the abyss and over the visible universe, and when thou openest them again, lo! there sweep around thee, as thoughts do around souls, new streams, surging up and down, composed of light waves of suns, of dark drops of earths, and new successions of suns stand over against each other in the east and in the west, — and the fire-wheel of a new Milky-Way revolves in the stream of time. — Ay, let an infinite hand remove me out of the whole heaven; thou lookest back and fixest thine eye on the paling, shrivelling sea of suns; at last the remote creation hovers now as nothing more than a pale, still cloudlet in the depths of night; thou imaginest thyself alone and lookest round thee and — — just as many suns and milky-ways flame up and down, and the pale cloudlet hangs still paler between them, and out around the whole dazzling abyss move nothing but pale, still cloudlets. — —

* Planets with their moons.

"'O Julius! O Julius! amidst the onward moving fire-mountains, amidst the milky-ways hurled from one abyss to another, there flutters a particle of blossom-dust made of six thousands of years and the human race, — Julius, who beholds and who cares for the fluttering particle of dust which consists of all our hearts? —

"'A star was just now cast down. Fall willingly, O star caught in the atmosphere of the earth; the stars above the earth also, as well as thyself, fall headlong into their distant graves, — the sea of worlds without shore or bottom wells up here, dries up there; the great moth, the earth, flies round the sunlight and sinks into the light and is consumed; — O Julius, who sees and sustains the fluttering particle of dust on the moth, in the midst of the fermenting, blooming, dissolving chaos? O Julius, if every moment witnesses the dissolution of a man and a world, — if time passes over the comets and treads them out like sparks, and grinds to powder the carbonized suns, — if the milky-ways dart only like returning flashes of lightning out of the great gloom, — if one procession of worlds after another is drawn down into the abyss, — if the eternal grave is never full and the eternal starry firmament is never empty: O my beloved, who then sees and sustains us little mortals made of dust? — Thou, all-gracious One, sustainest us, thou Infinite One, thou, O God, thou formest us, thou seest us, thou lovest us. — O Julius! raise thy spirit and grasp the greatest thought of man! There where Eternity is, there where Immensity is, and where night begins, there an Infinite Spirit spreads out its arms and folds them around the great falling universe of worlds and bears it and warms it. I and thou and all men, and all angels and all worms, rest on His bosom, and the roaring, beating sea of worlds and suns is an only child in his arms. He sees away through the ocean, wherein coral-trees full of earths sway to and fro, and sees the little worm that cleaves to the smallest coral, which is I, and He gives the worm the nearest drop, and a blissful heart, and a future, and an eye to look up even to Himself — yea, O God, even up to thee, even to thy heart.' —

" Inexpressibly moved, Julius said, weeping : 'Thou seest, then, O Spirit of Love, poor blind me also! — O, come into my soul, when it is alone, and it rains warm and still on my cheeks, and I weep at it and feel an inexpressible love: ah, thou good, great Spirit, it is surely Thou whom I have hitherto meant and loved! Emanuel, tell me yet more, tell me his thoughts and his beginning.'

" 'God is eternity, God is truth, God is holiness, — He has nothing, He is all, the *whole heart* conceives Him, but no *thought ;* and *we are only His thought, when He is ours.** —— All that is infinite and incomprehensible in man is his reflection; but beyond this let not thy awe-stricken thought go. Creation hangs as a veil, woven out of suns and spirits, over the infinite, and the eternities pass by before the veil, and draw it not away from the splendor which it hides.'

" Silently we went hand in hand down the mountain, we perceived not the storm-wind for the voice of our thoughts, and when we entered our cottage, Julius said: 'I shall always think the greatest thought of man, amidst the music of my flute, amidst the roar of the storm, and amidst the falling of the warm rain, and when I weep and when I embrace thee, and when I am dying!' — And thou, my beloved Horion, do so too.

"EMANUEL."

* Literally, He only thinks us, when we think Him. — TR.

* * * * * *

The petty woe of earth, the petty thoughts of earth, had now flown away from Horion's soul, and, after a devout look into the open starry heaven, he went, led by the hand of sleep, into the realm of dreams. — Let us imitate him, and come upon nothing further to-day.*

* Here ended Jean Paul's second volume. — Tr.

## 26. DOG-POST-DAY.

TERGEMINI. — ZEUSEL AND HIS TWIN-BROTHER. — THE ASCENDING PERUKE. — DETECTION OF KNAVERIES.

F I were in Covent Garden, and had wept over the tragedy, I would still stay to the epilogue, although I should have to laugh over it. Only, however, from tragedy does a cross-lane lead over to comedy, but not from the epic; in short, man can laugh after *tender*, but not after *exalting* emotion. I cannot, therefore, allow a fast reader, immediately after the twenty-fifth chapter, to begin this one. In fact, when one sees how they read a book, — namely, even five times as miserably, thoughtlessly, fragmentarily as it is written — (I speak merely of attention; knowledge is, of course, out of the question during the reading, and the author's pen cannot raise the spirits of the reader, any more than the piston can the water, beyond a certain level); how, at the best passages, they turn over two leaves at once, — now grapple two unlike chapters, and now spend four weeks in reading through a chapter which ought to have been finished in one sitting; how such classical readers often just before a visit, or during the twisting on or in fact the heating of the hair-roller, or during the combing out of the hair (which absolutely powders the sublimest chapter) how they take

that moment to read one of this last kind, or an affecting one while scolding at the whole room;—when one considers that such readers comprise most of those in Scheerau and Flachsenfingen, those female readers only excepted who know how to hit the way into all books and men, and to whom it is all one what they read or marry,— and when one actually learns by sad observation, that, if not even the reading-penny which they have to pay for the book has power enough to persuade them into the enjoyment of affecting and sublime pages, this long period will still less constrain them to it, — one must congratulate the German public, which is still nourished by works in which, as in turkey-fowls, the best part is the *white*.

As the *Vienna Magazine* is also such a turkey-cock, and I had a dream last week that my dog wrote for it, this will be a fitting place to revoke my error. The dream does not strike me as strange, — (since my bestial correspondent is likewise named *Hofmann*,*) — that this same beast was the Professor swaddled and chrysalized into the body of a dog. I certainly never should have hit upon the idea that a Professor of "practical eloquence" would in the form of a dog give the world printed things, had not once in Paris a fellow got himself sewed up with *contraband* goods in a poodle-skin, in order, thus disguised, to make his way through the gate. I might have known well enough, from the inequality of size between the two creatures, what was in the wind; † but I went so far in my crazy dream as actually to pinch and feel of the dog to probe him, when the Professor,

* Professor Hofmann as a throne-stormer, and his magazine, wherein at the beginning of the Revolution he took every free-thinker captive, are to be sure long since forgotten; but one may substitute for him any the nearest and newest German ultra.

† Literally, "What time o' day it was." — Tr.

whom I sought behind this mask, himself in person entered the door. He at once removed all confusion; I imposed on myself, however, as it were to give him satisfaction, the penalty of making the whole thing known, and of being, into the bargain, his fellow-laborer, i. e. his monthly pigeon, which hatches every month. . . . Many are actually said, therefore, to have looked in the Vienna Magazine (for in the first edition I forgot to state that I had only dreamed) for articles by me: is it possible, I ask? — —

We left our Victor in suspense under a cloud of dark conjectures: now we meet him again in the presence of an incident that confirms them all.

Whoso knows, though only by hearsay, the Apothecary Zeusel, around whom the whole occurrence revolves, knows that he is a hare's-foot.* The said foot — a hare and the Devil, though the whole skin is stripped off, still retain the foot — was delighted when a gentleman of the court got a dinner out of him and — a laugh upon him; he could not keep within the bounds of modesty, when a distinguished person made a fool of him. The noble Mat, therefore, often took away his modesty. From him he could, like the Flachsenfingeners, bear everything, from Victor nothing. I can explain it only by the fact, that Victor's satires were general and apt, and improving; but men sooner forgive lampoons than satire, slander than admonition, jests upon orthodox and aristocrats than reasonings about them.† Notwithstanding, though Zeusel was again this time the victim of practical jokes ‡

* I. e. a poltroon. — Tr.

† Hence in Athens it was allowed to ridicule the gods, but not to deny them.

‡ Literally, was *handselled* or *overhauled* (as young sailors on first crossing the line). — Tr.

and trouncings at Matthieu's hands, he could not fairly forgive him for it, but got the gout on the subject.

It was, namely, just before the first of April — many have three hundred and sixty-five first of April's every year — when the page made the apothecary an April fool.* In St. Luna three bathing and drinking visitors had already arrived, three wild young Englishmen, who announced themselves as *tergemini*, but were probably only brothers born in succession, not at once. Only their souls seemed three twins of the spirit of freedom and fraternity; they were so republican, that they did not even appear at court, and, like every Englishman, accounted us all, me and the reader and the Professor of Eloquence, as Christian slaves, and the enfranchised as turnkeys' assistants. The magic influence of a congenial heart soon drew the Regency-Councillor Flamin into their Cartesian vortex; they had hardly been there eight days, when they had held with him a club at the Chaplain's. He promised them for Easter a sight of their countryman Sebastian; and the noble Matthieu he had at the very beginning brought with him. Mat's liberty-tree was merely a satirical thorn-bush; his satires supplied the place of principles. Only a single one of the three twins, whom the very evil one with horns and buck's feet, — namely, the Satyr † — rode, could properly like the biting *Evangelist* and false *Apostle* of liberty; for in a clear, bright head every word of wit and lightning from another assumes a greater lustre, as glowworms gleam brighter in dephlogisticated gas.

When Matthieu saw the parsonage coachman and the hired lackey of the Englishmen, the bellows-blower

* Literally, "knocked him into April." — Tr.

† *Satyr* means a satyr, and *satyre*, satire. — Tr.

Zeusel, — the twin-brother of the Apothecary, — he devised something which I will presently relate. The Apothecary was notoriously obliged to be ashamed of his veritable brother, because he was a mere bellows-blower, and raised no other wind than musical, — and because, furthermore, he had bad inner ears, and, as to outer ones, none at all. Nevertheless, as respects the latter he had protected himself with a judicial certificate which stated, to his credit, that he had lost his acoustic volutes in an honorable way by a surgeon who undertook to help his difficulty of hearing. But his head was his ear. If he held a staff in contact with the speaker or his seat, or if one preached directly over his head, he heard very well. Haller relates similar examples, e. g. of a deaf person who always thrust a long stick against the pulpit as conductor and bridge of devotion. His deafness, which called him rather to the post of a highest state servant than to that of a hired servant, was the very thing which secured him the victory over the competitors, because Cato the elder — so the jolly Englishman styled himself — was pleased with the fellow's droll posture.

The noble Matthieu, whose heart had full as dark a hue as his hair and eyes, hung the three twins as bait-worms on his line, to draw the Apothecary between his arm and Flamin's to St. Luna. Zeusel went gladly, never dreaming of the misfortune that awaited him, namely, his brother, with whom he had years ago agreed, for a certain consideration, that they would absolutely not know each other in company. Besides, the bellows-blower, in his simplicity, could not at all comprehend how such a distinguished man as Zeusel could be his brother, and adored him in silence afar off; only one thing he could not endure, despite his stupid patience, namely, that the Apothecary should pretend to be the first-born. "Am not I," said he, "a quarter of an ell longer, and a quarter of an hour older than he?" He swore it was forbidden in the Bible to sell one's birthright, — and then, like all in whom a stupid patience gives out, he was no longer controllable.

The Apothecary, after his first terror at the presence of his brother, saw with pleasure that no one knew his fraternity; he proposed, therefore, to imitate the rest, and demanded of his servant-brother, as coldly as any one, something to drink. The bellows-blower, as he bowed down his head that his brother *overhead* might give his commands, surveyed with astonishment and real reverence the silver trellised-gates and shackles on the feet of his kinsman, and his hip-pendant of steel garlands of watches. Zeusel would gladly — if the page could have been trusted — have made believe to the Britons that he was deceived, and took the bending-down of the deaf man for overdone cringing before courtiers; he would then have been able to add, that *Opisthotonos* towards inferiors is a cramp of the same kind with *Emprosthotonos* * towards superiors; — but, as was said, the Devil may trust court pages!

Meanwhile the Britons hardly noticed the fool with his money-purse on his posterior, and merely wondered what he wanted there. Their republican flames blazed up together with Flamin's, and in fact in such a manner that the page would have taken them for Frenchmen and for travelling agents and circular-messengers of the French Propaganda, had he not been of the opinion

* *Emprosthotonos* is the cramp which bends men *forward*. *Opisthotonos* bends them backward.

that only a fool could have anything to do with or believe in that. Matthieu had acuteness, but no principles, — truths, but no love of truth, — sharpness of perception without feeling, — wit without purpose. What he was after to-day was, by letting fly grazing shot, to fix the Apothecary in the agonizing fear that some connection of ideas or other would lead him every moment to the subject of his present brother. Thus he incidentally with great success laid the poor hare's-foot on the rack of the "larded hare," when he contended ironically for nepotism.

"Popes and ministers," said he, "give important places, not to the first chance-comer, but to a man whom they have narrowly proved, because they have been almost brought up with him, namely, a friend by blood. They have too moral a way of thinking to let them, after their elevation, no longer know their kindred, nor do they hold the court to be a heaven where one never inquires about his fellow-trenchermen condemned to hell. Inasmuch as a minister can digest like an ostrich, one wonders that he does not also, like the ostrich, toss his eggs full of relatives into the sand under the burning sun, and trust the hatching to accident. But nothing accords less with genuine nepotism than this; nay, the very ostrich, by night and in colder places, broods in person, and only omits it where the sun broods better; so, too, the man of influence provides for his cousins only in those cases where great want of merit requires it. I confess, morality can as little command nepotism as friendships; but the merit is so much the greater, when without any moral obligation one covers, as it were, with his family-tree, half the steps of the throne." This smelting-fume and vapor of satire prepossessed the Britons in his favor, especially as the fume implied noble metals, that is to say, the highest impartiality on the part of a son whose father was minister.

While the Apothecary carved the *souper*, — Mat had begged him to act as *grand écuyer tranchant*, — his friend watched the moment when he had a great turkey-cock on the fork, to carve him in the air, as herons do fishes, and that, too, in Italian fashion; then the noble page took his way over the partitioned turkey-cock, and Poland, through the Electorates, till he arrived at the hereditary kingdoms, where he stopped to make the remark, that very naturally the first great Dictator will have raised up his own son to sit on his throne after him: "So had he often, at the Flachsenfingen shooting-matches, enjoyed seeing the children dance about with the crowns and sceptres which their fathers had shot down, and toss and play with them." The deaf man maintained by his gauging-rod and linstock, which he pressed against the table, the freest intimacy with the whole club, and watched his laboring brother, to see how he sawed and balanced. Matthieu, who loved the chief-carver, but the truth still more,* could not for his sake suppress his reflections upon crowned first-borns, but freely remarked, that "One should at least among the reigning family, if not among the people, have a free choice."

We do not now think even as the Jews do, with whom, to be sure, a half-bestial abortion has still the rights of primogeniture, but not, however, an entirely bestial one.† — The bellows-blower was impregnated through the

* "Sed magis amica veritas!" —Tr.

† See the weekly, called "The Jew," page 380, e. g. according to the Book *Lebusch Atteret Sahaph*, a man with a beast's head is a human first-birth, but not so an insect, an entire beast.

fallopian tube * of the staff with new ideas of primogeniture,—his brother was more dismembered with agony than the turkey-cock in the air. The Evangelist went on: "With the Jews, too, the bestial first-born, because it can never offer a sacrifice, has the best food, and is holy and inviolable,—the rest of the cattle belong to the class of *younger sons*." . . . .

—Thereupon he suddenly and smilingly pronounced the compliment: "Only my friend here with the turkey-cock makes the happiest exception to my assertion, and his respected brother with the staff there the wretchedest; they are, however, twins, and he is only a quarter of an hour older than the deaf one." He turned composedly to him of the staff, who had already mobilized † his face for war, "Am I not right, a quarter of an hour older?"

"Yes, may God punish me," said he, "if I am not. What says my brother?"

The Apothecary, fainting, had to let fall the dividend on the fork, though it had already been lightened by the cutting off of successive quotients. The bellows-blower took a flying survey of all faces, and detected on all a silent scepticism, which the page by his cold assurances made still more legible. "There is nothing in the whole joke," said Zeusel in a low tone, "that can possibly interest any one."

As the bellows-blower could not get hold, through his long auricular organ, of the low murmured exception,—but he did not see how even then he was going to maintain his case and his right of primogeniture,—he

* Anatomical term for a passage connecting with the uterus. — Tr.

† That is, as an army is put on a movable footing or in marching order for battle. — Tr.

entered upon his proof, and fetched out four long curses, as answering to just so many syllogistic figures, and bent his head before his brother, that he might hand in over it his replication. The Apothecary, who wanted to invalidate, not the primogeniture, but only the claim to be his brother, and who, on account of doubt as to his title, did not care to address him, said imploringly to Matthieu, "Concede the point to him, for he does not know at all what we have hitherto been talking of."

Quickly and abruptly, then, but with an incredulous look, the page said to him, "You shall be right, my friend," and added, under pretence of wishing to divert him, "You look right fresh and young."

"By heaven!" replied he, flaming up, "*he there is younger;* but he came behind me, as a fellow-traveller, into the world in the form of a tobacco-pouch: he is woven and twisted together out of the little beggarmen* that fell off from me."

The bellows-blower now fired off all the cannons on the wall of his head, exasperated by the vinegar-glances and poisonous looks and inaudibleness of his blood-friend: he therefore stretched out his thumb and his little finger, and set them like the feet of a pair of compasses on his own face by way of measuring it; then he set out to apply the two as a long-measure to the face of his blood-friend: he would then, as man is ten faces long, have held his own and the other face opposite each other, and then from their difference in measurement have easily inferred their respective statures; but the Apothecary wabbled, and the bellows-blower quite incorrectly planted his thumb above the jawbone. Here the thumb, which sought to press itself into the soft cheek, was stopped by

* So the spinners call the decayed part of the cotton-wool.

something hard and round, and the servant of the bellows, by the slipping down of the thumb upon the jaw, propelled out of the mouth a ball of wax with which the Apothecary had stuffed out as with a padding his sunken cheeks, in order to swell up the inlaid sculpture of his visage into relievo. The emerging ball knocked over, like a nine-pin ball, the Apothecary, i. e. upset his equanimity, and with flashing eyes he said to the deaf one, who was now on the point of absolutely striding on to a history of his bald head, only this much: "You, man, have no bringing up, and your elder brother must plane you down first."

But as the Calcant * had already made some headway in the natural history of the baldhead, Zeusel hurried off with the excuse that the Court-Physician Horion was awaiting him this evening. The most serious of the Englishmen stepped up very near to him and said: "Commend me to the Doctor, and as he makes such good cures, tell him, in my name, you are a great fool."

Hardly had he got out of the village, when the Calcant took pity on the Emigrant, and would fain have done with his history of the bald head. The Evangelist, therefore, despatched him after the enraged twin, to catch him now in the dark; and took up himself in his place the historic thread. On an evening — so the story ran — when the court was not at the play, the Court Apothecary — Heaven knows how — poked out his nut-cracker-face from one of the first boxes. Matthieu, who was then still page, posted the bellows-blower in the zenith of his peruke, namely, in the gallery exactly above him. The Calcant let down from above by an invisible horsehair a little hook, which hung like a bird of prey over

* The bellows' *treader* or blower. — Tr.

the out-looking peruke, which I hold to be an ideal of hair. For it seemed to have grown out from the head (from which locks and vergette* had long since fallen off) as an indigene and shoot, and no one took it for an adopted fur. The bellows-blower let the hook swing and sway like a pendulum above the peruke, till such time as there was a certainty of its having fastened into the vergette. Forthwith he made use of his hands as a drayman's windlass, and lifted up (as the frost does other growths) the whole frisure by the roots, and slowly drew the pig-tail wig like an ascending hair-balloon up into the air. The pit and the chief-lover and the lamplighter were turned by astonishment into lumps of ice, as they saw the tailed comet go up in right ascension to the gallery. Upon the Apothecary, who felt his head uncovered and blown upon by a cold wind, the few natural hairs lifted themselves up with terror, like the artifical ones, and when he turned round with his bald skull to look after the lifting of his head of hair on the cross, his twin-brother (in order not to be discovered) let the whole hairy meteor, which wanted to go after the hair of Berenice † in heaven, actually fall down before his face among the people, and looked composedly down at its culmination in the nadir, like the rest of the gallery.

During our recital the twins have been pommelling each other. The aspirant for primogeniture called out there, on the Flachsenfingen road, which was covered with the darkness of night, in one continued yell, "Mr. Court Apothecary!" and as he could not, of course, hear

* Bristles. — Tr.

† One of the seven stars in the tail of the Lion, named for the wife of Ptolemy III., whose hair was stolen from the Temple of Venus, where she had placed it in fulfilment of a vow. — Tr.

any answer, he was obliged to knock his ear-trumpet against every object, to hear whether it said anything. At last his probing-rod came in contact with the first-born, and he marched up to him to beg his forgiveness and return. But the Apothecary was in such a boiling and overflowing state, that, when the bellows-blower ducked his head to take in his answer, he made up his hand into a ball and let it fall like a bell-hammer on the sagittal suture of the bended head, whereupon the diving-bell gave out a regular tone. The Apothecary, if one had rightly understood him and given him time, would by this trip-hammer have made the sutures on the deaf-head considerably more prominent; but in this he was disturbed by his own brother, who bent his head down like a bush, — for the bellows-blower would have inserted his fingers like ornamental pins into the artificial hair and dragged him by that, if the peruke had been made fast on his head, — so that he could lay his hearing-tube as a second backbone so stoutly and yet so carefully along the twin's first, that no one came off with compound fractures, except the hearing-tube. — Thereupon he said good night, and recommended him to keep to the left, in order not to lose his way. . . .

— Had I known that this history would overshadow so many leaves, I would sooner have thrown it away. — The next morning the impudent Matthieu paid a visit to the cross-bearer, on whose hands the chiragra, warmed into maturity by wrath, was burning; he was going now — for he answered every reproach against his shamelessness with a greater — to make the gouty hands cat's-paws again to take fresh chestnuts of fun out of the fire. But the Apothecary, whose heart was only small, but not black, felt himself too sorely injured, and when Matthieu, laughing at his complaints, departed from him in silence, without even giving himself the trouble of an excuse, then the chiragrist swore — and there we have the fool again — to upset him.

Come forth again, my Victor! I yearn for fairer souls than these foolish brothers have! None of us lives and reads on so carelessly as not to know in what biographical period of time we are living; it is, namely, eight days before Easter, when Zeusel is on the way to St. Luna. — Flamin disclosed to our Victor the joke upon the sick Zeusel. It displeased him altogether, just as writings like the *Anti-hypochondriac*, the *Vade-Mecum*,* or the oral retailers of printed jokes, — the stalest of all companions, — disgusted him. He could never set on a bear-baiting between two fools: only the sketch of such a battle-piece tickled his humor, but not the execution, just as he loved to read and imagine cudgelling-scenes in Smollett (the master in that line), but never cared to see them. Even of the incarnate bon-mots and hand-pointings at another's body he thought too disparagingly, which I, indeed, should be disposed to call dumb wit (just as there are dumb sins), and which are the true attic salt of small towns; for true wit, methinks, must, like Christianity, show itself, not in words, but in works. He looked upon our follies with a forgiving eye, with humoristic fantasies, and with the ever-recurring thought of the universal lunacy of man, and with melancholy conclusions. When he had once deducted the bad point, that Zeusel came bending before every nobleman as his hired beast, till the latter cudgelled him back, as in Paris one can hire lapdogs to go to walk with, — then the vanity of

* From the connection, these books would seem to have been certain antidotes to melancholy, or *Cheerful Companions*, well known at that day. — Tr.

the man, especially as, in other cases, it was good-natured, indulgent, and often even witty, was something he had little to object to. No one tolerated vanity and pride more affectionately than he. "What does a man get by it, then," said he, much too spiritedly, "unless he is a fool, or where then shall he leave off being lowly? We must either think too well of ourselves, or not at all."

Victor, therefore, with his sympathetic soul, paid at once a friendly and a professional visit to his landlord. This mood of his fell in grandly with the Apothecary's plan of securing the Doctor's influence against Mat.

"For this I need nothing," said Zeusel to Zeusel, "except to let him see the intrigues which the Schleunes family is playing against him; for without me he is not *raffiné* enough for that."

For, in fact, he holds the hero of the Dog-Post-Days — who very willingly lets him — to be a little too stupid, merely because the latter was good-natured, humoristic, and confidential towards all men. In fact, life in the great world gave him, it is true, mental and bodily flexibility and freedom, at least greater than he would otherwise have had; but a certain external dignity, which he perceived in his father, in the Minister, and often even in Matthieu, he could never properly or long imitate; he was content to have a higher dignity within, and felt it almost ludicrous to be serious on the earth, and too small a thing to look proud. Perhaps it was for this very reason that Victor and Schleunes could not like each other; a *man* of talents and a *citizen* of talents hate each other reciprocally.

Before I allow the Apothecary to point out all the threads of the Schleunes spider-web, I will merely explain why Zeusel was so all-knowing on this subject, and yet Victor so blind. The latter was so, because in the midst of his enjoyments he never set himself at all to the guessing out of indifferent or bad people ; in fact, like a bird of paradise, he floated always in the air of heaven, far removed from the dirty ground, and, as all birds of paradise do on account of the looseness of their plumage, always flew *against* the wind; hence, from a want of communication, he did not get *oral* court news till all the Heyducs,* lackeys of pages, and stove-heaters had already read them black, — often did not get them at all. — The Apothecary is in the opposite case, because he has the bad eyes, it is true, but then the good ears of a mole, and because in the *camera-obscura* of his congenial heart the forms of kindred tricks more readily image themselves ; add to this, that he applies two long ear-trumpets — two daughters — to cabinets, or rather to their lovers, when they come out therefrom, and overhears by the tubes many a thing, of which I can avail myself grandly in the Third Part of this biography. There are men — he was one — who will hunt up intelligence without the least interest in its contents, and *personalia* without *realia*, and who, with no curiosity about learning, seek to become acquainted with all learned men, — without any care for politics, to know all great statesmen, — and without the least love for war, to know all generals, — personally and by letter.

It may be that many a reader of fine sense has already, from the foregoing, got wind of that which Zeusel will now disclose. I give the Apothecary's *exposé* in the following abridgment: —

" The Minister had never been able formerly to draw the Prince into his interest, seldom to get him to his

* Servants dressed in the costume of Hungarian soldiers. — Tr.

house; to be sure, he had sometimes not omitted to give in marriage a daughter who might please him; but either the diverse interest of the daughter's husband was always unpropitious to his own, or else the influence of his Lordship was. Hence he was more to be excused than condemned for espousing the cause of the *weaker* party, namely, that of the Princess, who at least, in all events, was something, and who perhaps was only concealing still her Italian arts. On the whole, then, it was not unjust, that one should endeavor through Matthieu to attach the Princess, who has much *frailty*, to the house of Schleunes, wherein they constrained themselves to walk after her external grandioseness of virtue, while they could make up to her by the court page for the coldness of her spouse." . . .

If the reader imagines to himself the worst, he will comprehend Victor's incredulous staring and cursing; but he will let Zeusel have his say out first.

"Fortunately the Court-Physician had done the family the honor of often visiting them; and the Schleuneses probably had encouraged him in *every* way to a more frequent bestowal of his visits, especially as he thereby made the Prince also a familiar guest. Deponent had a variety of information on this subject from good authority." . . .

Victor guessed, what Zeusel from politeness concealed, the allusion to Joachime. "Singular, — is it not?" thought he, "that my father writes me almost the same thing! But here is a fine complication of purposes! I make the Minister my cloak of concealment in my designs upon the Princess, and he makes me his in his designs upon the Prince." That is what he ought to have known without me, that bad men never seek good ones out of love, and that Joachime's heart is nothing but a bait in the hands of the Minister; but poetic men, who keep the wings of fancy forever on the stretch, are caught, like larks, by means of their *outspread* wings, even in nets which have the *widest* meshes, through which the smooth body of a bird might easily slip. Only one word more: why did Victor demean himself toward the best persons — towards Clotilda, his father, &c. — more finely, handsomely, and properly than the best man of the world; and yet towards mediocre and bad people conduct himself so clumsily; why? — Because he did everything from inclination and regard, and nothing from selfishness and imitation; worldlings, on the contrary, maintain always a uniform demeanor, because they never shape it after other people's merits, but according to their own designs. Hence his father, on the island, among those rules of life which, taken together, were a fine covert prophecy of his faults and fortunes, gave him this one: *One commits the most follies among people whom one does not respect.*

"Now, as Clotilda pleased the Prince, this Matthieu, who had been a suitor for her some years before, would seek to make her one of his conquests, in order, through her, to achieve much more important ones."

Fie! cried Victor's whole soul, now I see for the first time all the prickles of the crown of thorns which they are pressing upon thy heart, thou poor Clotilda!

"Matthieu would long since have got farther on with his propositions of marriage had he had his present prospects (of — an adulterous act) nearer before him. Perhaps, too, Matthieu was further anxious about the return of her brother (Flamin, on account of her diminished inheritance), although the death of his sister (the source of the inheritance, Giulia) slightly indemnified him. Hence the Princess loved Clotilda, since the marriage of the latter with Matthieu was only a matter of interest. But if it really came to an espousal, as was probable, since Matthieu, if only by coarseness, would extort it from the Chamberlain," . . . (it is a peculiar trait of the Evangelist, that towards the weak he was coarse, and often towards the same person rude and then again refined,) . . . "then might Matthieu and January exercise themselves in mutual forgiveness; and the band of friendship would bind at once four persons in different knots. This fourfold concatenation no one would then any longer be able to dissolve, and all would go to the Devil. The only *Deus ex machinâ* who could still prevent the tying of this knot was the Court-Physician. To him, perhaps, Herr Le Baut would not refuse his daughter, as he had helped her get the place of maid of honor, — 'which, at that time, when I was not at liberty distinctly to explain myself to you, was precisely my true intention, which you guessed quite as well as you executed,' — and as the fate of the son (Flamin, who, according to the general opinion, was not yet visible and acknowledged) really lay in the hands of his Lordship. Nor did he doubt about gaining the Princess, as he (the Doctor) had hitherto possessed her favor, and she preferred him to Dr. Culpepper. The loss of Clotilda and Agnola would clip the Schleuneses' wings." . . .

Scoundrel! was the curse which Flamin would here have vented; but Victor, who believed that only an entire life, not a single action, deserved this moral besom, and who to the greatest intolerance of vice joined a too great toleration of the vicious, simply said, — though with more heat than one will now expect, — "O thou good Princess, the *German* scorpions sit around thy heart and wound it with their stings, and for balm pour poison into the wound, that it may never heal! — Abominable, abominable calumny!" Victor loved to praise and defend his friends too ardently, — and, in fact, from his very inclination to the opposite; for as, in the matter of his *own* honor, he calmly and silently opposed to the libels of the world the commendatory letters of his own conscience, his inclination would, indeed, have led him to defend the honor of his friends as coldly as he did his own, but it was obedience to his conscience to do it (despite the feeling of its superfluousness) with the greatest warmth.

The polite and triumphant smile of Zeusel was a second calumny; the blockhead regarded Victor as a dial-plate-wheel or striking-wheel in the matter, and himself as the pendulum. Therefore Victor said, with a chagrin compounded of pride and melancholy: "My soul is too far exalted above your court-littlenesses, above your court-knaveries; your stuff inexpressibly disgusts me. — O thou noble spirit in Maienthal! — —"

He went away with transpierced heart. The night-watchman, who always reminded him in the higher sense of time, and of eternity too, called up his teacher's form before his weeping soul, — and Clotilda came with her pallid looks and said: "Seest thou not yet why I have such pale cheeks, and hasten so to the holy vale of Emanuel?" — and Joachime danced by and said, "I laugh at you, *mon cher!*" and the Princess veiled her innocent face, and said from pride, "Defend me not!"

The reader can easily conceive that Victor held the name of Clotilda too great to be so much as suffered to pass his lips in such a neighborhood, — as the Jews only in the holy city, not in the provinces, took on their lips the name of Jehovah. His soul fastened itself now on the after-flora of his love, the Agnola besprinkled by Zeusel. It was the thing he could have wished, that precisely at this time the merchant Tostato was to arrive from Kussewitz to make his Catholic Easter-confession in the city; he could at least insist upon his silence in regard to the masquerade-part in the shop, so that he might spare the abused Princess at least the pain she would feel at a well-meant offence; namely, the declaration of love pasted into the watch.

## 27. DOG-POST-DAY.

Eye-bandaging. — Picture behind the Bed-curtain. — Two Virtues in danger.

N Passion-week Clotilda, released by the Princess amidst caresses, went to St. Luna. In Easter-week she is to carry her heart, full of concealed cares, to Maienthal, to more congenial souls, when she has first passed through a purgatory, namely, through a brilliant ball which the Prince gives her — or, to speak more politely, to the Princess — on the third Easter-holiday. . . . If this flower shall be dug out and transplanted by the melon-lever of death from my biographical beds, — I throw away my pen and cudgel back Spitz, — I have come to be as much accustomed to her as to a betrothed, — where shall I again dis cover at court a female character which, like hers, unites *holy* and *fine* manners, *Heaven* and *this world*, virtue and *ton*, — a heart which (if it is allowable to compare it with anything small) resembles the heart-shaped *montre à régulateur* so tormenting to our hero, that with the index-hand of the court hours combines an index-hand of the sun's hours and the magnet of love?

Now, we are still together through all the Easter-holidays; for Sebastian must go to Pastor Eymann's, to see him and the three British twins, and his dear Chaplainess, and so much else that was dear. He would gladly have followed the Regency-Councillor thither on holy Easter-eve, (and it would have been as delightful to the biographer as an Easter-pancake, for he is more than sated with cities and courts on paper,) but the genius of the tenderest friendship beckoned to him for the sake of Flamin and Clotilda, who had both so long wanted and so longingly wished each other, and were now reciprocally bringing with them to the meeting new wounds, to stay behind at least only till the first Easter-day, as if he would ask, "Surely, the first glad looks of brother and sister so long held asunder, my unhappy Sebastian will not wish to disturb?" — "No, surely!" answered his tear.

The city was now emptied of his loved ones. — Passion-week was truly one to him, — not even the Princess, as it were the electrophorus of his love-flame blown back upon his own heart, had for a long time been visible to him, — for in this mood he could not go to Joachime's — — — when the father-confessor of the Princess, who to-day had confessed to him (on holy Easter-eve), called upon him and unfolded before him a medical bulletin of the state of her eyes, and scolded at him in a friendly manner, that the Court-Confessor, instead of bringing remission of sins to the Court-Physician, had to bring the sins themselves before his conscience. "I was on the point of making a journey to-morrow," said Victor. — "Very well!" said the Pater, "the Princess desires your help this very day."

On the way he said to himself: "Has, then, Tostato forsworn his Easter confession, that now at evening he still has not arrived? and where the devil will he be to-morrow?" — Here! answered — Tostato behind him. — Such a jolly penitent no sacristy had ever yet seen.

The child of fun and deviltry and penance told the reason of his wild delight: "The Princess had to-day, as his countrywoman, bought out half his shop." Before Victor had arrayed on his face in rank and file *those* serious looks, with which he was going to entreat of him silence on the subject of his mercantile vicariate, — I mean, his shop-keeping, — the skipping penitent gladdened him with the news, that the Princess had inquired after his and her countrymen, his *associés*, and that he had not at all concealed from her, that somebody had once been of the latter without being of the former, namely, her Court-Physician himself. — "Thunder!" said the . . .

The poor fool of a merchant meant it well, and there was nothing further to be done about it than to investigate, whether Agnola's questioning had not been mere accident; whether she still had the watch, or had ever opened it; whether no wind had blown away the declaration of love as a sister-wind!

After all it was a matter of grave consideration that the Pater and the Merchant, the evil eyes and the good news, should fall upon precisely the same time: this 30th of March, Easter-eve. As this visit is a very memorable one for my hero, I beg every one to settle himself down very comfortably, and split open beforehand the leaves of this narrative, stuck together with bookbinder's gilding, and to listen like a spy.

When Victor reached the palace, the Pater encountered him, who said he would go in too. It was fortunate; for without this guide he would hardly have found his path through a labyrinth of apartments into the altered cabinet of the patient. And with him went as a pewit through all the rooms the apprehension of seeing on the face of the Princess an indictment against the encased *Billet-doux;* but not so much as an initial letter or the *rubrum* of a sentence was seen upon her face, as he came before her, and his thunder-cloud had passed aside. At least his was repelled by one which hung over the Princess herself; that is to say, she was ill, but not merely in the eyes; and a second message which was sent to fetch him had just missed him. She received him in bed, — not on account of her sickness, but of her station; for with ladies of some rank the bed is the residence, — the moss-bank, — the high-altar, — the royal palace, — in short, the princely chair and seat. Like the philosopher Descartes, the Abbot Galiani, and old Shandy, they can think and work best in this hot-house. Although she lay in bed, nevertheless she was, as we said, not well, but was attacked with pain in head and eyes. She had therefore to-day sent away all her domestics, except a chambermaid who loved her very much, and the fly on the wall who plagued her, and our Doctor who omitted one of the two things. I should have been glad to reckon in a sedentary court-dame in a picture-cabinet that stood open; but she sat so dumb and motionless, that Victor swore she was either a knee-piece, or — a German lady, — or both. It spared the scalded eyes of the Princess quite as much pain as it gave well eyes pleasure, that the green light-screen, and the green satin tapestry, and the green satin curtains in the sick-cabinet conspired to shed an undulating *blue* clare-obscure. A single wax taper stood on a candlestick, which was enchased by all the seasons, that is, in sculpture, — upon which custom of the great not to enjoy nature except in counters, *in effigie* and copy-paper, never *in naturâ* itself, I can here state neither my opinion nor its reasons, because it would require a whole

EXTRA-LEAF

in order, among so many possible reasons why they everywhere — on tapestry, on the *dessus des portes, des trumeaux*,* *des cheminées*, on vases, on candle-sticks, on *plats de menage*, † on snuffer-stands, in their gardens, on every trifle — love to see a landscape which they never tread, a Salvator-Rosa rock which they never climb . . . I say, because among so many reasons why they do this and concede to old Nature this *jus imaginum*, the true one could be picked out only by an Extra-Leaf, as only such could fully decide whether it arose from the fact that Nature, at the eternal parting had given them her picture, as a mistress does to her lover, — or from the fact that the artists love best to offer them, as to the old gods, precisely what they hate, — or that they resemble the Emperor Constantine, who at the selfsame time abolished the true cross, and multiplied and consecrated images of the same, — or that from a finer feeling they fancy less the enduring but mosaic pictures of Nature, in which whole mountain ridges are the mosaic-pebbles, than the more delicate, but smaller puzzle-pictures of the artists, — or that they would resemble people (if there were such) who should cause to be painted on the theatre curtain the whole opera with all the decorations, in order to spare themselves the raising of the curtain and the seeing of the acts — — — and yet, if the Extra-Leaf were in the very midst of deciding, every one would, from canine hunger after mere incidents, take French leave and run out after nothing but the confirmation of the incidents, and the

*End of the Extra-Leaf.*

* Pier-glasses. — Tr.

† Household plate. — Tr.

The Princess had two coverings, of which he loved the one and hated the other very much. The beloved one was a veil, which was a healing-bandage to her inflamed eyes; but such a thing was to him the foil and setting of the female face, and he pledged himself to defend, as Respondent and Præses at once, the proposition, that virtue was never better rewarded with beauty than in St. Ferieux* at Besançon; for at the feast of morals there the best maiden gets a veil worth six livres. — The hated covering was the gloves, against which he universally threw down his glove of defiance. "Let a lady," he said in Hanover, "once dare to draw against me, that is her hand, and fight with that without the help of the Esau's hands against the Esau's hands, and say, one must not take them off except in bed. — There, at most, must she put them on, I might reply; but I will ask: Of what use then, finally, are the loveliest hands which I see, if they always lie under their wing-sheaths, as if we men were Persian kings? And is it then too severe, if one tells those persons to their faces, who wear such imitation-hands of silk or leather, that they resemble the Venus de' Medici, even to the very hands?† I pause for a reply!"

In fact, in this dark green cabinet, almost everything — except Agnola's beautiful Roman shoulders — is covvered up; even two images of saints were so. For a painted image of Mary with a real metallic crown — it was not meant for an emblem of princes with mockheads under genuine crowns — was hidden by the cedars of the bed-plumes, and over a very fine St. Sebastian by Titian — copied from the Barbarigo palace in Venice

* Probably a ward or school of the city.— Tr.

† The hands of the Medicean Venus are new and restored.

— (the man looked, with his arrows, like a hedgehog, and yet hung close by her pillow) — she had drawn the bed-curtain, when his namesake without the arrows arrived, who rather adored than was adored. Many have assured me since, that it was a Sebastian of Vandyk's, from the Düsseldorf gallery; but farther on I shall show why not.

Except a female eye reposing behind a veil, no finer specimen of nature's loveliness visits, methinks, us mortals (the Devil has got in here six final *S's* in succession) than one which is just in the act of laying it aside. The poor Doctor had to meet the out-flashing of such a lovely glow — when he was about to proceed as oculist — that he at once proceeded as Protomedicus* of her head, in order to take her hand and thereby save himself. For while she stripped off from her hand the glove-callus — they were, however, only half-gloves with bare fingers, or semi-wing-sheaths, i. e. *hemiptera*, — then was the Doctor, because she had to look down at what she was doing, in the greatest possible security, and the Greek fire shot quite by him. Hence has there been inserted with just forethought in the fire-regulations of morality a whole, almost too long article, which forbids young girls to go about with their eyes exposed, as if with an uncovered light, in a parlor of company, because there is so much inflammable stuff lodged there, — all of *us* in a body, — but they must bury them in a stocking, which they are knitting, or an embroidery frame, or a thick book — e. g. the Dog-Post-Days — as in a lantern.

— It is really a pity: since the public and I have been in the princely chamber, one tail — I mean one digression *à la Sterne* — has followed another. —

* Chief-Physician. — Tr.

The princely pulse went at a somewhat more feverish rate than even his who here describes it. Shortly before he came, she had taken off from her eyes a warm bandage of roast apples. She desired a temporary bandage, while they should be preparing that which the doctor prescribed. But now in the darkness, in this confusion of the twilight, he could not, in all the four corners of his brain, or the eight lesser brains of the fourth central chamber, muster up a single oculist except Dr. von Rosenstein, who started up within there and advised him to advise the spreading of powdered saffron, one fifth camphor, and melted winter-apples on lint of fine linen. The chambermaid was sent to oversee or order the preparation of the recipe, after she had first bound a black taffeta ribbon with the apple poultice before two of the most beautiful eyes, which deserved a more agreeable bandage and blindness. I am lively, when I write, that the poultice seemed to be made of the apple of beauty — and the black ribbon of beauty-patches pounded apart. The Pater also went away, so soon as he got from the doctor the hope of a speedy recovery. But for the Medicus it was verily now no child's play to sit opposite an Italian rose-cheek and Madonna-face, — and that, too, so near that he could hear the breath whisper, after having been able previously to see it grow, — to keep himself opposite to a face (methinks, was no sport) on which roses are engrafted upon lilies, like sunsets upon light lunar clouds, and which a picturesque shadow, namely a black order ribbon, a priestly fillet, a true *postillon d'amour*, so beautifully divides and sets off, — a bandaged face which he can contemplate in one steady gaze, and which supports itself (in a picturesque half-front) turned towards him, on the pillow and on the hand. . . .

I ought to have attempted a climax, have begun with Sebastian's soul, which to-day out of its own melancholy, out of its sorrows, out of its love for Agnola magnified by Zeusel's calumny, made nothing but lines of beauty and flowing tints in order to paint into his own face as beautiful a new one as ever a fair soul created on canvas, or on its own head or on another's.

Agnola may well have had this perception sooner than I.

It furnished, of course, to the couple slender assistance that they were (not under four eyes — for Agnola's were darkened — but) under only two eyes; for the two other eyes, of the Court-dame in the cabinet, about which Victor could not be sure, till now when the princely ones were shut, and he could without questions investigate by glances and smiles the stiff thing on the chair in there in the cabinet, were really *painted*, and so was the body which bore them.

It struck him as singular now, that, against all Court-order, he was suffered to be alone with the Princess; but, he said to himself, she is an Italian, — a patient, — a lovely little child of fancy — (this last was perceptible even in the unusual winter *negligé* and Sicilian fire). He could not possibly, therefore, (even to-day before the bandaging of the eyes,) hit the right tone with her; for as she was too fine for a German, — not tender enough for an Englishwoman, — too lively for a Spaniard, he would certainly have written on her *p. p. p.* (*passé par Paris*, which is inscribed on letters that come via Paris), he would have done it, I say, had she not again been too impassioned for a Parisienne. There was the rub. — But as two persons converse more courageously and freely when one or both sit in the dark — and that was

Agnola's case : — Victor was, after all, to-day not absolutely as simple as a sheep. Add to this that he took heart from the jewel-cupboard, in which to his joy — she could not see him look round so impolitely — he discovered among twenty watches no *montre à régulateur*. She asked him whether she should be so far restored by the third holiday, that she might contribute something to the Prince's pleasure at the ball. He answered affirmatively, though he knew that she would contribute still more to it by staying away, and although she knew it, too. Here he began to pity her, and he would fain make a clean heart. He would not exactly say plumply: "In Gross-Kussewitz I let the Devil so abuse my good nature as to prevail on me to smuggle into your Highness's watch a declaration of love"; but he would, in the finest outpouring of soul, fall down with his beating bosom and say: "Not from fear of punishment, but from fear lest the confession of my fault may contract some similarity to a repetition of the offence, I have hitherto concealed the fact that I once expressed, not so much too strongly as too boldly, a profoundness of esteem in which I am permitted to imitate only your Court, and not its sovereign; but the strength of feelings is easily confounded with their lawfulness."

He still delayed this falling down, because he perceived behind the curtain a gold strip which seemed to be the beginning of a picture-frame. This border-work must surely run round something, — round a picture, I fancy: and this was what he would like to know.

The cursed Court-Apothecary with his calumny had it to answer for, that he had this wish; not as if he supposed that Mat's face hung in a gilded frame behind the bed, but because to-day all sorts of things had startled him. He could do it very easily, as the arras-door and nunnery-grating of her eye was hung with black; he needed only to support his left hand softly on the edge of the bed, and thus, bending forward and hovering over her with suspended breath, reach across with his right over the bed (it was narrow, and he tall) and pull the curtain a little, — and then he would know what hung behind there. I repeat, but for the Apothecary it would never have entered his head. A slanderer causes one to demand of every action at least its passport, — one does it merely to effect a most patent refutation of the slanderer, — and as, often, the most innocent act has no certificate of health, one shakes one's head and says, It is a real calumny, but then I will still be on the watch.

He had made several attempts to reach over, but as she always had something to say and he to answer, it would not do, unless he chose to betray his nearness to her ears. The conversation related to the ball, — the presence and illness of her maid of honor, Clotilda, — the substitute of the latter, Joachime, upon whose appointment Victor expressed himself with decided coldness; he could never, with Agnola, get beyond court-news; all that was abstract and metaphysical she seemed to hate or to ignore; and as to *talking* of emotions with her, — which he generally loved best to do with women, and for which the husband's would have given him ample occasion and material, — that seemed to him not much better than actually to *have* them.

When he had given his cold answer about the promotion of Joachime, — a coldness which formed a flattering contrast to his present enthusiastic warmth and fulness of feeling for the Princess, — he would fain insert in the half-bar-rest which followed, and which Agnola filled out with thinking, the raising of the curtain. He rested on his hand, held his breath, drew the curtain, — but the St. Sebastian was behind it, which I have already mentioned above, and which was most certainly by Titian, and not by Vandyk, because he looked so like our Victor,* that it was credible to him that the Pater had copied it from his wax-statue at St. Luna. The Saint appeared to him still worse than the Evangelist, — not because he thought the portrait was his namesake, but because it occurred to him *why* the women in Italy sometimes *veil* the pictures of saints. Tho reason can, notoriously, form the subject of a wood-cut for the ten commandments — (Göschen and Unger ought to edit the catechism with more tasteful cuts to the prohibitions than the old ones are). Even the Mary over the bed was veiled with plumes and everything. . . . Zeusel! Zeusel! hadst thou not calumniated, this whole biography (so far as I can foresee) might well have had a different course!

He supported himself by resting his right hand against the wall, in a hovering posture above the blind fair one, because a little world-globe attracted his centripetal force and drew him out of his returning orbit. — For as the patient rested on her right side, one cloud after another of dishevelled hair had flowed down over the heart and over the lily hill which is lifted by sighs, and the locks falling towards the other hill had not been able there to cover up so much as they had here disclosed. The lace-veil sank slowly after the tresses, and the heart-leaves and the ripe blossoms fell away from the protruding apple-fruit. . . . Dear æsthetic hero of these Post-days, wilt thou remain a moral one, hanging, as thou art, unseen

* For Vandyk's Sebastian is said to resemble the painter himself.

over this veritable Belidor's *globe de compression,** — over this *waxing* moon-globe, whereof one never sees the other half, — near this commanding eminence, which, like other eminences, one should not suffer round a fortification, — and that too at a court where generally the *dress-regulations* suppress everything *elevated?*

When he is once away from the bed and the Paullinum, I will have a good quarrel with the reader about the whole occurrence, — but now it must first be related continuously and with a good deal of fire.

He was, as it were, fastened in the air. But at last it was time to withdraw from a position which was the torrid zone of all the feelings. Besides, a new circumstance enhanced at once the danger and the charm. A long sigh seemed to surcharge and heave her whole bosom, and to undulate like a zephyr through a bed of lilies, and the superincumbent snow-hill seemed to tremble with the swelling heart that glowed beneath it, and with the swelling sigh. The hand of the veiled goddess moved mechanically toward the imprisoned eye, as if it would press away a tear behind the bandage. Victor, in his fear that she would push aside the bandage, withdraws his right hand from the wall, and the left from the bed, in order, on tiptoe, to bend back, without grazing anything, out of this enchanted heaven.

Too late! — The ribbon is down from her eyes, — perhaps his sigh had been too near, or his silence too long.

And the unveiled eyes find above them an inspired youth, dissolved into love, hovering in the beginning of an embrace. . . . Stiff as a statue he hung in the petri-

* A furnace for destroying galleries of mines, invented by Belidor, a French military mathematician, born in 1697. — Tr.

fied posture, — her eyes, inflamed with pain, suddenly overflowed with the milder light of love, — ardently and softly she said, *Comment?* And too lame for apology, trembling, sinking, glowing, dying, he falls upon the hot lips and the beating bosom. He closed his eyes for rapture and confusion, and blind and love-intoxicated, bold and fearful, he grew to her lips with his thirsty ones . . . when suddenly his ear, on the stretch for every approaching sound, heard the night-watchman calling the hour of twelve, and Agnola, as with a strange, intruding hand repelled him from her, to throw aside a bloody chemise-pin.

Like a doomsday in the night-clouds the watchman's homely admonition to think of death and of the twelfth spirit-hour of this midnight of life, pealed into his ears, before which the blood-streams of the heart rushed by. The call in the street seemed to come from Emanuel, and to say: "Horion! Stain not thy soul, and fall not away from thy Emanuel and from thyself! Look at the linen over her diseased eye, as if death veiled it, and sink not!"

"I sink not!" said his whole heart; he unwound himself with respectful forbearance out of the throbbing arms, and stiffening at the possibility of an imitation of the wretched Matthieu, whom he had so despised, he sank down outside of the bed on her hand, which he had drawn out with him, and said with streaming tears: "Forgive a youth, — forgive his overmastered heart, — his dazzled eyes, — I deserve all punishments, any one would be to me a pardon, — but I have forgotten no one except myself." — "*Mais c'est moi, que j'oublie en vous pardonnant*,"* said she with an ambiguous look, and

* "But it is myself I forget in pardoning you."

he rose, and as her answer gave him the choice between the most agreeable and the most humbling interpretation, he gladly punished himself with the latter. Agnola's eye flashed with love, — then with anger, — then with love, — then it closed; — he stepped back to the most respectful distance, — she opened it again and turned her face coldly to the wall; and by a secret pressure against the wall which, I suppose, commanded a private bell in the apartment of the Chambermaid, gave the latter the order to make haste, — and in a few minutes she came in with the eye-band. Naturally (as in human life) they played out the fifth act, just as if there had been no third and fourth. — Then he politely withdrew.

There! — Now the reader and I begin to quarrel about the matter, and Victor to think about it. His embrace was not right, — nor were his voyage of discovery to the wall and his picture-exhibition, — but it was *discreet;* for he could not, of course, really throw a backward somerset, and say, "I thought Mat was hanging behind the bed." — To this, to be sure, people of experience reply, "We do not quarrel with him here for preferring discretion to virtue, but rather for this, that he did not do so again after the kiss. That kiss is too small a fault for Agnola to be able to forgive." I observe, these people of experience are adherents of the sect who, in my book, reckon the Princess, on account of so many half-proofs, among those women who, too proud and hard for the love of the heart, only let the love of the senses alternate flyingly with the love of domination, and who do it only for the sake of making out of Cupid's bandage a rein, and out of his arrows spurs and stirrups. I am very well acquainted, too, with the half-proofs with which this sect backs itself, — the bigotry of the Princess, — her confession-eve, — her previous attentions to my hero, — the covering of the painted Mary, and the exposure of the more living one, — and all the circumstances of my narration. But I cannot possibly believe such a thing of a friend of Clotilda (unless the latter, for this very reason, had taken leave of her, or from goodness of soul had not at all comprehended those couriers of the temperament more common with the male sex), until in the sequel manifest traces of a more *exasperated* than *afflicted* woman compel me to it.

I am getting quite away from my promise, to present some considerations, which would certainly, with impartial persons, if not justify, yet excuse my hero, for becoming, after the kiss, virtuous again, so to speak, and not full of the live Devil. I boldly set down among the grounds of mitigation his want of acquaintance with those women who, like the Spartans, bravely ask not about the *number* of the foes of their virtue, but about their *position;* he was often with them, indeed, and in their camp, but his virtue hindered them from showing him theirs. He is less excused by the influence of the night-watchman, and the remembrance of death; for this needs itself to be excused; — but then, on the other hand, it is only too certain, that certain men of a philosophical or even a poetic organization, precisely then, and in fact always, regard, instead of their own position, general ideas, when others can understand nothing at all, and be nothing at all but self: namely, in the greatest dangers, in the greatest sufferings, in the greatest joys.

A fair man will throw all upon the Apothecary, who was Victor's moral and mechanical bed-cord, or helper out-of-bed; for as he had prefigured to him the noble Mat in a similar situation (but without the bed-cord), of course the abhorrence which Victor, some days before, had felt of the Evangelist's conduct, became in him a laming incapacity of copying it in the least a few days after. — O if we could only, a couple of days beforehand, see every sin, to which we are tempted by ourselves or others, actually committed by a true scamp, whom we spit upon! Could we then eagerly imitate the scamp?

Finally, one needs only to cast a glance at Victor in his balcony, where he now sits in a singular barometrical condition, if one would pass judgment on his previous state. His present state, namely, is a mixture of emptiness, discontent (with himself and everybody), of increased love for Agnola, justification of this Agnola, and yet the *impossibility* of imagining her a near friend of Clotilda's.

For myself, I shall never repent the little which I have hastily brought together, if I have shown up therein by a few happy hints how well my hero, in regard to his conduct *after* the kiss, which must strike strict people of the world as singular, can plead a disagreeable combination of constraining circumstances, and if I shall, therefore, have succeeded in restoring to him, at the end of the twenty-seventh chapter, the respect which he had forfeited, by not wrapping round the princely ring, too large for his finger, the long silken threads of love, so as to make it fit. . . .

# 28. DOG-POST-DAY.

## EASTER-FESTIVAL.

A DOG-DAY so long and weighty as the twenty-eighth one may be allowed to break up into three holidays.

## FIRST EASTER-HOLIDAY.

ARRIVAL AT THE PARSONAGE. — CLUB OF THE THREE TWINS. — CARPS.

ON the first day of Easter, Sebastian, full of snow-clouds as the heavens above him, stole out of the farm-buildings of the passions, — I mean the residence-city, — but not till towards evening, in order not, to-day, with a heart whose very foundation had been washed away by a half-year's rain-storm, to be long a burden to any friend. On the mountain behind which Flachsenfingen drops down as by a sinking of the earth, he turned round toward the dusky city, and let the remembrance pass by as an evening mist before his soul, how, three quarters of a year ago, in the refulgence of summer and of hope, he had looked out so joyously over these houses, — I described it long ago, — and he compared his prospects of that time with his present desolation; at last he said: "Only say to thyself outright, what thou *hast* and what thou *meanest*, — namely, thou hast nothing more, not a loved or loving heart in the whole city, — but thou meanest once more to march to St. Luna, and, all impoverished as thou art, to take the *second* leave of the pale angel whom thy robbed and ruined heart cannot forget, as thou climbest after the sun, and, having already seen his setting from out a valley, once more seest him sink, from a mountain." . . .

Five half Sabbath-day's journeys from the village he espied the Court-Chaplain, pursued by a Catechumen (as well of the tailoring craft as of Christianity). In vain did he and the young tailor seek to overtake the hotly hunted shepherd of souls. The shepherd came not to a stand until the youngster had got into his house. A hundred-and-twenty-pounder (that is my physical weight) gets no addition to his æsthetic weight by keeping so long to himself the insignificant cause of this insignificant running, and not saying till now that the Chaplain could absolutely hear no one coming after him, because he was afraid the man would smash him from behind. Now the apprentice wanted to tread in the footsteps of his spiritual master and come up with him, — the more fiercely the master dashed forward through space to leave the other behind him, so much the longer leaps forward did the scholar take to overtake him, — that was the whole scrape, but so do men chase men.

Victor ran with outflying arms to a pair of hanging ones, which the owner in his agony could not raise. But in the parsonage two warmer ones folded themselves around his frozen bosom, those of his countrywoman; nor did the parson's wife disturb his and her resurrection-joy with a single complaint of his long absence, — this delicacy of friendship, which spared another unprofitable apologies, he reciprocrated with double warmth, and with a voluminous bill of accusation against his own follies. She led him up a stairway in the joyful parsonage, which to-night was one pierced-work of lighted stories, to her dear son's embrace, and into the presence of the three kindred sons from one mother-country, the three twins. . . .

O ye four men of one heart, press my forlorn Victor's to yours warmly, and make the good youth glad only for one evening! . . . I myself have verily been so, since the paschal Exodus from the Flachsenfingen Egypt: I will therefore make the twenty-eighth chapter as long as the watering-village itself is. A weightiness will thereby be imparted to my work with true critics, — but with postmasters, too, who, when I despatch it to the bookstore, will draw something considerable from me for their weighing. . . . But shall an author be so shabby as to abridge his sentiments, for the sake of postage, merely because a post-office clerk weighs them more according to his own than the postal rates? And am I not encouraged to the opposite course — that of protracting my emotions — by the electoral, princely, and city-benches in Ratisbon, inasmuch as the said benches by an imperial recess allow me a deduction of two thirds of my postage for printed matter, in order, as they hope, to give encouragement to literature and to sentiment?

The noble Evangelist, to be sure, was also up there among the rest, — he and Joachime having politely escorted the maid of honor to the house of her parents; — but here in the *country*, where there are fewer moral weeds than in *cities* (just as there are fewer botanical in *fields* than in *gardens*), and where one enjoys pleasures without *maîtres de déplaisirs*, — here where in Victor love of country appeased the longing for all other love, — no one could be unhappy but he who deserved to be. Mat disappeared there like a toad among tulips. Victor would have loved the English, even without the blood-relationship of nationality, and would have given a bad name to the Dutch, even with that relation; to this is to be ascribed his inconsiderate speech, that these nations pictured themselves in their tobacco-pipes, inasmuch as the English ones had *upright* heads and the Belgian *hanging* ones.

All three were of the opposition party, and lost the coldness of their blood at the ice-coldness of Pitt's. The correspondent of the Dog-Days does not write me, whether it was because the Minister had offended them, — or whether they took a nearer interest in the frightful judgment-day and resurrection of the dead in France, where the sun broods at once over Phœnix-ashes and crocodile's eggs, — or what the reason was. In fact he reports to me nothing further about them than their names, namely, Caspar, Melchior, and Balthazar,* which were the names of the three holy kings from the East.

The one who took the whim of calling himself Melchior concealed under a phlegmatic ice-crust an equatorial glow, and was a Hecla, that splits its ice-mountains before it flings out flames; with cold eye and languid voice and pale brow he spoke in a monosyllabic, sententious, condensed style, — he saw the truth only in a burning reflector, and his ink was a tearing waterspout. The second Englishman was a philosopher and German at once.

* According to the common opinion; for I am inclined to the other, which calls them Ator, Sator, Peratoras. These names distinguish the kings wholly from the shepherds, who were called Milati, Acheel, Cyriacus, and Stephanus, and who also preceded them, all which I copy here out of *Casaub. Exercit. ad Ann. Baron.*, II. 10, because I am not at all ashamed to know anything useless, provided a Casaubon is not, and provided it is something learned too.

The elder Cato, who likewise represented the Moorish king, every one knows. I am as glad as if it were I myself, that my hero was the very one who was distinguished from them all by a greater serene considerateness of free-thinking. I mean that Socratic bright eye which glances round freely over and through the garden of the trees of knowledge, and which chooses like a man, whereas others are exclusively impelled by instinct toward some one proposition, some one apple of these trees, as every insect is to its fruit. Moral freedom operates no less on our opinions than on our actions; and despite all grounds of decision in the understanding, and all grounds of motive in the will, still man *chooses* as well his system as his conduct.

Hence, almost even before supper, the three twins had become cold in affection toward Sebastian, merely because he was so in judgment. He was to-day for the first time in a case with them, into which he fell three times every day with Flamin; certain men can better worry down unlimited contradiction than limited concurrence. The case was this: Matthieu, by his satiric exaggerations, gave to the slight dissimilarity between Victor and them an ever-increasing prominence. He said (not for the purpose of making allusion, but only of seeming to) that princes to whom, as from the Chinese king, their subjects prayed for political weather, helped themselves like that rector who himself composed the almanac, and allowed his scholars (in this case the favorites of the princes) to make the weather for it. He said, too, that the poets could *sing* for Liberty, indeed, but not *speak* for it; that they imitated in a timid plight under the mask of tragic heroes the voice of the heroes, just as he had often witnessed a similar joke in the case of a roasted calf's head, which seemed to the whole table to bellow like a living calf, whereas there was nothing inside but a live tree-toad, which sent forth its croaking. "But it were a still greater cowardice," said Victor, "not even to sing; only I know men are now neither *barbaric* nor cultivated enough to enjoy the Poets and follow them; *Poets*, *Religion*, *Passions*, and *Women* are four things which live through three ages, whereof we are just in the middle age, — that of *despising* them; the past age was that of *deifying* them; the future will be that of *honoring* them." The indignant trio of twins were of opinion that religion, and women particularly, were merely for the state. Besides, Victor's republican sentiments were ambiguous in their eyes, if only by reason of his aristocratic relations. And now, when he actually added that the freedom of states had nothing at all to do with retrenchment of expenses, with greater security of property, with increased comfort of living, in short, with the promotion of material welfare, that all this was found often still more abundantly in monarchies, and that that for which one sacrificed property and life must of course be something higher than property or life; — when he further said, every man of culture and virtue lived under a republican form of government, notwithstanding his physical relations, just as prisoners in *democracies* enjoyed nevertheless the rights of freedom; — and when he made himself, not so much for the Minister and the Upper House as for the English people, armor-bearer and *Contradictor*, because the principles of the first two had from time immemorial combated those of the latter and not yet determined them; because the complaint of to-day was as old as the (English) revolution; because the ground-plan of this last could be torn to pieces only in a formal counter-revolution; because all acts of injustice were committed *according* to the *show* of law, which was better than a justice *against* the *show* of law; and because the *nunnery-grating* which had now been built around the freedom of the English press * was no worse than the Athenian prohibition of philosophizing, but better than the permission of the Roman emperors to make pasquils upon them,— —

The English love long coats and speeches. As he began with "when," so must, in his as in my period, a "then" follow. . . .

Then was there not a devil of them satisfied, and Cato the Elder said: "If he should deliver these principles in the Upper House, there would arise the greatest uproar on the subject, but from approbation, and every hearer would still cry, *Hear him!*" Victor said, with the modesty of a man of the world, he was as warm a republican and Old Briton as any of them, only he was incapable to-day of "proving from these principles that he resembled them;—perhaps at the next club!" "And that can be held," said the Court-Chaplain, "on my birthday, in a few weeks."—If we live to see it,—I and the reader,—it is to be hoped they will invite us, too, as old godfathers; the first time (on the sixth Dog-Post-Day) we were, as is well known, a part of the company.

My hero exacted of men (especially as he did not give himself the trouble) too little respect. He labored, to be sure, for these wages; but if they did not give him any, he knew how to make a thousand excuses for men, and drew out his mint-stamp and struck off for himself a medal of honor, swearing meanwhile, "I 'll be hanged, if the next time I don't behave myself more proudly, and

* The reference is all along to the years 1792 – 93.

less indulgently, and altogether more seriously, so as to excite a certain reverence." The next time is yet to come. He therefore forgave the twin-trio so beautifully, that they at last folded the philanthropist with passionate embrace forever to their souls.

After such a commencement-disputation there was nothing he loved to do better than something really nonsensical, gallant, childish, — this time it was going to the kitchen. Catinat said, he only was a hero *qui jouerait une partie de quilles au sortir d'une bataille gagnée ou perdue,** — or, after winning in a disputation, could go to the kitchen. "Either all or nothing has weight in this mock-life," said he. Into the kitchen, which was not so dirty as a French bedchamber, but as clean as a Belgian cattle-stall, another festal hare and envoy extraordinary had already made his entry, the Court-Chaplain, who had there his calling to attend to. He had to see whether his four-pound carp, — a native of the pastoral pond, and wintered expressly for the adopted son Bastian, — not so much whether it was properly scaled (he passed over that question entirely with very little philosophy) as whether the tail was properly tucked up. It could not surely be a matter of indifference to him, but as a man he must at once feel and fight down his sorrow on the subject, if a carp of as many pounds as a mortal has brains were so miserably slit open that the one quotum of the tail should be no smaller than a hair-bag, and the other no bigger than a fin. And this entire nominal terrorism † is after all of small consequence compared with another real terrorism (so much does important trouble fade be-

* Who would take a hand at nine-pins on coming out of a battle won or lost. — Tr.

† See Titan, Vol. II. p. 1, note. — Tr.

fore greater) which tormented the Parson with the threat that they would crush the four-pounder's gall-bladder. —— His own would have at once emptied itself after the other. "For God's sake, more considerately, Appel! *Embitter* not my first Easter-day," said he. Gall is, according to Boerhaave, true soap: hence the satirical kind washes half the reading world clean and shiny, and the liver of such a man is the soap-ball of a quarter of the world and its colonies.

However, it turned out gloriously. But, by Heaven! the world should for once perceive (after the printing of this book) that a carp of four pounds — so long fed in the fish-box, so skilfully gutted — weighs more in the fish-scales of *contentment*, than the golden *fish-bones* in the red field of the arms of Count Windischgrätz!

Could he then stay long in the kitchen, — that widow's seat of his old departed youth, — among so many female friends of Clotilda, who all bewailed to him her sinking and going away (in a double sense), without having the oxymel of regretted pleasures run over his lips, and the pang of sympathy shoot through his heart, — although he had to-day in the second story spread the disputation on Freedom, as a true scattering medicine, as an arquebusade-water,* at least as a bandage over his open veins? I asked whether he could long avoid thinking of the good soul. But I absolutely would not give the answer, from sympathy with the innocent Victor I absolutely would not disclose before so many thick-skinned souls — who in their empty breasts approve the poetical joys of love, and yet not its poetical sorrows — how often he again and again mixed fate's sugar of milk with memory's sugar of lead, were I not obliged to for the reason —

* A liquor made of sulphuric acid, alcohol, sorrel-juice, and water, once much used for gun-shot wounds. — Tr.

— that little Julia came back from the castle and brought with her the promise that Aunty (Clotilda) was coming to-morrow. This promised, then, that the Minister's daughter would leave to-morrow. Let no one think hardly of the parsonage-people for their importunity about Clotilda: for on the third holiday she goes to the ball, on the day following to Maienthal, — and all they had left was to-morrow and to-day. . . . Our Flamin had brought along with him little Julia herself, being well pleased with her office of penny-post. I am morally certain, the Chaplain's wife saw in my hero as much as I write of him, and she loved him so much, that, had she been obliged to decree instead of Fate, she would have died for sorrow, before she could have brought herself to bless the son at the expense of the friend. So very much did he win, by a beautiful blending of refinement, sensibility, and fancy, the fairest and tenderest hearts, — I mean those of women.

This tiny Julia, the after-flora of the faded Giulia, twined together in Victor's soul roses and nettles, and all his flowers of to-day's joy had their roots in tears deep buried in his breast. Even the kiss of Clotilda's friend, of Agatha, affected him. He thought of the Stamitz concert, and of their sitting side by side, and of the crape hat which veiled the grief of two beloved eyes. He begged Agatha to borrow that hat of Clotilda, and make him an exact copy of it, because he wanted to give it as a present. "When she is gone," he said to himself, — — "no, when she is dead, — then I will weep without concealment, and tell all men openly that I loved her." My dear fellow, at the *souper* — a parson can give one — they will ascribe the glistening of thine eyes more to thy self-discharging wit than to the repressed flood of tears, and, if I were at the table, I could not look upon thee for emotion, when during the hammering and "hardening" of the red eggs I saw thee try to fix thy overflowing and downcast eye, half shut, steadfastly on the pole of a red egg, and silently place thy egg-gable under the cross-block of Eymann's egg, in order to gain time for victory over thy voice and eye-socket! And yet I cannot see what important advantage thou wilt then think to gain by this mask, when Old Appel sends thee by the little Iris and express, Julia, — she can never, herself, undertake it, — a stained, tattooed egg, a real, boiled, allegorical picture, and when thou readest over in the fragile shell the flower-pieces etched into it with aqua-fortis, and thy name bordered with forget-me-nots; I say, what help can thy previous dissimulation be to thee, when thou now, in order not to think out the thought "Forget-me-not," hurriest from the room under the double pretext of having to thank Apollonia, and on account of exhaustion, to retire thus early to rest? Ah, the thanking thou wilt undoubtedly do, but rest thou wilt not! . . . .

## SECOND EASTER-HOLIDAY.

FUNERAL-DISCOURSE ON HIMSELF. — TWO OPPOSITE SORTS OF FATALITY TO THE WAX-STATUE.

THE snow-heavens had fallen and lay upon the landscape. The snow made me melancholy, and reminded one of the wintry lace-knots of Nature. It was the 1st of April, when Nature, so to speak, made the season itself an April fool. Victor had long ago learned manners (*mores*) enough to teach him that, when one is visiting a Court-Chaplain, he must go with him to sermon. And then, too, he loved to march to sacristies for the same reason that he loved to steal away to the huts of shepherds, hunters, and fowlers. It did not strike him as overwrought that the Chaplain (as he himself did at last) should place his mounting of the pulpit, — merely on account of the multitude of preparations he made for it, — in point of importance, side by side with the scaling of a wall. Nay, he disputed with him during the long hymn about the surplice-fees of a stillborn fœtus, and proved by a short argument that a parson could demand of every fœtus — and though it were five nights old — the appropriate burial-fees, whether the miserly parents bespoke a funeral sermon for the thing or not. The Chaplain made a weighty objection, but Victor removed it by the weighty proposition that a clergyman (for otherwise he would be cheated out of his best fœtuses) could make every couple pay him burial-fees as often as it could pay baptismal moneys. The Chaplain replied: "It is stupid that the best pastoral Theologies hurry over this point like a pinch of snuff in the wind."

With all the humor of my hero, and with all the gayety of my parson, — who on every holy eve scolded and condemned like a revolutionary tribunal, and who on every first holiday softened, till on the third he became absolutely an angel, — the world should promise itself something different from what nevertheless is coming: namely, that Victor saw gleaming out of every hour of the approaching evening, which was to bring Clotilda for the last time but one into his company, a protruding sacrificial knife against which he must press his wounded bosom. She was invited to-day, as it were to a farewell-supper, — the three twins of course.

At last she came at evening on the arm of the misunderstood Matthieu. — If, as Ruska asserts, the number of devils (44,435,556) who, according to the assertion of *Guliermus Parisiensis*, flank a *dying* Abbess, is made much too small,* one can readily imagine how many devils may form the escorting squadron of a *living*, a *blooming* one. I, for my part, assume as many devils around a fair one, as there are male persons.

When Clotilda appeared with that face of hers smiling down into its fading beauty, with the exhausted lute-voice, which sorrow draws from us, as a peculiar piano-forte variation, by the pressure of the stop, — but is it not with men as with organs, of which the *human voice* goes most finely with tremolos? — when she thus appeared, then had her noblest friend the choice, either to fall down before her with the words, "Let me die first," or to be, to-day, right funny.

He chose the latter (excepting with her) by way of drowning his dreams. He therefore flung about him with stories and healthy observations. Therefore he threw into the imperial military chest against sentimentalism this satirical contribution, that it was the March-gall or moist-gall in the human field, i. e. a spot that always remained damp, and on which everything rotted. As this availed nothing, he entered into alliance with whole states, and promised himself some help from remarking concerning them, that their summits, like forest-trees, had grown into each other, and that it had no effect to saw one through down below, — that the equality of kingdoms was a substitute or a preparation for the equality of ranks, — and that gunpowder, which had hitherto been the *sticking powder* of the great powers, would finally burn out and heal the hydrophobous wounds of the human

* Voetii Select. Disputat. Theol., P. I. p. 918.

race. At last, when he plainly perceived that it helped him very little, as he expressed the conjecture that Europe would one day become the *North India,* and the same North which had once been the breaking-tools and building-materials of the earth would be so once more, but the North in the other hemisphere, he struck, with his chemical process, into the wet road, and (like a secretary of legation) instead of politics took — punch.

But only cares, not melancholy nor love, can be drowned by drinking. The other spirits, dissolved in the nervous spirit, array themselves in a magically sparkling circle around every idea, around every emotion, which thou hast therein, as in breweries the lights, by reason of the steam, burn in a colored circle. The glass with its hot cloud is a Papin's digester * even to the densest heart, and decomposes the whole soul; the draught makes every one at once more tender and bold. A soft heart was of old ever associated with a bold, hardened fist. As it kept on snowing, he offered Clotilda for to-morrow his shell-shaped sleigh and himself (as he was, besides, invited to the ball) as knight-errant, — whereby he compelled the Evangelist to offer himself as sledge-gondolier to the stepmother.

Clotilda withdrew now from the merry male company into the adjoining room, where her Agatha and all were, — it was not done from disapproval of decorous, manly festivity, — still less from embarrassment, as it is, in fact, easier, and made easier for her sex, to behave itself naturally under forty eyes than under four, — still less from inability to disguise her sisterly love towards Flamin; for her flying soul had long since learned to fold to-

* Papin was a physicist and machinist, who invented a machine for softening bones to make a digestible food. — Tr.

gether its wings and hide its tears and wishes, brought up as she had been among *strangers*, trained in thorny relations and between discordant parents. She did it merely, like the Parson's wife, because it is a *British* custom, that the ladies shall take themselves away from the men and their incense-kettle of punch.

When she was out of Victor's sight, — and when, from her *present* look of *increased paleness*, he drew the conclusion that the vale of Emanuel would hardly restore her spring-colors, since the prospect of the journey had brought no healing influence, — and when this *short absence* held before him as it were in a pocket-mirror the death-apparition of an *eternal* one, — and when, at last, to be sure, the swelling heart carried away the dam of dissimulation, — then he rushed out into the winter, — bared his inflamed breast to the cooling flakes, and tore wider the clefts into which fate grafted its sorrows, — and ran up through the white night to the observatory; — and here, covered with the snow-avalanche silently descending from heaven, he looked out into the gray, whirling, trembling, flickering landscape, and in the broad snow-pierced night, — and all the tears of his heart fell, and all the thoughts of his soul cried: "So looks the future! So glistening fall the joys of men from heaven, and dissolve even while they fall! So does everything melt away! Ah, what air-castles I saw shine around me on this eminence, and how they gleamed in the evening red! Alas! all are buried under the snow and under the darkness of night!" He looked down into Clotilda's garden, in whose dark bowers, now whitened with snow, he had found and lost again the Eden of his heart. "The tones which flowed over this garden are dried up, but not the tears which streamed after them," thought he.

He looked down into her brother's garden, where the tulip-C had dropped its leaves, and the blooming names had passed away into obscurity.

With such a soul, which had looked into this landscape as into the charnel-house of mouldered days, he returned to the joyous club. The alternation of cold and warmth had kept up his similarity to the punch-union, which meanwhile had gone on drinking. He and all had touched the limits of drinking, where one laughs and weeps in the same breath; but I am glad that man can after all extract true nourishment of mind and heart (though not from a cloister-kitchen or cloister-library, yet) from a cloister-cellar; that he drinks the health of his wit; that every cup (not merely on the altar) spiritually strengthens him, and that, if serpents take off their crowns upon drinking,* he puts his on during the process; and that the vine sheds tears not merely of itself, or from the eyes of a Catholic image of the Virgin, but also from those of a man, who has drunk of it. The club hit upon the fancy of making parliamentary speeches. The Chaplain proposed occasional discourses. Victor jumped up in a chair and said: "I am going to deliver a funeral-sermon on myself, — I preached here long ago in my childhood."

All drank once more, even the corpse, and the latter began the following harangue: —

"*Most beloved and distressed hearers and brethren!*

"A mortal, deeply-afflicted hearers, may sink into the next world, without having a mourning-steed prance after him, just as he makes his entrance into this, without having a festive-nag trot before him. We, for our part,

* Writers on natural history deny that serpents *do* drink. But this may allude to some legend. — Tr.

have jointly taken the *funeral-cup* beforehand, in order to be able to go through it all; for man expands by moistening, and shrinks up when he is dry, I mean, when he takes only solid food, like the bloodsucker, which, when out of water, loses four inches in length. And I hope I and the deeply afflicted funeral-procession have *toasted* the deceased sufficiently.

"And so then I see before me" . . . — Here he beckoned to the Parson to toss out his nightcap, that something death-like might lie there on which his emotion could vent itself —

"I see lying before me him, the never-to-be-forgotten Mr. Court-Physician, Sebastian Victor von Horion, and dead he is and is about to go down under the covering of earth, into the place full of long repose. What do we see still lying at rest before us but the diving-bell, wherein the covered soul descended into this vapory life, — what but the dry shell of a kernel which is sown for the first time in a second planet, — what but his hull, — what but (so to speak) the cast-off nightcap of his awakened spirit?

"Behold, weeping hearers, this emblematic pale cap! Here it lies, the head is out of it, which once mused therein. Our Victor is gone and is hushed, who talked so often of mathematics, clinical medicine, heraldry, precautionary jurisprudence, *medicina forensis*, Sphragistics and their auxiliary sciences. We have lost much in him — who shall console you for this loss, excellent Herr von Schleunes, and the other gentlemen likewise? One has not however, absolutely, in this absurd life, which may well be a sort of ante-death, time enough to administer proper consolation. Not merely church-pews are often built on tombstones, but also princely chairs — *they* particularly — and even pulpits.

"Can it be supposed that thy soul, deceased Sebastian, in its intermediate state after death, should know anything of its body, from which it is unpacked, as out of its hat-box, and of the last honors which we here pay to its case? If it still has consciousness and an eye for this room, wherein it has been so often, then will it be glad that the three holy kings, of whom the Moor is Cato the Elder, are standing round its worm-bag, hardly willing to let the bag go; it must be pleased, that we are unitedly lamenting: where is his equal in common chemistry, in physiognomics and physiognomy, — in the modern languages, — in the *doctrine of ribbons*, from which he imbibed a love for all kinds of ribbons? Who sought less than he that strict concatenation of ideas, which misleads the Germans to cement good ones with bad ones, and to use more mortar than stones? Not even the Court — hence he never liked to go thither, when fun was going forward — could break him off from a certain serious sedate way, which he ran even into a ridiculous one, which last was always his aim. —— By heaven! through the hour-glass of death, through which he peeped, as through a pocket spy-glass, everything came out so small to him, that he knew not why he should be serious — I hope I may not be standing here alive and well, if in the aforesaid glass all the *steps* of the throne did not appear to him as diminutive as the thumb-long *wood-stair* of the tree-frog in his preserving jar.

"He was a very good preacher, particularly of funeral sermons, hence even a very good preacher asked him for godfather, and the godson stands among the present company and takes his part in the weeping, for the stomach-ache. . . . Only great court preachers, who deliver the princely funeral oration in the Cathedral-Church, can boast of what I, to my greatest satisfaction, now hear, that they make the mourning company laugh, and this is to me an earnest that my consolation is effectual. . . .

"And yet one who lies upon the death-bed has more consolation than one who only stands at the foot of the bed. The souterrain of the earth's crust is peopled only by still, reposing human beings, who draw close together; but above the souterrain stand their uneasy friends, and long to go down to the beloved arms of dust; for the linen on the eye of the dead is truly a padded hat for the cold brow, the coffin is a parachute to the unhappy, and the winding-sheet the last bandage of the widest wounds. Ah! why does weary man love better to sink into the short than into the long, undisturbed, sure sleep? Take, then, good Sebastian, the death-certificate as an eternal peace-instrument from the hand of gentle nature. . . .

"But, the Deuse! where then is our dead man? what has the white cap to do down there? I see the corpse in the looking-glass opposite — it must be somewhere — I must fetch it": —— with a shudder running through his soul he sprang down; an exalted frenzy passed, through the stages of tears, of smiles, of torpor, up and down his face. He ran behind a screen which had been placed before his wax statue — and brought out the waxen man — and threw him down as a corpse — and a veil was wound over the corpse — and with a distorted face he mounted the chair to proceed: —

"This is the night-corpse, — the scorified, carbonized man, — into such stiff lumps are conscious beings fastened and compelled to turn them round. Why do you tremble at me, hearers, because I tremble, to stare so at this overturned form of humanity? — I see a spectre hover round this corpse which is an 'I.' . . . . I! I! thou precipice that in the mirror of thought runnest back deep down into the darkness, — I! thou mirror within the mirror, — thou terror within a terror! Draw the veil away from the corpse! I will boldly look on the dead, till he destroys me."

Every one shuddered in response; but one of the Englishmen drew aside the veil from the dead. . . . Rigid, speechless, horror-struck and quaking, Victor looked upon the unveiled face, which also in a living shape hung round his soul; but at last tears gushed out down his cold cheeks, and then he spoke in a lower tone, as if his heart were melting: —

"See how the corpse smiles! why, then, dost thou smile so, Sebastian? Wast thou perchance so happy on the earth, that thy mouth stiffened and grew cold in a rapture of delight? . . . No, happy thou canst scarcely have been, — joy itself was often to thee a seed-vessel of sorrow. And thou saidst thyself very often, I am well contented and deserve hardly my hopes and wishes, to say nothing of their fulfilment. — —

"Flamin! look upon this assumed countenance here, — it smiles from friendship, not from joy. Flamin, this extinct breast was arched over a heart that loved thee without limit, and even unto death.

"And this, after all, is the only misfortune of the poor man now at rest. In and for himself, and so far as concerned his original condition and temper, the good Bastian might have fared well enough; but he was too sensitive for joy, — too inconsiderate, — too ardent, — almost too much a child of fantasy. He wanted even to love (during his lifetime), and it could not be done. The flower-goddess of love passed by him, she denied him the transfiguration of man, the melodrama of the heart, the golden age of life. . . . Cold form, erect thyself, and show men the tears that flow from a tender heart, which breaks for love and finds none! . . .

"If our Horion was not happy, then, of course, it may well be a comfort to him, if he is permitted even in the noonday of life to take his siesta, if he is permitted to die, and released from the hotly-beating heart, hushed by the death-angel, to lay himself down so early under the long shroud, which the genius of humanity draws over whole peoples, as the gardener draws the cover over the flower-bed to shield it from sun and rain, — against the glow of our joys, against the gush of our sorrow. . . . *Rest thou too, Horion!*" . . .

His grief at these words from the old dream so overmastered and so unmanned him that he passed over from it — by way either of excuse or of relief — into an almost frenzied humor.

"The whole joke, however, is half against my taste, which at court I wanted to cultivate. Life absolutely does not pay for one's scolding on its account at our good friend Death, or fumigating him with the incense of praise. The fear of dying excepted, there is nothing more pitiable than the fear of living. People of true talents should get drunk in order to see life in the right light, and afterward report it to us. The wretchedest of all (but so that *human* life in the comparison turns out still passable) is *civil* life, at which I could let fly for years, because it has nothing but long troughs for the stomach, from which hang down chains for the fancy, — because it perverts man into a cit, — because it turns our fleeting existence from a corn-field into a drill-plough, — because it exhales a pestilential vapor which lies thick before the grave and over the heavens, and in which the poor expeditionary committee-man, sweating, chewing, fat, and besmeared, without a warm sunbeam for his heart, without a streak of light for his eye, drives round, till the ramming-block of the pavior* pounds him down on the marshy ropewalk. The only advantage such a poor piece of marble has, out of which a *pavement* is made, instead of a *statue*, is that it looks upon the whole of human life as something really edifying, which it cannot sufficiently praise. And yet to us good fools the outer world could not appear so small, were there not something eternal and great within us, whereto we contrast it, — were there not a sunlight in us, which falls into this opera-house, just as the daylight, sometimes, when a door opens, falls in upon the nightly stage, — were it not that, like men in old pictures of the resurrection, we are half bedded in the earth and half out of it, — and if this ice-life were not an *Aiguille percée*,† and had not an opening out into an eternal blue. . . . Amen!

"I have, however, still to announce to the sorrowing assembly, that I have been making an April-fool of it; for the dead man, whose funeral sermon I have been delivering, is really myself." . . .

But here all his friends embraced him, in order to set limits to his ingenious frenzy, — and to press such an impassioned, true British heart to their own. The embrace softly warmed all his cold wounds, and he was healed, though exhausted; another's life grew into his, and love

* He calls Death, and the state, a pavior, though in different senses.

† The name given to a high rocky pyramid beside Mont Blanc, containing a hole through which one sees the heavens. It is to me a tender fancy to represent to myself beside the highest mountain, which takes in as much of heaven as of earth, a smaller one, which opens into a narrow prospect offering to our *eye* a blue telescope, out of which our *hope* builds the arch of heaven.

conquered death. The Englishmen, in whose eyes stood the tears of a double intoxication, could hardly tear themselves away from the humorous darling.

Clotilda, who with her female friends overheard the funeral oration in the adjoining chamber, at first held them back beseechingly from opening it. But when Victor said, " Cold form, erect thyself, and show men the tears which flow from a tender heart that breaks for love," — then she took leave of them with a hasty "good-night," unable to master an emotion which upheaved her whole being. When they reported to him the time of her withdrawal, then did he, who was now already so weary, weak, and tender, become inexpressibly so, — all the lights which his effort had brightened on his countenance seemed to melt away in love like moonlight in dew-drops, — he waited not for his chamber to be empty, but showed that which Clotilda in hers would conceal, — he could even contemplate the unveiled wax statue with softened spirit, and said smilingly: " I fancy, the reason why I have let the *whole* of me be repeated in wax is the same for which the Catholic does it with single limbs, in order to hang them on a saint, and thereby give thanks or pray for recovery; or like the Roman Emperors, whose wax statues the physicians visited after the death of the original." * The company went away, and he was at last alone. The moon, which had risen at 11 o'clock and 57 minutes, just began to throw its still low and waning light up against the windows of Clotilda's sitting-room. Victor put out his night-lamp, and, in order not to sink with his still toss-

* After the death of the Emperor, a wax image of him was kept for seven days in the palace, where it received as his representative ceremonious visits, and, among the rest, of course from the physicians. — Tr.

ing, dreaming heart into the dreams of sleep, seated himself at the window, almost in the wonted place of his wax copy and in a similar attitude —— when fate ordained, that he, who to-day had given out the wax mummy to be his own person, should now inversely be looked upon as the image — by Clotilda! She stood at some distance from her window, on which no light fell but that from heaven; Victor, as this latter could not yet reach him, was quite in shadow, and turned towards her with five quarters of his profile. Scarcely had he observed that she fixed upon him an unchanging glance, that seemed as if it would not only take him in but go through him, when he guessed that she confounded him with the man of wax; he also observed out of the corner of his eye that something white fluttered around her, i. e. that she often dried her eyes. But how would it have been possible for his fine feeling by the least motion to take away from her her error, and to make her blush with confusion for her innocent gaze! Another, e. g. the misunderstood Mat, would in such an emergency have composedly straightened himself up and looked indifferently out of the window; but he ossified himself, as it were, in his attitude of lifelessness. But only the night and the distance could conceal from her his trembling, when her tears shed for his corpse seized like a hot stream his dismembered heart, and softened and dissolved the little of it which this evening had still left whole into a burning wave of love. Children's tears flow more freely, when one shows them sympathy; and in this hour of exhaustion, Victor, who was generally made more hard by another's sympathy for him, grew softer; and when Clotilda seated herself at the window, to lean upon it her weary head, it seemed to him as if something exhorted him now to verify that which he had said to-day to the statue: Cold form, erect thyself, and show men the tears which flow from a soft heart.

Clotilda at length closed the curtains and disappeared. But he still cautiously acted for some time longer the part of his image, and just when he made less effort to play the statue he succeeded better. All his thoughts flowed now like balm over the lacerated spots of his inner man, and he said: "Though thou art only my friend, I am satisfied, and thou canst appease this bosom's tumultuous yearnings. O, besides, this full heart would fly to pieces, if it should entertain the thought that thou lovest me!" For the rest he took home to himself to-day for the first time the improbability of his recent supposition, that a person so reserved as she could have demeaned herself in so unreserved a manner towards the blind Julius, and he asked himself: "Is there not, then, sufficient explanation of her departure from the court, in January's and Matthieu's unholy love, and the holy love of Emanuel?" But that she might not in the morning discover her erroneous confounding of things, he gave his wax figurant exactly the position which he had occupied at the window.

## THIRD EASTER-HOLIDAY.

F. KOCH'S DOUBLE JEWS-HARP. — THE SLEIGH-RIDE. — THE BALL — AND . . . .

THE reader will wish, with me, that the third Easter-holiday ended something worse than the long 28th Dog-Post-Day.

The sleigh went tolerably, so far as could be foreseen. — — I however foresee yet something quite different:

that half a million of my reading-customers (for the other half I will answer) cannot find out what is in my hero. It is therefore my office to tell them only so much as this: Victor was never pusillanimous, man's subjection to the yoke of fortune disgusted him; once every day Death took him up on the Sublime Arm, and let him, looking down therefrom, remark how diminutive were all mountains and hills, even graves. Every misfortune hardened him to steel, the Medusa's head of the death's-head turned him to stone, and the melting sun-glance of joyful emotion always vexed him in the remembrance. His sportive humor, his ideal of female perfection, the want of opportunity, and the shield of Minerva, had helped him along over the wind-months of feeling, and he had hitherto worshipped no other sun than the one which is twenty-one million miles distant, — till Heaven or the Devil brought along the nearer one, just in the year 1792. Still things would have gone quite tolerably, and the misfortune would have been easy enough to get through with, if he had been discreet or cool; I mean, if he had not said to himself: "It is fine to weep never for one's self, but yet for another; it is fine to worry down every loss, except that of a heart; and which will a departed friend from his lofty place count greater, if I deliver consolatory sermons to myself on his decease with true composure, or if I sink, yearning, after the loved one, in voluntary, overmastering sorrow?"

Thereby, — and from unacquaintance with the overpowering influence of noble but untamed feelings, — and because he confounded his previous accidental calm of the heart with a voluntary one, — and from an overflowing love of humanity, — he had intentionally let the feelers of his inner man up to this time grow too large, — and thus, by the whirl of all the previous influences, the previous bereavements, the previous emotions of these Easter-days, of this fair village of his youth, he had been driven so far out of his course, that, notwithstanding his considerateness, his court-life, his humor, he forfeited (at least for Easter) somewhat of his old dissimilarity to those geniuses who, like the sea-crab, stretch out feelers which a man can hardly span with his arms. . . .

That sympathetic look of Clotilda which yesterday, after his previous heat, had been a cooling balm, was to him to-day a very burning one; the thought of her eye full of tears for him conjured up all the days of his love for her and her whole image in his heart. I am convinced that not even the Regency-Counsellor, who, for the rest, might by yesterday's funeral-sermon have lost something of his jealousy, as well as, by the republican diversion, somewhat of his love for Clotilda, failed to note the drunken and dreamy look of his eye. The parsonage itself was fortunately to-day an exchange, or a spiritual intelligence-office and recruiting-house; the Chaplain registered — not any of your French *car tel est notre plaisir*, but — the catechumens who were to confess at Whitsuntide.

He would not go over to the castle — his misunderstood friend Mat had already by ten o'clock called to him out of the window a morning-greeting and congratulation upon the snow-storm — until his sleigh had come from the city, so that he might start off at once, because he would not show over yonder any ridiculous emotion. Since the great world had become for him a work-day world, to disguise his feelings from it became harder; one conceals one's self most easily from those whom one respects.

But the three twins and Franz Koch carried him over earlier than he would have gone, as early as half past five o'clock in the afternoon.

The name of Franz Koch in the Dog's papers made me jump off of my feet. If any one of my readers is a guest of the Carlsbad waters, or should happen to be his Majesty, the King of Prussia, William the Second, or one of his court, or the Elector of Saxony, or the Duke of Brunswick, or any other princely person, he has heard the good Koch, who is a modest pensioned soldier, and travels round everywhere with his instrument and plays on it. This instrument, which he calls the double Jews-harp, or mouth-harmonica, consists of an improved pair of jaw-drums, or humming jaws-harps, played at once, which he shifts according to the piece he is playing. His handling of the buzzing-irons bears the same relation to the old Jews-harp playing as harmonica-bells do to servants' bells. I am under obligation to induce such of my readers as have wren's wings to their fancy, or at least, from the heart upwards are *lithopœdia* (petrified fœtuses), or have the ear-drum membrane for nothing but to be drummed on, — to induce, I say, with the little oratory I have, such readers to tumble the aforesaid Franz out of the house, if he undertakes to come and buzz before them. For it amounts to just nothing, and the wretchedest bass-viol or rebeck screams louder in my opinion; nay, its hum is so low, that he played at Carlsbad before not more than twelve customers at once, because one cannot sit near enough to him, particularly as in his leading pieces he has the light carried away, that neither eye nor ear may disturb the fantasies. If, however, a reader is differently constituted, — a poet, perchance, — or a lover, — or very tender, — or like Victor, — or like me; then, indeed, let him without scruple listen with still and melting soul to Franz Koch, or — for to-day is just the time when he is not to be had — to *me*.

The jolly Englishman had sent this harmonist to Victor with the card: "The bearer of this is the bearer of an echo which he carries in his pocket." Victor preferred, therefore, to take him over to the friend of all sweet tones, that her departure might not deprive her of this melodious hour. It seemed to him like going through a long church, when he entered Clotilda's Loretto-chapel; her simple chamber was like Mary's sitting-room, enclosed with a temple. She had already completed arranging herself in her black ornamental dress. A black costume is a fine eclipse of the sun, wherein one absolutely cannot take one's eyes away from it: Victor, who, with his *Chinese* regard for this color, brought with him to-day to this magic a defenceless soul, an enkindled eye, grew pale and confused at the radiant face of Clotilda, over which the trace of a trouble that had rained out, hovered like a rainbow over the bright, blue sky. It was not the cheerfulness of light thoughts, which every maiden takes on when she dresses herself, but the cheerfulness of a pure soul full of patience and love. He trembled lest he should tread on two kinds of thistles, — on the painted ones of the floor, over which he took care to step, and upon the satirical ones of the fine observers around him, with which he was always coming in contact. Her stepmother was still upon the stucco-work and finishing of her worm-bag,* and the Evangelist was in her toilet-chamber as assistant-priest and collaborator in the finery department. So that Clotilda had still time

* Meaning her body. See p. 78. — Tr.

to hear the performer on the mouth-harmonica; and the Chamberlain offered himself to his daughter and my hero — for he was a father of good breeding towards his daughter — as part of the audience, although he could make little out of music, table- and ball-music excepted.

Victor now saw for the first time, by Clotilda's delight in the musician he had brought with him, that her harmonious heart loved to tremble in unison with strings; in fact, he was often mistaken about her, because she — like thee, dearest * * * — expressed her highest praise as well as her highest censure by silence. She begged her father, who had already heard the mouth-harmonica in Carlsbad, to give her and Victor an idea of it, — he gave it: "It expressed in masterly manner, not so much the *fortissimo* as the *piano-dolce*, and, like the simple harmonica, was best adapted to the *adagio*." She answered, — leaning on the arm of Victor, who led her into a still chamber darkened for the occasion, — music was perhaps too good for drinking-songs and for mirthful sensations. As sorrow ennobled man, and, by the little cutting pangs which it gave him, unfolded him as regularly as they do the buds of the carnation, which they slit open with a knife that they may bloom without bursting; so music as an artificial sorrow took the place of the true." "Is the true so rare?" said Victor in the dark chamber which only *one* wax-taper lighted. He came close to Clotilda, and her father sat opposite to him.

Blissful hour! thou that didst once, with the echo-strains of this harmonica, pass through my soul, — glide along by me once more, and let the resonance of that echo again murmur around thee!

But scarcely had the modest, quiet virtuoso put the

instrument of enchantment to his lips, when Victor felt that now (before the light was removed) he should not dare to do as at other times, when he pictured to himself at every adagio appropriate scenes, and underlaid every piece with peculiar fantasyings for its texts. For it is an unfailing method of giving tones their omnipotence, when one makes them the accompanying voices of our inner mood, and so out of instrumental music makes as it were vocal music, out of inarticulate tones articulate ones, whereas the fairest series of tones, which no definite subject arranges into alphabet and speech, glides off from bathed, but not softened hearts. When, therefore, the sweetest sounds that ever flowed over human lips as consonants of the soul began to well forth from the trembling mouth-harmonica, — when he felt that these little steel-rings, as if they were the setting and touch-board * of his heart, would make their agitations his own, — then did he constrain his feverish heart, on which, besides, all wounds came out to-day, to shrink up against the tones, and not picture to itself any scenes, merely that he might not burst into tears before the light was gone.

Higher and higher swept the drag-net of uplifting tones with his heart in its grasp. One melancholy remembrance after another said to him in this short ghostly hour of the past, "Crush me not out, but give me my tear." All his imprisoned tears were clustered around his heart, and in them his whole inner being, lifted from the ground, softly swam. But he collected himself: "Canst thou not yet deny thyself," he said to himself, "not even a moist eye? No, with a dry eye receive this sad, stifled echo of thy whole breast, receive this resonance from Arcadia, and all these weeping sounds, into a broken

* Or neck (of a violin, for instance). — Tr.

heart." — Amidst such a secret melting away, which he often took for composure, it always seemed within him as if a breaking voice from a far region addressed him, whose words had the cadence of verses; the breaking voice again addressed him: "Are not these tones composed of vanished hopes? Do not these sounds, Horion, run into one another like human days? O, look not on thy heart; on the dust-cloud of the crumbling heart, as on a mist, the gleaming forms of former days cast their image." — Nevertheless he still answered calmly, "Life is truly too short for two tears, — the tear of woe, and the other." . . . But now, as the white dove, which Emanuel saw fall in the churchyard, flew through his imaginings, — as he thought to himself, "This dove, truly, once fluttered in my dream of Clotilda, and clung to the ice-mountains; ah! it is the image of the fading angel beside me," — and as the tones fluttered more and more faintly, and at last ran round in the whispering leaves of a death-garland, — and as the breaking voice returned again and said: "Knowest thou not the old tones? Lo! they sounded in thy dream before her birthday festival, and there made the sick soul beside thee sink up to her heart in the grave, and she left nothing behind for thee but an eye full of tears, and a soul full of grief" — — "No, that was all she left me," said in broken tones his weary heart, and all his suppressed tears gushed in torrents from his eyes. . . .

But the light was just then carried from the chamber, and the first stream fell unseen into the lap of night.

The harmonica began the melody of the dead: "How softly they slumber." Ah, in such tones do the far-wandering waves of the sea of eternity beat against the hearts of darkling mortals who stand on the shore and yearn to put forth! Now art thou, Horion, wafted by a wave of harmony out of the mist-rain of life over into the light of eternity! Hear, what tones murmur round the broad fields of Eden! Do not the strains, dissipated into breaths, reverberate from distant flowers, and float, swollen by echo, round the swan-bosom, which, blissfully dissolving, swims on pinions, and draw it on from flood to flood of melody, and sink with it in the distant flowers, which a cloud of fragrances fills, and does not in the fragrant dusk the soul glow again like a ruddy evening, ere it sets in bliss?

O Horion, does the earth still abide under us, drawing its circle of death-hills round the breadth of life? Do these tones tremble in an earthly air? O Music! thou that bringest the Past and the Future with their flying flames so near to our wounds, art thou the evening-breath of this life, or the morning air of the life to come? Ay, thy sounds are echoes, which angels snatch from the second world's tones of gladness, to convey down into our mute hearts, into our dreary night the faint spring-melodies of heavens flying far above us! And thou, dying harmonica-tone! verily thou comest to us out of a peal of exultation, which, driven from heaven to heaven, dies at last in the remotest mute heaven, which consists of nothing but a deep, broad, tranquil, and eternal bliss. . . .

"Tranquil and eternal bliss," repeats Horion's dissolving soul, whose rapture I have hitherto made my own, "ay, *there* will lie the region where I shall lift up my eyes toward the All-gracious, and spread out my arms toward *her*, toward this weary soul, toward this great heart. Then shall I fall upon thy heart, Clotilda, then shall I clasp thee forever, and the flood of tranquil and eternal bliss will close around us. Breathe again toward life, earthly tones, between my breast and hers, and then let a little night, an undulating shadowy outline, swim along on your light waves, and I will look toward it and say, That was my life; — then shall I say more softly, and weep more intensely, Ay, man is unhappy, but only on the earth."

O, if there is a human being over whom, at these last words, memory draws great rain-clouds, to him, to her, I say, Beloved brother, sister, I am, to-day, as much moved as thou; I respect the sorrow which thou hidest, — ah! thou excusest me, and I thee. . . .

The tune stopped and died away. What stillness now in the dark! Every sigh took the form of a long-drawn breathing. Only the nebulous stars of sensibility sparkled brightly in the darkness. No one saw whose eye had been wet. Victor looked into the still, black air before him, which a few minutes ago had been filled with hanging-gardens of tones, with dissolving air-castles of the human ear, with diminished heavens, and which now remained a naked, black firework-scaffold.

But the harmonica soon filled this darkness again with meteorological apparitions of worlds. Ah, why, then, must it needs strike precisely that melody which woke such restless yearnings in my Victor, the "Forget-me-not," which sounded out to him the verses, as if he repeated them to Clotilda. "Forget me not, now that fate sternly calls thee away from me. Forget me not, when the cool earth one day rests lightly upon this heart, that fondly beat for thee. Think it is I, when some soft voice shall whisper to thy thought, Forget me not." . . . And O, when these tones intertwine themselves with waving flowers, when they flow backward from one past to another, when they ripple more and more faintly through the past years that repose back of man's memory, — at last only murmur under the dawn of life, — only well up inaudibly under the cradle of man, — and stiffen in our cold twilight and dry up in the midnight, when each of us was not, — then does man, deeply moved, cease any longer to conceal his sighs and his infinite pangs.

The still angel at Victor's side could no longer veil them, and Victor heard Clotilda's first sigh.

Ay, then he took her hand as if he would sustain her, hovering over an open grave.

She gave up her hand to him, and her pulse throbbed trembling in unison with his.

Finally only the last lingering tone of the song still flung out its melodious circles in the ether, and its wake undulated away over a whole past, — then a distant echo wrapped it up in a fluttering breath of air, and wafted it away through deeper echoes, and finally over to the last which lay round about heaven, — then the tone expired and flew as a soul into one of Clotilda's sighs.

Then the first tear escaped from her, and fell like a hot heart on Victor's hand.

Her friend was overpowered, — she was carried away, — he pressed the soft hand, — she drew it out of his, — and went slowly out of the chamber, in order to come again to the help of the too tender heart, over whose sweet signs night hung her veil. . . .

The light which was brought in took away these dream-worlds. Matthieu and the Chamberlain's lady appeared also. We will not, however, in this soft mood, when one is precisely the severest against evil natures, say or think anything about the new couple which cannot help its contrast to our tenderness. Victor said this to himself, too, but more than once; because the Apothecary's lyingly alleged engagement of Clotilda to Matthieu impressed itself upon him in the liveliest colors, as resembling that platonic union, in which the pure spirit, driven out of its ether and with crooked-up wings, is immured in an unclean body. Clotilda came back. She was in a state of embarrassment towards Victor, merely because he was in one, or was to be still more so by her side in the sleigh, — the swollen ball of her eye she withdrew from the light. As condensation of tears, like inspissation of milk, oppresses and destroys; his sadness, repressed and drawn back into his innermost being, sought an outlet through the voice, which was vehement and abrupt; through the motions of the body, which were quick; even through vivacity of expression; — in short, it was well that they started.

He thought the opposite again, when he stood behind her on the sleigh. The night seemed to have withdrawn behind the clouds, whose wide arch occupied the heavens. He could not hunt up any subject of conversation, let him think as much as he would, — he ran through Clotilda's, Victor's, all his acquaintances' lives, — nothing occurred to him. The reason was, that his thoughts, which he sent out on this errand, returned every minute without his knowledge, and hung like bees on Clotilda's noble profile, or on her soft eye, or buried themselves in that tear of hers which had fallen on his hand, and in the whole ethereal sea of to-day's tones. The dark heaven above him finally put into his head Emanuel's last communication, and he could relate to her out of that the blind youth's initiation into the highest thought of man. Clotilda listened to him with delight, and at last said: "No one is more fortunate than a pupil of such a teacher: but he must never go into the world, — there he will be so no longer. His teacher has given him too soft a heart; and a soft heart, as you yourself say, hangs, like soft fruit, so low down, that every one can reach and wound it; the hard fruits hang higher."

They had arrived now at the hard fruits of the capital, and her remark was her own history. But the new scenes, — the rattling carriages and rustling dresses, — the much ado about little or nothing, — the hall-lights like systems of fixed stars, — the double mouth-*un*harmonicas, — the masculine court-fauna, — the feminine court-flora, — the whole mobilized pleasure camp, — this din of a fair drowned the muffled echo which passed to and fro between two harmonious souls.

Our hero was received by the Princess in a more friendly manner than even by the Prince. Joachime, Clotilda's lieutenant in office, had, in addition to her cold angry friendliness, a *montre à régulateur* rich in jewels. In a public place it costs less than in a cabinet to cover the inner man with the outer as with a theatrical mask. Victor, on whom, besides, every *sorrow* produced the witty effect of *intoxication*, betrayed the former at most by the exuberance of his vivacity.

A woman betrays herself by the opposite, — Clotilda by nothing. He expressed to her in the singular stunned state into which outer tones of joy and inner fantasies put one, when they come together like two streams meeting, the following ideas: "Were I the Goddess of delight (if there is one), I would have it strike three; round the chandeliers I would draw prismatic colors, or in fact would hang them up in the cabinets and diffuse through the dancing-hall with incense a magic twilight, — then I should have to set back the tones of the orchestra through so many apartments, that nothing of the music should find its way hither but a soft echo, — and then if, in the glimmering maze, breathing throughout with melodies, the people did not, after some silent movements, feel like sinking away with ecstasy, I greatly mistake." .... "Add further," said she, "in order that we too may have one, that we stay here and observe the dissolving."

But his composure hardly ever at any ball survived the minuet. After the first din was over, at least about the witching hour, his whole soul was always dissolved into a poetic melancholy which hardly left him the mastery of his eyes. Besides the tones, I can further adduce the *motion* as an explanation of this phenomenon: all motion, in the first place, is sublime, — that is to say, of great masses; or rather every quick motion imparts to the object the greatness of the space hurried through: hence, in contrast with the end in view, objects in motion are more comic than those at rest. Secondly, the movement of men imaged to him their fluttering by, their fleeing into graves; often at night he would stop in sad musing under the windows of houses, where they were dancing in the second story, and look up, and the gliding by of heads in their movement was to him the mad dance of *ignes fatui* in the churchyard.

To-night, with his melted, overflowing soul, he felt this sooner than ever. The Anglaise, in which one couple after another disappears from the column, was the very image of our shadowy life, into which we all march out with drums, and encircled with thousands of playmates, and in which we grow poorer and poorer every year as we move onward, every hour more solitary, and in which we hurry to the end forsaken by all except a hired man, who buries us behind the goal. But death spreads out, as it were, our arms, and folds them around our beloved brothers and sisters; a human being feels for the first time on the brink of the tomb, when he comes upon the realm of unknown beings, how much he loves the known ones who love him, who suffer like him, and like him die.

As a woman in no way discloses to us more touchingly the whole blessed past, than when she lifts her eyelids and shows us her beaming eyes, accordingly he could not well help, during the dance, at least, looking into an eye, which pictured to him nothing but heavens that had set, — and to-night all was to set for him, even the eye itself. And as Clotilda usually grew pale with dancing, he entered through her eyes into her innermost being, and counted there the tear-drops that hung undisturbed on the still soul, — the many incisions made by the grafting-knife of fate for new virtues, — the clipped roots which fate shortens in this flower as we do in lowlier plants, before transplanting into another soil, — and the thousand honey-vessels of sweet thoughts. And as he thought on all her hidden virtues at once, on the supremacy of her womanly reason over her sensibility, on her easy consent in regard to the ball which the Prince now imposed upon her, as well as in regard to the rouging on which the Princess had before insisted, and on her ready compliance, whenever she had to sacrifice nothing but herself; — and as he held the thought before his mind how she, not like the women of court and city, who, like shrubs at the window of the greenhouse, spread themselves out after the light, but like spring flowers, loved to bloom in the shade, and yet made as little show of her fondness for country life as of her modesty; — he had to turn away his eye from the delicate, upright flower, on which death threw down the gravestone; from that loveliest soul who never yet saw her worth in the glass of an equal; from the dying heart, which nevertheless was not happy.

And then, to be sure, the thought before which he shrank into himself sprang up like a storm: "I will tell her to-day how good she is, — O, I shall certainly never see her again, and she will die, otherwise unknown to herself! I will fall at her feet and confess my inexpressible love. She cannot be angry; God knows I crave not her holy heart, which no man deserves; I will only say, Mine shall never forget thee, but it desires not thine, only it will break more gently when it has trembled and bled and wept and spoken before thee." . . .

Close behind this thought came to him Clotilda herself, hand in hand with her step-mother, and, the face robbed of its color by the warmth as roses are by the sun, the tired and more sick-looking features put forth the silent prayer to come out into the fresh air and go home.

She went; her step-mother followed her at a distance. What a change of scene! Under the eastern gate of heaven stood the moon, who had taken off the funeral veil of cloud from the milky-way and the whole blue abyss. She gradually laid out a ground of silver, and sketched upon it with gleams and shadows a growing night-piece. The frost seemed to condense her light into body, into white meadows, into tumbling streams, into floating flakes; it hung glistering as white blossoming foliage on the bushes, it glimmered up the eastern mountains, which the sun had cast into ice-mirrors. And all above man and around man was sublimely still, — sleep played with death, — every heart rested in its own night.

And here, at this entrance, as it were, out of the turmoil of earth into the still twilight-shrouded underworld, cold thrills and after them glowing thrills ran over Victor's nerves. This happens when the soul of man is too full and too sorely agitated, and all the threads of the trembling web of the fleshly organism sway with it. His sleigh became now a flying gondola. The night-air blowing against him kindled all his flames. O the stream full of ice-points, if it had only swept over him! the cool coverlet of snow, if it were only laid upon him! A voice was continually crying within him: "Thou art bearing the still, the patient one with her black veil to death; it is her hearse: the noble pearl-diver has given heaven her sign that she has collected here below enough sorrows and virtues, that it may draw her up again to itself." The procession of mountains gliding by, the trees that whirled past, the fields that fled away, this flight of nature seemed to form together one great cataract that carried all before it, and man first of all, and left nothing behind it but time. And as he rolled down into the valley, where the city disappears, as did a year ago his female escort, and the moon behind the trees began seemingly to scud through the heavens, then he lifted his eyes toward the stars, and, bent backward in a rigid gaze, spoke aloud as out of a shattered heart to the heavens: "Deep blue grave over men, thou hidest thy broad nights behind crowded suns! Thou drawest us and our tears upward like vapors. Ah, cast not poor short-sighted mortals so far asunder, so infinitely far! And why cannot man look up to thee without thinking: who knows what loved heart I may not a year hence have to seek up yonder!"

His darkened eyes fell painfully from heaven — upon Clotilda's, which were lifted over against his. The tear which had just fallen from her eye down to her cheek she could neither conceal through the veil, nor make believe to be a snow-flake which had melted on her face, since the veil kept off the flakes; but such a tear needed no veil. Clotilda had thought he meant merely Emanuel, and therefore she was touched and softened. . . . . Like two parting angels, the two now beheld each other with tearful eyes. But Clotilda withdrew hers, and her sinking head bent. Nevertheless, she turned round again, and with her heavenly face and heavenly voice presented to him the sweet prayer: "Bestow this warm friendship upon my brother also; and forgive his sister today this prayer, as I may not for a long time have an opportunity to renew it." He bowed himself down low, and could not answer.

But when now her place of residence and her castle, from which the silver rain of the moon ran down, gleamed before their eyes, — as the moment came on, darker and darker, in which the parting (perhaps the mask of death) was to take this still angel from his side, — as every indifferent formula of leave-taking which he could imagine to himself lacerated his sick heart, — as he saw how she leaned her head on her hand and on the veil, in order, unobserved, to remove or check the first signs of her farewell, — then did the whole cloud which had so long been letting fall single drops into his eyes, rent asunder, rush down upon him and flood his heart. . . . Suddenly he stopped. . . . He looked with still gushing eyes toward St. Luna. . . . Clotilda turned round, and beheld a colorless face, a brow full of sorrows, and a quivering lip, and said bashfully, "Your soul is too good and too tender." Ay, then his over-full heart burst in twain. Then gushed up all the depths of his soul in which old tears had been so long accumulating, and lifted up from the roots his swimming heart, and he sank down before Clotilda, radiant with heavenly love and streaming sorrow, — mantled with the flame of virtue, — transfigured by the moonlight, — with his true, helpless breast, with his veiled eyes, — and the dissolving voice could only utter the words: "Angel of heaven! the heart breaks at last which loves thee inexpressibly. O, long indeed have I been silent. No, thou noble form, never canst thou pass out of my soul. — O soul from heaven, why have thy sufferings and thy goodness, and all that thou art, inspired me with an eternal love, and with no hope, but with an eternal sorrow?" Her agitated face lay bent aside from him in her right hand, and the left covered only her eyes, but not her tears. A dying sound implored him to rise. They heard the second sleigh far off. "Never-to-be-forgotten one! I torment thee, but I will remain where I am till thou hast granted me a token of forgiveness." She extended to him her left hand, and the gesture disclosed a holy countenance full of emotion. He pressed the warm hand to his flaming face, into his hot streams of tears. Trembling, he again asked: "O, my fault grows greater every moment! Will you, then, wholly forgive it?" . . .

Then did the blushing face bury itself in the folded veil, and, turning away, stammered: "Ah, then I must share it, noble friend of my teacher."

Blessed, blessed man! After this word, the whole of earthly life has no greater heaven to offer thee! Rest now in silent rapture with thy overpowered face upon the angelic hand, into which the noblest of hearts pours the blood that kindles for virtue! Shed all thy tears of joy upon the dear hand which has given them to thee! And then, — if thou canst for rapture or for reverence, — then lift up thy pure, glistening eye, and show her therein the look of sublime love, the look of the love which is eternal and speechless and blissful and unspeakable!

Ah! he, who had ever been loved by a Clotilda, could now read no farther, — write no farther, — for ecstasy . . . or else for pain!

Silent and sanctified he now sped along the fair road; the moon hung down from heaven like a dewy morning overlaid with white blossoms; spring stirred its meadows and its flowers under the veil of snow; rapture throbbed in Victor's heart, swelled in his breast, shone in his eye; but speechless reverence controlled his rapture. . . . They arrived. And when, in the harmonica-chamber, where in the evening he had grasped her hand for anguish, they now stood alone face to face, so changed, so blest for the first time, two such hearts, — she like an angel who had descended from heaven, he like a mortal who had risen from the earth, to fall on the heart of the timid angel, and, speechless, to go back with her to heaven. . . . What an hour! O, only for you, ye fair souls, who have never experienced such an hour, and yet have deserved it, do I go on picturing this one! . . . Like two risen ones before God, they look into each other's eyes and souls, — like a zephyr, which two swaying roses prolong, breathes between the trembling lips the speechless sigh of bliss, drunk in by the bosom in quick inspirations, and issuing with a tremulous thrill of glad awe in long expirations, — they continue silent, to look at each other, they lift their eyes, to see through the drop of joy, and cast them down again to dry it away with the eyelid. . . . . No, it is enough: O, there is another tear that now lies heavily on the fair heart, which is silent and would say, I was never happy, nor ever shall be!

Victor had so much to say to her, and had so few

minutes more left for it; and yet not so much joy as reverence made him dumb, — for sacred to the loving heart is the form that has said to it, I am thine. But think not he would make any such rude request to her, as that she would stay here on his account; only the *question* whether he might visit her in *Maienthal*, only the *prayer* that she would take thought of her recovery, can he venture upon. Clotilda had only one to make to him, which she could not sufficiently veil over, namely, that, for the sake of her jealous brother, he would not see her in Maienthal.

During the lingerings of rapture, they hear the bells of the second sleigh. Haste necessitated courage. Victor transformed his *prayer* into the *wish* that spring might favor the design of her journey (restoration to health), and the *question* into the *joyful thought* how happy she would be in Maienthal by the side of Dahore, how blest he had once been there, and how little he had once dreamed that one could ever be still more so there. Clotilda answered (probably to his wish of following her thither): "I leave behind quite as much to you, — my *brother* and your *friend;* forget not my former prayer."

Not until the approaching parents reminded Clotilda to throw back her veil, and admonished her beloved to take his first leave of the heart which he had won, — not till then did they both look far into the great Eden which had opened around their life, — and the bright moment which now darted by in the stream of time projected into eternity the images of two heavenly forms, — one unveiled, pale-red, transfigured with tears, and one glorified by love, radiant with the reflection of hope. And now let no longer the hand sketch souls, which not even the great, glowing eye of love can portray. . . .

5*

When the parents came, he felt, but he forgave, all possible contrasts. He soon took his leave, that he might at home, in the silence of night, throw the first prayerful glance over the stream of his future life, which now glided on toward the grave in lines of beauty, and in which gay minutes played like goldfishes.

In the stillness of night, not far from his wax-mummy, the happy one thought to fall down before the Infinite Genius and thank him, with new tears, for this night, for this friend, of whom he is the first love. But the thought of doing it is the deed, and O, how could our touched heart, which even before men is dumb, find any other words before the Infinite than tears and thoughts?

And in this resigned frame, full of deep tranquillity, wherein I lay down the pen, mayst thou, dear reader, lay aside this book, and say with me, There may well be more sad days that will conclude like the Twenty-eighth Dog-Post-Day.

## PREFACE TO PART III.

*(Which in the first edition came on a dozen sheets earlier.)*

AS the Intercalary Day this time falls in with the Preface, and as it begins, too, with the letter V,* both indeed can, with uncommon felicity, be despatched together.

* *Vorrede* being the German for Preface. — Tr.

## SEVENTH INTERCALARY DAY.

### END OF THE REGISTER OF EXTRA-SHOOTS.

### U. V.

UNFEELINGNESS OF READERS. — VOL. III. (PREFACE TO.)

THERE were once happy times, when one had nothing to suffer from his fellow-savage and neighbor, except being struck dead, — when the hail was the only knout-master of the skin, whereas now the trade-wind of the visiting-fan is to us a whirlwind, and the cool breath over the teacup a sea-breeze, — when one took less interest in another's trouble than in his fodder, — when the ladies never wounded the gentlemen in bear-skins in any way (least of all with glances, charms, tresses), except with clubs, and when, to be sure, they possessed themselves, as well as to-day and to-morrow, of the heart of an honest man, but only in this way, by first stretching out the proprietor of it on an altar and regularly slaughtering him, before they cut out the heavenly globe from his chest.

These times we have now all forfeited; in those which are upon us, things look badly. By heaven! one really needs not much less than everything to make him happy, and little more than nothing to make him unhappy, — for the former he requires a sun, for the latter a particle of sun-dust! We should be well off, and have the key to large apartments in all pleasure-castles, if fate had provided for us that we should endure, say as many degrees of torture as the Jurists have, namely, three, — no more plagues than the Egyptians underwent, namely, seven, —

no more persecutions than the first Christians stood out, namely, ten. But for such drawings of fortune a man of sense does not look; at least, no one promises himself such prizes, who like me sits down and considers our humming-bird stomachs, — our soft caterpillar skins, — our ears tingling of themselves, — our eyes which are their own tinder, — and our *culs de Paris*, which can be pierced, not by a crumpled rose-leaf, but by the very shadow of a thorn, — and our fine complexion, which without a moon-umbrella would blacken in the moonlight. . . . And yet in this account of our troubles, — because I am diligently intent upon lessening them, — I have not included other quite different, most accursed items, but have left out riches, e. g., entirely, that smart-money for so many thousand gashes and fractures of the breast, and in fact millions of wounds which would make our riddled self absolutely transparent, were it not fortunately clothed from head to foot in English court-plaster. . . . But I left out all such stuff, because I knew it would after all amount to nothing, if I should set it off against a quite different purgatory and tempest into which we male-kind particularly are thrown, if we are so unfortunate as to keelhaul ourselves, that is to say, fall in love, which in my poor opinion is a slight foretaste of hell, as well as of heaven. Let the best peeress in this department write to me, and enclose it post-paid to the publishing office in Berlin, and give me her name, if she was capable of not flaying and impaling her poor *pastor fido*, nor persecuting him with backbitings, nor filling his heart full of bruises with the compression-machines of her hands, his head full of fissures with the bastinado of the fan, his breast full of blisters with her eyes, nor of giving him, as they do to tobacco, a mellowing with her tears. . . .

At least I myself at this present moment come straight from such a house of correction and baiting-house, and my skin looks as pitiably as if I had a scalped one over my limbs.

We will say no more of this. My intention in all this is to brace up the reader, because a wholly new rainy-constellation (Pleiad) which I have not at all named is rising in his horizon, to snow upon him. This will rage worse than all that has gone before. What I mean is this: An imperial citizen may be just giving the finishing touch to everything, — his coffers * and his enemies may have been already overturned, and his labors right well received by the public or the board, — his pleas for delay have been allowed, and the quinquenniats † of his debtors refused, — his youngest daughter, who, like the eldest of the French king's brother, is called Mademoiselle, may already have got through with the measles and her betrothal afterward; it avails him nothing, the worst of all, a whole Gehenna still awaits him on his book-shelves; for there may the fair spirits (let him have swallowed as he may all bitter salt of fate) have sliced for him, under the name of romance-manna, a hard tear-bread, which I, for my part, should be glad neither to bake nor to chew, — truly they may (to use another metaphor) have composed and placed in readiness for him dead-marches and funeral cantatas, which shall utterly upset him and make him so warm that his eyes shall run over.

And unfortunately warm-blooded and soft-skinned excellent men are just the ones least remarkable for steadiness and moderation in bearing the poetical sorrows which

* *To turn over the strong-box* means *to count the cash.* — Tr.

† Outlawry of debts after five years. — Tr.

authors send them. I cannot, therefore, possibly leave this third part, which will too easily affect people, wholly without a preface in the way of counterpoise, unless I am willing to be myself the cause of innocent persons weeping over the best scenes of this part, and suffering from sympathy. Such too sensitive persons, to whom Nature has denied æsthetic apathy to cases of great distress in tragedies and romances, should, — unless they are fat, for sorrow is good for fatness as a fasting-cure and *lapis infernalis*, * — these should make themselves cold, and arm themselves against the tragic poet with philosophy; they should console themselves during the reading of a great affliction and say: "How long does such a printed misery last? How soon a book and a life are over! To-morrow thou wilt think very differently. The unhappy condition into which I am here brought by Shakespeare exists, in truth, only in my own imagination, and my sorrow over it is indeed, according to the stoic, only illusion. One must not, says Epictetus in his handbook, bewail that which lies not in our will, and the sad scene of Klopstock here is, in fact, an external thing, which thou canst not alter. Wilt thou let thyself be shamed by a North American, by a saltwork-man of Halle, by the rabble, by the Cretin from Gex, † who bore that whole scene from Goethe's Tasso quietly and composedly, without the moistening of an eye?"

I assure the readers that I take the field here only against their wives and sisters; for among readers of our sex stout-hearted spectators of æsthetic woes have never been wholly wanting, and still less than among the vulgar themselves; and least of all would I have the appear-

* Hell-stone, or lunar caustic. — Tr.

† The district in which Voltaire's Ferney lay. — Tr.

ance of disputing the great majority of business-people, reviewers, criminal-lawyers, and Dutchmen, the possession of great composure during the reading of sad crape-clad scenes, which I and others give to the press. Much rather do I fondly persuade myself that — if there ever was hope of the like — it is precisely now, when the German promises to put on that Belgian stoicism, that noble insensibility, which so becomes him, and through which he is made bullet- and blade-proof against Melpomene's dagger, and goes through Dante's hell, as Christ did through the real one, without suffering. We never, to be sure, had the sensibility of the French, and their Racine would never have been for us anything more than a prince's jester; but we are now, if an author does not absolutely push the matter too far and bring in too many battle-fields, and cups of rat-poison, and gallows-trees, — for that takes hold of us, — but if he only half good-humoredly trots along — I seem really to see him at this moment riding — on a mourning-steed, and shakes with one hand a death-bell, and with the other swings (ah, woe!) a funeral-marshal's baton; or if, finally, he only delineates the invisible, stanched gashes of the tenderer, more delicate soul; — then are we now already in a condition to maintain our merry humor, and to show what a German can endure. People of more moderate force *sleep* at least, so as not to *suffer* over a Goethe's *Iphigenia*, because sleep sets sufferers right; or we absolutely forget such elegies, because, according to Plattner, we have no memory for sorrows, and because oblivion — as a prince wrote — is the only remedy for sorrows; or Heaven sends us, as after sorrow joy, after a Messiad (of which a good travesty were to be desired for us) a

Blumauer's parody, over which we can easily forget the preceding epopee.

W.

Women. — Ye sweet, soft spring flowers and angel shoots by the side of us hard winter-cabbage-stumps, I have indeed already, under the former letter, remembered you and your tenderness in contrast to the German *immeltableness!* What shall I further say, except that, when you are good, you are so in the highest degree, and that you and the Cornwall tin have one and the same kind of stamp, — namely, the figure of an angel?

X (see I K S). — Y (see I). — Z (see T S).

Tz.

Spitz. — Poor Spitz likes as well to be in Prefaces among Extra-Shoots as his Master, and comes in just right with the Twenty-ninth Chapter. I can talk for hours with Pomeranian dogs, as Yorick did with asses. I will now set the messenger of the gods on his hind-feet and hold him by the fore-paws, that he may listen to me in an erect posture. — — — "Stand, nimble beast! — I talk with thee about something only that I may place thee in the third Preface. It deserves, Spitz, to be remarked, that thou art a rogue as men are, and like them wilt not remain *straight*, but *crooked* and bowed down, merely for the sake of eating well; thou and they will, like Faro-cards, win by *bending* and *crooking*, as the common English bend their bad silver money that it may not be passed for less, namely, two pieces for one. Thou hast false eyes, but nevertheless thy actions are good. The reviewers, impatient cattle, say, if they were in thy place, they would bring along the biographical building-stuff more industriously, that the biography might be over before it snows; — meet them not with the counter-assertion, that I might do like Baronius, who began his annals without a beard and ended them with a gray one. In that can only reviewers (but not I) imitate him, who have time to polish, and who can begin a work beardless, on shaving day, and not till three days after finish it, when they are lathered. — — Just fall down, Hofmann, and eat; thou art at least not wholly without sense, and givest more heed to an harangue, after all, than a Dauphin-fœtus, and at least waggest thy tail, which the fœtus does not. I have now to talk with quite other people, and the fewest possible among them wag their tails in token of appreciation, Spitz!"

JEAN PAUL.

## 29. DOG-POST-DAY.

CONVERSION. — BILLET-DOUX OF THE WATCH. — CRAPE HAT.

N the morning Clotilda went off to her poplar-island, and at noon Victor departed to his Pontine marsh, — both contented with a separation which made them worthy to enjoy a reunion.

The first thing to which the court-physician gave himself in Flachsenfingen was — afterthought, or rather after-feeling. Man is the Iceland-spar of time, which shows all scenes twice, side by side. Memory caught once more in her mirror the moonshine of last night, and the angels which floated in it, and turned the mirror with this lustre, with this perspective, towards my Victor. He thought over Clotilda's past conduct, in which he — as I hope my reader has — discovered the traits of the purest love, which looks with only one eye out of the veil, together with the traces of a decided mastery of woman's feelings over woman's wishes. She comes on the 1st of May from Maienthal with a weeping heart, which, torn away from a dead companion, still bleeds on from its open wounds. — The pupil of Emanuel meets her, and she hastens back again to the grave, there to quench in tears of mourning her first love. — But Emanuel communicates his holy fire to this love by his own, by his praise of the beloved, by his open letter full of germinating love, which the latter had written to him on the birthday festival of the 4th of May. — She returns unrestored, towards the time of his approaching departure. — But her good Emanuel, with the cruel kindness of friendship, impresses the image which makes her heart too uneasy still more deeply into its wounds, by reporting to her Victor's life in Maienthal and his confession that he loves her. Victor is silent before her, but she thinks he is so because he has no permission from his father to speak with her about Flamin's relationship. — He goes to court, and seems to forget her, nay, he puts upon her the chains of the court office, which nevertheless, as he knows, oppress her soul even to blood. Her parents, either by way of sounding her, or of flattering her secret suitor Matthieu with her female veiling of herself, extort from her by a tyrannical question the unhappy No, which deceives her brother and repels her friend. Victor steals away, on her festal evening, from the garden, without speaking to her, thereupon visits her parents again, and grows entirely cool. Now she hears nothing more of him excepting, at most, of his pleasures at court and his visits to Joachime. — — — Ay, thou good soul, thus, in conflict with wishes and with troubles, in sick pining after the loved soul, must all thy joys go to sleep and thy hopes die out, and thy innocent cheeks grow pale! — — As, now, Victor thus thought over this sad past, and remembered how, in the playhouse, where he revealed to her his knowledge of her sisterly relation, the last bloom of her cheek, the last twig of hope, fell off, because she could regard his previous silence as owing to a command of his father, — and as all these traits conspired to form the image of a heavenly queen before whom it is easier to kneel down than to embrace her, — and as he further reflected that this noble heart, improved by an Emanuel and worthy of an Emanuel, nevertheless gave itself with all its heavens to the fickle heart of the pupil — — and that the good soul could not have even this modest wish fulfilled, because fate delayed the blossoming of her love like that of a rose-bush by transplanting it, by setting it in the shade, by clipping the buds in *spring* and *autumn*, — and as he saw that nevertheless this noble one had gone off to Maienthal with her finger on her lips, with her hand on her heavy heart, without a hint of her bitter disappointment, and that moral coldness *lifted up* this flower, as physical cold does other flowers, but tore from it thereby the roots of life, — and as, finally, his dream on the third Easter-holiday, when it appeared to him as if he saw her rise singing from the earth on a light veil of mist, passed by before him like a great rain-cloud, and the dream with her faded hues paused before his pining soul, and a voice out of the dream asked him, "Wilt thou long continue to love her, when angels yearn for her and lift her out of her sorrow, and leave thee nothing but the grave of the too long misinterpreted heart?" — — As all these thoughts, in glowing procession, like mountain chains of ruddy evening clouds, moved around his soul, then was his heart, like an altar, covered by a sacrificial fire falling from heaven, and all his earthly desires, all his stains, were consumed in this fire, — in short, he resolved to amend himself, in order, by virtue, to be worthy of a virtuous woman.

He was converted on the 3d of April, 1793, towards evening; when the moon — and the EARTH — were under his feet in the Nadir.

The reader may have laughed at this chronometer; but every man in whom virtue is anything higher than an accidental *water-sucker* and wood-shoot, must be able to tell the hour wherein she became the Hamadryad of his inner being, — which the theologians call conversion and the Moravians the *breaking-through.* Why should not time mark off our spiritual sensations, when in fact it is only they that mark off its periods?

There is — or comes — in every man who is more solar than planetary, a lofty hour when his heart, amidst violent commotions and painful rendings, at last, by a lifting-up, suddenly turns round towards virtue, in an indescribable transition like that in which man lifts himself over from one system of faith to another, or, suddenly, from the highest point of wrath to a melting forgiveness of all faults; — that lofty hour, the birth-hour of the virtuous life, is also its sweetest hour, because it is to man as if his oppressive body were taken off from him; because he enjoys the bliss of feeling in himself *no contradictions;* because all his chains fall; *because he fears nothing more* in the awfully sublime universe. — The spectacle is great, when the angel is born in man; when, thereafter, on the horizon of earth, the whole solar warmth of virtue falls upon his heart unobstructed by a cloud.

But poor mortal man, the prisoner man, immersed in blood, encased in flesh, soon feels the difference between his raptures and his powers; he who was going to subdue the promised land, when its clusters of grapes came to meet him, hesitates, when he has to march against its giants (the passions). I do not, however, reject even the extravagance of that enthusiasm; Man, like buildings, must be *screwed up into the air,* in order to be *rebuilt;* a syllogism does not lead off the blood streams of our desires. It is singular that the devil in us must have alone the right to spend blood, nerves, beverage, passions, upon his military operations and for his imperial treasury, but the angel not. . . .

So it is, however; men are vicious, because they look upon virtue as too hard, and they again become so, because they held it easier than it is. Not reason (i. e. conscience) makes us good: that is the outstretched wooden arm on the road to virtue; but this arm can neither draw nor drive us thither,—reason has the legislative, not the executive force. The power of loving these commandments, the still greater power of giving one's self up to them, is a second conscience by the side of the first; and as Kant cannot indicate with ink that which makes man bad, so neither can that be set forth which keeps his heart upright above moral filth or lifts it out of it.

Who can explain the fact, if there are men who, from youth up, either possess or do without a certain sense of honor, — in the female sex this line of division is still sharper and more important,—if there are men who, from youth up either experience or forever live without a certain yearning for the super-earthly, for religion, for the nobler principle in man (and for systems which seal this nobler quality instead of disputing it)? — — (With children a warm feeling for religion is often a sign of genius.) Man does not become good (though he does grow better) because he is converted, but he gets converted because he is good.

Were virtue nothing but stoicism, then it were a mere child of reason, whereas it is at the highest her foster-daughter. Stoicism represents virtue as so useful, so reasonable, that it is nothing more than a conclusion; it gives one nothing to conquer but errors. As (according to the stoical principle) it is, not the highest, but the only good, — as, according to that principle, all desires aim at an empty nothing,—it follows that virtue is no merit, but a necessity. E. g. if there is nothing odious: then love and the victory over anger towards an enemy are not harder or more meritorious than towards a friend, but all one.

What then has the Stoic to sacrifice to Virtue according to his notion, but mock-goods, air-castles, and fever-images? Nevertheless Stoicism renders Virtue, as criticism does genius, negative services; the stoical *chill* calls forth no spring, but it destroys the insects which gnaw it; the stoical winter, like the physical, removes the *pestilence*, ere the warmer months come, which bring new life. . . .

Although Victor said: "Thou dear one, no heart can be pure, still, tender, and great enough for thine, but the weak one which thou endurest will sanctify itself through thine and come to thee improved"; still mere love was not the source of his virtue, but the reverse was the case, only virtue could manifest itself by such a love. But even without taking that into account, a half-selfish change of purpose becomes by action a disinterested one, as the love which starts from beauty of face ennobles itself at last into love for beauty of soul.

His separation from Clotilda gave him joy in the thought that so long as it lasted he should spare the delusions of her jealous brother. *General love* now led the way to friendship for the better sort of women, and tolerance toward the worse. He annulled his satirical intolerance — which, however, was not half so great as that of young wags of authors — by toleration-mandates of his own. He read Gulliver's last journey into Horse-land (Houynheim), as a recipe against lying when one goes to court. His Kubach* and jewel-casket and his *collegium pietatis* consisted of three dissimilar volumes, — Kant, Jacobi, and Epictetus.

* Probably some *vade-mecum* of Jean Paul's time. — Tr.

I could wish, however, that he would not make himself ridiculous. Of a man who had been nine months at court, one was surely justified in expecting that he would behave differently, and not offend against that equality of ranks and of vices; as men practise sins best in common, as in Swiss churches the hearers must cough simultaneously, or as recruits on their march must make water at the same time. At least, the well-bred man seeks to conceal his love for his religion, as well as that for his wife. — I return to the story.

Victor determined now to make only visits that annoyed himself and pleased his neighbor. The first was an extraordinary tribute of a visit to the Princess (for his daily portioning-tax * of calls on her now ceased). To be sure, the thick hour-watch of old Bee-father Lind was every minute an alarm-clock to hold up before him his former foolhardy jokes, his watch-enclosure, and love-letter to Agnola. I cannot avoid the apprehension that the reader may make a slip, and not dream with what heart Sebastian went to the Princess; — O, with one full of dumb apologies and — exculpations, with a distended breast full of proud confidence, and yet full of sympathetic mildness. Whence came this? — It came from the fair soul which now, reconciled and filled up with another's *love*, could wish nothing more but *friendship*, and which was now too happy to be inexorable. But he found in her apartment two cold, refined faces, which it is quite as hard to apologize to as to forgive, — namely, her own and that of Count von O. from Kussewitz, in whose house her transfer had taken place. Victor blushed; the Count appeared not to have the least knowl-

* Contribution levied on subjects when the sovereign's daughter is to be portioned. — Tr.

edge of him, — they were not introduced to each other, — but talked together as genially as if they had been (especially as it made no difference), — and so, with cold feelings, and with the greatest indifference about their own and each other's anonymousness, they politely separated. Only Victor afterward worried himself with doubts whether he had not sooner than Agnola called the unknown Count by that title.

For the rest, he now, for the first time since he had loved Clotilda, found the partition-wall between *love* and *friendship* with women to be very *visible* and very *thick:* before that he could see through the partition-wall well enough. A woman cannot choose for herself a firmer or purer friend than another woman's lover.

Victor must now also, and for still more urgent reasons, visit Joachime. The evil spirit, which, like the youngest councillors, always gives its voice first in man, made the motion that "he should indulge Joachime in the slight illusion of believing that he loved her." — As this did not pass, the *filou** took another voice, and proposed that "he should punish her for her former ambiguity by the most unambiguous signs of his hatred." — But he followed willingly the good spirit which led him by the hand, and said on the way, "Go now to her, — disengage thyself from her without giving her any pain, — let thy hand glide gradually out of hers, and clear one finger after another, as maidens do with their natural hand, and assume the attitude neither of her enemy nor of her lover." He went to her house without any selfish consideration; for the latter would rather have prompted him to stay at home, and enjoy and turn over the leaves of the past and future, or else to quit the house and go to St. Luna, to

* Knave. — TR.

sit down by Agatha beside the crape hat of Clotilda which she was studying.

In order, however, not to let his visit have too much weight in the eyes of Joachime, he proposed to himself to beg of her for some weeks the views of Maienthal, which hung in her room. O Maienthal, how much thou must have, if the very sketch of thee makes one so happy!—But his visit turned out singularly. He wished on the way that he might find in her toilette-chamber the fine fool and the fragrant fool and more stuff;—there was nothing there. She received him with a careless gayety, as if she were the Columbine * and the Medicus the clown. He, however, was going merely to execute the gradual weakening or *diminuendo* of his moral dissonances; therefore he became, by his constant looking off at his note-stand, and at the score of his inner harmony, somewhat stiff and awkward in his playing. Women easily distinguish the coldness of reason (if only by the very want of extravagance) from coldness of mood. Now he asked for the views. Joachime did not grow cooler, but warm, i. e. serious, and lifted up her watch in the hollow of her hand, and said, looking at it, "I give you as many minutes' grace as you have stayed away days, to excuse your staying away." Victor accepted without embarrassment—like every one who acts only according to *one*, either good or bad, principle—the allowed time for decision, and took the *montre à régulateur* from under the looking-glass, that Joachime might not cheat him. This cursed watch of the Princess grinned at him everywhere, like a percussion-ball and powder-mine under his feet. He wound it up just to have a chance to open this Nuremberg egg

* Ballet-dancer. — "The brisk locomotion of *Columbine*." (Johnson's ghost in "Rejected Addresses.") — Tr.

(as they used to call watches), and finally for once to examine whether the love-declaration, i. e. the *punctum saliens* of love, or the Cupid, — who also, according to Plato, came out of an egg, — was still in there. "I know well enough — he said to himself — it has been gone this long time, but I 'll just try it."

There might have been, indeed, a question whether it was the same watch, as the one in Tostato's shop had no diamonds, — had there not come fluttering out from this Pandora's box, so soon as it was opened at the window, a little thin piece of paper half as big as a butterfly's wing, and as long as the stamen of a tulip. — The little leaf took flight at every breath of wind. —— Joachime caught the thing, — read the thing, — found the declaration of love still there, — took it for one which he was just making to *herself*, by way of atoning for his absence, and which, for the sake of the wit (he might allude to its heart-shape), he had been trying to incorporate into the watch. . . .

Every one can imagine how he felt about the matter. — He would have got through it very well, if he had dared to lie terribly, or if he could have ventured at least to imitate the few courtiers who, into the twenty-eight pounds of blood which irrigate their bodies, have not instilled twenty-eight drops of honest blood, — of which a single one may, as a *liquor probatorius*, leave behind in the remaining mass confounded precipitates. But his soul loathed this new bait to lure him to a lie. The reader cannot possibly yet know that Victor shot aside from the mark, — that is to say, that, on account of the remoteness of Joachime's suspicion, he did not guess it at all, but fell upon the nearer one, that Joachime had nosed out his whole whimsical trick upon the Princess. He was never capable of holding up another's body as a shield against the arrows which were aimed at his own, — a habit on the Court-Moriah, which, not, like the Old Testament plan, redeems an *Isaac* with a *ram*, but a ram with an Isaac; he was to-day least of all capable of sacrificing the Princess to save himself; but neither could he bring himself even to *this*, to sacrifice Joachime for the sake of saving *her*, i. e. to recoin the devil's-billet into a sweet-billet (*billet-doux*) to Joachime. The Satan in him screamed himself hoarse to get him only so far along, that he at least would lie by silent expression of countenance, and justify hers, wherein there began to be less and less appearance as if she supposed it directed to another lady.

He told her right out plainly what he was, — a fool. He narrated the whole business in Kussewitz. He concluded by saying that it was lucky for him that the Princess had not at all detected the crazy insertion into the watch. . . . As now he recited all this monotonously without a single flattery, out of which some sort of a new and improved edition of the insertion might possibly have been made, he was fortunate enough, at his departure, to leave the enlightened Joachime in a state which, after such magnetic passes, expresses itself with cultivated women in a fine, proud *exaltation*, and with uncultivated ones in the attempt to put the sculptor's last touch to a man, just as the Greek artists did to their models, — namely, with the finger-nails. Victor took his leave with two very different sorts of *views*, those of the future and those of Maienthal. —

She kept the billet. Not fear, however, but the bitter feeling that his former follies ended only in another's heart with an abortive hope, this trickled with bitter drops into the sweet, rejuvenating sensation of having acted right at his own expense. An emotion, a tear, is an oath before Heaven that one will be good; — but a single sacrifice steels thy soul more than five tears of penitence and ten penitential sermons.

I have not the courage to guess why the Princess should have given the watch with the enclosure which she (even by the showing of her conversation with Tostato) must have read, into the hands of Joachime; but to the suspicious knaves whom I thought of when writing the chapter of her eye-bandaging and kiss, this is a windfall: the present of the watch confirms them entirely in their knavish creed; for they can now — despite all my efforts to the contrary — allege the gift as a sign of the Italian revenge which Agnola had proposed to herself to take upon her rival Joachime (to whom she must needs ascribe Victor's resistance) in the fact of communicating to her his declarations of love in other quarters.

Victor proposed to himself, as he took the greatest physical strides homeward, to take similar politic ones, and to confess plumply to the Prince: "It is not much over nine months since I troubled your Illustrious Highness's bride with a flimsy declaration of love, which she certainly cannot have ever read, and which now changes hands." But at present the opening of the affair of the watch-letter was impracticable: January was a little vexed at Clotilda's withdrawal; Victor had also for some time been less about him than usual, which certainly with an honest favorite ought not to be so, as, e. g., the famous Count von Brühel * watched, like a mother, around his master from morn to midnight. January seemed in this loneliness to think more of his children, and Victor

* 1700 – 1763. A famous, extravagant German statesman attached to Augustus III. of Saxony. — Tr.

had no tidings to impart to him from his Lordship. The main thing, moreover, was his spring sickliness, which made him again the credulous disciple of Dr. Culpepper and the gout. This doctor's trunk under a doctor's hat, whose brain-fibres were twisted to bass-strings, extolled his simplicities, merely by the solemn pomposity with which he delivered himself of them, beyond their value; of certain persons, e. g. physicians, financiers, economical-agents, even people of fine manners require stiff ones, and make more account of a pointed wig than of a hair-bag as big as a buckle or a Titus's-head.* Sebastian appeared to people much too waggish to allow them to think that he had learned anything. In the article of physicians — as in every main article of property or of life — the most distinguished vulgar think as the lowest, and prize men and lapdogs according to shaggy wildness of exterior. Besides, Victor had the fault of bringing himself and the physicians under suspicion of a thirst for glory, in that he praised them outright; e. g. "By their impressment of sailors and dead men they were a sort of buyers-up of souls for the next world, and served for nut-crackers to the good angels, who desired the kernel without the bodily shell, in order to transplant it. How often do we not obviate," he continued, "the most dangerous *transfers of maladies* by an easy *transfer* of the patient? I might appeal to the *refugiés* from this world, whether our sand-box and inkstand (the implements of our receipts) are not the sowing-machine and waterpot of the winter-crop of humanity; but the survivors shall speak and answer whether, for the benefices, the regiments, the estates in fee, the order-ribbons, which fall to them, they have not

* Heads of short, frizzled hair, modelled after the busts or portraits of Titus. — Tr.

to thank our recipes and Uriah's-letters, and whether they or even kings would sit *high and dry*, without our frequent *ditching* and draining in the churchyard. — And yet, methinks, our renown in the way of healing and bringing to life is quite as great, if not greater; this glory — as well as the lists of mortality on which it is based — has remained for many centuries the *same*, — our theories, specifics, judgments, may *change* as they will."

Such satires made the Prince right merry and incredulous. Dr. Culpepper, on the contrary, stood upon his dignity, and would have drawn his sword against a satirist who had talked of the slow decimation of physicians, and by a swifter one have completely refuted him. I advise every one who wants to be anything in the world (that is anything different from what he is) to appear among men as a funeral-bidder, — with women, as a godfather-bidder. — The Prince in the sickly spring held himself, for two reasons, to be possessed with the gout again: first, because I have never yet known a nervous weakling who, when I had talked a disease out of him in summer, did not the next sickly winter get it into his head again; secondly, because January calculated that he had fallen on his knee before ladies often enough to feel the traces of his adoration still lingering in the shape of *gonagra* or knee-gout.

So stood matters, when a little accident made our Victor happy again. Only I must say beforehand that, independently of that, he was not at all unhappy: for a lover never worries himself about anything, certainly not about a court; he has on Cupid's bandage, and willingly forgives Fortune and Justice theirs. And the moral Easter-eve bonfire melted — just as superstition ascribes to the physical one a peculiar power — all the ice wherewith they dammed up Victor's blood into the lymph of joy; the Easter-wind — which, according to the weather-prophets, continues till Whitsuntide — set his old joy-flowers in motion, and wafted forth from them the pollen of future ones; the snow dissolved on the hot spring awaking from its winter sleep, and the first flowers and the thousand buds gave all hearts energies and hopes and love. O when Victor looked out of doors toward the green-growing path which, with fresh sap-colors, (for in spring the foot-paths grow green first,) would fain lure and lead him out of the midst of the after-grass heath to the Eden of Maienthal, — and then when he turned round glowing and thirsting, and ran over into the sketched Maienthal, into the borrowed views, and there climbed every colored mountain, and encircled every dotted-out garden with his fingers and fancies, — then he did not think himself that a little accident could make him still more joyous. — And yet it did.

It is not well done of me that I always — and it is a thing I have become very much accustomed to in this biography — call that an *accident* which is a direct great-grandchild by blood of former chapters, and which really must come. For the crape hat — that was the accident — must indeed come, because it was bespoken. It was, however, the — original itself. Besides, in so small a time no hat could have been made by the nimblest master-builder of finery; and yet Sebastian never would have thought, had not traces of powder and opened lace-lattices compelled him, to distinguish the old hat from a new one. In short, Clotilda had given it to Agatha, who could not conceal from her for whom she was taking the copy, *before* the *third* Easter-holiday, for the purpose of letting her copy it, and *after* the aforesaid day had written to her to send her the copy and pass off the original upon the Medicus for the imitation, (as in the case of the wax-statue,) — and why, perhaps? — O, of that her friend had a sweet consciousness; she was sorry that she could not give a shy, delicate heart anything, not a sound, nor a glance, nor a joy, nor a reminiscence of the fairest evening, except its mere autumnal after-flora, mere silk-flowers sewed together in imitation of that flower of joy, the taffeta shadow of a taffeta-shade. . . . No, she did violence to herself, in order to give the mute darling at least more than a copy of the shadow. O, if the loving, closed heart of a good woman should open before a man, how much controlled tenderness, how many veiled sacrifices and dumb virtues, would he see reposing therein!

— One must, at any rate, with the German Diet and its cross-benches, make no mystery of the fact, that Victor would not accept the ninth Electoral hat, or in fact the eighth and last, on condition of parting with the *crape hat*. . . . . What can the thickest, heaviest crowns, said he, which have been exhibited to me in my travels, weigh in the one scale, — even supposing one should throw in also several tiaras and doges' caps with bows and papal hats, — if Clotilda's crape hat weighs down the other? As the reader has quite as much intelligence as I, let him decide the question. — This hat gave him an inexpressible longing for Maienthal, and was to him a dedicatory copper-plate which (as by an *investitura per pileum*) first presented Clotilda to him; he stood before this crown as an heir to the crown — every minute drew his coronation-chariot — with two big drops of joy, which the happy eye could not hold, and said slowly, gently shaking his head: "No, kind destiny gives me too much. — Ah, how can I deserve this soul from heaven? — I will merely say to her, I am thine! and by and by, some day, Thou art mine!" And when his fancy actually opened behind the crape-lattice-work the two great eyes which had once concealed behind it the tears of a rejected heart, and when he let the remote voice discourse again out of shadowy threads behind this nunnery-grating, then he could no longer restrain himself from writing, — so that he might thus go to Maienthal, — as he sat opposite the hat, his first letter to her, which I shall certainly get from the dog by to-morrow evening's post. —

I believe I have not yet said that Agatha handed him the hat, and that she invited him — it is now towards the end of April — to the birthday of her father on the 4th of May. Victor thought on the melancholy 4th of May of the year '92, and grew still more full of yearning for the friend who was torn from him.

Before closing the chapter, I will only say to the younger Clotildas, the Vice-Clotildas, the illegitimate Clotildas, and the Counter-Clotildas, who have me and my chapters in their laps: Be cool. You cannot possibly carry the coldness of virtue too far, unless you absolutely set no limits to it. I will, on your account, dress up this doctrine in wise sayings and witty sentences, that it may be the better adapted to fans and albums.

Love, like the seed of the Auricula, must be sown on snow; both are warmed through by ice itself, and then spring up so much the more vigorously. — You must never give yourselves as a mere present, but as a lady's acknowledgment of thanks to her knight. — You receive and deserve exactly as much respect as you demand, and you can, though you should be *alloyed* as much as you pleased, take your mint-die or coin-stamp out of your pocket and coin yourselves therewith as a *lady d'or* for one gentleman, or as a miserable little *fat-mannikin* * for another. — A rake indicates in a company, like a measurer of the purity of the air, by the different degrees of his boldness, the different degrees of female merit, only in inverse relation. * . .

Even if it did not belong to the female point of honor, one must still desire, merely for the sake of having one trouble more, — because my sex thinks on this subject entirely with me, who desire a daughter from no recruiting-house of sons-in-law, where at least the parents have not something against me; — and let it hereby be known (therefore I do not insert it in the newspaper) that I expect of parents, who in their auction-room of daughters, in their love-inoculation-hospital, have one or two subjects to dispose of, and to whom a Mining-Superintendent, Justice, Music-Master, and Biographer — such may be my few offices — is no too contemptible match, — that I [I repeat] expect of such parents, that (if they mean the thing seriously) they will at least forbid me the house or frequent correspondence: — that enlivens sons-in-law.

* A small Cologne coin, so named from the image of a little fat man or monk (some thinking *fettmännchen* a corruption for *fettmönchchen*) stamped on it. — Tr.

## 30. DOG-POST-DAY.

### Letters.

HAD I or any one else been lying in wait behind a bush or in a narrow pass, and had we darted out in the nick of time, we might have taken away the two letters, sealed up one into the other, which Victor was sending to Maienthal, from the hands of the messenger, who understood no German, namely, his Italian servant. The letter to Emanuel was the wrapper of the letter to Clotilda, — friendship is always the envelope of love. Of the wrapper I will give only an extract before I communicate in full the letter to Clotilda. He begged his Emanuel to take this only as a letter-cover, and to hand the enclosed to Clotilda alone; — he told him without further explanation he was held not by his own wishes, but by flowery chains which drew him back from the other chains of flowers in Maienthal, and that a manifold fettering with garlands was something one *could* not break through, because one *would* not, — he was intentionally obscure in regard to his new connection with Clotilda, because he could not presume upon her permission of the contrary; — he playfully begged his friend to beg his lady-friend to command him to make the journey to Flachsenfingen, that they might get a sight of each other, — (I lose my way in this period if

I show the design of this way of putting the thing); — he erased again in his head the question, whether Clotilda still needed the physician, merely because he was one for her in a double sense, and only asked whether she had recovered. — Finally he concluded thus : —

"And thus then I flutter with tolerably dusted butterfly's * wings in the immense temple which to our butterfly * eyes breaks up into smaller ones, and the leafy ornaments of whose columns we take for the columns themselves, and whose rows of pillars become invisible from their greatness; there flutters the human butterfly * up and down, — strikes against windows, — rows through dusty cobwebs, — flaps his wings at last around a hollow flower, — and the great organ-tone of the eternal harmony tosses him about with merely a *dumb*, rising and falling tempest, which is too great for a mortal ear.

"Ah, now I know life! Were not man even in his desires and wishes so *systematic*, — did he not in all things aim at roundings-off as well of his Arcadias as of the kingdom of truth, — then he might be happy and brave enough for wisdom. But a looking-glass wall of his *system*, a living hedge of his *paradise*, neither of which lets him *sally* or *see* into the infinite, fling him back forthwith to the opposite side, which receives him with new railings and throws in his way new limits. . . . Now, when I have gone through such various states, passionate, wise, foolish, æsthetic, stoic; now that I see that the most perfect of them crooks and cripples either my earthly roots in the earth, or my twigs in the ether, and that, even if it did not do that, still it could not last over an hour, to say nothing of a life; — as, therefore, I

* The one word *butterfly* is expressed by three different words here in German: *Schmetterling*, *Phaläne*, and *Zweifalter*. — Tr.

clearly see that we are a fraction only and not a unit, and that all reckoning and reduction of the fraction is only an approximation between numerator and denominator, a change of the $\frac{1000}{1001}$ into $\frac{10000}{10001}$, I say: "Well, for all me — be it so! Let wisdom, then, be for me the *finding out* and *enduring* of merely the *least* gaps in our knowing, enjoying, and doing." Accordingly, I no longer let myself be led astray, nor my neighbor either, by that most common illusion, that man regards every change in himself — every improvement at all events, but also even every deterioration — as greater than it afterward proves.

"— Enough! but since this observation — and still more since high destiny has given me joys, *in order that* I might deserve them — new morning-light has fallen on my shady path, and I have new courage to improve myself. The clear stream of time runs over a sloping flower-bed of fair hours, on which I once stood, and upon which I can distinctly look down. — O when this Eden-lawn once comes up again, and I can take thy hand and walk upon it, and kneel down beside thee and look gratefully now to the morning-sky and now over the waving flower-fields of this life; then will I fall back upon thee speechless, and gratefully embrace thy breast, and say: 'O my Emanuel! only through thee do I indeed deserve it all.' Nay, I say it to-day, beloved teacher, and do thou stay a good long while by the side of thy scholar on the earth, even until he is worthy to accompany thee out of it." —

*   *   *   *   *

Long as this letter was, still Victor after all loved his teacher too much, — and hated too much the princely rudeness of making men tools, — not to have told him outright, that this letter owed — not so much its origin as — its birthday to the letter to his beloved. Here is the one to Clotilda, into which with the following words he brings his request to see her: —

"If I knew that I should even for a moment oppress or disturb by this sheet the beloved soul, which will now be enjoying itself by the side of the lofty Emanuel, in the presence of spring and amidst its fair thoughts, O most gladly would I sacrifice this blessed hour, in order, perhaps, to deserve it. But no, my friend forever! your tender heart desires not my silence! Ah, man must so often conceal coldness and bitterness, why, too, even love and joy? — Nor should I be able to do it to-day.

"O, if an inhabitant of earth had in a dream gone through Elysium; if great unknown flowers had waved above him; if a saint had handed him one of these flowers with the words, 'Let this remind thee when thou awakest that thou hast not dreamed!' — how would he pine for the Elysian land, as often as he looked upon the flower! Never-to-be-forgotten one! you have, in the glimmering night, when my heart twice succumbed, but only once from pain, given a mortal an Eden, which reaches out beyond his life; but to me it has seemed till now as if I were waking more and more out of the receding dream-night, — when, lo! I received from the paradisiacal dream a flower,* which you left behind for me, that I might remain inexpressibly happy, and that my longing might be as great as my bliss. Why does this crape draw up all the hot tears out of the depth of my heart, why do I see behind this woven lattice the eyes open, which are so far from me, and which so move

* The crape hat.

my inmost being to sadness? O, nothing appeases the loving soul, but what it shares with the loved one; therefore do I gaze upon the spring with such a sweet stir of emotion; for she enjoys it, too, I say, — therefore it is that thou pleasest me so, dear moon, with thy evening star; for thou weavest the web of thy silver-threads round her shadows also and her May-flowers, — therefore it is that I so love to bury myself in every shaded dell of your Eldorado; for I think, in the magnified shadows, in the fragrance-breathing blossoms of these pictures, she is now roaming, and the moon-sickle deflects the softened lightnings of the sun upon her eye. Then when I am too full of joy, when the *evening-rain* of memory falls upon the hot cheeks, when my rapture rocks up and down on a single long trembling tri-clang of the harpsichord, then does the trembling and the silence and the infinite love too heavily oppress with woe the tumultuous heart, then do I yearn for the least sound, wherewith I may tell the beloved of my heart how I *love her*, how I honor *her*, that for *her* I will live, for *her* will die! — — O my dream, my dream steals now like a tear into my heart! In the night of the third Easter-holiday I dreamed: Emanuel and I stood in a dusky nocturnal region. A great scythe on the western horizon flung flying, reflected flashes at the high lawns, which forthwith dried up and turned pale. But when a flash flickered into our eyes, our hearts, sweetly fainting, drew themselves up in the breast, and our bodies grew lighter for soaring away. 'It is the scythe of Time,' said Emanuel, 'but whence does it, haply, catch the reflection?' We looked toward the east, and there hung far in the distance and high in the air a broad dark-glowing land of vapor, which occasionally lightened. 'Is not that Eternity?' said Emanuel. Then fell before us light snow-pearls, like sparks. We looked up and three gold-green birds of paradise poised themselves overhead and swept round incessantly in a little circle, one after the other, and the falling pearls came from their eyes, or were their eyes themselves. High above them stood the full moon in the blue, but on the earth there was still no light, but a blue shadow: for the blue of heaven was a great blue cloud, opened only in one place by the moon, which poured down radiance on the three birds of paradise, and down below on a bright form averted from us. — *You* were that form, and turned your face toward the East, toward the hanging landscape, as if you would presently see something there. The birds of paradise sprinkled their pearls faster and faster into your eyes; 'They are the tears which our friend must shed,' said Emanuel; and then, too, they fell from your eyes, but more brightly, and lay glittering on the flowery ground. The blue on the earth suddenly grew brighter than the blue in the heavens, and a steep cavern, whose mouth yawned towards Eternity, sank back deeper and deeper through the earth towards the west, down even to America, where the sun shone from below into the opening, — and a stream of evening-red, broad as a grave, shot upward out of the earth, and diffused itself with its evening sheen over the far haze-land of the vapory Eternity like thin flames. Then trembled your outspread arms, then trembled your songs full of blissful longing, then could we and you see perfectly the illuminated Eternity. But it shifted with playing colors under the gaze, we could not retain even in thought what we saw; they were elusive forms and dissolving hues, they seemed near, seemed far, seemed to be in the midst of our thoughts. — Little clouds going up from the earth floated around the glowing Eternity, and each bore a human being, standing upon it and singing, up to that luminous island, which clove itself open toward the earth, with only an endless row of white trees, moulded of light and snow, and instead of blossoms putting forth purple flowers. — And we saw our three shadows lying sublimely projected on the radiant white grove; and on Clotilda's shadow the purple flowers hung down as garlands; an angel hovered round the lovely shadow and smiled upon it tenderly and touched the place of the heart upon it. Then didst thou suddenly tremble, Clotilda, and turn round towards us, fairer than the angel in Eternity; thy whole ground gleamed under the fallen tears and became transparent. And now when thy dropping pearls dissolved the ground into a rising cloud, then didst thou hastily reach thy hand to us, and say, The cloud takes me up, we shall see each other again. — Ah! my fainting heart no more retained its blood: I knelt down, but I could say nothing; I would fain have melted my soul into a single sound, but the fettered tongue could not frame one, and I stared at the ascending immortal with infinite and inconsolable love. — Ah! thought I, life is a dream; but I could perhaps say to her how I love her, were I only awake.

"Then I woke. O Clotilda, can man say how much he loves?

"H."

* * * * *

His character and the contents of this dream shut out the suspicion of invention. — For the rest, even if Clotilda refuses his veiled wish to see her in Maienthal, still she must do it with a leaf of paper and three lines, which he can then read a thousand times over, and with which the cabinet of pictures and seals, wherein already are contained the hat and the views, will be considerably enriched. Meanwhile he stood in his fair Alpine valley between two high mountains, on each of which was mustering material for an avalanche, — one is perhaps already started up there in its crushing course, and he is not yet able to see it. The first avalanche, which the least sound of his may topple down upon him, is his crazy relation with his court acquaintance. He can boast of having angered them in a body: the Princess, Joachime, Matthieu. But, even independently of that, some conductor or other — merely because he stands not with the rest on the social isolating stool of the throne — must soon dart a diminished flash at his fingers or his eyes; at boards and at courts no one can stand upright without connections; it is there as in galleys, where all the slaves must move their oars together, if no one is to feel the cutting of the chain. But Victor said to himself, "Be not a child! be not the reversed fox who pronounces *sour* grapes, because he cannot reach them by leaping, to be *sweet!* I flatter myself, thou canst dispense with courtly hearts, which like their viands must first be warmed over a chafing-dish full of flickering spirits of wine. — By heaven! a man will surely be able to eat, even though that which he puts on the spit is not fetched by a guard from the kitchen, then handed to a page, then served up by a chamberlain or some other regulation-cavalier. — Only my father, — if it makes no difference to him!" That was just it: in the son there was nothing to be felled, but there was in the father,* for

* Because courtiers herein also resemble the first Christians, who destroyed only such statues as had received adoration in the place of *God.*

whom they will probably let the uplifted woodman's and sacrificial axe hover, till he stands under it with his head, which without his return is not to be had.

But deuse a bit does a Pastor-fido care for the first avalanche. On the harmonica-bells of his fancy the external dissonances of fate, as the rolling of carriage-wheels over the pavement does on the strings of a musical instrument, die away in softly ascending murmur. With him, as with the astrologers, April, like my book, was dedicated to the evening-star, i. e. to Venus.

On the contrary, the other avalanche lay already beforehand on his breast, — the possibility of a breach with Clotilda's brother. A jealous man the twelve Apostles and the twelve minor Prophets cannot convert; — if he is cured on Sunday, then on Monday he is sick again, on Tuesday he is raving mad, and on Wednesday you can loose him again; he is weak and cunning and — — only lies in wait. The cancer of jealousy on the breast can never wholly be cut out, if I am to believe great masters of the healing art. This time, furthermore, there was something true at the bottom; and then too the jealous man insures it in good season ; jealousy enforces infidelity, and the provoked woman will not, so far as in her lies, leave the man in *error.* I cannot give myself the trouble (but the reader may) to enumerate in my biography all the little crannies and wood-holes through which he has hitherto let his Flamin see and *hear* into his love-smitten heart: these knot-holes are so much the larger, as he was *before* the *third* Easter-holiday more improvident, for the very reason that he was more innocent, or, rather, more unhappy.

To this add, that Flamin — who every day thought the dear Evangelist Mattheus more honest and *open* (like a burnt-out *touchhole*) — every day looked upon his faithful Bastian as more artful and impenetrable. I could wish the Regency-Councillor were more discerning; but crowded souls like Victor's, that have more powers, and for that very reason more sides, than common, seem, of course, to be less *porous*, just as authors full of meaning seem less clear. A man who exposes to you with frankness all the colors of his heart playing into each other, loses thereby the glory of frankness; — one who like Victor, from humor, collects and shows up other people's tricks, seems to imitate them; — a changeable, an ironical, a fine man is in the eyes of narrow ones a thorough-going false thief. Then, too, Victor, when it could be done without noise, jumped out of the way of any long mentionings of Clotilda, i. e. long dissemblings; and this very flight from artifice, even his present increased human-kindliness toward Flamin, precisely overshadowed his noble form; and nothing consoled him for the distortions of suspicion, but the sweet reflection that to please the brother of his beloved and of his heart he had turned his back upon the fairest days in Maienthal.

## 31. DOG-POST DAY.

CLOTILDA'S LETTER. — THE NIGHT-EXPRESS. — RENTS AND GASHES IN THE BAND OF FRIENDSHIP.

I WAS going to have inserted in the Magazine of Literature, that I needed *Herrnschmidt's osculologia* * for my (learned) labors, — that is for this Chapter. I wanted to find out from it, how in Herrnschmidt's times they managed with women. In Jean Paul's times, they treat them miserably, that is to say in romances. Only an Englishman can portray excellent women. In the hands of most German romance-founders, the women turn out men, the coquettes w——, the statues lumps, the flower-pieces kitchen-pieces. That the fault lies more with the artists than with the models, not only the models themselves know, but also the Mining-Superintendent, even from the fact, that the female readers of romances are all even more romantic than the heroines of them, — more refined and reserved. The Mining-Superintendent will here — without any design of having eight distinguished women in Mayence bear him to the grave, as they did the women's minstrel and meister-singer, Henry Frauenlob — swear a printed oath (or simply *swear* in print) that he has found most of his contemporaries better than the good,

* Doctrine of kissing. — TR.

open, but empty and rough head of the author of the Alcibiades and Nordenschild * can draw them. In fact, if women did not forgive men everything, even authors, (and in truth they do it seventy times a day, and offer the other cheek, when one has been offended by a kiss,) then no circulating-library keeper could explain how it is that human beings, whose head nevertheless is heavier, whose pineal gland is smaller, and who have six more annular cartilages to the windpipe, — that is, in all, twenty, probably for the sake of their more speaking, — whose breast-bone is shorter, and whose breast-bones are softer than men's, — how such human beings of the female sex can still send their maid or footman to a circulating library with the commission: "A romance of chivalry for my mademoiselle!" My colleagues of the quill — in reference to women I am, according to miners' language, one of the *feather*,* not of *fire* nor of *leather* — are elected for the education of female readers, as, according to Lessing, the Jews were for the education of the nations, for the simple reason that they are ruder than their pupils.

Every woman is finer than her station. She gains more by culture than the man. The female angels (but so also the female devils) are kept only in the highest and finest human drawers; they are butterflies, on whom the velvet-wing between two rough man's-fingers becomes a naked, skinny flap; they are tulips, whose colored leaves a single grasp of fate rubs down into a smutty leather. — —

I bring forward all this, in order that Herr Kotzebue

* Carl Gottlob Cramer, who died in 1817, was a very prolific, and in his day popular, romance-writer.

† In miners' language the *men of the quill* are the superintendents, clerks, &c., in the Mining-office; those of *leather* are those who wear the hind aprons of that stuff for sliding down into the mines; those of *fire* are the men that smelt the metal.

and the shameless Poets'-corner in Jena* and the whole romantic crew may not take it ill of my Clotilda that she imitates more her own sex than the aforesaid tribe, and so much the more, as she can allege in her defence, that she has not yet read this.

Through Agatha came very soon an answer from Clotilda, superscribed by Emanuel, which was inwardly sealed in the style of ambassadors, geometrically cut, and calligraphically written, because ladies execute all things that require the attention of the senses better than we, and because they — for hardly four of my acquaintance need I except — are exactly the opposite of men, in that the better they think, the finer they write. Lavater says the handsomest painter produces the handsomest pictures; and I say, fair hands write a fair hand.

Clotilda's letter sets itself with an ornamental belt and a live hedge full of blossoms across our Doctor's path and shuts him off from Maienthal. For it runs thus: —

"Most Worthy Friend, —

"Perhaps no maiden is so happy as a poetess; and I think, here in this charming valley one at last becomes both. You are happy everywhere, for you can be a poet even at a court, as your beautiful poetic epistle shows me. But fancy loves to paint from paint-boxes, — the true Maienthal cannot give yours so much as you know how to put into the three landscape-pictures of it. As often as you and I are obliged to make good the absence of the same things by imagination: only with you is the compensation greater than the sacrifice.

"If I could by persuasion have procured you the pleasure of seeing Herr Emanuel, gladly would I have done

* That is to say, in the years of *Lucinda*, the anti-Herders, &c.

it; but I was at last, from conscientious scruples, not eloquent enough to induce him to make the journey, which would expose his weak breast to the danger of bleeding to death. Regard him as a Spring, for which every year one must wait nine months.

"Ah, my anxiety for my unforgetable and irreplaceable teacher casts a shadow over the whole present Spring, as a monument does over a flower-garden. I have never looked upon a Spring so gladly and joyfully as on this. — I can often, even by moonlight, go out along the brooks, and look for a flower which trembles beside the liquid mirror, and around which a moon above and another below fling their lustre, and I represent to myself the floral festival in the East, at which (as they say) a mirror and two lights are placed by night around every garden-flower. And yet I cannot look over to the flower-beds of my teacher, without being too much affected by the thought, Who knows whether his tulips will not stand longer than his crippled form? Has then the whole medical art no remedy that shall frustrate his hope of death? — It seems to me he is gradually attuning me to his melancholy tone, whereby I should make myself ridiculous before any other than the friend of Emanuel; but a still, hidden joy loves to break out even into melancholy. 'Only in the cold, not in the fair season of our destiny,' you once said, 'do the warm drops pain us, which fall from the eyes upon the soul, just as only in winter one must not sprinkle flowers with warm water.' And why should I not disclose to your open heart all the weaknesses of mine? This chamber, wherein my Giulia ended her beautiful life, even this looking-glass which, when I turned away for pain from her dying, showed me once more my pale and fading sister, the windows, from which my eye so many times a day must fall upon a mournful, thornful rose-bush, and on an eternally closed mound, all these may, indeed, cause my heart some sighs more than a happy one should otherwise have. I know not whether you or Emanuel said, "The thought of death must be only our means of improvement, not our end and aim; if the earth of the grave falls into the heart, just as when it falls into the heart-leaves of a flower, it destroys instead of fructifying it'; — but on my leaves fate and Giulia have already thrown some earth. — And I gladly bear it, as I can now, since gaining your friendship, flee for refuge to a heart, before which I may dare to open mine, in order to show it therein all the woes, all the sighs, all the doubts, all the questions of an oppressed soul. O, I thank the All-Gracious, that as much as he threatens to snatch from me in the person of my *teacher*, so much he gives me again already in advance in the person of his *friend*. — My friendship will reach after our Emanuel even into the next world, and will accompany his darling through this; and if one day the double stroke of his death should fall on us both, then would we shed more patiently our united tears, and I should perhaps say, Ah! his friend Sebastian has lost more than his friend

CLOTILDA!"

* * * * *

The beating of my own heart, a stranger's, is to me a measure of the beating of the happier one. But before I relate what at the outset disturbed, and then doubled Victor's joy over this letter, let me be allowed to make two good observations. The first is: the enhanced sensibility, in a proud bosom (such as Clotilda's), which otherwise would call back sighs and send out only female satires at us lords of the creation, is the fairest token that her heart is melting in the sunshine of love. For this sentiment reverses women; it makes out of a Columbine a female Young, out of an orderly a disorderly one, out of a fine woman a frank one, out of a maker and wearer of finery a female philosopher, and so *vice versâ.* And do thou, dear Philippina, prove the second remark, for thou answerest here as well as thy own brother: Is not the concealment of love the sweetest confession of it? Does not a veil — a moral one, I mean — show the whole face, and is it not permeable to everything except the wind, — the moral wind, I mean? — Does not the glass case of a lady's watch reveal the whole varnished watch-portrait at the bottom, and exclude merely *soiling*, not *seeing?* And what observations wilt thou make, when I rehearse to thee these two!'

The letter strengthened at once Victor's wish to be about Clotilda, and his power to give it up, — until, the next day at supper-time, an accident changed all. Matthieu, who paid almost more visits to enemies than to friends, came up from the Apothecary's. He saw the views of Maienthal and the crape hat; and as he knew that his sister Joachime had both, he said jokingly, "I fancy, you are going to dress yourself up in borrowed robes, or somebody has been disrobing." Victor fluttered away over the subject with a gay, vacant "Both." He was unwilling to take upon his lips the name of love or of a woman before a man who had no faith in virtue, least of all in woman's, who, to be sure, as other spiders do on other music, let himself down by his threads upon love, but who, as mice do, from love for the tones, crept over the strings and snapped them. Victor never loved (before his court-life) to be with such philosophical defamers among blameless maidens, because it pained him even to be reminded of their point of view. "They must not," said he, "learn so much as the existence of a daughter of mine, because they insult a father in the very act of imagining her to themselves."

Matthieu spoke of the next Patriotic Club (on the 4th of May, the birth-day of the Parson) and asked whether he would be there. Agatha, however, had already reminded him of it yesterday (the last day but one of April). At last Mat proposed his question, "Whether he would not also be of the party at Whitsuntide. He had planned a little excursion with the Regency-Councillor (Flamin), who always needed holidays for that purpose, to Grosskussewitz to the Count of O.'s. He had business there, to pay for some lodgings of the court to the Kussewitzers, and put the Count of O. in tune for an amicable adjustment of the recent misunderstanding; therefore he must have the lawyer with him. Perhaps the Englishmen would be at this Congress, — the travelling corps might then have as great entertainment as a *corps diplomatique*, after having first had just such occupation as theirs. The Count of O., in fact, loved Englishmen very much, though he did not like to ride English horses, — for he had been very sorry that he had lately talked with the distinguished Court-Physican at the Princess's without knowing you." Sebastian had concluded his long, dumb attention with a cold "No!" because the perspiration of this false, flying cat * overspread his unprotected heart with an eating poison. "What have I done to this man," thought he during that invitation, "that he pursues me eternally, — that with a knife, of which one side is poisoned, or both, he cuts away,

* Jean Paul reminds us in the Preface to "Quintus Fixlein" that "Flying *Dogs*" is a name for *Vampyres*. — Tr.

amidst the double pangs of both of us, my youth's friend from my soul, — that he runs out his mines even to strange places, in order in all situations to have me over his powder?" Victor had, namely, after all, reason to fear that the Whitsuntide journey was a voyage of discovery, upon which Joachime might propound to her brother, as Chevalier Michaelis * did to the Oriental travellers, questions about the case of the watch-letter, about Tostato, &c., in order, perhaps, to form out of it all an impeachment before the Prince. He held the lower side of his card, i. e. of his *virtuous pain*, in such a way that Matthieu could not quite see it, so as to deprive him of a *malicious pleasure*. The latter, who wore not a lace mask, but an iron one, and besides one with a neck, showed often such coldness, that one did not comprehend his furious wrath and *vice versâ*, — but the one (the coldness) he had in camp, the other (the wrath) in the fight against the foe. If any one immediately enraged him, it was a good sign, and meant that he had no design against him.

After the evacuation of the Evangelist, — when he had done scolding at himself for letting him find the crape hat, which, in fact, he would have kept more concealed if Flamin had came oftener, — he looked round for Clotilda's profile, that the charming shadow might cool his wrath. It was not to be found: his first hypothesis was that Mat had quietly stolen it, which was the more likely, as he had cut it. If he has really pocketed the profile, then must the Evangelist — for, as is well known, the silhouette was made over *to me* at the very beginning of this story — be actually my corresponding fellow-member Knef, and it is

* John David Michaelis (knighted by the King of Sweden) planned, in 1756, a journey to the East, in the cause of biblical and philological science, for which he prepared a series of questions. — Tr.

he who sent me the advice-boat, — namely, the Pomeranian dog. — Odd enough it is that my correspondent himself by such intelligence sets me upon the suspicion.

While Victor took the dear crape hat into his hand as a compensation for the likeness, and dreamily contemplated it, there sprang forth on the hat wholly new, fresh flowers for his soul. "What!" he said to himself, "must I then have only the profile to look at? Can I not choose the — original itself for that purpose?" In short, the hat became an urn of fortune, from which he drew a joyous hour, that is the determination to travel on Whitsuntide, but to — Maienthal. He seriously reflected, that for him and Clotilda this excessive indulgence of a jealous brother, whose mistaken hopes no sister indeed was obliged to strengthen, was besides aggravated and frustrated by the misanthropic suggestions of Matthieu, — that, therefore, their separation was as little of an alleviation as their meeting was a crime, — that, meanwhile, it would be a fine thing to spare the brother and to take merely the time of his absence for a suspicious excursion, till one day the drawing down of the bandage should disclose in the unfaithful one the sister, and in the rival the forbearing friend, — and that it was at all events better to talk with her in Maienthal than, at his return, when he was near, — and that a brother enlightened in regard to his origin would certainly one day have nothing to reproach him with, except that he had taken from him no other illusions than, at most, disagreeable ones. — O, Love and Virtue have a naked conscience, and apologize for their heavenly pleasures longer and more than other qualities do for their infernal ones!

When Victor further thought on *this*, how soon leaf and blossom drop off from the days of love, and that

Emanuel, and even Clotilda, were two flowers moved close to the brink of the grave, whose loose, naked roots already hung down dead, then was his resolution fixed, and he wrote to Emanuel the intelligence of his intended arrival at Whitsuntide, in order not to anger Clotilda by a surprise, and in order, besides, to allow her the opportunity of a countermand. The way in which he put it was this: "If his Socratic genius would allow it (i. e. Clotilda), who always told him what he must *not* do, then he was coming on Whitsuntide, as, besides, the town would then be deserted, as Flamin was to be gone for four or five days to Kussewitz, &c."

When he had finished the letter, it occurred to him that this very day a year ago, on the 29th of April, he had travelled all night, in order with the first of May in the morning to enter through the mist into the parsonage. "I can, verily, again spend the sultry zephyr-night, not under the coverlet, but under the stars. I can take one steady gaze into the evening-red towards Maienthal's mountains. I can, indeed, better still, go half the way over them, — or in fact the whole. I can post myself on a hill and look down into the hamlet. Truly I can then deliver my billet here incognito to some Maienthaler, and take flight again before it is yet day."

At seven o'clock in the evening he went, like the sea, from east to west. Orion, Castor, and Andromeda glisten in the west, not far from the evening-red, over the fields of the loved one, and, like her, will soon sink from one heaven into another. His heart agitated by nothing but hopes, the *heated* chambers of his brain, on whose walls Maienthal sketched with *sympathetic* ink came forth in ever clearer outlines and brighter colors, this inner and almost painful din of joy deprived him at first of the power of taking in the temple of Spring, built up in Grecian beauty, with a still, luminous soul. Nature and Art are best enjoyed only with a clean eye, from which both kinds of tears have been wiped away.

But at last the outspread *night-piece* covered over his hot *fever-images*, and heaven with its lights, and earth with its shadows, made their way into his expanded heart. The night was without moonlight, but without clouds.. The temple of nature, like a Christian temple, was sublimely dimmed. Victor could not make his way up out of the trenches of long valleys, out of the glooms of woods, and out of the mists of meadows with their play of colors, till the midnight hour, when he climbed a mountain like a throne, and there lay down on his back in order to plunge his eyes into the heavens, and cool off from his dreaming and racing. The low-hanging blue of heaven seemed to him to be a thin blue cloud, a sea dashed into blue mists, and one sun after another with its long rays slightly parted this blue flood. Arcturus, who stood over against the reclining man, was already descending from the battlements of heaven, and three great constellations, the Lynx, the Bull, and the Great Bear, marched far in the van under the western gate. — These nearer suns were encircled by remote milky-ways with a swimming halo, and thousands of vast heavens flung into eternity stood in our heaven as white vapors a span in length, as faintly luminous snow-flakes out of immensity, as silver circles of hoar-frost. — And the strata of suns crowded together, which only before the thousand-eyed eye of Art let fall their misty veil, played like streaks of *our* little particles of sun-dust in the glowing sunbeam of the Eternal that burned through the immeasurable space. And the reflection of his throne, glowing through and through, lay bright on all the suns. ——

— Suddenly, nearer at hand, molten cloudlets of light, nearer mists, which had flown upward out of dew, take their stations, during their silvering, low down before the suns, and the silvery gleam of heaven comes on apace with scattered dark fleeces. — — Victor cannot comprehend the supernatural kindling, and starts up, enchanted, to his feet . . . . and lo, our good neighbor and kinsman, the moon, the sixth grand division of our little earth, had silently, and without the morning's cry of joy, entered *beside* the triumphal gate of the sun into the night of her mother earth with her *half-day*.

And now, when the shadows ran off from all the mountains, and glided through the discovered landscapes only in brooks between trees, and when the moon gave the whole dark spring a little morning in the midnight, — then did Victor, not with nightly melancholy, but with morning rejuvenescence take the great round play-room of the annual creation into his awakened eyes, into his awakened soul; and he surveyed the spring with an internal cry of joy in the midst of the wide realm of profound silence, with the feeling of immortality in the circle of sleep. — —

Earth also, and not Heaven only, makes man great!

Enter into my soul and into my words, ye May-feelings that throbbed in the bosom of my Victor, as he looked over the budding, swelling earth, covered with suns above his head, enclosed in a net of green life that reached from roots to tree-tops, from mountains to furrows, and borne up by a second spring under his feet, as he imagined to himself behind the transpierced earth-crust the sun standing with a day of splendor under America. — Climb higher, moon, that he may see more easily the gushing, swollen, dark-green spring, which with little pale spears crowds upward out of the earth, till it has lifted itself out, full of glowing flowers, full of waving trees, — that he may descry the plains which lie under rich leaves, and on whose green track the eye ascends from the upright flowers on which the cloven charms of light grow and fix themselves to the bushes bursting into blossoms, and to the slow trees whose glistening buds sway up and down in the spring-winds. —— Victor had sunk into dreams, when all at once the cold fanning of the spring-air, which could now play more with little clouds than with flowers, and the murmur of the spring brooks, which darted away beside him from all the hills and over every patch of darker green, woke and bestirred him. — There was the moon that had gone up unseen, and all the fountains glistened, and the lilies of the valley came out in white bloom from the green, and round the lively water-plants danced silver-points. Then did his bliss-burdened look lift itself in order to rise to God from the earth and from the green borders of the brooks, and climb up the curved woods, out of which the iron-sparks and smoke columns * leaped above the summits, and far up the white mountains where winter sleeps in clouds; —— but when his holy sight was in the starry heaven, and was about to look up to God, who has created night and spring and the soul, — then, weeping and reverent and lowly and blissful, he fell back with drooping wing. . . . . His heavy soul could only say, He is! —

But his heart drank its fill of life from the endless, welling, breathing world around him, above him, under him, wherein force reaches to force, blossom to blossom, and whose fountains of life shoot from one earth to another, and whose void spaces are only the paths of the finer powers and the residence of the lesser ones, — the whole immeasurable world stood before him, whose dis-

* From the iron-forges and colliers' huts.

tended cataract, spraying into fragrances and streams, into milky-ways and hearts, between the *two* thunders of the summit and the abyss, rapid, starry, flaming, descends out of a past eternity, and leaps down into a future one, — and when God looks upon the cataract, then the circle of eternity paints itself thereon as a rainbow, and the stream does not discompose the hovering circle. . . . .

The blessed mortal rose up and journeyed on in the feeling of immortality through the spring-life pulsating around him; and he thought that man, in the midst of so many examples of immutability, erroneously translated the distinction between his sleep and waking into the distinction between existence and non-existence. Now his vigorous, exuberant feelings welcomed every noise, the stroke of the trip-hammer in the woods, the rush of spring-waters and spring-winds, and the whir of the partridge. —

At three o'clock in the morning he looked down on Maienthal. He came upon the mountain relieved by five solitary fir-trees, on which one can see through the whole village, and again over to the other mountain, where the weeping birch shades his Emanuel. The embowered cell of the latter he could not discern, but all the windows of the convent where his loved one dreamed glistened in the sparkling moonlight. The rapture of night was still in his breast, and the burning glow of dreams on his countenance; — but the valley drew him out to the earth, and only gave his flowers of joy a *firmer* soil; and the morning-wind cooled his breath, and the dew his cheeks. The tears rose into his eyes, when they fell upon the white-curtained windows, behind which a lovely, a wise, a loved and loving soul was completing its guileless morning-dreams. Ah! dream, Clotilda, of thy friend, that he is near thee, that he is turning his overflowing eyes toward thy cell, and that he will vanish, if thou appearest, and that, nevertheless, he is growing more blessed from moment to moment, — ah! he too, indeed, is dreaming, and when the sun rises, the beloved vale will have sunk like thy dream with the starry heaven. — O, the mountains, the woods, behind which dwells a beloved soul, the walls which enclose her, look upon man with a touching magic, and hang before him like sweet curtains of the future and the past.

The mountain brought before him the image of the painter who had once been here for the purpose of sketching Clotilda's charms, like a golden age, as it were, only from a distance, and so of drawing them nearer, — and this again led his eye into the days of her earlier youth and her still, pure life at the convent, and it grieved him that a time had once been, and been lost, in which he had not been able to love her. As he looked around him, and thought to himself that on all these paths, by these brooks, under these trees, she had walked, the whole region became to him holy and living, and every bird that glided over it seemed to seek his friend, and to love her as he did.

But now with every star that sank back into heaven overhead, a flower and a bird woke down on the earth, — the way from night to day was already laid with half-colors, — little clouds came up on the coast of day, — and Victor was still on the mountain. His fear that the white window-veil might stir and betray him, was as great as his wish that the fear might grow greater and greater! Occasionally a curtain swayed, but none rose. — All at once the throats of the birds woke a magic flute at the foot of his mountain, and the still Julius came to meet the sun, that no more shone for him, with his morning-tones. Then, suddenly, Clotilda's window unveiled itself, and her fair, bright eyes took the freshened morning into her holy soul. Victor, not considering the distance, stepped behind one bush after another; but his flight from the beloved eyes led him nearer to the flute; he was, however, full as unwilling to appear before Emanuel, whom he supposed to be in the vicinity of the blind one, as before Clotilda herself. When now only a few bushes separated him from the tones, he espied on the mountain his friend Emanuel under the weeping birch. Now he hastened, glad and trembling, down to Julius, whom he found, with his lily-face, fair as the younger brother of an angel, with birds flying and singing around him, leaning against a birch-tree: "What forms, what hearts," thought he, "adorn this Paradise." How could he, on such a morning, on such a holy spot, toward so good a youth, have disguised himself, and handed to him, say, with the imitated voice of his Italian servant, the letter to Emanuel! — No, that he could not do; he said with a low voice, in order not to alarm him, "Dear Julius, it is I!" — Then he sank slowly upon the tender being, and embraced in one breast three hearts, and handed him the letter with the words, "Give it to thy Emanuel!" and with the warmest pressure of the dear hand flew farther down the mountain and away. —

Just at this hour, on this day, a year ago, Giulia also disappeared from Maienthal, and took nothing with her of the fair flowery ground but a — grave-mound.

And now when he had escaped behind bushy avenues from the place of the blessed, his nightly elation gave way to an uncontrollable sadness. The rising sun drew all the bright colors out of his nightly dream. "Have I then really seen Maienthal and Julius and all the loved ones, or is it all only a play of shadows that passed by before me on a cloud whose colors flickered in the moonlight, and which has melted away?" said he, — and the brooding day warmed the fresh night-air of his soul into the sultry fanning of a south-wind. Whereas man generally, like Raguel,* hews out graves in the midnight, and in the morning sun fills them up again, Sebastian to-day reversed it. ——

Strictly speaking, it was not quite so: but the swift emerging and reabsorption of the beloved forms, the aggravated longing for them, the touching contrast between the din of morning and the pause of night, between the fire of the sun and the moon's twilight, and the dreary exhaustion of sleeplessness joined to the weariness of the fancy and the body, all these things wrung from the heart and the tear-glands of our somnambulist involuntary sweet tears, which had no object, which flowed neither for joy nor for sorrow, but for yearning.

All at once the fair, cloudless first May-day made to pass before him the remembrance of the one a year ago, when, like a spring and an Homeric god, he arrived in a cloud, — and the good man looked with dew-drops in his eyes upon the dew-drops in the flowers, and said, inexpressibly touched: "Ah! a year ago I came so happy, became so unhappy, and now am so happy again, — O ye flying, playing, echoing, trembling years of man!" — and the holiday-hum of bells from all the villages (it was St. Philip's and St. James's day) with the soft thrill of an echo set all his mourning-strings into a responsive quiver.

"O, a year ago," all the bells sang to him, "we escorted Giulia, as we now do thee, out of Maienthal." Then, as the sun unfolded his white blossoms in the sky, the warm thought dissolved his heart: "A year ago this morning

* See Apocrypha: Tobit viii. 3.

thy Flamin went to meet thee, and shed on thy glowing breast so many tears of joy, — and at the end of this very day he drew thee again to his heart, and said as if with a presentiment, 'Forget me not, betray me not, and if thou wilt forsake me, then let me perish with thee!' —

"O thou faithful one," said all his thoughts, "how it consoles me to-day, that I once gladly sacrificed all my wishes to thine, in order to continue true to thee.* — No, I cannot conceal anything from him, I will go to him at once." — He went straight to Flamin, in order (though without perjury towards his Lordship, and with forbearance toward jealousy) to confess that he was going at Whitsuntide to Maienthal. His dismembered heart needed so much an eye that should weep responsive to it, — his delicate sense of honor scorned so much to make another's journey the screen of his own, — his renewed love was pained so at the thought of the least concealment from his friend, — Matthieu was so completely thrust out from this heavenly-blue Eden under the walls of the brain, — that the longer he thought and ran, the more would he lay open. He would, namely, even disclose to his Flamin that he had this very night delivered with his own hands the note of invitation to the blind youth: by an illusion, the future Whitsuntide journey was made more certain through to-day's, and this his own point of view he looked upon as another's.

But his dreamy and *night-intoxicated* soul did not carry so far its dangerous effusion, which might do so much the more harm, as Flamin in his anger was unable to listen any longer to distinctions and justifications, and even re-

* It was when he spoke with his father in the arbor in behalf of Clotilda's union with Flamin, — and when he proposed to himself, *before* the event, to renounce even her friendship.

jected again old ones which he had before allowed. For at his entrance a May-frost on Flamin's face closed a little the opening blossom-cup of his heart. He begged Flamin with his contrasting warmth of face to take a walk on this bright day. Out of doors the contrast grew still more sharp, as Flamin thrust his cane into the ground even to the point of cracking it, beheaded flowers, whipped off leaves, stamped out footprints with the heel of his boot, while Victor sought to discourse in one steady stream, in order to maintain his soul in the warmth which he had brought with him.

One thing about him gratifies me, that he was going to pour out his heart, overrunning with to-day's renunciations, into the very one which he had to charge with those renunciations. At last he said, hurriedly, just for the sake of throwing off from his soul the confession which had become so hard to utter, "At Whitsuntide I am going to Maienthal," — and then flyingly passed over to the words, "O just a year ago to-day thou wentest with me."

Flamin interrupted him, and his icy face, like a Hecla, was cloven with flames: "So! so! — at Whitsuntide? — Thou dost not go with *us* to Kussewitz! — Let me once for all speak right out, Victor!" — Then they stopped. Flamin stripped the blossoms and leaves from the branch of a wild plum-tree with bloody hand, and looked not at his gentle friend, lest he should be softened himself. "A year ago to-day, sayest thou? Yes, that very evening I went with thee up to the watch-tower, and we promised each other either truth or death. Thou sworest to me to throw thyself headlong with me, whenever thou shouldst have taken all from me, all, — or, say, *her* love; for in thy presence she hardly looks at me any more. — By the Devil, am I then blind? Do I not see, then, that the machinery of her journey and thine has been all planned out?—What hast thou to do just now with the Maienthal landscapes? To whom does the *hat* belong?—And what am I to infer from all this?—To whom, whom? say, say!—O God, if it were true!—Help me, Victor!"—In the eyes of the misused, to-day exhausted Victor stood the bitterest tears, which Flamin, however, who exasperated himself by his own talking, could now bear. Never did the latter in a rage accept remonstrances: nevertheless he expected them, and was astounded at his being in the right, and at the other party's silence, and desired to be contradicted. He crushed in his bleeding hand the sloe-thorns. His eye burned into the weeping one. Victor bewailed his firm oath to his father, and looked on the trembling balance wherein the oath and indulgent friendship hung in equipoise. He collected once more all his love into his breast, and spread his arms wide open, and fain would draw with them the struggling one to himself, and yet could say nothing but "I and thou are innocent; but till my father comes, before that I cannot justify myself."—Flamin repelled him from him: "What is this for?—So it was at the garden-concert, too, and thou hast since that been daily with her, and at Easter-balls and in sleighs, without me. Say rather outright, wilt thou marry *her?*—Swear that thou wilt not?—O God, hesitate not,—swear, swear!—Ay, ay, Matthieu!—Canst thou not yet!—Well, then, lie at least!"

"Oh!" said Victor,—and eclipsing blood-streams shot through his brain and over his face,—"thou shalt not insult me quite too much; I am as good as thou, I am as proud as thou,—before God my soul is pure"—
—But Flamin's blood on the sloe-bush repressed Victor's

indignant exaltation, and he merely lifted a sympathetic eye full of the tears of friendship to the brighter, softer heaven. — "Only marriage, forsooth, dost thou not forswear? —— Good, good, thou hast strangled me, — my heart hast thou trampled on, and my whole happiness. — I had none but thee, thou wast my only friend, now will I go to the Devil without one. — Thou dost not swear? — Oh, I tear myself away from thee bloody and wretched, and as thy foe — we part — only go — away! it is all up — all! — Adieu!" He rushed away, striking his stick into the ground as he went, and his distracted friend, lying at the feet of Truth, who lifts the flaming sword against Perjury, and dying in tears before Friendship, who casts upon the soft heart the melting look full of entreaties, — Victor, I say, cried, as with dying voice, after the fleeing friend of his soul: "Farewell, my faithful Flamin! my never-to-be-forgotten friend! I was indeed true to thee! — But an oath lies between us. — Dost thou still hear me? — do not hasten so! —Flamin, dost thou hear me? I love thee still, we shall find each other again, and come when thou wilt." .... He cried after him more vehemently, although with stifled, smothered tones: "Honest, precious, precious soul, I have loved thee very much, and do still and still, — only be right happy. — Flamin, Flamin, my heart breaks now that thou art my enemy." — Flamin looked round no more, but his hand seemed to be on his eyes. The friend of his youth vanished from his sight like youth itself, and Victor sank down *unhappy* under the fairest heaven, with the consciousness of innocence, with all the feelings of friendship! — O, Virtue itself gives no consolation, if thou hast lost a friend, and the heart of a man, stabbed by *friendship*, bleeds on mortally, and all the balm of *love* avails not to heal or to soothe! —

## 32. DOG-POST-DAY.

PHYSIOGNOMIES OF VICTOR AND FLAMIN. — BOILING-POINT OF FRIENDSHIP. — SPLENDID HOPES FOR US.

HO would have thought it of Cicero (if he had not read it) that a man of so many years and so much sense would sit down in his St. John's Island, and manufacture *beginnings*, introductions, pre-existing germs in advance for the market? However, the man had this advantage, that when he wrote a torso on any subject, he had his choice among the heads lying ready made to his hand, of which he could screw one on to the trunk according to the corpuscular philosophy. — As to myself, who have nothing sedate about me, no one can wonder that I on my Moluccian Frascati * have reeled and twisted beforehand whole skeins of beginnings. When Spitz afterward brings a Dog-day, I have already commenced it, and have nothing to do but just to clap the historical remnant on to the introduction. — This very beginning itself I have selected for to-day.

At first, however, I had a mind, to be sure, to take this one: —

Nothing torments me about my whole book except my anxiety as to how I shall be translated. This anxiety is not to be blamed in an author, when one sees how the

* Frascati was a summer residence of the Roman Emperors in the Campagna, on the Tusculan Mount, eight miles from Rome. — TR.

French translate the Germans, and the Germans the Ancients. At bottom it really amounts to one's being expounded by the lower classes and their teachers. I can compare those readers and these classes, in respect of their spiritual fare, which passes first through so many intermediate members, to nothing, except to the poor people in Lapland. When the rich in that country intoxicate themselves in the tippling-room with a liquor which is decocted out of the costly toadstool, the poor people watch around the house-door, till a Lap in easy circumstances comes out and makes ——; this translated beverage, the *Vulgate* of distilled liquor, the poor devils enjoy greatly.

This beginning, however, I am keeping for the Preface to a translation.

It is one of the juggling tricks and *lusus naturæ* of chance, of which there are very many, that I should begin this Book just in the night of St. Philip's and St. James's day, 1793, when Victor undertook the witch's-journey to the Maienthal Blocksberg, into the midst of the enchanters and enchantresses, and when, in 1792, he arrived from Göttingen.

I cannot say, The reader can easily imagine how Victor lived or grieved through the first May-days; for he hardly can imagine it. Perhaps we all held the bands which bound him to Flamin to be a few thin fibres or unsensitive cords of custom; in fact, however, delicate nerves and firm muscles form the lattice-work * of their souls. He himself knew not how much he loved him, until he was compelled to cease doing so. Into this common error we all fall, hero, reader, and writer, on the same ground: when one has not been able for a long time to

* Architectural term. — Tr.

give a friend, whom one has long loved, any proof of that love, for want of opportunity, then one torments one's self with the self-accusation of growing cold towards him. But this accusation is itself the finest proof of love. With Victor yet more things conspired to persuade him that he was becoming a colder friend. The vesper-tilts about Clotilda, those disputations *pro loco,* did, besides, their part; but he was always afflicting himself with the self-criticism that he had sometimes refused his friend little sacrifices; e. g. the neglecting of a pleasure-party on his account, the staying away from certain too distinguished houses which Flamin hated. But in friendship great sacrifices are easier than small ones, — one would often rather sacrifice to it life than an hour, a piece of property than the gratification of some petty bad habit, just as many people would rather present you a bill of exchange than a piece of *blank* paper of the same size. The secret is, great sacrifices inspiration makes, but little ones, reason. Flamin, who himself never made little ones, demanded them of others with heat, because he took them for great ones. Victor had less to reproach himself with on this point; but Clotilda shamed him, for her longest and shortest days, as is the case with most of her sex, were nothing but sacrificial days. — Then, too, his natural delicacy, which had now gained by his court-life the addition of the conventional kind, was wounded more deeply than ever by his friend's sharp corners. — The fine people give to their inner man (as to their outer) by bran of almonds and night-gloves soft hands, merely for the sake of feeling better the under side of the cards, and for the sake of giving neat ladylike half-boxes-in-the-ear, but not in order, like the surgeons, to handle wounds with them.

Unfortunately this delusion about his growing cold prescribed to him a friendly external effort to show warmth when with Flamin. Now as the Regency-Councillor did not consider that even *constraint* may full as often arise from *sincerity*, as unconstraint from falseness: accordingly the Devil had more and more his game of Bestia (in which a friendship was the high stake) till on witches' day he actually won it.

But on the 4th of May he is to lose all again, I think. For Victor, whose heart at the least motion bled through the bandage again, undertook not only, on the 4th of May, to be present at the birth-festival of the Court-Chaplain in St. Luna, but also to celebrate a birthday of renewed friendship with Flamin. He would gladly take the first, second, third, tenth step, if his friend would only stop where he was, and not take a step backward. For he cannot forget *him*, he cannot get over a compulsory renunciation, however easy for him generally the voluntary one was. He pressed every evening Flamin's fair image, which was made out of his love for *him*, out of his incorruptible honesty, his rock-like courage, his love for the state, his talents, even his excitability, which originated in the double feeling of injustice and of his own innocence, — this glowing image he pressed to his lacerated heart, and when in the morning he saw him going to his public duties, his eyes ran over, and he congratulated the servant who carried his papers behind him. Had not the 4th of May, the great day of reconciliation, been so near with its expiatory offering, he would have been obliged to accustom little Julia to himself, as a third estate between the two others, as a key-note between conflicting tones. Only the hope of May applied to his thoughts, instead of burning stings of nettle-points, at least rose-briers. — The friend of thy youth, dear reader, thy school-friend, is never forgotten, for he has something of the brother about him; — when thou enterest the school-yard of life, which is a Schnepfenthal educational institute, a Berlin scientific school,* a Breslau Elisabethanum, a Scheerau Marianum,† — then for the first time thou meetest friends, and your youthful friendship is the morning divine service of life.

Victor was sure beforehand of Flamin's placability; he even saw him very often standing at his window, and glancing across toward the balcony, from which a friendly eye, untroubled by all the misconstructions of the point of honor, looked freely and directly toward the Senior's; — this, however, did not take away his tender yearning, but it was increased by the first returning sight of the face, so fair, so lamented, and so loved. Flamin had a tall, manly form; his compact and receding narrow forehead was the eyrie of spirit; his transparent blue eyes — which his sister Clotilda also had, and which harmonize very well with a fiery soul, as, indeed, the old Germans also and the country people have both — were kindled by a thinking intellect; his compressed, and for that very reason the more darkly red, over-full lips, were settled into the kindly elevation for a kiss; only the nose was not refined enough, but was juristically or Germanly built. The nose of great jurists looks sometimes, in my opinion, as wretchedly as the nose of Justice herself when its flexible material is drawn out and twisted and tweaked under too long fingers. It is not to be explained, by the way, why the faces of great theologians — unless, indeed, they

* *Real-schule:* practical school, for the learning of things. "Res, non verba, quæso," was Spurzheim's motto. — Tr.

† This Institute is of course out of Jean Paul's brain; the others are historical. The one at Schnepfenthal (in Thüringen) was founded by Salzman, who died in 1811. — Tr.

are something else great — have about them somewhat of the typographic magnificence of the Kanstein Bibles. Victor's face, on the contrary, had, less than any other, either these Bursch-like trivial features of many jurists, or the dead-gold of many theologians; his nose — its edge and the indentation of the nasal bridge deducted — descended in Grecian straightness; the angle of the thin, closed lips was (in case he did not happen to be laughing) an acute angle of 1'''', and formed with the sharp nose the order-sign and order-cross, which satirical people often wear; — his broad forehead arched itself to a radiant and roomy choir of a spiritual rotunda, wherein a *Socratic* equally illuminated soul dwells, though neither this brightness nor that brow consort with *inborn* wild tenacity, though they do with that which is acquired; — his fancy, that great prize, had, as often happens, no lottery-device on his face; — his eyes, colored like Neapolitan agate, spoke and sought a loving heart; his soft, white face contrasted, like court with war, against Flamin's brown, elastic countenance, which served as the ground for the two glowing cheeks. — For the rest, Flamin's soul was a mirror which flamed under the sun from only a single point; but on Victor's several powers were ground out into flashing facettes. Clotilda had all this tinder-box and these sulphuric mines of temperament in common with her brother; but her reason covered all up. The rushing blood-stream, which with him dashed from rock to rock, glided along with her still and smooth through flowery meadows.

I should be glad to see it, if he were to renew again with the Regency Councillor the treaty of friendship: I should then get to describe his Whitsuntide journey to Maienthal, which perhaps is the Septleva * and the best

* Septleva (Sept-le-va) is an old French term applied to the case in

thing to which the human understanding has yet attained. But nothing will come of this Septleva, unless they make peace again; by the side of every flower in Maienthal, by the side of every delight, the grief-worn face of his friend would appear and ask, "Canst thou be so happy, while I am so far from it?"

It were a wiser course, if both were monks or courtiers; then they might be expected, as friendship is the *marriage* of souls, to remain continent in a *celibacy* of souls. . . .

Just at the very conclusion of this chapter the dog brings the new one, and I simply weave both together and go on: —

Without any remarkable vexation at the delay of the answer from Maienthal, Victor went alone on the 4th of May to St. Luna, and with every step that brought him nearer, his soul grew more soft and placable. — When he arrived: — —

There are in every house days, which were forgotten in the Litany, — cursed, devilish, deused days, — when all goes criss-cross, — when everything scolds and growls and wags its tail, — when the children and the dog dare not say, Pugh! * and the liege-and-manor-lord of the house slams-to all the doors and the house-mistress draws the bass-register of moralizing, † and strikes the silvery tone of dishes and the bunch of keys, — when one does nothing but hunt up old grievances, all forest-offences of mice and moths, broken parasols and fan-sticks, and that

the game of faro where the player gains seven times the number he laid down. — TR.

* In German, Muck! like the snapping noise of the dog when flies torment his sleep. — TR.

† Most women are not gallows-*paters* [confessors] properly, gallows-maters and female barrack-preachers, until they are full of the Devil, as Sterne had the most conceits when he was not well.

the gunpowder and the perfume-powder, and the elegant note-paper have become damp, and that the sausage-sledge is worn out by sitting to a wooden hobby-horse, and that the dog and the sofa are shedding hair, — when everything comes too late, everything is roasted to death, everything is over-boiled, and the chamber-donna sticks the pins into my lady's flesh as into a doll, — and when, after they have, in this *scurvy sickness where nothing is the matter*, vexed themselves to their hearts' content without cause, they become good-natured again without cause. — —

When Victor arrived at the parsonage, he heard the birthday hero of the day, the parson, lecturing and screaming in his study. Eymann was pouring out his holy spirit into the long ears of his catechumens, into whom no fiery tongues were to be got. He had in hand a female dunce from a hermitage (a solitary house in the woods), and was trying to explain to her the distinction between the loosing-key and the binding-key. Nothing, however, could be done with her: the chaplain and the convert had already spent a half-hour over the school-time with the explanation; the dunce was constantly confounding the keys, as if she were a — *lady of the world.* The chaplain had set his head upon illuminating hers; — he set before her every consideration that might have moved iron-wood and iron-stone, — his birthday festival of to-day, the embittering of the general joy, the surplus half-hour, — in order to persuade her, that she must comprehend the difference, — she did not, she could not see it; — he condescended to entreaties and said: "Jewel, Lamb, Beast, daughter penitent, understand it, I beseech thee, — do thy spiritual shepherd the pleasure of repeating to him the extraordinary difference between binding- and loosing-keys. Am I not dealing fairly with thee? — But my office as parson requires of me not to let thee go like a cow, without knowing a key. — Only take courage and just say after me, word for word, dearly-bought christian beast." — She did so at last, and when she had done, he said joyfully, "Now thou pleasest thy teacher, and attend further." — Out of doors she recapitulated it all, and had comprehended it all very well, except that instead of "Bind- und Löse-Schlüssel" (keys) she always caught it "Bind- und Löse-*Schüssel* (dishes). —

The three-twins had a miserable plan of not coming till after dinner. — The soul of the red Appel was exhaling for this very occasion a wild-game flavor, and smelt like burnt milk-porridge, and complained that she alone had all the labor on her shoulders, and when Agatha offered to fly to her assistance, she said: "I can do it, thank God! as well as thou!" The Regency-Councillor had arrived, but unfortunately had run out into the fields again till dinner-time, — Agatha's face had been crystallized into a rock-cellar by the coldness of her brother towards Victor, — only the parson's wife was the parson's wife; not merely one mother-country, but one breath of love linked her heart to his, and it was impossible for her to be angry with him. She loved a maiden, if he praised her; had she been without a husband, she would have been either his love-letter-writer or his letter-carrier. — Thus do women love — without measure! often, too, they hate in the same way. — To this my correspondent adds further, that he could draw from the watering-village a whole protocol of depositions in evidence that the Parson's wife not merely always, but even on the present Ventose and Pluviose* day, was able to endure and live

* Sixth and fifth months of the French Republican calendar. — Tr.

through it with the unvarnished composure of a Christian woman, if any one let anything fall, a cup or a word. For such a state of mind, — for apathy under the present, entire loss of a soup-tureen, or rinsing-bowl, or fruit-dish, — there is needed perhaps as much health as reason.

— At last in the evening, the Page came in and said, Flamin was still in the garden. Victor received it, as if it were said to him, and went out carrying his oppressed heart to meet another troubled one: Flamin he found in an embowered nook staring up with all his eyes at the wax-image of the rejected friend; Victor's heart moved heavily as if through tears in his overladen breast. Flamin's face was covered, not with the panoply of wrath, but with the funeral veil of sorrow. For here in the foreground of a bright, warm youth, as it were on the classic soil of a former, irreplaceable love, he became too warm and too tender, — in the village he revoked his hardness in the city, — and what was still more, only friends of his friend, only affectionate eulogies on the despised darling, overwhelmed and warmed his impoverished heart, and he could here still more easily excuse than spare him. Victor welcomed him with the soft voice of a subdued heart, but he only half spoke either his thoughts or his words. Victor gazed deep down into the soul which mourned for friendship; for only a heart sees a heart; so only the great man sees great men, as one sees mountains only from mountains. He held it therefore as no sign of resentment, when Flamin slowly walked away from him; but he must needs, left so alone there, turn away his eyes from the consecrated corner of the garden, where their friendship had once opened its blossoms, and from the sacrificial bower where he had interceded with his father for Flamin's and Clotilda's union, and from the high observatory, the Tabor of friendship's transfiguration, from all these burial-places of a fairer time he must needs avert his eyes, in order to endure the poorer present. But that which he would not look upon, he represented so much the more vividly to his mind.

Now the Vesper-bell extended its melancholy vibrations even to the hearts of men, — past times sent the tones, and the evening-lamentations sank like ardent entreaties into the souls of the sundered friends: "O be reconciled and walk together! Is then life so long that men may venture to be angry with each other? Are then good souls so numerous, that they can fly from each other? O these tones have floated around many a heap of the ashes of mortality, around many a stiffened heart full of love, around many closed lips full of fury, — O transitory creatures, love, love each other!" — Victor followed willingly (for he wept) after his friend, and found him standing by the bed whereon Eymann caused the F of his name to grow green on the cole-rape-plants, and he was silent, because he knew that for all *sympathetic* cures *silence* is needed. O, such an hour of deepening silence, when friends stand beside each other like strangers, and compare the silence with the old outpouring, has too many heart-stings, and a thousand smothered tears, and for words sighs!

Victor, so near to his friend, and as during the talking his better soul, like nightingales during concerts, grew louder and louder, would fain, from minute to minute, have fallen upon that noble face, on those lips rounded for the kiss of reconciliation, — but he started back at the thought of the recent repulse. He saw now how Flamin stepped farther and farther into the bed, and slowly trod down the heart leaves of the cole-rape, and crushed them asunder; at last he observed that this trampling out of the blooming name was merely the dumb language of disconsolateness, which wanted to say: "I hate my tormented self, and I could crush it as I do my name here: for whom should it stand here?" — This snatched blood from Victor's heart and from his eye tears which had been brushed away, and he took gently the long withdrawn hand, to lead him away from the suicide of his name. But Flamin turned his quivering face side-wise toward the waxen shadow of his friend and rigidly crooking his head away stared up at it. — "Best Flamin!" said Victor with the tone of the deepest emotion, and pressed the burning hand. Then Flamin tore it out of his, and with his two fists pressed back the tear-drops into his eyes, — and breathed loud, — and said in a choked voice, "Victor!" and turned round with great tears and said in a still more muffled tone, "Love me again!" — And they rushed into each other's arms, and Victor answered, "For ever and ever do I love thee, thou hast indeed never offended me"; and Flamin, glowing and dying, stammered, "Only take my beloved, and remain my friend." — For a long time Victor could not speak, and their cheeks and their tears united burned on each other, till at last he was able to say: "O thou! O thou! thou noble man! But thou art in error somewhere! — Now will we forsake each other no more, now will we remain so forever. — Ah, how inexpressibly shall we *one day* love each other, when my father comes!"

At this moment the Parson's wife, who was perhaps anxious about both, came to call them in, and Flamin in his softened mood honored her, which he seldom did, with a filial embrace; and from four eyes swollen with weeping she read with delight the renewal of their imperishable covenant.

Nothing moves man more than the spectacle of a reconciliation; our weaknesses are not too dearly purchased by the hours of their forgiveness, and the angel, who should never feel wrath, must envy the mortal who conquers it. — When thou forgivest, then is man who inflicts wounds on thy heart the sea-worm that drills through the shell of the mussel, which closes the openings with pearls.

This reconciliation drew after it one with fortune, as it were, — the *Brumaire*-evening became a *Floréal** evening, — the three-twins ate of the remains of Appel's roasted glory, — the Parson had nothing to do any longer with any other keys than the loosing-keys, the spiritual music-keys, — and the birthday feast had bloomed out into a feast of the covenant, an opposition club, where all, but in a higher sense than that of Quakers and merchants, called each other *friend*. The three-twins delivered old-British speeches, which only freemen could understand. Victor wondered at the universal frankness before such a stinging gad-fly as Matthieu, — but the Englishmen cared for nothing. The Parson sent off heart-felt prayers, and said: "He, for his part, took little notice of what they did, and only begged them to harangue more softly, that he might not get the name of allowing pietistic conventicles in his parsonage; meanwhile he relied entirely upon Messrs. the Court-Physician and the Court-Page, who would certainly insure him against a fine; otherwise he would not let wife and son join in the conversation." The Parson's wife preferred reminiscences of her free native land to the best calumnies and fashions. Victor must needs to-day keep his promise of putting his Republican Orthodoxy beyond question; and as he gave the same in our hearing, we will also help see how he keeps it, and whether he is an old-Briton.

* February changed to August. — Tr.

He imitated mostly the style which he had last read or — as to-day — heard; therefore he spoke in the sententious manner of the burning-cold Englishman of the three.

"No state is free but that which loves itself; the measure of patriotism is the measure of freedom. What, then, is now this Freedom! History is the *Place La-Morgue* * where every one seeks the dead kinsmen of his heart: ask the mighty dead of Sparta, Athens, and Rome, what freedom is! Their perpetual festival days, their games, their eternal wars, their constant sacrifices of property and life, their contempt of riches, of trade, and of mechanics, cannot make the fiscal prosperity of a country the goal of freedom. But the logical despot must assiduously promote the material well-being of his negro-plantation. The tyranny or the mildness, the injustice or the virtue of an individual, constitute so little the distinction between a servile and a free form of government, that Rome was a slave under the Antonines, and free under Sulla.† — Not every Union, but the object of the Union, not the uniting under common laws, but the import of those laws, give the soul the wings of patriotism; for otherwise every Hansa, every trade-league, were a Pythagorean Society and would create Spartans. That for which man gives blood and goods must be something higher than either; — not in defence of his own life and property has the good man so much valor as he has when he contends for another's; — the mother risks nothing

* A grated Place in Paris, where they expose the dead found during the night, that every one may find his relative.

† Great is the soul which, like him, with none but enemies around him, renounces all power, — greater is the people, before which one could venture to do it. Another people would have anticipated Sulla's lice. [Alluding to a loathsome disease which beset him late in life, called the *morbus pediculosus*. — TR.]

for herself and everything for her child; — in short, only for what is nobler than self in himself, for virtue, does man open his veins and offer his spirit; only the Christian martyr names this virtue *Faith*, the Barbarian, *Honor*, the Republican, *Freedom*.

" — Take ten men, shut them up in ten different islands: neither of them (I have not selected cosmopolites) will love or defend either of the others, if he meets him in his canoe, but will merely, like an innocent uncultivated beast, let him pass unharmed. But throw them together on *one* island,* then they will make mutual conditions of living together, of common defence, &c., i. e. laws; now they have more frequent enjoyment of use and right, consequently of their personality, which distinguishes them from mere tools, consequently of their freedom. Before, on their ten islands, they have been rather *unrestrained* than *free*. The more the objects of their laws rise in dignity, the more they see that law concerns the inner man more than the rubbish heap it protects, right more than property, and that the noble man fights for his goods, his rights, his life, not on account of their importance, but on account of his own dignity. — I will look at the matter on another side, in order to defend the proposition with which I began the discourse. When a people hates its constitution, then the object of its constitution, i. e. of its union, is lost. Love of the constitution, and love for one's fellow-citizens as fellow-citizens, are one. I start with this principle: If all men were wise and good, then they would be all alike consequently friendly. As that is not so, accordingly Nature makes up for this goodness by similarity of

* Victor took for his union ten persons, perhaps because exactly that number is required to make a riot. Hommel, *Rhapsod. observat.* ccxxv.

motives, by community of object, by living together, &c., and by these bonds — of connubial, of brotherly and sisterly and of friendly affection — holds our smooth, slippery hearts together at different distances. Thus she educates our heart to the higher warmth. The State gives it a still greater, for the citizen loves the man even more in the citizen, than the brother loves him in the brother, the father in the son. The love of country is nothing but a restricted cosmopolitan love; and the higher philanthropy is the philosopher's enlarged patriotism for the whole earth. In my younger years the mass of men was often painful to me, because I felt myself incapable of loving 1000 millions at once; but the heart of man takes more into itself than his head, and the better man must needs despise himself, if his arms should reach only round a single planet. . . ."

* * * * *

— Now, as in a drama, I set only the names of the players before their remarks. The coldly-philosophical *Balthazar:* "Then must the whole earth become one day a single state, a universal republic; Philosophy must approve wars, misanthropy, in short all possible contradictions to morality, so long as there are still two states. There must one day be a national convention of Humanity; the kingdoms are the municipalities."

*Matthieu:* "We are only just living now, then, in the 11th of October and a little in the 4th of August." *

*Victor:* "We see, like David, our Solomon's Temple only in dreams, and in our waking hours the tabernacles of the Covenant; but it were a sorrowful philosophy which

* The 4th of August, 1789, was the memorable night in which all the represented upper estates formally renounced their old privileges. — Tr.

should require nothing of men but what they had hitherto rendered without philosophy. We must fit reality to the ideal, not the reverse."

The ardently-philosophical *Melchior:* "Most modern movements are only the starts of one sleeping under the ear-wig* and grasping at his bloody scalp. — But the falling stalactite of regentship forms at last with its drops one column with the ascending stalagmite of the people."

*Flamin:* "But do not Spartans imply Helots, Romans and Germans Slaves, and Europeans Negroes? — Must not always the prosperity of the whole be based upon individual victims, just as one class must devote itself to tilling the soil, that another may apply itself to knowledge?"

*Cato* the elder: "Then I spit on *the whole* if I am the victim, and despise myself if I am the whole."

*Balthazar:* "It is better that the whole suffer voluntarily for the sake of a single member, than that he should against his just vote suffer for the whole."

*Matthieu*: "Fiat justitia et pereat mundus."

*Victor:* "In plain English: the greatest physical evil must be preferred to the least moral evil, the least unrighteousness."† —

*Melchior*: "The physical inequality of men produced by nature no more excuses any political inequality than pestilence does murder, or a failure of crops corn-monopoly. But inversely political equality must be the very compensation for the want of physical. In a despotic state enlightenment as well as prosperity may be greater in inward contents, but in the free state it is greater in outward contents, and is distributed among all; for freedom and enlightenment reciprocally beget each other." —

* Literally *brain-borer*. — Tr.

† Job xxxvi. 21: "Take heed, regard not iniquity; for this hast thou chosen rather than affliction." — Tr.

*Victor:* "As unbelief and tyranny do. Your assertion shows to nations two ways, one slower, but more just, and one which is neither. Wild clutchings at the *dial plate-wheel* of Time, which is turned by a thousand little wheels, dislocate more than they expedite it; often they break off its teeth.* Hang thy own weight on the *weight* of the clock-work, which drives all the wheels; i. e. be wise and virtuous, then wilt thou be, at the same time, great and innocent, and be building up the city of God, without the mortar of blood, and without the stone blocks of death's-heads." —

Here we strike the bell that closes this political sermon, during which Victor, despite his Socratic continence and moderation, made all these wild heads friends of his own. With Matthieu alone jest was the only object, to which he turned everything serious, instead of the reverse. He had in a characteristic degree that shamelessness of rank, at the same time to commit and to ridicule certain follies, to seek and to despise certain fools, and to avoid and praise at once certain philosophers. Wherever he could, he covered the good Prince of Flachsenfingen with satirical cockle-buttons † which he threw at him, and showed hostility to the husband, which is generally the sign of too great a friendship for the wife. Thus he said to-day in reference to Jenner's or January's *penchants*, which contrasted with those of the month and saint from which he derived his name: "For the St. Januarius in Puzzolo ‡ a fish was the Dr. Culpepper." —

* For there is no great event from a little cause, but only great events from a million little causes, of which one always assigns the last as the mother of the great result. Is then the priming the charge of the cannon?

† Thistle-knobs. — Tr.

‡ That is to say, no sculptor could make a second nose to fit this

I confess, I have, during the whole session of the Club, again had the freakish thought, which, wild as it is, I have often before been unable to drive out of my head, — for it is, to be sure, a little confirmed by the fact that, like an atheist, I know not whence I am, and that with my French name, Jean Paul, I was impelled by the most wondrous accidents to a German writing-desk, on which I one day will copiously report them to the world, — as I was saying, I hold it myself to be a folly, my sometimes getting the conceit in my head, that it is possible — since thousand-fold examples of the kind are extant in Oriental history — that I might be actually the unknown son of a Kniese* or Shah, or something of the sort, that was trained for the throne, and from whom they concealed his noble birth the better to educate him. The very entertaining of such an idea is of itself folly; but so much is nevertheless correct, that the examples are not to be erased from universal history, in which many a one, even to his twenty-eighth year, — I am two years older, — knew not a word of it, that an Asiatic or some other throne awaited him, wherefrom he afterward, when he came to it, wielded a magnificent sway. But let it be assumed I was changed from a Jean Lack-land to a John Withland, — I should go forthwith to the billiard-room, and tell everybody whom he had before him. Were one of my subjects there joining in the game, I should forthwith govern him on the spot; and if it were a female subject, without scruple. I should proceed with considerateness, and invest only subjects from my billiard-shire with the weightier offices, because the Regent must be

statue, — for the first had been broken off. At last, after four hundred years, a child found in a great fish the marble one which belonged to it. Labat's Travels, Fifth Part.

* Old designation of a Russian or Polish Prince. — Tr.

acquainted with him whom he appoints, which, as is well known, he can best become at the gaming-tables. I would strictly command my vassals and all by a general *règlement* for all times to be happy and well-off, and whoever was poor, him I would put as a punishment on half-pay; for I think, if I interdicted poverty so emphatically, it would come at last to be the same as if Saturn and I ruled together. — Like a Sultan in his harem, so I in my state, would desire no physical mutes or dwarfs, but, as occasion required, moral ones. — I confess, I should have a peculiar predilection for geniuses, and should appoint to all, even the wretchedest places, the greatest heads. — I should fear nothing (enemies excepted) but dropsy on the brain, of which a crowned or mitred head must always be in an agony of dread, if, like me, it has read in Dr. Ludwig's, or else in Tissot's, treatises on the nerves, that it comes on at first with close *bindings* around the head, which I should fear still more from my crown, especially if the head which was forced into it was *thick* and *it* was *tight*. . . . .

We come back to the story. The next day Victor and Flamin, in the fair, newly assumed bonds of the covenant of friendship, returned to Flachsenfingen. Now could Victor enter through the heavenly gates of Maienthal, if Clotilda did not bolt them. All depended on Emanuel's answer. The May-airs breathed, the May-flowers exhaled, the May-trees rustled. O how this fanning kindled the longing to enjoy all these blisses in Maienthal, and to get from his friend the admission-ticket to the finest concert-hall of nature. None came; for it had already — come through the Bee-father Lind of Kussewitz, who as feudal-postilion had been sent by Count O. to Matthieu, and had taken the route through Maienthal. It was from Emanuel: —

"Horion!

"Come sooner, beloved! Hasten to our valley of Eden, which is a summer-house of nature, with green-growing walls between nothing but avenues running out of heaven into heaven. The light, flowery hours move by before the eye of man as the stars do before the optic tube of the astronomer. Blossom-snares of honeysuckle are laid for thee, and covered with fragrances; and when thou art caught in them, the up-welling incense envelops thee in a cloud, and unknown arms press through the cloud, and draw thee to three hearts full of love! I have already taken up lilies of the valley out of the wood, and planted them near me. — Thy city is indeed also a wood around thee, still lily of the valley! I have already transplanted two balsamines and five summer carnations; but my first transplanted Balsamine was Clotilda. Thou seest how spring, with its exuberant, swelling juices, penetrates through my budding soul also, and May splits open therein, as I am now doing on the carnations, all the buds. — Appear, appear, ere I become melancholy again, and then tell thy Julius who the angel was that handed him the letter for me.

"Emanuel."

Julius had probably thought on this occasion of that other letter which a hitherto unknown angel had given him to unseal on this Whitsuntide. — But what have I to do here with angels and letters? Write by courier is what I will now do, that so I may have got through the 32d Chapter before the dog appears with his 33d Whitsuntide Chapter, which, not merely because it has thirty-two ancestral chapters, but on account of the probable effusion therein of a holy spirit of joy, or on account of a whole dove-flock of holy spirits, and on account of the historic pictures it will contain, — and by reason of my own exertions, — must be (it is believed) a chapter like which in each Dionysian * period hardly half a one, and in each Constantinopolitan hardly a whole one, can be written. — The Whitsuntide dog-day may turn out long, but it will be good and divine, — Philippine will shake her brother and say (she loves to flatter): "Paul! St. Paul was *also* in the third heaven, but he never described it like this in his Epistle to the Romans!" I myself could wish that I might read my 33d dog-day before I had made it. . . . .

The much in little which, with my previous haste, I have still to throw out, is, according to the gourd-documents, this: Victor set his heart full as much as I do on the Whitsuntide-gospels. His conscience placed not the thinnest pasture-bars, not the lowest boundary-stone, in the way of his enjoyment, and he could go like an innocent pleasure to the beloved Clotilda, and say to her, Accept me. He paid now his farewell and professional visits regularly at court, and cared nothing for any word full of human caustic, or any eye full of basilisk's poison. He redoubled his fairer visits to Flamin, in order to reward his noble reconciliation with a warmer friendship, and he stamped upon the past history and on the subject of jealousy the privy-seal of forbearing silence. His dreams did not, to be sure, on their stage full of shadow-plays and airy apparitions, present Clotilda's form (the most loved faces are just those dream denies), but by conducting him into the old, dark, rainy months, when he was again unhappy and without love and without the dearest

* Dionysius the Little, a Roman abbot, invented the Christian era. — Tr.

soul, they gave him by means of the rained-out night a brighter day, and redoubled melancholy became redoubled love. — And when in the morning after such dreams of the past dream he walked out through the May-frost, and by the swollen joy-drops of the vine-leaves, and under the morning wind, which rather wafted than cooled him, in order to touch with his yearning eyes as precious relics the fixed western woods, which hung a green curtain before the opera-stage of his hope, — — a reviewer, who shall put himself in my place, cannot possibly expect me with this shortness of time, and in my extra post-coach to the carriage of Phœbus (now in the shorter days), to give this long antecedent member of the period its conclusion.

Even the perpendicular climax of the barometer, and the horizontal streams of the east wind, swelled the sails of his hope, and wafted him into the silent sea of the Whitsuntide-future, and into the Almanach of 1793, to see whether the moon fulled on Whitsuntide. — By Heaven, it will at least be half full, which is much better still, because one will have it at hand in the middle of heaven when one is about to begin his evening . . . . .

I have, after all, by extraordinary racing, brought matters so far, that I have done with the 32d dog-post-day before Spitz with his goblet of joy on his neck has made his way across the Indian Ocean. — And as, besides, according to the *capitulatio perpetua* with the reader, (at which, notoriously, the benches of princes and cities bite the dust,) I must now make an Intercalary Day: I will spend the Dog's vacation in that way; but I earnestly beg all my day-electors, those of my subscribers who have hitherto skipped across the Intercalary Days on the leaping-pole of the index-finger, not to do it in this case, first, because I agree to be shot, if in this Intercalary Day I in the least exercise my intercalary-day privilege, though confirmed under several governments, of delivering the wittiest and weightiest matters, — and, secondly, because the dog even on the Intercalary day may run into port, and bring me facts which I may serve up not in the 33d Dog-post-day, but already in the —— VIIIth *Intercalary day*, or in the VIIIth *Sansculottide*. — The contents of this, like the present, are a rambling overture to the Future. —

I must say, if, in the first place, as Bellarmin (the Catholic champion and contradictor) asserts, every man is his own Redeemer, — whence follows, in my judgment, that he is also his own Eve and serpent for his old Adam, — if, secondly, the pen of an extraordinarily good author is the snuffers of truth, just as, inversely, to Herr von Moser in prison the snuffers were a pen, — if, thirdly, Despotism may at last, instead of the living tree-stems (for it saws right into the world as if blind,) saw into the throne-saw-horse itself, — further, I must say, if, fourthly, every action (even the worst) has, like Christ, two unlike genealogies, — if in fact, fifthly, one and another reviewer carries his critical eye, wherewith he surveys everything, not on the apex of his skull (as Mahomet's saints are said to, in order not to see *beauties*), nor, like Argus, before and behind, but actually in front, under the stomach, over the gut, in the midst of the navel; if this man, in addition thereto, possesses no other heart than the linen one which the seamstress has stitched in the corner of the shirt-frill, and which lies over the pit of the heart, which one would call more sensibly the pit of the stomach, — finally I must say (at least I can do so), if, in the sixth place, true coherence, strict *concatenation* of paragraphs, is perhaps the greatest ornament and soul of the so-called *unbound discourse*, or prose, which, however, is like a *bound* harpsichord, and if, therefore, the sense, like an epic action, must begin at the end of the (rhetorical and temporal) period, because otherwise there would not be any at all. . . .

— But neither will there be any to come.—These four points, however, look like the *hare's tracks* in the snow.— In short: the Pomeranian dog, my biographical hod-bearer and forwarder, is already lying under the table, and has discharged some Elysian fields and heavenly kingdoms.— As, besides, I did not wholly know in the above paragraph what I was after (I hope not to sit a well man before the public, if I knew) — accordingly the dog did me a true labor of love in actually biting off, so to speak, the tail, or second member. It was, besides, my plan merely to make caprioles in a period of an ell's length until the dog should have removed my anxiety about the doubtfulness of the Whitsuntide journey. — In fact, I never wanted to lay out words and thoughts together, but to save the *latter*, while I spent the *former;* Peutzer wrote long ago to the men of Ratisbon and Wetzlar, Many thoughts need a small stream of words, but the greater the brook is, so much the smaller can be the mill-wheel. — An honest reviewer is offended also by a laconic book if only for this reason, (not merely that the public does not understand it but) because a German has in the jurists and theologians the very best models before him for writing prolixly, and indeed with a diffuseness which perhaps — for the thought is the soul, the word the body — establishes among *words* that higher friendship of men, which, according to Aristotle, consists in this, that *one* soul (one thought) inhabits several bodies (words) at once. — —

— I now begin Victor's vigils, the holy eve of Whitsuntide. It was already Saturday, — the wind (like the sciences) came from the east, — the quicksilver in the barometer-tube (as it does to-day in my nervous-tubes) almost leaped out at the top. — Flamin had parted in peace with his friend on Friday, and was not to return for five days. — Victor will to-morrow, on the first day of Whitsuntide, sally forth before the sun, in order to come back again on the third, when he alights in America. — (I wish he would stay longer.) — It is a fine *blue-Monday** in the soul (every blue day is one), and a fine dispensation from the mourning of life, when one (like my hero) has the good fortune on a holy even-tide, during the tolling for prayers, and when the moon is already up above the houses, to sit tranquil and innocent in Zeusel's balcony in the presence of the prospects of the fairest Whitsuntide-days and the fairest Whitsuntide-faces, to take a first cut of all the preparatory dishes of hope, to gather all the bosom-roses and signs of the fairest morning, and, amidst the noisy booth-preludes to the Festival, to read the second part of the *Mumien* † precisely in the Sectors of joy in which I sketch my own and Gustavus's entrance into the heavenly Jerusalem at Lilienbad. — — All this, as was said, my hero had. . . . .

But when he who found out so much affinity between his Whitsuntide-journey and that journey to the watering-place in the book, came at last with his agitated soul to the destruction of that Jerusalem; then, with the first sad sigh of to-day, he said: "O thou good Destiny, never lay such a sacrificial knife on the heart of my Clotilda; ah, I should die, if she became so unhappy as Beata." — And he

* Working-man's holiday. — Tr.

† *Mummies*, — one of the titles of the "Invisible Lodge," given in allusion to mixing up of serious and jocose scenes and ideas, as the Egyptians introduced a skeleton at their merry-makings. — Tr.

further reflected how the ruddy morning clouds of hope are only high, hovering rain, and how often sorrow is the bitter kernel of rapture, like the golden Imperial Apple of the German Emperor, which, to be sure, weighs three marks and three ounces, but inwardly is filled up with earth. . . .

By Heaven! we are here needlessly embittering with night-thoughts the holy evening, and none of us knows why he sighs so. — I assure the reader I have the whole Whitsuntide-festival before me in copy, and there is not a single misfortune there, unless Victor joins on a fourth Whitsuntide-day as after-summer, and in that there should something be developed. I confess I like to be an æsthetic *frère terrible*, and to point the sword at the breast of the world, which is reading deep into my Invisible (mother) Lodge, and play other like tricks, — but that comes from the fact that in youth one reads and owns the Sorrows of Werther, of which, like a mass-priest, one prepares a bloodless victim before one enters the Academy. Nay, if I this very day were composing a romance, I should — as the blue-coated Werther has in every young Amoroso and author a quasi-Christ who on Good-Friday puts on a similar crown of thorns, and ascends a cross — myself also do the same over again . . . .

— But it is time I opened my Maienthal, and let every one in. Only I will no longer make a mystery of it that I am minded to present outright this whole Paphos and knightly seat to the reader, as Louis XI. cast the Duchy of Boulogne at the feet of the Holy Mary. I think thereby to tower, perhaps, above other writers, who bestow only their quills upon their readers, full as much as the king does above old Lipsius, who made over to Mary only his silver-pen. In the beginning I meant to retain for myself this Elysium with thrice-mowed meadows and pine-groves, because I am in fact a poor devil, and really have no more income than a Prince of Wurtemberg formerly, namely ninety florins Rhenish of appanage-money, and ten florins for a coat of state, and because, as to the two square miles of land set off to me by God and equity, — for so much does the whole earth at an equal division, according to a good plan, lay off to each man, — verily I make so small account of that, that I would gladly give up my two miles to any one for a miserable sheep-fold. — And what most kept me back from making this presentation of my Maienthal to living men, was the fear that I should turn over a *feudum* to people, readers, provincial deputies, who are possessed of a thousand times greater palatinates and patrimonial estates, and whom one would provoke, if one should make them resemble the holy Mary, who from a Queen of Heaven became a Duchess of Boulogne, or the Roman Emperor who must on the day of his coronation become at the same time a member of the Order of Mary at Aachen.

But what then can all their *majorats*, — their Teutonic-knights' estates, — their mesne-tenures, — and their *patrimonia Petri* (an allusion to *my patrimonium* PAULI), — and their grandfathers' estates and all their cargoes stowed into the ship of earth, — in short, their European possessions on the earth, — what, I say, can all these Dutch farms yield, in the way of products, that could stand even at a distance before those of Maienthal? And do there grow on their crown-estates heavenly blue days, evenings full of blissful tears, nights full of great thoughts? No, Maienthal bears loftier flowers than those which cattle pluck off, fairer apples of the Hesperides than are laid up in fruit-cellars, super-terrestrial treasures on subterranean rival-pieces to Eden, like Clotilda and Emanuel, and all that our dreams paint and our tears of joy bedew. —

— And this is just my excuse, if I deny the Maienthal domain of joy to a thousand rival claimants, if I as its fee-provost cannot invest with this Swabian reversionary fief such people as are not fit for a proper *feudum*, morally blind, lame, minors, eunuchs, &c. — And here I must make myself many enemies, when, from among the vassals and joint subjects of investiture to whom Maienthal, with all its poetic privileges, is given in fee, I expressly exclude old gabblers who can no longer make the *knight's leap* of fancy, — forty-seven inhabitants of Scheerau and one hundred of Flachsenfingen, whose hearts are as cold as their knee-pans, or as dogs' noses, — the greatest ministers and other grandees, in whom, as in *great* roasted lumps of meat, only the middle is still raw, namely the heart, — one half billion economists, jurists, exchequer and finance-counsellors, and plus- i. e. minus-makers,* in whom the soul, as in Adam's case the body, was kneaded out of a clod of earth, who have a pericardium [or heart-bag], but no heart, cerebral-membranes without brain, shrewdness without philosophy, who, instead of the book of nature, read only their papers for law-cases and their tax-books, — finally, those who have not fire enough to kindle at the fire of love, poetry, religion, who for *weep* say *blubber*, for *poetry*, *rhyme*, for *sentiment*, *craziness*. . . . .

Am I then crazy that I work myself up here into such a rage, as if I had not before me on the other side the finest college of readers, which I am promoting to the *primus adquirens* of the freehold and apron-string-hold of Maienthal; a mystical, moral person, who discerns

* Financial speculators. — Tr.

that utility is only an inferior beauty, and beauty a higher utility? — It is peculiar to all emotions (but not to opinions) that one thinks he alone has them. Thus every youth holds his love to be an extraordinary celestial phenomenon which has been only once in the world, as the star of love, the evening star, often looks like a comet. But the world is not all Flachsenfingenites and Dutchmen, who climb the Alps less to have great thoughts and *elevations* than to get *sedes*,* or go to sea, not to throw a poet's glance over the sublime ocean, but to escape consumption . . . . but there are everywhere to be found, in every market-town, on every island, fair souls who rest in the bosom of nature, — who reverence the dreams of love, though they themselves have awaked from their own, — who are encased with rough men, before whom they have to veil their idyllic fantasies about the second life, and their tears over the first, — who give fairer days than they receive, — to this whole fair society I finally make a present of the *Feudum* of Maienthal, of which there has been already so much talk, and go in at the head with some friends of both sexes and my sister as investing fief-provost.

*Postscript* or autograph bull of dispensation: — The Mining Superintendent cannot deny that the S. T. author of this biography, by the fact that the dog is lazy, and that these post-days are more than commonly voluminous, and that in this chapter he has actually melted two into one, is sufficiently excused with those who have the right to ask him why he has not ended the 32d Post-day till the middle of September or Fructidor. He still sits with his description four months distant from the history, 1793.

J. P.

* According to Scheuchzer, Alps are the best remedy for constipation.

## 33. DOG-POST-DAY.

### FIRST WHITSUNTIDE-DAY.

POLICE-REGULATIONS OF PLEASURE. — CHURCH. — THE EVENING. — THE BLOOMING-CAVERN.

ARDLY had Victor waked from his sleep, though not from his dreams, when the low talking of all his thoughts, the Elysian stillness that pervaded his whole heart, told him that to-day his *Sabbatical weeks* came on. Without reproach or design of a misstep, without a sigh of his conscience, he went guilelessly to meet joy and love. The tenderer and more delicate a flower of joy is, so much the clearer must be the hand that plucks it, and only cattle pasture can bear filth; just as those who pick Imperial tea deny themselves beforehand all gross fare, that they may pluck the fragrant leaf unsoiled. — Vctor had, out of doors, hardly dawn enough to see on his broad hour-watch of Bee-father Lind's the first hour of his Sabbath; but this watch, the step-marker on the so beautiful road of the Bee-father's life, and the morning-service of nature, which consists in stillness, fortified his purpose of prefixing his present life to the second life after death as a still, cool, starry spring-morning.

"By you I swear," — said he, as, by degrees, more and more larks soared up singing out of their dew into the morning-hora,* — "I will even in joy remain composed for thirty whole years together, at least for three whole Whitsuntide days, — I will be a university-friend and house-friend, but not a Wertherish lover of enjoyment. — Does not man act as if his path of life must be a bridge of connected honey-combs, through which he has, moth-like, to chew his way, as if his hands were only sugar-tongs of pleasure? — I will again apply the sportive faculty as a bridle to my pleasures and my pains. The warm tears of melancholy, especially those of rapture, a sort of hot vapor which propels and decomposes more mightily than gunpowder and Papin's † machines, I will indeed shed, but cool them a little beforehand. — And if I do not get sight of Clotilda every forenoon, I will simply say, A man cannot be always in the third heaven, he must also sometimes stay over night in the first." — He has, perhaps, more reason than power; but, it is true, health of heart is equally removed from hysteric spasms and from phlegmatic torpor, and rapture borders more nearly on pain than on tranquillity. But no tranquillity or coolness is worth aught but that which is *attained*, — man must have at once the *capacity* and the *mastery* of passion. The *freshets* of the will resemble those of *rivers*, which for a time muddy all the *springs;* but take away the rivers, and the springs are gone too. —

The increasing dawn veiled one distant sun after another; and when at last the near one had risen, or rather nature, then could Victor see and read and take my work

* *Horæ* are the matins in the Catholic convents. — Tr.

† Papin, the inventor of the machine for dissolving bones to make them digestible. — Tr.

(the well-known *Mumien*) out of his pocket. A book was for him, in the midst of free, stimulative nature, a pair of *garden-shears* to his wantonly up-shooting dreams and joys. This morning sparkling with a whole spring, this flashing on all brooks, this humming out of blossoms into blossoms, — this blue hanging sea, over which the sun sailed like a Bucentaur,* in order to throw on the bottom of that sea, the earth, the marriage-ring, — such a Present beside such a Future would even now at the third hour have deprived him of the strength, in obedience to his new constitution, to rule over his ecstasy, and to preserve steadily so much repose as is needed for a *mezzotint* between a rapturous and a dull day, — I say he would not have had that power without his biographer, I mean, if he had not had my book before him, in the second part of which he had still the schoolmaster Wutz † to read. But this learned work — I venture without self-conceit to flatter myself — set the proper limits to his rapture. For thus, — as he walked along reading, — (as others, e. g. Rousseau and I, read while eating, and take a bite now from the plate and now from the book,) — as he contemplated the life of the schoolmaster till a new valley or a new wood opened, — as he listened now to this printed chorister, and now to a living one before whose Whitsuntide songs he passed by: in this way he could keep his ideas, with all their rondos and knights'-jumps, in such a fine ball-room-order and church-discipline, that he was as happy as the Wutz he was reading of. Besides, I was still crying to him on the stretch out of my *Mumien*, to be discreet, and to give heed to my little schoolmaster as a

* Galley in which the Doge of Venice wedded the waves. — Tr.

‡ Richter's Idyl, "The Life and Death of the contented Schoolmaster Wutz." — Tr.

file-leader in the arts of happiness, and to *get the kernel* out of every day, every hour. "Besides, I am a reprobate," said he, "if I do not do it; good God, is not then the very sense of existence,* and the first sweet breakfast after every waking, a *standing* enjoyment?"—He reflected, to be sure, that culture gives us spectacles, and takes away in return the papillæ of the tongue, and compensates to us for our pleasures by the better definitions of them (just as the silk-worm, as caterpillar, has *taste*, but no *eyes*, and, as butterfly, has eyes without taste), he confessed to himself, indeed, that he had too much understanding to have so much contentment as the Auenthal schoolman Wutz, and that he philosophized too deeply besides; but he also insisted upon this: that "a higher wisdom must nevertheless (because otherwise the all-wise would be necessarily the *all-unhappy*) find a way again out of the sweltry parterre of the lecture-room into a parterre of flowers. Lofty men produce, like mountains, the sweetest honey." . . .

Although, even while he was in the last village, the suburbs as it were of Maienthal, he heard the last tolling, still he was not provoked at the belated arrival. Nay, to show himself that he was the philosopher Socrates, he passed on with a diligent increase of slowness, and did not, like the Athenian, make a libation of the cup of joy, but did not, in fact, yet fill it up. "Float on," he said to a little cloud formed of collected lily-pollen, "and be wafted before me in advance over the *good hearts*, thou pillar of cloud at the entrance of the promised land!—And may thy little shadow silhouette

* "The very sense of being would then be a continued pleasure, such as we now feel it in some few and favored moments of our youth."—Shelley's Notes to Queen Mab.

for them the more fixed one, which follows more lazily, and which is absorbed later by the blue of heaven!" — And ere the winding footpath placed him before the flower-curtained gate of the valley, wherein stood the beloved cradle and nursery-garden of his fair three-days future, he was arrested by a closed thistle, around whose sealed honey-cups a white butterfly was drawing his third parallel, — and the mosaic thistles on Le Baut's floor started into life before him, and showed him the stings of the past; then he felt it incomprehensible how he had been able to endure his sorrows, and easier to bear the heaven of joy. . . .

He took out Lind's watch, in order to know the birth-hour of his honeymoon or honey-week, — precisely at 11 o'clock he came out before the neat village, before the green-house of his heaven, before the colony of his hope, before Eden. . . . Ah, the murmuring little village buried in foliage seemed to throw all its blooming twigs, like arms, around, and knit himself to itself; it was green and white and red, — not painted, but overspread with leaves and blossoms. And when, as the ringing died away, — in order avariciously to hoard up for himself the embrace of his Emanuel, and in order to come upon the Maienthal church music with a heart opened by Nature, — he stole into the long, clean village, and ran Friendship's toll for a few minutes at Emanuel's house, it seemed to him as if his peacefully glad heart in the still lanes rocked with the birds on the cherry-twigs that latticed the window-panes, and hovered with the bees in the cherry blossoms. "Come right in," all seemed to say, "thou good man, we are all happy, and thou shalt be so too." — He approached the shining church, whose dazzling stucco flung by contrast upon the blue of the sky a sublime darkness, and his beating heart trembled blissfully with the waves of the organ within, and with the rustling birch-tree fixed in the ground before the church-door, and with the dry May-pole, in the middle of the village, bowed by the morning-wind. . . .

"But," says my reader," could then his eye so long deny itself the fairer prospects, and his heart the more beloved beauty, and, instead of the Abbey, seek out only the church?" — Oh, he looked after that the very first thing of all, and his eye ran trembling around all the windows of his sun-temple; but as he found all of them open and empty, and all the curtains drawn up, he guessed that its fair conclave of sisters, and among them the conclave-sister of his heart, were there where he sought — and found them, — in the temple. He went up unheard, during the tramping down of the church-goers, into the front-stall of the nobility, which from without appeared empty, that flower-stand of the convent-nuns. There was nothing there but dropped birch-leaves; for the body of nuns and the Abbess and Clotilda stood — below in the Church, and encircled the altar with a choir of singing angels, and took the sacrament there. — With a thrill of joy he beheld the queen of his heaven, the so dearly loved and undeserved, the shining angel, melting her vestment of earthly snow with heavenly warmth to tears, in order soon to become invisible. —— His spirit bowed itself as she knelt: "Drink heaven's peace," he said, "out of the sacred chalice of the great man, among whose thoughts was never a cloud nor a sigh, — and may the thought which thou now contemplatest with such steadfast devotion be destined to become more and more luminous and immovable, like a sun, and always to throw a warm evening-light over the weary soul!" — This angel in mourning-attire called forth in his inner being by an awakening of the dead all the virtues of his life and all its faults, and gave those a heaven and these a hell; he was, therefore, now too holy to disturb a saint by making his appearance, even supposing her tranquil eye, absorbed in pious emotions, which did not so much as fall on the nearer devout beauties to the height of the waist, had been able to lift itself to him. The birch at the first window of the loft he kept before him as a leafy fan;—this green veil playing on his cheeks covered his attentiveness and his tears of joy from the whole church. The place where he was so happy seemed, to judge from an inscription on the glass, to have been once the usual stand of Clotilda; for Giulia's was near by, as I know for certain, because on the stall-window a G and C, enclosed by a wreath, had been cut in with the words by Giulia: "Thus are we united by the flowers of life and the circle of eternity." . . .

Victor slipped away unseen and early out of this niche of removed goddesses, and bore his heart filled with love to the open breast of friendship,—to Emanuel. He saw already the latter's tabernacle of the covenant in the temple of Nature,—when his rapture was delayed by one of earlier date. Julius lay in the blooming grass with its waves rippling over him, and holding a cherry-twig full of open honey-cups in his hand, in order to draw the bees to him, and to delight himself with their murmurous hovering over the blossoms. Victor embraced him, and forgot in the ecstasy to name his name,—"Art thou my angel?" said he.—"I am only thy Victor!"—"O come! O come!" said the blind youth, trembling like a melody, and drew his friend to Emanuel's house; but he led him, behind the cloud of his blindness, the longer way, and, besides, he turned round at every fourth step for a renewed embrace.

When they came to the water-wheel, which loudly emptied its sprinkling-cans on the flower-beds, and whose shivered lightnings flitted against Emanuel's windows and ceiling, then the blind one said, "Embrace me once more right heartily." — But amidst the din of the rain-shower, and amidst the stupefaction of love, they were pressed together by other arms than their own, and the two young hearts were linked to a third, and the East Indian gazed like a god of love from one to the other, and said: "O ye good youths, remain ever thus, and weep on in your blissful love! — Blessings on thee, my Horion, and a welcome in the great spring round about us!" — And when Emanuel and Victor sank on each other's necks, then was it as if all the flower-beds bowed down for rapture, as if all the waves flamed more radiantly under super-earthly lightnings flying over them, as if the zephyrs swelled with sighs of love, as if higher beings must needs whisper in the over-measure of joy: O ye good human beings, verily ye love like us! —

An arm out of a river of Paradise lifted and bore this loving trinity into the leafy rooms, and here, for the first time, Victor saw that the spring was on Dahore's cheeks and the summer in his eyes, as well as twelve May months in his heart. The white mourning-roses on his cheeks, which always seemed to bloom like *mural crowns* of death against St. John's-day, had given place to the red ones, — in short, Emanuel's face gave the hope that he had been, in regard to his death, a false prophet. —

In this waving apartment, whose golden wall borders were linden-boughs, and whose splendid tapestries were linden blossoms, and over whose door, as door-paintings, flickered the reflection and the mock-suns of the flashing water-wheel, in this four-walled island, surrounded by Nature's roaring sea of joy, through whose open windows the zephyrs flung bees and butterflies over the window-flowers among the lindens, my hero, to whom, besides, the noonday hum of bells appeared like a ringing call to a peace-festival of the earth, felt himself wading through flowers of joy up to his heart. — Emanuel's poesy sounded to him, in this epic intoxication, like prose; he was, as it were, sunk in a thicket of flowers, and, lifting his eyes, saw overhead a healed immortal who bent apart the blooming envelopment, — and still higher up an eternal Whitsuntide sun in the infinite blue, — and nearer above him the sprouting of the flower-leaves, and above this the swarming of bees, — and a golden morning-red, wound as a living frame round about the whole variegated incense-breathing woodland. . . .

— By Heaven! only to lie in a *literal* flower-wood of this kind were of itself something, — to say nothing of lying actually in a *metaphorical* one! — Victor was devout with joy, still from overfulness, contented from gratitude. The aspect of their common teacher gave, it is true, to Clotilda's image warmer colors, and to his soul higher flames, but imparted to his wishes no insatiableness and no impatience.

Emanuel immediately began speaking of that beloved pupil of his; not at all as if Clotilda had clearly described to him the third Easter-holiday, or as if Emanuel had guessed it, but this guileless man simply knew not the difference between love and friendship, and he would have said of himself as well as of Victor, that he loved her. And just this childlike *naïveté*, which, through the open chamber of a woman's heart, watched for no right of transit nor for any breaches, but laid bare his own, and which fished for no confessions, found fault with none, took advantage of none, — this quality must have been just what would bind with the Gordian ganglion of sympathy the shyest female soul to so open a manly one. Nay, I believe Clotilda could more easily have made known her love to her teacher than to her beloved. — As this Emanuel now told him how he had pictured to her all the scenes of his former sojourn here, — and all his raptures, — and his confession of friendship for her, — how he had read to her his letters, and how the second (that disconsolate one on the night of the Stamitz concert) had forced so many tears into her eyes, — and as Victor saw how very much his friend had by his breathing on it drawn her love open like a closing tulip-cup, — all this kindled his love for her, his friendship for him even to devotion, and in a blissful embarrassment he kissed the blind one. By this double love he now explained to himself Clotilda's easy consent to his Whitsuntide journey.

He would have held it an Angel's- and a Peter's-fall from friendship, not to propose directly the question to Emanuel, when he might see this beloved — of Virtue. — "Now!" said the latter, who, despite his respectful East-Indian gentleness toward women, knew not the nose-rings, binding-keys, and dampers of our Harem-decency. But Victor acted otherwise and yet thought just so. He had already asked when abroad: "Why do they suffer the wretched police-regulation to stand for maidens, that they, e. g., must never walk out singly, but always, like Nuremberg Jews, under the escort of an old crone, or like the monks, in pairs? Not as if this would in any manner embarrass me, if I acted a romance, but that it would, if I wrote one, where I should have to keep to the female rules-of-march at the expense of the critical, and trail round with me a convoy of auxiliary-women through the whole book as an abattis to my heroine. Should I not be obliged, if I would so much as get her out beyond the house door-steps, to march along beside her with a crown-guard of female keepers of the seal? Should I not be obliged by this confounded co-investiture and trading in company with Virtue — there would be no such thing as doing business on one's own account — to foist female friends on my heroine contrary to all probability? I should think hard, to be sure, of a Spanish maiden if she showed me her foot, and of a Turkish, if she showed me her face, and of a German, if she went *alone* to see the best young man; but just because the most fanatical *blue laws*, which surely are blue vapor on blue Mondays, become a real moral law for them, therefore am I vexed at this deplorable pusillanimity, and wish to see nothing forbidden but — waltzing and falling! . . . . He has here, perhaps, satire *in petto;* for, to speak seriously of the matter, this sanitary-ordinance, that maidens must with us, as petitions with princes, always present themselves in duplicates, has manifestly the design of accustoming them all to one another, because they must have each other's friendship for visits; — secondly, brothers and sisters must be out of each other's hair, because they do not know whether they shall need each other as collateral securities of their virtue and second exchange-bills of love; — thirdly, these human ordinances give to female virtue by the *minor* moral-service (because great temptations are too rare) daily exercise in religion, and higher importance, and bear the same relation as the articles of the Talmud do to the Bible, although a right Jew would sooner transgress the Bible than the Talmud; — fourthly, we owe to these symbolic books of propriety the earlier culture of that female acuteness for which we unhappily furnish no other opportunities of attention than the oath they swear on those books affords.

Victor at once blamed and followed, like a good girl, the female rules of the order; court life had made him more courageous, but also more refined, and, like the court itself, he was, among women, reconciled to the writing-lines of the ceremonial. Therefore he purposed not until the second day of Whitsuntide to make his regular diplomatic appearance at the Abbess's, since to-day it was too late for anything, and besides that he would not fly into the sweet, holy emotions over yonder like a comet. And then too, his contentment told him, indeed, how little the *neighborhood* of a loved heart differs from its *presence*, which, besides, is nothing but a nearer neighborhood.

Meanwhile he mastered himself at least so far as to go out with his twin-brothers of the heart into the Colosseum of Nature, although he did not conceal from himself that he should be in dread out there of meeting Clotilda. And Emanuel lessened this fear but poorly, when he confessed to him that she had hitherto with her wounded life gone every day round the ponds as around magnetic healing-tubs, and through the lawn as through field-apothecaries'-shops. — Hasten forth at last, ye three good souls, into the Jubilee of Spring, which the Earth celebrates yearly in memory of Creation. Haste, ere the minutes of your life, like the broad waves on the two brooks, now still fleeting, and flashing, and sounding, fly to pieces and extinguish themselves on a weeping-willow, — haste, ere the flowers of your days and the flowers of the meadow are veiled by evening, when instead of the vital oxygen they shall exhale only poisonous air, — and enjoy the first day of Whitsuntide ere it trickles away!

— And it has trickled away, and a summer already lies upon it to-night as a grave; but the three dear hearts have hastened and enjoyed it, before it faded. . . . They sauntered on among the zephyrs, those sowing-machines of the flowers, as they came fluttering out of all the bushes, — they came before the five pocket-mirrors of the sun, the ponds, (the rivers being pier-mirrors and the gay shores the pier-tables,) — they saw how Nature, like Christ, conceals her miracles, but they saw also the bridal torch of the marriage-making May, the sun, and a bridal chamber in every singing tree-top, and a bridal bed in every flower-cup, — they, the wedding guests of the earth, turned not away the bee, who drunk with honey revelled around them, nor did they scare up the food-bringing mother, before whom the young bird with trembling wings melted into invisibleness, — and when they had climbed all the earthly steps of the eternal temple, whose columns are milky-ways, the sun sank, like the thoughts of men, to meet another world. . . .

The fountain in the *garden of termination*,* which rears itself half-way down the declivity of the southern mountain and gleams away high over the mountain, already bore on its thin crystal column a shaft recast by the evening sun into a ruby, and this glittering, full-blowing rose contracted itself, like other flowers that had gone to sleep, to a red point, — and the hanging columns of gnats in the last beam seemed to say: To-morrow it will be fair again; go back; ah, you play longer in the sun than we. —

They went back; but when Victor saw the five high

* Such was the name given to the park in the Abbey which Lord Horion in his romantic taste had begun but not finished, because he hit upon the Island of Union. I weave this description of it only fragmentarily in with the incidents.

white columns at the western end of the beloved garden blink in the light of evening, his exalted heart felt a yearning and a burden, and he restrained it not from sighing: "Good Clotilda! ah, I should be glad indeed to see thee even to-day; my heart is full of tears of joy over this holy day, and I would fain pour it out before thee." — And when the whole park of the Abbey reared itself proudly beside the evening-heaven, and took possession of their hearts, then all at once said Emanuel, — who was always like himself even in his raptures, — "I will tell the Abbess this very day, so that Clotilda may lay up joy for to-morrow," and he separated from them. . . . Noble man! thou that in four weeks hopest to leave this flowery spring and mount to the stars above thee, — thou thinkest more of immortality than of death, — no threatening Orthodoxy, but the Indian love of flowers, hath trained thee, hence art thou so blessed; thou art free from wrath, like every dying man, free from greed and from anxiety; in thy soul, as at the Pole when every morning the sultry sun stays away, the *moon* of the *second* world never sets day nor night! —

Victor, alone, led the blind youth home, and both were silent and embraced each other with brotherly tears behind every screen, and asked each other neither for the reasons of the embrace nor of the tears. When they had passed through the still village, and as they came along by the park of the Abbey, Victor saw his Emanuel pass out of the last bower into the dazzling convent. It seemed to him as if every one therein already recognized him, as if he must hide himself. The garden of inspiration was to be in the valley only the flower-bed in a meadow, and not violently contrast itself with nature by sharp limits, but hang over into it softly as a dream into waking hours with blooming, embowered borders, and flow over into it with hop-gardens, with green thick-set hedges around corn-fields, and with sowed-over children's gardens. A large wide colonnade of chestnuts, set in silver by two brooks, opened broad and free toward the five ponds with their pierced work of blossoms. The northern mountain lifted itself up over against the park like a terrace, and seemingly continued the Eden over unseen valleys.

Victor avoided every opening window of the convent by means of the chestnut-trees under which he led his blind one, and behind which he could, unobserved, observe more nearly. On the shed-roof of the avenue woven of green roof-laths the evening lay like an autumn gleaming through with red streaks of splendor. He went, despite the danger of detection, to the very middle, where the avenue divides into two arms; but here he chose the right arm of the leafy hall, which bent away with him from the convent, as well as from a nightingale which, in the midst of the garden, sent out from a consecrated thorn-hedge her young and her tones. The arbor rendered to him by its softening distances from the bravura-airs of the feathered Prima Donna the services of a pedal and lute-stop; — gently was he led on by the windings which the gradual darkening and narrowing of the alley concealed, through the tones of the nightingale that floated after him, through the thinner trickling of the evening rays among the leaves between the two brooks, which now glided away *inside* of the chestnut-lane. — The brooks came closer together and left room only for love. — The portico closed in more coseyly. — The scattered flowers of the two banks crowded together and passed over into bushes. — The bushes grew up into a garden wall and touched each other at first in summits hanging towards each other, loose and transparent, and at last darkly knit together. — And the avenue and the arbor which had grown up under it blended their green together, so as to make with their coinciding blossom-veils only a single night. — Then in the green twilight was the arbor stopped up by a web of honeysuckle and nest of blossoms, but five ascending steps invited to the tearing asunder of the blooming curtain. And when one parted it, one sank into a blossom-cleft, into a narrow, tangled vault, as it were into a magnified flower-cup. In this Delphic cave of dreams the cushion was made of high grass, and the arms of the seat of blossoming-twigs, and the back of flowers massed together, and the air of the breath of dusting dwarf-fruit-trees. This flowery Holy of Holies was peopled only with bees and dreams, illuminated only with white blossoms; it had for evening-red only the purple of night-violets, for heaven's blue only the azure of elder-blossoms, and the blest one therein was lulled only by bees' wings and by the five mouths of the brooks meeting around him into the slumber in which the distant nightingale struck the harmonica- and evening-bells of dream. . . . .

— And as Victor to-day, beside the blind one, trod the five steps, and opened the blossom-woven tapestry door of the heaven: lo! — there — O man beatified this side of death! — reposed a female saint with weeping eyes, absorbed in Philomela's expiring plaints. . . . It was thou, Clotilda, and thou thoughtest of *him* with softened soul and heightened love, — and he on thee with reciprocal love! O when two loving ones meet each other in the *selfsame* emotion, then and not till then do they respect the human heart and its love and its bliss! — Hide not, Clotilda, with any blossoms the tears under which thy cheeks blush, because they should fall only before solitude! Tremble, but only for joy, as the sun trembles, when he comes out of a cloud on the horizon! Cast not down yet thy eye curtained with flowers, which for the first time falls so calmly opened and with such a stream of love on the man who deserves thy fair heart, and who rewards all thy virtues with his own! . . . . Victor was struck with the lightning of joy and must needs remain immovable in the sweet smile of rapture, when the beloved rose behind the flower-clouds like the moon behind an Eden standing in full bloom, and in the womanly transfiguration of love resembled an angel dissolved into a prayer.

The blind youth knew nothing as yet of the third blessed one. She moved her hand, in sweet confusion, towards a too thin twig to raise herself from the deep grass-bench; it seemed to her lover, as if this hand reached to him out of the clouds of the second life a second heart, and he drew the hand to himself and sank with his mute, overflowing face down through the blossom on her throbbing veins. But hardly had Clotilda bade *both* a stammered welcome during the coming out from the green closet, when there appeared to them the angel — Emanuel, who had hastened from the convent to seek his friend. He said nothing, but looked on both with a nameless rapture, to find out whether they were right joyful, and as if to ask, "Are you not, then, now right happy, ye good souls? do you not, then, love each other inexpressibly?" —— Oh, only a mortal is needed for sympathy in sorrow, but an angel for sympathy in joy; there is nothing more beautiful than the radiant Christ's head, on which the laying aside of the Moses' veil shows the still, glad interest in another's blameless joys, in another's pure love; and it is quite as godlike (or still more so) to contemplate the love of others with a mutely congratulating heart, as to have it one's self. . . . Emanuel, thy greater praise is kept in kindred souls, but not on paper! —

On the cross-way of the alley the fair society parted, and the left branch of the same led Clotilda along by the nightingale back to the abode of gentle hearts. Victor, dissolved by his heightened love for three human beings at once, arrived at the dusky apartments of Emanuel, lighted only by setting stars, and found there a spread table which the refined Abbess had sent to the guest or to the host, for Emanuel at evening ate only fruit. One wishes to share everything with one's love, even the kitchen. Emanuel after Easter never lighted a light. In the clar-obscure, made of the fusion of lunar silver and linden green, the blissful trefoil * bloomed under the evening star. Victor, by his professional pictures of the night-cold, put his invalid friend out of conceit with night-walks, and went alone with the blind one at this late hour out to the dormitory of hushed Nature. . . . Blessed is the evening which is the fore-court of a blessed day. The May-frost had cleansed the stars from the warm breath of the vapor, and deepened the blue of the celestial hemisphere, to make a beautiful night the earnest of a beautiful day. All was silent around the village, except the nightingale in the garden and the rustling May-chafers, those heralds of a bright day. — And when Victor went home with an upward sigh of thanks for these Whitsuntide hours, of which each handed the next the box of powdered sugar to sweeten the short moments of a still mortal; as he passed along before the muffled confession-hymns, which here a twelve-years-old little man who to-morrow was to take the sacrament, and there one

* Trio. — Tr.

by the side of his mother, sang; and when, finally, a vesper-hymn breathed out from the Abbey, and, swimming forth as it were on a single lute-tone, brought the fair day with a swan-song to its close, and when nothing more was left of the soft day except its resonance in the heart of the happy one and in the evening song of the convent, and its reflection in the fleeting evening-red of heaven, and in the contented and still smiling face of the sleeping Emanuel; — then did the mute joys in Victor's face look like prayers, the undisturbed tears like overrunning drops from the cup of gladness, his stillness like a good deed, and his whole heart like the warm tear of joy shed by a higher genius.

Victor led the beloved blind one softly to his place of slumber, where dream restored his disordered eyes and arrayed the little landscapes of his childhood, with morning hues, more brightly around him. — He then laid himself down without undressing himself, opposite to the moon which hung low above the horizon, and sank to sleep on the building-ground of our fairer air-castles, on the sounding-board of childhood, where morning-dreams lead consecrated man out of the wilderness of day to the mount of Moses, and let him look over into the dark, promised land of Eternity. . . . .

The first Whitsuntide day, dear reader, in this tri-clang of rapture, has died away; but in these three high festivals of joy, as with those in the almanac, the second is still fairer, and the third the fairest of all. I shall not at all hurry with the movement of my pen through these three heavens, — nay, if I could certainly know that the acting persons in this history would never get to see my work, I should shift the boundaries of this Eden, by adding much that, on nearer inspection, would not prove historically true. —

# 34. DOG-POST-DAY.

## SECOND DAY OF WHITSUNTIDE.

MORNING. — THE ABBESS. — THE WATER-MIRROR. — DUMB ACTION FOR LIBEL. — THE RAIN AND THE OPEN HEAVEN.

T two o'clock the morning-wind swept in more loudly and coolly through Victor's open chamber, and shook already dew-drops from shiny foliage, and the near whisper of leaves murmured through his ears into his dreams. The lark, as the overture of the day, flung herself high up into the gray of heaven, and rang in the morning's feast of trumpets. This alarmist became in his dreaming the hovering after-echo which blended with the morning; amidst the soft in-fall of the neighboring sounds he slowly opened his eyes and dreamed on, and closed them again, and was more awake, and sleep did not pass off like a thick shroud made of night, but floated upward like a veil of morning perfume; and his soul, without making a single movement of the body, opened with the still awaking of a flower-cup in the presence of the morning. . . . .

— Now I am again already at boiling and blazing point, — and yet, as often as I dip my pen in the ink, I make up my mind to gain the good graces of the critics, and to write with my pen as with an icicle. But it is impossible for me, — in the first place, because I am getting into years. With most men, it is true, as with birds, singing ceases when love does; but with those who make their head a hot-house of their ideas, years, i. e. the days of drill therein, give the fancy as well as the *passions* a higher growth. Poets resemble glass, which, when it is old and breaks, takes on motley colors. — But secondly, though I were just blooming in my twentieth year, still I could not now write frostily, seeing winter is at the door. Rousseau says that in prison he produced the best poem on Liberty, — hence the French, those state's-prisoners, used to write better prose on the subject than the free Britons, — hence Milton poetized in winter. I have often carried out my writing-tablets in summer, and undertaken to press it to this silhouette board, and then take its profile; but fantasy can lay only Past and Future under its copying-paper, and every actual Present limits its creative power, — just as, according to the old naturalists, the water distilled from roses loses its virtue precisely at the time when roses bloom. Therefore I always had to wait till I became unfaithful, before I could go at love with my drawing instruments. . . . On the contrary, a man who now, towards after-summer, on a Molucca Island, primes and sketches the spring, must, for the foregoing reasons, and for the further one that the flying-summer is the regretful after-echo and silver-wedding of spring, hand it over to the Gallery-inspectors with much too bright sap-colors. —

The gayly-embroidered description of Victor's sojourn in Maienthal may well get to be as long as that of Voltaire's in Paris, with the publisher's compensation for which the lean wag might have cleared the rent of his *chambres garnies.* For just at this moment the dog has actually handed in a fourth Whitsuntide day, and expanded the trinomial root of the given *power* of joy into a quadrinomial. As in this quadruplicate of joy again, there is no wailing, no murder, no pestilence, but only good, I joyfully catch the remaining images of this spring in my camera-obscura, nor hover in anxious suspense, lest I should have to drag out my hero (Knef has made over to me all the Whitsuntide-days, and is only to send a little supplementary page afterward) somewhat as I did my Gustavus,* from the collapsed rubbish of his pleasure-palace and summer-house. —

Emanuel despatched in the forenoon his day's work of writing in his astronomical tables, in order to spend the whole afternoon with his guest at the Abbess's; he also offered him a little collaboratorship at his flowers, namely, to pluck out the rosemary blossoms, and spread the sunshade over the carnation-stand. With Emanuel, even in the prosaic repose of the day, the wings always protruded far out from under the half-wing-shells. Victor took the requests of his teacher as gifts. As he picked away out there at the rosemary, the rising sun opened the valves of the wind, and then, under its breath, all the registers of the great organ of being began to go, and the tremolo of the brooks rolled its waves on his ear, the flute-work of the birds pealed, and the thirty-two footed pedal-register of the woodland roared. One little parishioner's head after another, as he carried his twelve years together with the same number of Herculean labors of memory to the Holy Sacrament, creeping along behind its father, embroidered and stiffened up with a wreath-knob, and generally with gold-spangles, passed by before him. What

* In the "Invisible Lodge." — Tr.

a beautiful second Whitsuntide-day, which is generally full of rain-clouds, have you, ye little folks, to-day! — Victor right gladly indulged the grandees of the village, i. e. the drivers of a full span and the schoolmaster's son, the hair-modeller and queue-preacher Meuseler, who on the second Whitsuntide-day frizzled the neighboring villages, and who with his holy-(powder)-sprinkler effected the last effusion upon the little heads, which the Parson had been moistening these six weeks. Victor's heart beat for joy, as if he had a child, or were himself a child among them, when the motley, powdered, animated chain, with dancing spangles, with long-stemmed nosegays, with black-glistening spiritual *Musen-annuals*, marched in under the commander's staff and shepherd's crook of their two consuls, singing and besung and rung in and trumpeted in through the triumphal gate of the church. — Ah! joy sits still more beautifully on children than on us, just as an unhappy, a begging child, whose first child's-garden fate has trampled down, and before whose eyes, at the first bursting into existence, nothing hangs but black, misshapen morning cloud, afflicts our heart more than his father beside him. —

"Pluck, like a berry, *every* minute of your first day of triumph, ye good children, and I wish the sermon would be right long, that you might keep on so much longer your handsome dress!" said Victor, and looked round toward the convent, whose windows were full of unrecognizable spectatresses; he proposed to himself, on the return of the juvenile procession, to seek out for himself from among the windows with a pocket spy-glass the one with the fairest contents. — Just go, kindly man, who lovest fair souls like fair nature, and endurest cold ones like the winter-landscape, and who never revengest, just walk up and down by the brooks, for there is the footpath of the fishers, and because on thy poetic ring-races thou wouldst not harm a peasant by trampling down so much as a forked wagon of hay, such as the children braid out of hazel-rods! Fill the interval between the first heaven and the third, when thou wilt sit down not with Abraham, but with thy Clotilda at the table of the Abbess, — fill it up with a second, namely with the embrace of all nature, which never looks more sweetly into the soul, than when on it, not far from the soul, a beloved dwells! —

A stroll between two brooks that mingled their flashings and between their lackered willows snowed over with foam-worms * overspread the whole inner man even to every corner of a dark tear with morning-splendor. — In addition to that Victor kept looking across the meadow up at Emanuel's open window, and letting a smile float down from it like a running wave full of light. — In addition to that, he did not stop there, but went up twice and disturbed him in the midst of his writing with a child-like embrace. — In addition to that, he put seven-leagued boots on his eyes, and ran over the whole landscape, here rising, there sinking, here shining, there shadowing, in order to catch and size even here in anticipation a postal and travelling map of the finest places for the afternoon-rambles with Clotilda, because in the afternoon the raptures themselves will perhaps spoil the choice of raptures! — And thus did Nature create over again in his spirit her morning and her spring out of the earth-clod of the first spring, i. e. out of the hot sun, out of the cool brook, out of the butterfly, whom May shelled out of his hull, from the motley flies which the prolific earth hatched out of the larva-seed like winged flowers. — Then he closed his eyes amid the din of sparrows and swallows in the village, and

* Worm-shaped clots of foam. — Tr.

amidst the watch-cries of the larks, and against the dazzling waves of the brooks, and let his soul dive down into the ringing sea and into the chiaroscuro painted by the eyelid; but then would his heart have been overwhelmed by creation's flood, which swept over it out of all pipes and beds and mouths of life around him, out of the tangled vein-work of the stream of life, which shoots at once through flower-runnels, through tree-channels, through white flies' veins, through red blood-canals and through human nerves, . . . he would, in the impotence of enjoyment, have been drowned in the deep, broad ocean of life, which life-streams cross and fill, had he not, like every drowning man, heard a peal of bells far down into the waves.

In short — church was out, and he had to go behind a leafy hunter's-screen, in order, when the Panists * of the Lord's Supper should march by out of the church, whose organ-music still followed, and under the tower that still trumpeted after them, that then he might see with his pocket-glass *who* looked out of the convent. Clotilda's face floated, as if called forth by magic out of the second world, close to the glass, and he could, without fear of being driven away, close his butterfly-wings around this flower; he could freely sink into her great eyes, as into two flower-cups filled with the splendor of dew. Never did he see so pure a snow of the white around the blue heaven's-opening, which went far into the soul, now fairer than ever; and when she cast down her eye toward the garden, the great veiling eyelid with its trembling lashes stood just as beautifully over it as a lily over a fountain. *Love*, like *drawing* and like the germ of man, begins at the *eye*. — When the children had gone by, then Clotilda

* Originally those who bore a ticket from the Emperor recommending them to receive bread (*panis*) from a monastery.—Tr.

slowly and freely turned her face toward Emanuel's cottage, and gazed across with the far-reaching, longing look of love. . . . .

And with such a love, beating like a heart in his innermost consciousness, Victor with his two friends arrived up at the convent. The Abbess (her name is not reported to me at all, not even her pseudonyme) received him with a stately air, which her station had not imparted to her, but had attempered. Her soul was born crowned. The Princess of ——, whose chief governess she was, loved sometimes to play the child (children inversely reciprocate, and represent their representatives): but although she possessed a pride of thirty years, she checked her hobby-horse so soon as the monarchical chief governess appeared, than whom no one in the land (the swans excepted) carried her head back so high. A lady like her, whose looks were throne-insignia, and her words *mandata sacræ cæsareæ majestatis propria,** had from the hands of Nature herself the allegiance-medals and the throne scaffolding, so as to weigh her imperial apple against young maidens' apple of beauty,—such a one could rule and mould a Clotilda. Her soul was painted by three masters:—the back-ground by the world,—the fore-ground by the church,—the middle-ground by Virtue, Her æsthetic parts placed her in a singular manner in a certain elective-affinity with Emanuel's East Indian ones.

I know nothing more touching and beautiful than a woman's obeisance when it springs from that deep respect with which alone good maidens venture to speak their love.—Happy Victor! thy Clotilda received thee with as much reverence as her teacher. Only the coquette is made by love more dictatorial † (a silicious juristic word!);

* "Proper mandates of the sacred imperial majesty."—Tr.

† *Befehlhaberisch* is the German word.—Tr.

but the proud one it makes modest and gentle. Never did he take a meal more delightedly than in this bright pleasure-villa, before whose open windows reposed a blue horizon and nearer at hand murmuring avenues, filled with music, than in this decorated orangery of blooming girls, — (whereas a gymnasium is a menagerie and a house of sisters an aviary.) — Victor, who understood how to manage women even better than men, felt himself as well in the busy ant-hill of these lively maidens, as in an ant-bath,* and he was a second Bee-father Wildau, who constructed for himself out of the swarm of bees now a beard and now a muff. More manly sense is required for a certain refined gallantry, than they have who in their satires confound it with the insipid kind; just as only mountains afford the sweetest honey. Earnest must be the groundwork of jest; respect and kindliness, of praise. Victor could more easily before two than before thirty-two female eyes fall into embarrassment, which, by the way, is the grossest blunder and Germanism in female grammar. He had long since learned to combine the volatile salts of woman's wit with the fixed ones of man's, as well as the art, in great circles, of setting every soul, every caterpillar, on the right leaf for its nourishment.

To him who had once said, "I wish I had to converse at least four times a year with ladies, with whom one should have to apply so much *tournure*,† that one actually would not know what he wanted, and who were fine even to nonsense," — to him a high lady like the Abbess, whom, since the laying down of her high governess-ship, one could confound a very, very little with a *précieuse*,‡ was a true

* Defined by Grimm, "a medical warm-bath prepared over ants and ant-hills." — Tr.

† Readiness at turns, repartee, &c. — Tr.

‡ A prim, affected person. — Tr.

refreshment; for he could sketch her at least the physiognomical fragments of the court with a thousand turns, i. e. a full face with *five* dots. But he had in this the still nobler design to draw off his adoring attention, his heart that sometimes started in the shape of a tear to his eye, from his beloved Clotilda, in order to spare her a wholly different attention from his own. In a singular manner his satirical feeling, precisely, always drew off the Moses' veil from his serious feelings, from his softened soul,— that is to say, he was not ashamed of a tear, simply because he knew that his humor could protect him against the suspicion of exaggeration and against the mocker; just as, on the other hand and inversely, his playing and flashing of wit under tears, like phosphorus under water, conserved and nourished its light.—

Fortunately, at this point, Emanuel, who in the midst of dinner had gone out into the garden, came back and proposed taking a walk. For in his soul great ideas were all that remained standing of life, as of old Egypt only temples were left behind, no houses; and his ignorance in little things must be ridiculous to little *things*.* — The Abbess had taken Clotilda beside her on the throne as under-queen of the fiery nuns. Victor represented in his single person the board of wards of the Electorate of Brandenburg among these fluttering graces. Clotilda gave over the blind one just to a whole dove-flock of the liveliest way-guides, because they all sued for the boatman's and forefinger's-office with the blind youth; they all loved him on account of his heavenly beauty, but (as he could not see theirs) only in the same way as they would caress a beautiful boy of five years. . . . At another time

* I. e. light girls. Jean Paul uses *Dingen* for the dative in the first instance, and *Dingern* in the second.— Tr.

Victor would certainly have looked round and made the fine allusion that *beauty* was leading *blindness;* but to-day he only looked round for other reasons.

— At last the Island of the Blest, which had already gleamed far, far out through the mist of his childhood's dreams, was now the ground under his feet, and he made the voyages of discovery through his heaven; — he and Clotilda were silent for some minutes, because their hearts began to be softly agitated with joy, that they were at last alone together and stood before the great esplanade of spring. Amidst the blissful smiles, the dumb alphabet of rapture, and amidst trembling respirations, that holy sanscrit of love, they had already arrived at the first pond, over whose crystal mirror a bridge winds like gilded foliage-work. — They stopped dazzled in the midst of this moon-disk and looking-glass, because the parasol could not screen from two suns at once, reckoning the one in the water; they turned half round, and sought with their eyes in the picturing water the deeper heaven's-blue, and two still, blissful forms, that looked at each other with their moist eyes. O, his eye rested warmly in her reflected one, like the sun upon the subterranean sun, and his trembling look was the long tremolo and continuance of a single tone; for the goddess dwelling in the water sank with her eyes to meet his soul, because she would fain avail herself of the doubled distance of his form, which amounted to ten feet. — To conclude at last the overmastering rapture, he withdrew his eyes from this glass-painting and directed them (i. e. he merely redoubled it) to the archetype itself; and the mutual inflowing of glances, the trembling together of souls, threw into the short moment the fields of a long heaven. — And they saw that they had found each other, and that they had loved each other, and that they deserved each other. As they went on, Victor could only say, "O that you might be to-day as inexpressibly happy as I am." — And she answered softly, softly as a zephyr exhaled from among tender, leafless blossoms, "I am so indeed." . . . . Ah, I have often pictured to myself, if we all loved one another as two lovers do, if the emotions of all souls, as these are, were *tied* notes, if Nature drew from us all at once, the resonance of her strings stretching even beyond the stars, instead of moving only a loving couple as a double harpsichord, — then should we see that a human heart full of love contains an immeasurable Eden, and that Deity itself created a world in order to love one.

But I will write again, as Clotilda spoke, who manifested the poetic spirit only by actions, not by words, like players who know how in speaking to evade the rhyme and metre of their poet.

The village, or rather the inn, gave their Jacob's ladder a *fourth* round, the fourth Whitsuntide-day. — The Englishman, Cato the elder, who had run away from Kussewitz and from his club with a travelling orchestra of virtuosos from Prague, came out to see Maienthal also. He could never in his life wait for anything. He told Victor he was coming to see him to-morrow, to-day he should survey the cultivated prospects and he was waiting with the overture of the Prague musicians only for the close of the vesper-sermon. At last he told him that Flamin and Matthieu were going a journey day after to-morrow, and were going back again to Kussewitz, and consequently would stay there longer than they had intended. This presence of the Englishman and the delayed return of the jealous one settled all at once in Victor his last will, to stretch the fourth Whitsuntide-day also as the fourth string on this tetrachord of joy. And as on this fourth day the riddle about the angel running through all the parts of this book is brought into the deciphering-office of time, because Julius delivers the letter of the said angel to Clotilda to read, he could make believe to himself he stayed merely for that reason, and say to himself: "For the novelty's sake surely one should tarry, to see what the state of the case is about the angel." — Good hero! thou confoundest every angel with thine, nor do I know why thou shouldst not! . . .

Now a shadow of a cloud flitted over them, a sort of forerunner of a darker one which was seeking their souls. For Victor, who before a fair heart could never shut up his own, who in the consecration of love scorned all dissimulation, related to Clotilda, with that heartiness which so easily marries itself to refinement, the reasons of Matthieu's journey, namely, his own little folly in Kussewitz, when he played into the Princess's hands the little billet-doux. He would at any rate have been obliged, too, to make this disclosure, by way of obviating the extraneous one of an accuser. But he presupposed too hastily on the part of Clotilda a calculation of the chronology of his little annual registers, and did not remark that he had written the billet before he knew that Clotilda was not Flamin's *sweetheart*, but only his *sister*.* She was silent for some time. He feared this pantomime of anger, and did not dare to convince himself of it by looking into her face. At length, on her favorite green spot, where in the greatest depth the vale's green shadow rocks its painted twigs in the sheen of sun and water, there she begged him with a voice neither cold nor proud, but almost a voice of emo-

* For not until he came back from Kussewitz did he learn on the island, from his father, Clotilda's relationship.

tion, to let her rest a little on her favorite grass-bench, whose arms were great flowers. As he stood before her, he saw with alarm in her animated face — not a resentment wrestling with courtesy, but — the touching struggle against the destiny which darkened for her the darling of her soul, the unselfish grief at the closed scar, which she wished away from his virtue. She felt, he felt, as if the former year lifted itself up again from its death-pillow of flowers of joy, which it had trampled on for both; they were right sad, — Clotilda had hardly the mastery of her eyes or Victor of his tongue, — till at last upon the latter the misunderstanding dawned. He therefore said softly to her and in English: "Had his father made all his disclosures to him earlier, he would have spared him more than one conflict, more than one dark hour, and first of all the foregoing folly."

In the higher love anger is only sorrow over the object. Clotilda continued, however, the solar-eclipse of her fair features; but it proceeded not from the continuance of the previous sigh, nor from the usual inability to carry over at once a reconciled soul into an angry face, but her discontent with her own hastiness always looked like that which has another's for its object. She rose up therefore to give him back her arm, and, as it were, the heart which lay near it. Victor did not allow himself to break the doubled-voiced silence. — Emanuel came after, and then Clotilda said with emotion, as if she were just answering what had been said before: "Ah, I am only too closely related to my brother on the side of my faults." — Did she mean Flamin's jealousy, or suspecting nature, or more probably his temperament? — Victor turned to her, as if to beg her pardon for what she had said, — and her eyes said, "O, I ought not to have misunderstood thee," — and his said, "I ought not, even though unknown, to have denied thee," — and their hearts made peace, and the olive-branch twining among the old flowers of joy bound their souls to each other.

Emanuel led them, as their guiding star, to his dear mountains, those front boxes of the earth, — only from his mountain with the weeping birch he kindly turned them aside for unknown reasons, — and his easy climbing gave them joy over the restoration of his breathing. At last they came out upon the throne of the region, on the mountain where Victor, on the morning after the night spent in travelling, had looked down upon Maienthal. O how the living plain of God, the foreground of a sun and of an Eden, stretched far away in such untamable, blooming, breathing, undulating masses! How did heaven hang full of mountains of incense, full of ice-fields of light! And a gentle morning-wind stole out from the eastern gate overhung with cloud-bloom and played with heaven and earth, with the yellow floweret and with the broad cloud above them, with the eyelash under a tear and with the cornfields it searched through! — How the eye dilates, when chased night-pieces of cloud-shadows cut through the bright sunshine of the earth! how the heart enlarges, when the morning-wind hurls the winged shadows now over mountains, now into ponds of splendor, now into bowed grain-fields! — But round upon the woods still ice-mountains of clouds had settled themselves. — Ah, this field flecked with day and night, this wall of nebulous glaciers, put Victor's heart into the old dream again, in which he saw Clotilda on an ice-mountain with outspread arms! — Ah, on this rocky peak rising above the southern mountain he could see the *Isle of Union*, lying darkly with its tree-tops and its white temple, and the thirsty heart staggered full of the mingled draught of yearning and melancholy and love. —

Then he was glad to tell her that he had seen her that morning when he gave the blind youth the note to Emanuel, and yet that he had denied himself a visit to her, — only give him, Clotilda, a great, warm, thankful look for his sparing of thy brother, for the nobleness of his loving, and for his hiding of that love with a veil! She looked on him, and when her eye grew warm with a tear, heaven bowed itself and came down to them on a sunny cloud and touched the kindred beings with hot, fluttering drops. — O thou good earth! thou good Nature! thou sympathizest oftener (and always) with good men, than good men do themselves! — Before him the dream passed in which Clotilda's tears resolved the ground into an uplifting cloudlet. . . . .

But the approach of evening and the little shattered pearl-strings of rain-drops rattling down called the fair group back to the cottage. The girls, who with the blind one had not even quite climbed the mountain, went no farther, but turned about and took the advance. Emanuel withdrew himself to his hill of mourning, in order there to uncover his flowers to the rain. When our loving couple reached the smoking vale below, how heavenly was the evening and the earth! — In the great evening-heaven above them waved tulip-beds of red clouds, between which ran blue strips like dark brooks. — Behind them stood under the sun mountains like Vesuviuses in flames, and the woodland like a burning bush, and the prairie-fire running over the flowers caught the cloud-shadows. — And all the larks hung with their ***ripieno*-voices of Nature near the red ceiling-piece of

* Complementary or completing, a musical term. — Tr.

evening, and every deeper sunbeam held a humming chain-of-being made of happy insects. — And in the sheep-fold on the mountain a hundred mothers at once called lovingly to a hundred children, and every sheep hastened bleating to its thirsty kneeling lamb. — —

Great evening! only in the Vale of Tempe thou still bloomest and dost not fade; but in a few minutes, reader, all its blossoms for the first time will open magnificently! —

Clotilda and Victor went along more closely and warmly, linked together under the small sun-shade, which walled *both* in from the transient shower. And with hearts which beat more and more strongly, and, instead of blood, sent round as it were devout tears of joy, they reached the park; the warm tones of the nightingale came to meet them, the tones wafted away from the musical retinue wherewith the Englishman was just passing across the mountains floated after them like perfumes exhaled from flowers. — — But lo! while the earth still wore its gilding in the fire of the sun, while the evening-fountain still blazed up like a torch, when in a great oak-tree of the garden, in which motley glass globes had been grafted instead of fruit, twenty red suns sparkled out of the leaves, — then a warmed cloud melted asunder and came all down in drops into the fire of evening and on the gleaming water-column. . . . .

The nuns who were nearer to the trees flew under the foliage; but Clotilda, who deemed a slow gait more beautiful and becoming for a female soul, went without haste to the neighboring "Evening-bower," which, raised above the garden, nowhere opens its thick leaf-work except to the setting sun. — No, it was an angel, it was Clotilda's sister, Giulia, who reposed on the tender cloud and let fall through it her tears of joy, in order to compel her friend, whose arm rested on her lover's as in a bandage, to the glimmering bower, where two blessed hearts were to be most blest. Clotilda still lingered under the rain of pearls and golden sand, and resembled the still doves around her, who on all the roofs flung open their pure wings like variegated umbrellas and held them under the bath, — and before entering Victor drew her back, who said, oppressed with bliss, "Thou all-gracious one!" and looked over to Emanuel's bower, on which the gate of Paradise built up of mosaic stones, the rainbow, abutted itself and arched across through heaven over the evening-bower and enclosed in its heavenly magic circle the three loving souls.

And when they stepped into the dark bower which had only a small opening toward the sun that blazed in through the rain, there lay before the opening the evening-field, with the swaying fiery columns, between which dashed the golden flood of the molten sun, and with the lawns which stood even to the flowers in a sea of luminous globules. — And fallen rainbows lay with their ruins on the blossoming trees. — And little airs fanned the running-fire in the meadow flowers and threw sparks out of the blossoms. — And the heart of man was swept onward by the stream of rapture and swam burning in its own tears.

Like a transfigured saint Clotilda looked into the sun, and her countenance was exalted at once by the sun and by her soul. And her friend disturbed not the fair soul; but he took the white handkerchief out of her hand and softly wiped away the colored particles dropping from the foliage, encircled with flower-dust, and she gave him voluntarily her hand. When she turned her eyes full of tears upon him, he let the tears stand; but she herself removed them, and looked upon him with a love over which soon the old ones glided, and said with a smile that flowed forth blissfully: "My whole heart is inexpressibly moved; pardon it, dearest friend, to-day everything in which it has hitherto not been like yours!" . . .

— Lo, then was the warm cloud emptied into the garden as if it were a whole river of Paradise and on the streams angels playfully floated down, . . . and when bliss could no more weep and love could no more stammer, and when the birds screamed for joy, and the nightingale warbled through the rain, and when the heavens, weeping for joy, fell with cloud-arms on the earth, aye, then two inspired souls met trembling and rushed breathless on each other with quivering lips and cheek pressed to cheek in glowing, trembling ecstasy, — then at last gushed forth, like life-blood out of the swollen heart, great tears of bliss out of the loving eyes over into the loved ones. — The heart measured the eternity of its heaven with great throbs heavy with bliss, — the whole visible universe, the sun itself had sunk away, and only two souls throbbed against each other alone in the emptied, glimmering immensity, dazzled with the glistening of tears and the splendor of sunshine, stunned with the roar of the heavens and the echo of Philomel, and sustained by God in dying of rapture.

Clotilda bent her head aside, to dry her eyes; and her mute darling sank down and knelt before her, and pressed his face upon her hand, and stammered: "O thou heart out of my heart, O thou for ever and ever beloved one, — ah, that I could bleed, could die for thee!" — Suddenly he rose, as if lifted by an immeasurable inspiration, and said in a lower tone, looking upon her: "Clotilda, I love thee, God, and virtue forever."

She pressed his hand and said softly: "Oh, how could man and fate wound such a heart? But mine, Victor, she said still more softly, "will never more do it wrong." —— They came out from the bower, — heaven, like their hearts had exhausted itself in tears of joy, and was merely serene, — the sun had gone down simultaneously with the great moment.. Victor went *slowly*, as if he were passing along before a wide Elysium, bearing in his heart the received Eden, home to Dahore's quiet dwelling. Dahore, who had sunk to sleep in a sitting posture, swayed softly to and fro, and Victor, although he would gladly have let his heart cease its beatings on a second, congenial bosom, nevertheless denied himself, — and slowly leaned against his swaying teacher. He held for a long time the slumbering head on his tumultuous breast. His tempest of joy cooled itself off into serene sky, and the refreshed flowers of joy opened the incense-cups of memory. Dahore flung his arms around his darling, and then, and not till then, woke up: for he had dreamed he was embracing him, and when he woke, he was delighted that it had not been merely a dream.

Enough! — And you, O ye human beings whom I love, take your rest on the lap of memory or of hope, when, as I do, ye lay down these little leaves!

## 35. DOG-POST-DAY.

### THIRD DAY OF WHITSUNTIDE,

OR

### BURGUNDY-CHAPTER.

THE ENGLISHMAN. — MEADOW-BALL. — BLISSFUL NIGHT. — THE BLOOMING CAVE.

ITH men, as with misers, it never strikes anything but quarters of the happy hour; like a bad clock, it never strikes full the Arcadian hour of our hope. But in respect to the Whitsuntide days this is utterly false, — they are magnificent, and as the outpouring of the Holy Spirit was formerly represented in the old churches by the flinging down of flowers, so do we shadow forth those of Maienthal by throwing out flowers of speech. I have therefore actually unsealed a flask of Burgundy, and set it beside my inkstand, in order, in the first place, by my greater fire in this chapter, to bring over the critics of art and nature to my side, who would rather break the staff over authors than a lance with authors, — and secondly and simply to drink the wine, which of itself is final object and teleology enough. A true Paradise and kingdom of heaven we should have, if the reader also would himself take something spirituous in such chapters. When

the author alone gets drunk, half the impression goes to the d——ogs; and it is a misfortune that the reviewers have nothing to nibble and nothing to drink, else they might minister to me as to a star by refracting me through their *atmosphere* and show me *higher* and *broader* than I stand.

Victor had hardly run out into the wet grass of the morning, when he came upon the Englishman with his head under the sprinkling-pots of the water-wheels. He gladly forgave this Cato the elder all his singularities and the idiosyncrasy of his extravagant nature and his comet-course; for he had himself in his eighteenth year been such a hairy star, and so looked upon this man as a comet-medal struck for himself. Although the Briton *affected* singularity, Victor knew from his own experience that it arose not from vanity, (one can, if one will, extract vanity from all, even the most innocent, actions, as well as *air* from all bodies,) but it proceeded from humor, for which the enjoyment of an eccentric part, whether we shall *read* or *play* it, has full as many charms as it has for the sense of freedom and of inward power. Vain men succumb to the ridiculous, which the whimsical man defies; and the former hate, the latter seek their likenesses. The only thing which Victor had against him was that he would not show others little indulgences, for the simple reason that he never desired any either; and this very war, inseparable from humor, with all the little weaknesses and expectations of men, had given the humane Victor a dislike to this eccentric path. Misfortune, therefore, more easily makes odd men than prosperity.

His delight at the pictures which Cato drew him of Flamin's similar heavenly ascensions and *feux de joie* inspired him with the thought of earning his Quatraine* of beautiful days in some other way than by his foregoing gloomy ones, — namely, by making those of others like his own. In short, he concerted with the elder Cato, — to whom the idea was most agreeable, — to employ the Prague company for some useful purpose, namely, in giving in the cool of the evening a ball on the green to the Maienthal children. What needed either for this purpose more than — which they immediately did — to thrust their hands into their pockets and their fingers into their purses and give the night watchman *loci* more than the hay of his great meadow might be worth on St. John's day, which would have to be mowed to-day for a ball-room? Besides, the man gave it with a thousand pleasures, because his son was to-day to be — married. The twenty May-poles which Cato proposed to plant in the hall stood already incarnate there as autochthones. And when they had, further, gone to the parents of the neat village, — generally, however, the poor ploughman resembles the swine, which, according to Ælian,† invented his ploughing for him, — and unitedly and with the greatest earnestness — for peasants and ladies do not understand singularities — begged and extorted from them the young dancing-partners: then all was right.

The trio of friends found, at the dinner-table of the Abbess, yesterday over again. Victor was immediately at home in all points; he would not continue a guest, so that the other might not continue the host. In general, maidens are seldom found again as one left them, just as their reception is always warmer or colder than their note

* Four points in Lotto, next to the highest. — Tr.

† The Roman who wrote much on husbandry and natural history in a gossiping style. — Tr.

previous; but in Clotilda's dissolving features an infinite charm announced the memory of yesterday, when she had, for two reasons, surrendered her heart to all his flames consecrated on the altar of nature and of virtue. In the first place, she was warmer yesterday, because she had previously been colder in the little quarrel which only her face had had about the Kussewitz watch affair: nothing makes love sweeter and tenderer than a little previous scolding and freezing, just as the grape-clusters acquire by a frost before vintage thinner skins and better must. Secondly, in a high degree of emotion and love the best girls behave just like — good ones.

I have only taken three coffee-cups of Burgundy, because I shall not perhaps need any more for the carnation and red crayon drawing of the afternoon — but O heavens! the night! — It is not my fault if it does not get to the ears of posterity, that most persons in the afternoon, on account of the heat, stayed out of the garden. But they see from the chambers the meadow, the timber-yard of a beautiful evening, where the children were already running round beforehand, carrying off the grass, and opening the feast of trumpets with horn-blowers on beer-siphons. It would be too trifling, if I should remark that several youngsters were stretched out dead by having red caps or crowns shot at them, because they represented hares, the cap-shooter the hunter, and the rest greyhounds; one can, however, take it metaphorically, and then it becomes satirical and edifying enough.

The joy of tender natures is bashful; they would sooner show their wounds than their raptures, because they do not think to deserve either, or they show both behind the veil of a tear. So was it with Victor, and in every joy he looked with a sigh to the west; I know not whether he thought of the setting of stars and of men, or of the blacks whose chains clank across even to our hemisphere, or on the nearer whites whose sundered chains they resolder with blood. — — But this looking towards his *Keblah* * constrained him to *earn* his rapture. That of yesterday and of to-day was so great, that he said with emotion to the genius of the earth: "Such greatness my feeble virtue cannot attain." — It availed him naught, that he sought to magnify himself to his conscience, and represented to it how many fair moments and happy pulsations he here in this *Valley of Seifersdorf* imparts to his friends and to her, his friend, who through him regains her health, and to the children whom he sees already skipping about and who at evening will do so still more, — it had some effect on his conscience, but still not enough, when he asked it whether, then, he should stop his ears to the sphere-music of these days; whether he had not conquered his passions, and whether the enlargement of a man's sphere and the increase of his activity were not simply in proportion to the greater number of passions he had mastered; so that, accordingly, a maid of honor, nay, even a king, possessed no smaller circle of efficiency than the most useful citizen; and whether man, like very small children, had not been sent into the school of earth to learn to be *still*, — but the sacramental religious war between the old and the new Adam was ended merely by a delight, namely, by the determination, so soon as his father should release him from the manacles and ankle-fetters of the court, to do more cures than the city and country physicians and all *gratis* and mostly among the poor. — —

* The spot in Mecca to which every good Mussulman turns in prayer. — Tr.

Only one word, reader! Virtue cannot make one *worthy* of felicity, but only *worthier*, because existence of itself with us as with the non-moral creatures gives a right to joy, — because Virtue and Joy are incommensurable qualities, and one knows not whether a happy century is earned by a virtuous decade or the latter by the former, — because the years of pleasure forerun the years of virtue, so that the virtuous man, instead of the future, would have first to deserve the past, — instead of heaven, would have first to deserve the earth.

The afternoon glided away like a bright rill, over motley trifles as over golden sand, over little joys and over great hopes, over delicate attentions and over the flower-dust of benevolent refinements which is the best sticking-powder of the heart. Victor felt that a mistress who has much intelligence imparts to love a peculiar piquant taste; she herself felt, that the heart which one has plucked with soft, covered hands, and not with rough clutchings, keeps better, just as Borsdorf apples keep longer which one has picked only with gloves on. Although, according to my tables, love stands the highest precisely on the day after the first kiss, that is at 112° Fahrenh. or 10° De l'Isle: with Victor's love, however, his reverence had risen at the same rate, — and love exalts, when the favors which are shown therein make one not bolder but shyer! —

Our friend felt how happy in joy *self-continence* makes one, and how much the foaming beaker of joy is cleared up and improved by throwing in a few knife-points of sedative-powder. After an afternoon when the whole hours were charming, without one's being able to single out into prominence any extraordinary minutes, — as the feathers of the pheasant shine not singly, but in whole bunches, — after such an afternoon all went into the garden, but Emanuel first. The East Indian, like ground-sparrows, could not endure the confinement of a room, and was silent therein or only read, and that too merely — which does not surprise me — the tragedies of Shakespeare. . . . .

Under the great evening-sky, which no cloud limited, their souls opened like night-violets. Emanuel was the cicerone and gallery-inspector of this picturesque garden. He led his friend and the others to his little flower-garden, which lay highest in the park. That is to say, the park ran down the mountain with *five* landings and stories slid out as it were from the latter in the manner of drawers. These five plains, these cut-in green steps, bore just so many different gardens, orchards, and shrubbery-gardens, &c., — hence with every new point of view, as by a kaleidoscope, a new garden was put together out of the old one. The sloping park was enclosed on both sides by two serpentine walks of tall, flaunting, flaming flowers, like two balustrades flowing downward, and behind each flowery serpentine line curled down from the mountain above silvery veins of bright, thin water leaping up and down,* which in the evening sun became a gold-snake or artery of ichor lying there in upright sinuosities. On the last and uppermost terrace stood the *evening-* and the *morning-arbors*, like the poles of the garden, opposite to each other, and the *evening-fountain* gleamed up over the former, and the *morning-fountain* over the latter, and the two looked across at each other like sun and moon.

* One took the silver thread rising and falling in arcs for one continuous rill trickling downward; but the arcs of several diagonally leaping fountains were set at such distances, that one became a coninuation of the other.

And just at the evening-fountain Emanuel had his middle-garden. For he loved, as an East Indian, physical flowers as he did poetic ones, and to him in December a book of flowers was a gently waving flowery lawn, and a catalogus of carnation leaves was to him the hull and chrysalid of summer. He conducted his loved ones over the flowery region of the mountain away through the innocent flowers, which, like good maidens, take neither sun nor soil from another's life for their own, — along by the gold tassel of the tulip, — by the miniature-colors of the forget-me-not, — by the many-colored bells, which are also, like those that *sound*, cast in the moulds of the earth, — by the ear-roses * of August, namely, the roses, — by the Cato, not the jolly Englishman, but an auricula that does not flame, (to be had of Herr Klefeker in Hamburg,) — by the beloved Agatha, which reminded one of the other in St. Luna, and which is a beautiful cowslip. . . . .

At last they arrived at the evening-bower and at Emanuel's flowers, namely, at the snow-white hyacinths, in whose shadow the irradiated evening-fountain tinged a pale red. O, how sweetly, how sweetly, there, breathed the warmth of the evening sun and the coolness of the evening wind ! — But why droop thy eye and head, Clotilda, so sadly here toward the flowers ? Is it because the water-column is extinguished, because the sun goes down ? — No ; but because the white hyacinths, in the language of the florists, mean *Julia*, — O because the churchyard looks over hither, whose tall, swaying wild-flowers stand with their roots over two beloved eyes, over the eyes of the pale hyacinth Giulia, who has not lived to see to-day's festival. —— But Clotilda concealed herself, so as to disturb nothing.

* A term for the ear-flaps. — Tr.

The last sparkling gold of the water-columns and the evening-blaze flung back from all the windows, turned all eyes toward the sun, who sank behind his stage.— But a rolling fire-wheel of the allegro, with which the harmonists on the meadow accompanied the retiring sun, brought down the eyes to the level of the ears, and below on the veiled meadow there rose a new theatre of joy with new players. . . . Two roses were planted in heaven, the red, the sun, which unfolded its buds over the second hemisphere, and the white, the moon, which hung low in ours; but sun-gold and lunar silver and evening-slags were as yet absorbed by a smoking magic-haze, and one could not separate the shadows from the silver ground of the moonlight, and blossoms fluttering downward were still confounded with night-butterflies.

The happy party went down through the chestnut avenue to the younger happy ones, the children, who, made more bold by the presence of their mothers, encircled and girdled twenty liberty-trees in changeable groups, and waited only for deeper shadows to dance more briskly. The Englishman was welcomed by Clotilda as a friend of her two friends. The bridal pair, to whom the meadow belonged as an inheritance, had exchanged their own music for this, and their feast of the covenant in its solemnity brought nearer to our hero the joyous day when he too should be able to call his Clotilda a bride; but he had not the courage to turn his blushing face towards her, because he thought she was thinking the same thing, and was red also. Only a lover can sympathize with the inspiration of a bridal pair; and never did fairer wishes go up for one than ascended for this one in two souls full of love. A four-years-old sister of the bride attached herself to Clotilda,— the former was the little Luna of this Venus in her walks,—and the latter gladly discharged her love into the little hand which gave hers the preference over a dancing partner.

And now the moon, by the reflection of the sun wherewith it silvered this children's paradise, gave joy brighter colors, and under the deepened shadows of the May-trees the children's courage grew. All was happy,—all unfettered,—all peaceful,—no poisonous eye flashed lightnings,—not a single roughness disturbed the metrical life,—in melodious march the minutes went sounding onward with silver tone, and sang themselves away, and lingered in the bursting rose-thicket of the evening red.—The bland, fluttering ether of Spring drank its fill of perfume from the blossoms, and bore it like honey into the breast of man.—And as pulses beat fuller, dumb, cooling lightnings played round the clouds of the horizon, and the moon drew vital air * from the leaves, in order to convey more healthily thereupon the abstracted spirit of their cups.

Victor and the Englishman and Emanuel and Clotilda, together with some of her female friends, stood below as patron gods of joy beside the children, and were intoxicated by the enjoyment of the young people's delight. Our friend had too holy a love to show (especially to so many strangers and to the Englishman), and laid a bridle on his unmanageable, dancing heart. In noble love the sacrifice—and though it were that love itself—is as agreeable as the enjoyment; but still easier is it near an Emanuel, who—that is the gleaming order-cross of the higher men—precisely in the hour of joy lifts his eyes to the higher life and to the truth.

* In the moonlight, plants secrete oxygen gas or vital air.

This time, moreover, the feeling of his improving health redoubled his pining after the predicted departure. His glorified countenance, his super-earthly wishes, and his still resignation, constituted, as it were, the second and higher moonlight which fell into the more dim; and he disturbed not in the least the growing elysium, when he said, for example: "Mortal man regards himself as eternal here, because the human race is eternal; but the propelled drop is confounded with the inexhaustible stream; and were it not that new human creatures always spring up after us, each one would feel more deeply the fleetingness of his second* of life"; — or when he said: "If man is not immortal, then no higher being is either, and the conclusions are the same; in that case the abiding God would burn solitary out of the struggling and expiring sense, like the sun which, if there were no atmosphere, would blaze out of a black heaven, and pierce, but not illuminate, the vaulted night"; — or when he said: "The gait of mankind toward the holy city of God is like the gait of certain pilgrims, who, wayfaring toward Jerusalem, always after three steps forward take one backward"; — or, finally, when, upon his Victor's remarking, that amendment only removed the great faults, not the fine stings of remorse, and that a saint got as many reproaches from his conscience as the bad man, when he said to this: "Our *distance* from virtue, like that from the sun, by exact reckonings we always find only *greater;* but still, notwithstanding all our changeable calculations, the sun always pours into our faces the *same* warmth."

Suddenly the Englishman ran to the players and demanded of them — in order to see the pranks and cranks

* *Third* in German, — the musical division of time, not however used in our common arithmetical tables. — Tr.

of his ideas set to music — the best adagio, and hastened up to the "Crape-Tent," which Lord Horion had had built of iron arches, over which was stretched black double crape, in order to convert, for his eyes, which were at that time ailing, the sunshine into moonshine. As every heart at the first touch of the adagio must needs dissolve in tears of bliss, the consequence was that the rapture which sought to veil itself broke up the tranquil circle, and all glided away from each other, in order (each under his own arbor) to smile unseen and sigh unheard, — like patients visiting a medicinal spring they parted, met, avoided each other in accidental directions.

The beautiful blind youth was reclining above not far from the nightingale, as it were at the fountain-head of the streams of harmony, and Clotilda looked upon him pityingly, as often as she passed by him, and thought: "Poor overshadowed soul, the sighs of music distend thy yearning heart, and thou never seest whom thou lovest and who loves thee." — Emanuel went up slowly the long way to his mountain with the weeping birch and back. — Victor roamed about the whole garden; he passed along before veiled obelisks, columns and cubes which better filled the place of stone Fauns; he stepped into the dark evening-bower shaded only by the evening-red, where he was yesterday too happy for a mortal, and too susceptible for an immortal; he pushed through a ring of bushes, out of which and above which towered a gleaming fountain, and closed his eyes to the dazzling light, when he saw therein in artificially embowered pier mirrors a water-bow saturated with lunar silver, arched over a million times in receding and paling curves, and reduced from white rainbows to moonsickles, and at last to shadows. — —

Oh, how often in the dreams of his childhood, in his landscape-pictures which he sketched to himself of the days of Paradise, had he not seen this night and hardly wished for it, because he never hoped to live to see it on the rough earth; and now did this Eden-night, with all blossoms and stars hanging round it, stand out created before him? — And who of us has not in some magically illumined spot or other of his fancy and his hope set up just so grand a night-piece of a future vernal night, when, as in this one, he is made happy *with all friends* at once (not always alone), — when, as in this one, the night is only thrown as a transparent veil over the day, when the red girdle which the sun laid down on stepping into the sea remains lying till morning glowing on the margin of the earth, — when the long, soul-like tones of the nightingale float aloud through the adagio that melts asunder, and start up out of the echo, — when we meet none but friendly souls, and look on them with rapture, and ask by our smiles, " O thou too art surely as happy as I? " and when the other's smile answers in the affirmative, — a night, O God, when thou hast made our hearts full and yet tranquil, when we neither *doubt* nor *hate* nor *fear*, when all thy children repose on thy bosom in thy arms, and hold each other's hands as brothers and sisters, and slumber only with half-closed eyes, in order to smile on each other? — — Ah, inasmuch as the sigh wherewith I write and you read this reminds us how seldom such spring nights fall upon our earth, take it not ill of me that I only slowly execute the voluptuous picture of *this* night that so I may some time in my old days refresh myself by the painted hour of the present inspiration,* and

* Remember the Author's " Recollections of Life's fairest Hours against the last." — Tr.

may haply be able to say: Ah, thou knewest then, perhaps, that thou shouldst never live to experience such a night, and for that reason wast thou so copious. And what else than petrified blossoms of a clime which is not on our earth, do we dig up out of our fantasy, just as in our North they exhume fossil palms? . . .

Victor went to the still Julius at the hedge of the nightingale and laid night violets in his hand, and kissed him on the curtained eye, which could not see, yet could weep for joy, — and neighbor nightingale paused not during the kiss. He came up the garden, as Emanuel came down; they looked on each other near the morning fountain, and Emanuel's face gleamed in the reflection of the waves, as if he were standing before the angel of death and dissolving, to die, and he said: "The Infinite One clasps us to-day to himself, — why can I not weep as I am so happy?" — and when they had separated again, he called back to his Victor and said: "See, how blooming-red the evening goes forth toward the morning like a dying man, as if the tones moved it onward, — see, the stars, like blossoms, hang down out of eternity into our earth, — behold the great deep, how many springs bloom to-night on so many thousand earths wheeling therein!" —

The maidens, after short walks, had soon seated themselves on the grassy banks of the terraces in pairs or in the number of the Graces. Clotilda, who had strolled alone, at last did the same, and seated herself beside a solitary friend on the fourth terrace, near the gay solar rainbow of flowers, behind which the lunar rainbow of water glistened. This friend appealed to Victor, approaching, as umpire of a virtuous quarrel: "We have been disputing," said the friend, "which is sweeter to good souls, to forgive or to be forgiven. I absolutely assert, forgiving is the sweeter." — "And to me it appears," said Clotilda with a touched voice, which betrayed all the affectionate thoughts of her indulgent heart, all her grateful remembrances of their last variance and of his beautiful forgiveness, "that it is more beautiful to receive forgiveness, because love toward the forgiving soul is made by its own lowliness *purer*, and by the other's goodness *greater*." Never, perhaps, was anything lovelier said to our Victor. His emotion and his gratitude made the decision hard for him; but Clotilda prompted or corrected his dreams by this turn: "I have reminded my good Charlotte already of *day before yesterday*, but she sticks to her opinion." She meant the day of confession and communion, when the fair hearts all asked and received forgiveness of each other. Victor finally answered at once truly, significantly, and delicately: "You both, I think, suppose impossible cases; no human being is either all right or all wrong; and whoever forgives is at the same time forgiven, and the reverse; — thus two beings who are reconciled always share the joy of forgiveness and the joy of *purified and increased* love with each other." —

Victor went off, in order to conceal an emotion through which he too much heightened another's. But on his far and near ways among tones and blossoms, feelings clung to him which doubled and glorified his love; he felt that the *strongest* expression of love takes not so firm and deep a hold of the soul as the *finest*. But as he passed along by the sun-dial, which with its measuring-rod of shadow counted out for us other shadows our narrow fortunate islands, and as the moon weighed out on the scale with her shadowy beam in equipoise the last minutes of this glad hour, because she pointed toward midnight, as if she wrote, It will presently be over, — just then the Englishman passed out alone slowly and with downcast eyes from the crape-tent, and went in among the tones, to lead them away with the whole heaven around them. Victor, who in the still sea of the deepest joy no longer steered for countries, but contentedly tossed or rested upon it, and desired nothing in the future but the present, only paced now to and fro on the long terraces, instead of ascending and descending the garden, — he stood just on the uppermost, on the flower-terrace, at the morning-fountain, and looked along the glimmering way over to the evening-fountain, and the fallen snow of the moon lay deeper and whiter down along the blissful slope, and this blooming sugar-field appeared to his dreaming heart like a point of land with which the island of the blest stretched over into this earth, and he saw on all this enchanted field nothing but blessed ones walking, reposing, dancing, here alone, there in pairs, yonder in groups, and innocent men, quiet children, gentle, virtuous maidens, and he looked up to the starry heaven and his tearful eye said to the All-gracious, O give my good father and my good Flamin also such a sight! — — when all on a sudden he perceived that the tones were wafted away, and saw the Briton moving on with the children, and the swan-song of a Maëstoso was borne along before the fleeing youth. . . .

Victor went up with the tones that swam away, and the stars seemed to swim with them, and the whole region to go with them; — all at once he stopped at the end of the terrace of flowers, before the emblems of Giulia, the white hyacinths, before the friend of Giulia, before — Clotilda . . . . O moment! repeated only in eternity, wear not too strong a lustre, that I may be able to endure it! move not my heart too intensely, so that I may be able to describe thee! — Ah, move it only as thou dost the two hearts to which thou appearedst; thou wilt meet none of us any more . . . And Clotilda and Victor stood innocent before God, and God said, Weep and love as in the second world with me! — And they looked on each other speechless in the transfiguration of night, in the transfiguration of love, in the transfiguration of emotion, and tears of bliss closed their eyes, and behind the illuminated tears transfigured worlds rose around them out of the dark earth, and the evening-fountain spread itself gleaming like a milky-way above them, and the starry heaven closed sparkling over them, and the receding and dying sounds washed their uplifted souls away from the shore of earth. . . . . Lo! then a little breath of air brought the escaping sounds more warmly and closely to their hearts, and they wiped the tears from their eyes; and as they looked round in the actual scene, the melodious waving agitated all the blossoms in the garden, and the great night, which with giant limbs slept in the moonshine on the earth, stirred for rapture its wreaths of shadowed tree-tops, and the two beings smiled trembling in unison, and simultaneously cast down their eyes and simultaneously raised them without knowing it. And Victor at last was able to say: "O may the noblest heart that I know be as unspeakably blessed as I, and still more blessed! I have not deserved so much!" — And Clotilda said in a soft tone: "I have remained the whole evening mostly alone, merely for the sake of weeping for joy, but it is too beautiful for me and for the future. . . ." — Her companions turning round came up the garden, and the two had to part; and when Victor added with stifled sounds, "Rest well, thou noble soul, — may such tears of joy have always to stand in thy eyes, may such melodious tones be destined always to float around thy days! — Rest well, thou heavenly soul!" — and when a look full of new love and an eye full of fresh tears thanked him; and when he bowed himself low, low before the saintly, still, modest one, and from reverence did not so much as kiss her hand; — then in the invisibleness did her genius embrace his genius for delight, that their two children were so happy and so virtuous..

O what comfort did his overwhelmed soul now find in his beloved Dahore, whom he followed under the loud chestnut-trees, and on whose neck he could fall with all his tears of ecstasy, with all his caresses of a raptured heart: "My Emanuel, rest softly! I stay to-night under this good, warm sky round about us." — "Aye, stay, good heart," said Emanuel, "such a night will never pass through any spring again. . . . . Hear'st thou," he continued, as the tones receding into immensity, like evening stars, as it were, of the sunken glory, like autumnal voices of the departing summer-song, sent their call into the yearning soul, "hear'st thou the sweet dying away of the strains? Lo, even thus may my soul die away on the longest day, even so may thy heart lie on mine and say as now, Rest well!" . . .

Sinking from the arms of his last remaining loved friend, Victor went reeling back in the confused twilight of inspired sadness through the avenue pierced by moonlight, as it were dropping with rays, in order to recline, in the blossom-cave, where he had here first found Clotilda, his dreaming head on a pillow of blossom-cups. . . . And as he slowly and alone and with Elysian remembrances and hopes staggered along through the arbor which had grown into the avenue, between the lulling rivulets, low waves of the departed melody still swam more into his fancy than into his ears, and only the nightingale reigned aloud over the inspired night. Then, unspeakably blest and burdened with ecstasy, the last man of this night glided from the five steps of his heavenly bed through the lattice of twigs into the dark thicket of blossoms. — — Bedewed leaves fell, cooling, on his fevered brow, he laid his two outstretched arms on two supports of dwarf-trees, and closed in rapture his burning eyelids, and the continuing tones of the nightingale and of the five fountains around him wafted him some spaces onward into the glimmering illusion of dreams, — but the nightingale, screaming out in the jubilee of joy, warbled through his dream, and when he opened his eyes, drifted away into half-dreams, the glimpses of the moon shot through the white shrubbery, — — nevertheless, satisfied with the previous scenes, he only smiled half beside himself, and closed his eyes again and sank completely into the harmonious slumber . . . only a few broken tones he still sang to himself, — only a few times more he stirred his prostrate arms for embraces . . . . and in the euthanasia of slumber and rapture only obscurely stammered once more, Beloved ! . . .

And so sweetly, great All-gracious One, let the rest of us mortals sink to sleep in the last night as Victor does in *this*, and let our last word also be, Beloved ! —

## 36. DOG-POST-DAY.

### FOURTH AND LAST DAY OF WHITSUNTIDE.

HYACINTH. — THE VOICE OF EMANUEL'S FATHER. — LETTER FROM THE ANGEL. — FLUTE ON THE GRAVE. — SECOND NIGHTINGALE. — FAREWELL. — PISTOLS. — GHOSTLY APPARITION.

HE appendix to the fourth day of joy has just come in. — Pausing only to breathe the sigh wherewith one usually says, on the day after festal days, that he is burying them, I come back again before the blooming bed of my friend, and open the living-green curtain; not till toward nine o'clock did a ground-sparrow twittering close to his hands draw him with difficulty out of a deep sea of dream. But the shadowy shapes, which the concave mirror of dream had erected in the air, were all forgotten; only the tears, which they had wrung from them, still stood in his eyes, and he could no longer remember why he had shed them. To-day was Ember-day, which, like other changes of moon and weather, makes the echo of our dreams louder and more polysyllabic. — In a singular lassitude he opened his eyes before the white twilight of the canopy of apple-blossoms, before the maze of the green web, — his hand chased the ground-sparrow through the bushes, — it was sultry around this shade, the tree-tops were mute and

all the flowers erect,—bees bent down from grains of sand into the springs around him and sipped water,—white flocks dropped from the willows, and all the smelling-bottles of the blossoms and the censers of the flowers diffused over his place of slumber a sweet, sultry steam. . . . .

He raises his right hand to his moist eye and sees therein, to his astonishment, a white hyacinth, which some one must have placed there. . . . He suspected Clotilda; and she it had really been. Half an hour before she had stepped up to this bed of flowers,—had gently let the bushes immediately close again,—but then, however, drawn them apart again, because she saw the tears of the forgotten dream run down the face of the glowing sleeper,—her whole soul became now a tender look and blessing of love, and she could not refrain from laying the memorial of her morning-visit, the flower, on his hand,—and then hastened softly back to her chamber.

He stepped hastily into the beaming day, to overtake the giver, whose morning-offering he unhappily, for fear of destroying it, could no more press to his heart than he could herself. O how it saddened him, when he stood in the open air before the Moravian churchyard of the heavenly night which had *gone home*, before the reposing garden, and when he looked upon the bald, close-shaven, trodden-down dancing-floor, and on the silent nightingale's-bush, and on the hills where the children were tending sheep, disrobed of yesterday's finery! Then the forgotten dream again appeared and said: Weep once more, for the rose-feast of thy life concludes to-day, and the last of the *four* rivers of Paradise in a few hours will utterly dry up!—"O ye fair days," said Victor, "ye deserve that I should leave you with a tenderness that knows no measure and with unnumbered tears!" — He fled from the too harsh daylight into the cell of crape, that it might recolor the brilliant foreground of the day into a dim back-ground, overspread with the moonshine of yesterday; and under this pall of the pale dead night he proposed to himself to indulge his heart, so soon to be impoverished, with its last joy, namely, its yearning, in utter overmeasure. He stepped out of the tent, but the nocturnal moonshine faded not from the lawn; he looked up into the blue heaven, which touches us with *one* long flame, but the veiled stars of the wintry night sent little outwelling rays to the eclipsed soul; he said to himself, indeed, "The ice-mountain on which hitherto my reason has delivered half sermons-on-the-mount, has shrunk up under the glow of joy to a mole-hill," but he added, "To-day I care for nothing."

He came to Emanuel with wet eyes. The latter told him that the first link of yesterday's chain of flowers, namely the Briton with his people, had already loosed itself in the night. But the longer he looked on Emanuel and thought of the morrow, — for to-morrow before day he too would softly close the garden gate of this Paradise behind, and this afternoon he is to take leave of the Abbess and this evening of his beloved, in order not to hinder her in the reading out of the well-known angel's-epistle, — so much the more painful was the straining of his eyes, and he preferred to go out, with a heart bleeding itself full, into the open air, and led the blind one with him, who suspected nothing, saw nothing, and before whom, besides, one loved to lay bare his innermost heart as before a child.

But this time Julius was in the same softened state, because he had all the morning seen the angel playing and hovering in his darkling soul. The yearning for the angel brooded over his reposing heart and warmed it even to beating, and he said with an unaccustomed sorrow, "If I could only see, only something, only my father, or thee!" The dust-covered remembrances of his childhood were shaken up; and out of this cloud-enveloped period emerged before him into special prominence one day, bright with morning, blue and full of song, and bore three forms on its cloud-floor, Julius's own and those of the two children, from whom before their embarkation for Germany he had parted, — drops escaped from him without his perceiving it, when he described to this Victor, the very one who had done what he described, how he had been kissed and hugged and cried after by the one child, that loved him most, and always carried him. "And I think," he continued, "that every one whose voice I love to hear has the face of that good child, and that *thou* hast too. Often when I contemplate this form alone in my darkness, and feel warm drops on my lips, and fall into a languishing, slumbering rapture, I fancy it is blood trickles from my lips and my heart is boiling, — but my father says if then my eyes were suddenly opened, and I should look upon my angel, or the good child, or a beautiful human being, I should have to die for love." — — "O Julius, Julius," cried his Victor, "how noble is thy heart! The good child whom thou lovest so my father will soon lay in thy arms, and he will kiss thee and love thee and clasp thee just as I do now." —

He led him back to dinner; but he himself remained till afternoon under the open heaven, and his heart put on silent mourning under trees full of bees, near thickets full of feeding birds, on all the former walks and ecliptics of this dying festival, — and all the hours of childhood rose out of the winter-sleep of memory and stirred his heart, but it dissolved.—O when far distant moments sound on our ears with their chime, then great drops fall from the softened soul, as the increasing nearness of far-off bells sounding across betokens rain. I blame thee not, Victor,—thou art, after all, only *feminine*, but not *effeminate*,—if thy biographer can describe thy emotion and thy reader can feel it, without relaxing the firm muscles of the heart, thou canst do it quite as well, and only a man who can wring bitter tears from others will scorn sweet ones and shed none himself.

At length Victor went to take his last pleasure, to the garden of termination, in order to take leave with tender tears of all his female friends at the Abbey. A singular incident delayed it a little: for as he left Emanuel, he encountered Julius coming from the garden, who told him, "if he wanted to find Emanuel, he was in the garden."—This raised a friendly dispute, because each of them insisted on having just talked with him. Victor went back with him to Emanuel, and Julius related to his teacher every word of the alleged garden-talk with him: "e. g. about Victor, about Clotilda, about the farewell he was to-day taking, about his previous happy days."

During the narration Emanuel's face grew radiant, as if moonlight flowed down from it,—and instead of representing to the beloved child the impossibility of his appearance in the garden, he humored his notion of the apparition, and said with delight: "I shall die, then!—It was my departed father,—his voice sounds like mine,—he promised me when he died to come back from the next world to this before I should go hence.—Ah, ye beloved ones beyond the graves over yonder, ye still then think of me. — O thou good father! break through even now into my presence with thy fatal radiance, and release my spirit in thy lips!" —

He was still more confirmed in his conclusion, because Julius added that the shape had demanded of him the angel's letter, but given it back again after a short whisper. The seal was uninjured. Emanuel's joyful enthusiasm at these telegraphs of death implied that he had drawn dissatisfying inferences from his previous health. Victor never set himself in opposition to the exalted errors of his teacher; thus, e. g., he never arrayed the reasons he had, and which I will show in the next Intercalary day, against the innocent delusion, that "from dreams, and from the independence of the personal consciousness on the body, one could infer its future independence after death," — that "in dream the inner diamond dusted itself and drank in light from a fairer sun." — Victor was alarmed about the matter, — but for other reasons, Julius took them both along with him to the place of the interview, which was in the darkened avenue near the blossoming hollow. No one was there, nothing appeared; leaves whispered, but no spirits; it was the place of bliss, but of earthly bliss. —

Victor went into the other place of bliss, the Abbey. Clotilda was not over there, but in the intricate labyrinth of the Park, probably for the purpose of facilitating for its possessor, Julius, the opportunity of hearing read the angel's letter. Just as the sun blazed over against the window-panes, he took leave of the good Abbess with that refined, feeling courtesy to which in her position the highest enthusiasm was limited. The refined Abbess said to him: "The visit was so short, that it would be inexcusable, if Victor did not make it good by persuading her second spring guest (Clotilda) to lengthen hers; for she too was going soon to leave them." — He took his leave of her with a heart-felt respect: for his tender heart knew, quite as well behind the lace mask of refinement and knowledge of the world as behind the leather-crust of roughness, how to feel the tender heart of another.

But as he hastened to the garden, the tears of his heart gushed up higher and warmer, — and he felt as if he must here in the face of the sun embrace the rising moon, as he thought: "Ah, when thy pale fleece hangs this evening brighter overhead there, when thou lookest down alone, I shall have departed or be in the act of departing from my pastoral world." — And below near the nightingale's hedge reposed his Julius, shedding bright streams of tears, — for this whole evening swarmed with greater and greater wonders * of chance, — he hastens down to him, the letter of the so-called angel is opened in his hand, Victor says softly, "Julius, why weepest thou so?" — "O God," said the latter in broken tones, "guide me under a bower!" — He conducted him to the crape one. Julius said, when they were under cover: "Good! here the sun does not burn!" and flung his right arm around Victor, and gave him the letter, and folded his arm round even to his heart and said: "Thou good soul! tell me when the sun is down, and read me once more the letter of the angel!"

Victor began: "Clotilda!" — "To whom is it?" said he. — "To me!" said Julius, "and Clotilda has already read it to me; but I could not understand her on account of her weeping, and besides I also was too much distressed. — I shall die for sorrow, thou good Giulia, why

* "*Sea*-wonders" is the German expression. — Tr.

didst thou not tell me of it before thy death. — The dead one wrote it, read on!" — He read:

"Clotilda!

"I cover my blushing cheeks with the funeral veil. My secret lies hidden in my heart, and will be laid with it under the grave-stone. But after a year it will force its way out of the mouldered heart. O, then let it rest forever in thine, Clotilda! — and forever in thine, Julius! — Julius, was not a silent form often about thee that called itself thy angel? Did it not once, as the death-bell tolled for the burial of a blooming maiden, lay a white hyacinth in thy hand, and say, Angels pluck such *white* flowers? Did not a mute form once take thy hand and wipe away its tears therewith, and it could not tell why it wept? Did not a low voice once say, Farewell, I shall no more appear to thee, I go back to heaven? That form was I, O Julius; for I have loved thee and even unto death. Lo! here I stand on the shore of the second world, but I look not over into its infinite fields, but I turn my face, while I am still sinking, back to thee, to thee, and my eye grows dim over thy image. — Now I have told thee all. — Now come, quieting death, crush slowly the white hyacinth, and rend the heart asunder speedily, that Julius may see the love enclosed therein. — Ah, wilt thou then take a dead one into thy soul? Wilt thou weep, when thou hearest this read? Ah, when my covered, sunken dust can no more touch thee, will my remote spirit be loved by thine? — But I conjure thee, O ever-remembered one, go, on the day when this tearful leaf is read to thee, then go, at sundown, up to my grave and offer to the pale face below, which the old mound is already crushing asunder, and to the dissolved heart that can beat for nothing more, then present to the poor heart that has loved thee so much, and on thy account has hid itself under the earth, thy funeral offering, — bring to it on thy flute the tones of my loved song, 'The grave is deep and silent.' — Sing it softly to the accompaniment, Clotilda, and thou too visit me. — Ah, poor Giulia, lift up thy soul, and sink not now, as thou imaginest thy Julius on thy grave! — When thou bringest thy offering to the dead, my spirit will, it is true, already have gone up higher; I shall have lived a year beyond the earth, I shall already have forgotten the earth, — but nevertheless, but, O God, if Thou shouldst let the tones above my grave penetrate into Elysium, then should I sink down and shed hot tears and stretch out my arms and cry: Yes! here in eternity I love him still, — may it fare well with him on the earth, may his soft heart repose softly and long on life below there! — No, not long! Come up hither, mortal, to the Immortals, that thine eye may be healed, and see the friend who died for thee!

"GIULIA."

* * * * *

"I will go," — said Julius hesitatingly, but with quiverings in his face, — "although the sun is not down. My father shall console me till sundown, that my heart may not beat so violently against my breast, when I stand at the grave and make the offering to the dead." — — Let me say nothing, reader, of the choking heart with which I proceed, — nor of this too sensitive Giulia, who like a morning sun-dial was ere noon in shade and coolness, who, like a dove, unfolded her wings to the rain and to tears, — nor of her soul's-sisters, who in the second decade of life hang the skeleton of death all over with flowers, that they may not be able to see its limbs, and who rest their white arm merely on a myrtle-twig of love as upon a bleeding-support, and watch calmly the bleeding to death of its severed veins!—

I could not have said even this, if Victor had not thought it, whose heart was mortally distraught by an infinite grief and an infinite love; for ah! how far on the way was not his irreplaceable Clotilda already, to follow her friend and hide her unloved heart in the earth, as they lay down carnations in the frost?

The sun sank lower, the moon mounted higher,—Victor saw Clotilda, like an ethereally embodied angel, reclining in a niche that opened towards the west,—the little girl mentioned yesterday played, in her lap, with a new doll,—it seemed to him as if he saw her soaring toward heaven, and when she lifted her great eyelids, weighed down with tears for the departed friend, whose secret she had long since guessed and concealed, towards him, who to-day increased them by his departure; and when she saw his face also melted in emotion; then did like sorrowful thoughts drown in both even the first sounds of welcome, and both turned away their faces, because they wept for the parting.——"Have you," said Clotilda, at least with a composed voice, "just spoken with Julius?"—Victor did not answer, but his eyes said yes, in the simple fact that they streamed more passionately and looked on her fixedly. She cast hers down with a slight blush for Giulia. The little child took the falling of the eyelids over the great drops for a sign of sleepiness, and drew the little hay-stuffed pillow away from the doll, spread it out for Clotilda, and said innocently, "There, lie down on it and go to sleep!" A shudder thrilled through her friend, as she answered, "Not to-day, dear; on pillows of hay only the dead sleep." He shuddered, as he saw a snow-white pink, in the centre of which there was a great dark-red point, like a bloody drop, trembling on her agitated bosom. The fearful pink seemed to him to be the lily which superstition formerly found in the choir-seat of the priest, whose death was said thereby to be predicted.

She fixed her gaze painfully on the low sun and the churchyard, behind which in the May days it sank like a mortal. "Leave this prospect, dearest," he said, though without a hope of obedience, — "a tender integument is most easily destroyed by a tender soul, — your tears make you too sad." But she replied: "Only in earlier years — but long ago it ceased to be so — did they make my eye-sockets burn and benumb my brain." — Suddenly, as the thought of the beclouded perspective of her eyes exhausted with weeping wrung his heart out of his bosom, the sunlight died upon her cheeks, — streams of tears broke violently from her eyes, — he turned round, — over on the churchyard the veiled youth had prostrated himself on the grave-mound of the veiled one beneath, — the sun was already below the earth, but the flute had as yet no voice, sorrow has only sighs, — no tones. . . . . At last the beautiful blind one raised himself erect, amidst convulsive sorrows, for the funeral-offering, and the wailings of the flute went up from the closed grave into the evening-redness, — three hearts melted away like the tones, like the fourth heart that was buried below. But Clotilda lifted herself up by force out of her dumb woe, and sang low as an offering to the dead the heavenly song, for which the departed one had entreated her and which I give with inexpressible emotion: —

The grave is deep and dismal, —
  How solemn there to stand!
Below, in gloom abysmal,
  There lies an unknown land.

There sounds, when daylight closes,
  No nightingale's sweet tone ;
And Friendship strews with roses
  The mossy mound alone.

In vain the bride, forsaken,
  May wring her hands and weep :
Nor orphans' wail may waken
  The dead one from his sleep.

*Yet* nowhere else can mortals
  Attain the wished repose,
And through these gloomy portals,
  Alone, man homeward goes.

O Salis! in that *yet* are all our expired sighs, all our dried-up tears, and they lift the aspiring heart from its roots and veins, and it fain would die!

The voice of the noble singer gave way to sadness, but still she sang the last of the strophes of this song of the spheres, though lower under the weight of overmastering sorrow: —

The weary heart, storm-driven,
  There, where all tempests cease,
Finds home at length and heaven,
  And everlasting peace.*

Her voice broke, as an eye breaks into tears or a heart in death. . . . . Her friend veiled his head with the leaves of the bower, — the whole of earthly life passed before him like a dirge. — Clotilda's sad past, Clotilda's dark future, drew together before his vision, and cast, in the darkness, the funeral veil over this angel, and bore her

* The translator feels how much he has sacrificed of the simplicity of the language in this song, in endeavoring to keep the rhyme and the silvery rhythm.

shrouded into the grave of her sister. . . . He had even forgotten his farewell. . . . He had not the heart to look upon the great scene around him and the bowed form beside him. . . . .

He heard the little one go and say, " I will fetch thee a larger pillow to put under thy head."

Clotilda stood up and clasped his hand, — he turned round again toward the earth, — and she looked on him with eyes worn with weeping, yet tender, whose drops were too pure for this unclean world, but in those large eyes stood something like the terrible question, " Do we not love each other in vain for this world ? " And her beating heart shook the bloody pink. The moon and the evening star gleamed solitary, like a past, in heaven. — Julius lay mute and prostrate, with outspread arms, on the low mound which had been rolled upon the dust of his shattered paradise.

The tones of the nightingale throbbed now like high waves on the night, — then he gathered up his courage to bid her farewell. . . .

Reader! raise not thy spirit to any pitch of rapture, for it will soon stiffen in a spasm, — but I raise my soul thereto, because even the fatal stumble at the gate of paradise is not unlovely when one is going out of it!

The first call of the confiding nightingale was suddenly answered still higher by a new nightingale that had fluttered along and whose voice was muffled by thick blossoms, who kept flying as she sang, and now made her languishing melody flow out of the blossoming hollow. The two lovers, who delayed and dreaded parting, wandered confusedly after the receding nightingale, and were on the way to the blessed blooming hollow; they knew not that they were alone; for in their hearts was God;

before their sight shone the whole second world full of risen souls. At last Clotilda recovered herself, turned round before the nightingale, and gave the mournful sign of separation. — Victor stood on the shore of his late blissful island, — all, all was now over, — he lingered, took both her hands, could not yet look upon her for anguish, bowed down with tears, raised himself up again, when he was able to say softly: "Farewell, — my heavy heart can say no more, — fare thee right well, far better than I, — weep not so often as thou usedst to do, that thou mayest not perchance have to leave me utterly. — For then I too should go." — Louder and more solemnly he continued: "For we can no more be separated, — here under Eternity I deliver to thee my heart, — and when it forgets thee, then may a sorrow crush it which shall reach over the two worlds." . . . . In a lower and tenderer tone, "Weep not to-morrow, angel, — and Providence give thee rest." Like a transfigured one to a transfigured he inclined himself modestly to her holy lip, and in a gentle, devout kiss, in which the hovering souls only glide tremulously from afar to meet each other with fluttering wings, with a light touch he took from the yielding, dissolving lips the seal of her pure love, the repetition of his late Eden, and her heart and his all — — —

— But here let the gentler soul, which the thunderbolts of fate too sorely agitate, turn its eye away from the great yellow flash which suddenly darts through the still Eden!

* * * * *

"Scoundrel!" cried Flamin, rushing out with sparkling looks, with snow-white cheeks, with locks hanging down like a mane, with two pocket-pistols in his hands, — "there take, take; blood I want," and thrust the deadly weapon towards him; Victor forced Clotilda aside, saying, "Innocent one! do not aggravate thy sorrows!" — Flamin cried in a new kindling of fury, "Blood! — Faithless one, take, fire!" — Matthieu fell upon his right arm, but the left, trembling, forced the weapon upon Victor. — Victor snatched it towards him, because the muzzle was swaying about Clotilda. — "Thou art in truth my brother," cried the tortured girl, whose deathly agony alone kept her by its rack from the death of a swoon. — Flamin with both arms flung all from him and said with a horribly low and long-drawn voice in his raving exhaustion, "Blood! — Death!" — Clotilda sank to the ground. Victor looked at her and said, turning to him, "Only fire, here is my life!" — Flamin cried aloud, "Thou first!" — Victor shot, lifting his arm high up, so as to shoot into the air, and the splintered top of a branch was brought down by his ball. — Clotilda came to. — Emanuel flew to the spot, — threw himself on his pupil's heart, — from his breast for the first time in years rent with passion the sickly blood gushed out. Flamin proudly hurled away his pistol and said to Matthieu, "Come! it is n't worth the trouble," and went off with him.

When Clotilda saw Emanuel's blood on her lover's clothes, she supposed him to have been hit, and laid her handkerchief on the blood and said, "Ah, you have not deserved this of me!" — Emanuel breathed again through his blood, no one could speak any more, no one could think, every one feared to give consolation, the mortally crushed hearts parted with suppressed woe; only Victor, whom the horrible word "scoundrel" at every recollection of it pierced through like a dagger, said to the sister: "I love him no more, but he is unhappier than we; ah! he has lost all and kept nothing but a devil."

Namely, Matthieu. It was he who had to-day imitated the voice of Emanuel, which had seemed to speak with Julius, and whose voice Dahore had taken for his father's, and afterward the voice of the nightingale, which Victor had followed, in order to convince the Regency Counsellor through his own ears and eyes of Victor's love for Clotilda.

Victor led his weak teacher to the Indian cottage. He felt his nerves now after so many relaxing days cooled and steeled by this tempest; his anguish of soul and sacrifice had made his blood, as the confinement of narrowing channels does streams, more swift and impetuous, and his love for Clotilda had been made manlier and bolder by the thought that he now entirely deserved it. There is nothing more beautiful than magnanimity and gentleness, except the union of the two.

Emanuel was nothing more than faint, and, as the evening brooded with a sweltering influence over all, he seated himself with Victor on the grassy bench of his house in order to keep his palpitating breast in an erect posture, and a tender joy gleamed in his features at every fallen drop of blood, because each was a red seal upon his hope of dying. But when Victor took the good man's weary head to his bosom and let him go to sleep thereon, then in the still evening sadness came over him again, and for the first time his heart pained him. He thought to himself all alone there, how over at the Abbey hot swords would pass hissing through the innocent bleeding soul, — he felt how now the two-syllabled, two-edged word of Flamin's wrath had cut through the whole bond of their friendship, — he represented to himself the blooming theatre of beautiful days beside him deserted and desolate, and the sweeping by of joys, which only play round us like butterflies in wide circles, while the hair-worm* of grief bites deeply into our nerves. At last he leaned weeping on the slumbering father, and pressed him softly, and said, "Ah! without friendship and love I could not bear the earth." — And at length his distracted and exhausted soul also was weighed and dragged down by the heavy body into the thick atmosphere of sleep.

* * * * *

Reader! the last moment in Maienthal is the greatest, — raise thy soul through awe and mount up on graves as on high mountains, in order to look over into the other world!

At midnight when fancy draws the buried dead from their coffins and sets them upright in the night round about her, and unknown shapes drift to us from the second world, — just as indistinguishable corpses driven from America to the coasts of the Old World announced to it the New, — in the ghostly hour Victor opened his eyes, but with inexpressible serenity. A forgotten dream had sunk far away to-day's past with all its din and cloud; — the bright moon stood overhead in the blue dark like the silvery fissure and sparkling fountain-like mouth, from which the stream of light out of the other world breaks into ours and comes down in ethereal vapor. — "How still and radiant is all!" said Victor. "Is not this glimmering region a relic of my dream? is not this the magic suburbs of the supernal city of God?" — A voice hurrying over said, Death! I am already buried.

Emanuel opened his eyes at that, sent them through the foliage over to the churchyard that overlooked the village and said, with a convulsion of his being, "Horion, wake up; Giulia has left eternity and is standing on her grave."

* "*Nerve*-worm," literally. — Tr.

— Victor cast a feverish glance up thither; and all the warm thoughts and nerves of life grew hard and stiff in a cutting ice-cold shudder, as he saw up there a white, veiled form resting on the grave. Emanuel snatched himself up, and his pupil, and said: "We will go up to the theatre of the spirits; perhaps the dead one will lay hold on my soul and take me with her." . . . Fearful was the silence of the regions around their way. . . . Men start up out of the ground like dumb-waiters, like serving-machines, and drop down again when they are emptied. . . . . . The human race darts like a flying summer through the sunshine, and the bedewed web hangs fluttering on two worlds and in the night it passes away. . . . So thought both on their pilgrimage to the dead one; they wondered at their own heavy incarnation and at the noise of their steps. Emanuel fastened his gaze on the veiled form that now knelt down; he thought she heard his thoughts and would fly over to his heart through the moonlight. . . .

The hearts of the two men rose and fell as if under two gravestones, as they climbed the long, grass-grown steps to the churchyard, and touched and opened the heavy gate which was painted with forms of risen saints, half effaced by the weather. The warm earthly blood congeals and the soft brain runs to a single image of terror, when the great cloud rolls away from eternity and from the gate of the spiritual world; on the stage of the dead Emanuel called as if beside himself: "Awful spirit, I am a spirit like thee, thou too standest below God, — wilt thou kill me, then kill me not by a stroke of horror, not by a crushing form, but smile like men and quietly wring off my heart." — Then the veiled form rose up and came, — Emanuel wildly grasped his friend, buried himself in his face, and said clinging to him: "On thee I die, on thy warm heart, — O live happy, unless thou wilt grow cold with me, ah! go with me!" . . . .

"Ah, Clotilda!" said Victor; for she was the form. She was dumb as the realm of spirits, for the dead one whom she had visited still clung around her heart; but she was great as a spirit from that realm: for the ethereal luminous nebula of the moon, the standing over the dead, the look into eternity, the lofty night, and the mourning exalted her soul, and one almost forgot that she wept. — Emanuel still held his wings spread out over the scene, and looked sublimely over the graves: "How all sleeps and rests here on this great green death-bed! I would lie down there and die. — Did not something just speak? — The thoughts of mortals are words of spirits. — We are night birds stealing through the dubious atmosphere, we are dumb night-walkers who fall into these pits, when they awake. — Ye dead! crumble not so mutely into dust; ye spirits, ye that come forth out of your buried hearts, flutter not so transparent around us! — O, man were vanity and ashes and a plaything and vapor on the earth, did he not feel that he were so * — — O God, this feeling is our immortality" † — —

Clotilda, by way of drawing him down from this desolating inspiration, took him by the hand and said: "Farewell, O worthy of veneration! I bid farewell this very day, because to-morrow I leave Maienthal. Live happily, — happily till we see each other again; my heart will never forget your greatness, but I shall see you again soon." . . . . Her melancholy at the thought of his

* Pascal.

† "Man's littleness is grandeur in disguise
And discontent is immortality."

YOUNG.

predicted death, her fear of an eternal parting, stifled her remaining words, for she wanted to say more and thank him more warmly. Emanuel said: "We shall never see each other again, Clotilda; for I die in four weeks." — "O God! no!" said Clotilda with the most heart-felt and impassioned tone. — "My good Emanuel," said Victor, "torment not this tormented one. — Cheer thyself, O tortured one, our friend will certainly stay with us." — Here Emanuel raised his eyes to heaven and said with a look in which a world lay, "Eternal One! Couldst thou hitherto have so deceived me? — No, no, on the longest day thy stars will draw me upward, and thy earth will cool my heart. — And thee, thou good Clotilda, thou soul from heaven, thee, then, I certainly see to-day, God knows! for the last time with thy lovely cheeks and in thy earthly form, — I bless thee and bid thee farewell, but heavily and sadly, because I must still live so many days without thee. Go through life with soft influences breathing around thee, keep thy heart high above the many-colored mist of earth and above its storm-clouds, — indeed, thou hearest me not, thou bitterly weeping face; God pour solace into thy soul, let thy parting be more glad! — Thy friend will be with me when I go hence." — Here Victor grasped the hands of the trembling form, exhausted with weeping, who vainly wiped away her tears to see her teacher once more and press his image on her soul; and when Victor cried wildly, "Giulia! sainted one! mitigate the woe of thy friend in this hour, hold this breaking heart," then said Emanuel, looking on both with indescribable tenderness: "I bless you, like a father, holy pair of souls! never forsake, never forget each other! — O ye blessed spirits here above the glimmering mould of the crumbling coffins, give these two hearts peace and happiness, and when I am dead, I will float around your souls and quiet them. And Thou, Eternal One, make these two mortals beneath thy stars as happy as I, — O take nothing from them, nothing on the earth, but life. — Good-night, Clotilda!" . . .

— The Whitsuntide days are over! —

And I thank thee, kind Destiny, that Thou hast given me health for the joy of sketching such a fleeting golden age, since my weak, unequally beating heart deserves not to paint such raptures. — And for thee, my dear reader, may the Whitsuntide feast have sweetened some ash-Sunday or passion-week of thy life!* —

* Here ended Richter's third volume. — Tr.

# FOURTH PREFACE,

## OR, EXTORTED ANTICRITIQUE AGAINST ONE OR ANOTHER REVIEW, WITH WHICH I MIGHT POSSIBLY BE DISPLEASED.

LEVER Romance-writers create out of writing-ink and printer's-ink a new and terrible tyrant, give him a throne either in Italy or the Orient, — and then (unlike children who run away from the figure they have drawn) they step up courageously before the painted, crowned tyrant, and tell him the grandest, but boldest truths to his face, which betray the free man, and which no crooked courtling could well repeat before his sovereign. Such dare-devils remind me so often of two abecedarians, when I pass a gate in Oat Lane in Hof, on which a painted lion rears himself and his mane, and curls and sways his tail and his tongue. For one of the aforesaid abecedarians said to the other as I was hurrying by: "Hear me, I tell you I'll seize him by the tail, I'm not a bit afraid." But the other tyro, who had a much bolder thought, coolly mounted a corner-stone and said: "I first, Sir, I thrust my fist right into his jaws, — so!" —

It is the same boldness with which an author often attacks on paper, not only the aforementioned grim king of beasts, but also the critical *feline race*, — which Linnæus reckons in the royal line of lions, — while he shakes judicial chairs as coldly and boldly as if they were painted thrones, and so in general scolds and assails Journals in his Prefaces. A writer of power can do this. I, for my part, am perhaps as audacious in this as any one, and paint out for myself expressly the following review-cat, in order to grapple with her freely and fearlessly, and to show by her what courage can do.

In the first place, the Reviewer who charges me with being indebted to the amount of two whole Intercalary Days, — the one after the Fortieth and the one after the Forty-fourth Dog-Post-Days, — cannot have seen this Second Edition at all; the two Prefaces with which I have enriched it, the first and this, will answer with all sensible men for true Intercalary Days.

Secondly, my Reviewer will find fault (in future) with my indulging my *manner.* But let him hear now the Philosopher (namely, myself) : Manner is of itself nothing but what follows : the æsthetic ideal and integral, like every other, is reached only by an infinite power, but we with our finite strength are incessantly coming *nearer* to it, never so much as *near ;* Manner is, therefore, as the Philosopher takes it, a finite mirror of infinity, or the expression of the relation in which every *temperament* and number of strings of any given Æolian harp stands to the score of the infinite music of the Spheres, which it has to echo. Every combination of human powers gives only a manner ; and higher spirits would find in Homer and Goethe the *human* manner at least ; nay, the higher angelic hierarchy would find the lower manneristic, the seraph the angel of the churches. But as I am not even an ordinary angel, — not to say a seraph, — another Reviewer than he who will criticise me would have presumed beforehand that I should have a manner. — And such I manifestly have. —

But yet more: as the *degree* and the *relation* of our powers change from year to year, — and consequently the product and proceeds of the same also, the manner —: accordingly and unfortunately the manner of the fiftieth year generally sets itself as the corrector of that of the twenty-fifth; or rather there ensues a heterogeneous adoption of children of two marriages, in which both are losers. Such a simultaneous Hysteron-Proteron * is still worse than if one should undertake to clip and grind down the Grecian statues of one of Winkelmann's ages of art according to the statues of another. Pour rather a pure, flowing work into thy present mould, and do not wait to force it in when it is cast and hardened! — Even granting I should become hereafter another and a wiser man, I would never graft the old man upon the youth.

Man regards himself in the concert-hall of the universe, if not as the solo-player, yet as one of the instruments, — instead of a single *tone,* — as in fact the Prince looks upon himself as an Oberon's or at least hunter's horn, — the poet as an oaten pipe, — the author as a composing-instrument, † — the Pope as the organ-works, — the belle as Bestelmeier's hand-steel-harmonica, or as a quail-whistle, — my reviewer as a pitch-pipe, — and I on myself as Maelzel's great Panharmonicon. But we are all only *tones,* as in Potemkin's orchestra every one of the sixty metallic flutes gave only *one* tone. Therefore I am glad of every individuality, of every manner, as of a new semitone in the church music of natures.

Thirdly, I know nothing by which I can see more clearly my future reviewer's perplexity for want of *mate-*

* Last-First, or *the cart before the horse.* — Tr.

† The name given to a harpsichord which notes down everything that it plays.

*ria peccans* to censure, than this, that he sticks to such pitiful trifles — in future — as the following evidently are, that I, e. g., have appended this Preface, that I have bound the work in four separate Parts, and by this fourth part have made, for an earlier possessor and bookworm, the sheet-worm * of the old edition wholly useless. From the like specimens and sayings, wherewith such a Spartan Ephor Emerepes will rob me of the fourth and highest string, which I stretch on my fiddle full of rising fifths, let the indulgent reader form an idea how the whole of the Review must look. I am ashamed to go on.

Fourthly, I find universally, that, if an author in his Preface charges himself with a slight fault, which, however, he himself hardly believes, then the critics forthwith adopt and double this charge, as, among the Romans, a suicide who failed to accomplish the act was afterward regularly executed. If the author, having his eyes thus opened, strikes into another line, and bestows upon himself, beforehand, some praise, — and that not apparent, — *this* is not even accepted, not to say doubled. In that case the Devil may be speaker of the prologue! —

Meanwhile he seems also to be only Reviewer, and less a sly than a coarse customer. Many and really glaring incivilities, however, I willingly forgive my future reviewer, whereas I pardon nothing to a Gallic or British one, because he knows how one should treat people. — I play with him myself in this anticritique in no specially polite manner, nor do I, as the peasant doffs his hat before higher lightnings, doff mine before his. Besides, the judges after the Special Recension address the defendant

* The term applied to the abridged title of a book recurring at the bottom of every sheet.

as "thou." A mild (critical) winter is unwholesome to him upon whom it comes. For the rest, I simply wait and watch for the hour when I shall be celebrated and have on laurel-leaves: then I shall not, any more than other contemporaries who have now set up laurel-trees, suffer any one to find fault with me; and few will undertake it, just as on pictures which have been smeared with *laurel oil* no flies alight.

Fifthly and finally. It is well known that the deceased authoress, Ehrmann, when the advocate Ehrmann had accepted and noticed with much approbation one of her works in the Strassburg Gazette, married him on account of the review. If the editor of some journal play his cards so adroitly that a female coadjutor in the magazine shall welcome and announce my Second Edition of Hesperus (or Star Venus) with the admiration which the First Edition universally receives on account of its charms; and if he will only tip me a wink as to the sex of my reviewer, — in which connection, however, *this* must be looked to, that the critical person shall be, on the whole, still in the best blooming period of a reviewer's life, wherein one can still readily feel and impart and favorably review the fire of the Evening Star or Venus, and so much the more, as even in physics only green wood is a conductor of the electrical flame, but dry a non-conductor, — if the editor will see to and execute all this, then the author of this anticritique pledges himself with his signature to wait upon the coadjutress immediately after the receipt of the review, and with the usual ceremonies to marry her.

JEAN PAUL FR. RICHTER.

Hof in Voigtland, June 8, 1797.

## NINTH INTERCALARY DAY.

### VICTOR'S ESSAY ON THE RELATION OF THE SOUL TO THE ORGANS.

VICTOR was an enemy to the exclusive taste in philosophy quite as much as in poetry. On all systems — even of the heretics of Epiphanius and of Walch — the form of truth is imprinted, as the human form is in the bestial kingdom, although in bolder and bolder lines. No man can believe in nonsense proper, although he may speak it. Singular it is, that precisely the *consequent* or consistent systems, without the atomic *Clinamen* * of feeling, deviate from each other the most widely. Systems, like the passions, only at the focal distance throw the brightest point of light upon the object; — how pitifully, e. g., does the great theory of self-subjugation run out of *Christianity* over into *Stoicism,* — then into *Mysticism,* — then into *Monachism,* till the stream spreads out and oozes away into *Fohism,* as the Rhine loses itself in the sand! — The theory of Kant, with all logical systems, has this tendency to run into sand, and has that deflection † of feeling in common with the inconsequent ones, which brings together the wasting arms again to a renewing fountain-head. The two hands of the Pure Reason, which in the antinomy ‡ scratched and beat each other, the Practical Reason peacefully joins together, and presses them, folded, to the heart, and says, here is a God, a Conscious Person, and an Immortality! — —

* The gradual sapping of logical strictness by moral freedom. — TR.

† The getting of its Eastings through the Practical Reason.

‡ Opposition of laws. And yet *antinomian* is an opponent of law. — TR.

Victor first fructified his soul with great Nature or with poets, and then, and not till then, awaited the dawn of a system. He discovered (not invented) the truth by soaring and surveying, not by penetration, microscopic inspection, and syllogistic groping from one syllable of the book of nature to another, *whereby one gets its words indeed, but not their sense.* That creeping and touching belongs, he said, not to the *finding,* but to the *proving* and confirming of truth ; for which he always took lessons of Bayle : for no one is a poorer teacher in the discovery of truth, or a better one for the proof of it, than acuteness or Bayle, who is its mint-assayer, but not its miner.

* * * * *

## THE ESSAY.

IF I wrote it in Göttingen, I might make it in paragraphs and more thoroughly, because the Flachsenfingen folks would not disturb me. Meanwhile it must still be written here, in order that I may have a patron and advocate in my own person against the court-gentlemen, who want to transform my soul into my body.

The Brain and Nerves are the true body of the "I" ; the rest of the environment is only the body of that body, the nourishing and protecting bark of that tender pith.— And as all the changes of the world appear to us only as changes of that pith or marrow, accordingly the pith- and pulp-ball with its streaks is the proper world-globe of the soul. The inverted nervous tree springs from the swollen brain of the fœtus as from a kernel, which it also resembles in appearance, and ascends with sensitive branches as spinal marrow, even to the anatomical summit of the horse-tail. This marrowy growth is grafted upon the venous tree as a consuming parasitic plant. And as every twig is a tree in miniature, accordingly — for all this is not a correspondence of wit, but of nature — the nervous ganglia are fourth cerebral chambers in small. The terminations of the nerves, in their development, open out on the retina, on the Schneiderian * membrane, in the gustative knot, &c., into leaf and flower. Hence, e. g., we see not with the continuation of the optic nerve, but with the delicate unravelling of its stamina; for the great dissolving picture-gallery on the retina cannot possibly, by a movement of the nervous spirit, (or whatever one will assume — for after all it comes back to motion,) be slid back to the brain; in which case, besides, the two galleries of the two eyes would have to pass through the two prongs of the visual nerve and coincide at its handle to one picture.

Consequently the image in the eye, ear, &c., if it is to serve any purpose, must be felt forward on the point of the nerve, — in one word, it is even more absurd to shut up the soul in the locker † of the fourth ventricle of the brain, i. e. in a pore of this tubercular plant, than it would be if one who, like me, ascribes an animating soul to the flower, should imprison the same in the ground-story of the dull kernel. Rather would I, surely, locate the soul in the finest honey-vessels of the senses, the eyes, than in the insensible brain, if I did not, in fact, believe that, like a Hamadryad, it inhabits and warms and stirs every nervous bough of this animal plant. The under-tied or severed nerve conveys, it is true, no further sensation, not however on account of the

* Named after its discoverer. — Tr.

† The *Zwinger* is originally the narrow interval between the town-wall and the town itself. — Tr.

interruption of the connection with the soul and residence chamber in the brain, but because the nutritious spirit of life is cut off from it; for the nerves, like all finer organizations, need so much a continuous supply of food, that the arrested beating of heart and artery suspends in one minute all their powers.

I go further and say outright, beforehand, — by way of contradicting two errors: these organs do not feel, but are felt; secondly, the organs are not the condition of all feeling in general, but only of a certain kind.

The last first: as the organ (i. e. its changes), which is as much a body as any gross object, whose own changes it brings in contact with the soul, is nevertheless felt by the spiritual nature immediately and without a *second organ:* accordingly all corporeal substances give the spiritual essence sensations as well as the nerves do, and an unembodied soul is not possible, for the simple and sole reason, that in case of the dissolution of the body it would then wear the whole material universe as a heavier one.

My first assertion was, one should not say the *perceptive,* but the *perceived* organization. The nerves do not feel the object, but only change the place where it is felt, and their changes and those of the brain are only *objects* of sensation, not *instruments* thereof, nor in fact sensation itself. But wherefore? —

I have more than one Therefore. A body is capable only of motion, although, to be sure, that motion is only the show of the aforementioned combination and the result of the powers concealed in simple parts. The string, the air, the auditory ossicles, the auricular nerves, vibrate; but the vibration of the latter no more explains the sensation of a tone than the vibration of the string could, if the soul were chained to that. Thus, despite all images in the eye and brain, the *discernment* of them is still not yet made out or explained; or will you say, perhaps, that for some such reason as this, because the senses are *mirrors* full of images, therefore the spiritual *eye* is dispensed with or made good? And does not the change of the nerve presuppose a second in a second essence, if it is to be perceived? Or does another motion in this essence represent the first motion?

This brings me to the brain. That greatest and grossest nerve — the sounding-board of all the others — shows up to the soul the delineations of those images which are introduced by the rest. Upon the whole, I am of opinion that the brain serves more the nerves of the muscles, the veins of the limbs, which meet in the hand of the soul, and all, in fact, more as nourishing root, than it serves as a case of instruments to the pictorial soul. As most of our ideas are served up on visual images, and take from them their ground color, it is probable we think more with the optic nerve than with the brain. Why is it, as Bonnet has observed, that deep-thinking wearies the eyes and sharp-seeing the brain? Why do certain excesses blunt at the same time the memory and the eyes? The fever-images playing their antics outside of the eyes of the sick and people of lively fancy, like Cardan, who saw in the dark whatever he thought vividly and glowingly, are explained in my hypothesis.

In regard to the brain there are two errors; but Heaven save my friends only from one of them. For from the other Reimarus can guard them, who has fully proved that the brain is no Æolian harp with trembling strings, nor a camera-obscura with sliding pictures, nor a barrel-organ with pins for every idea, which the spirit turns, in order of itself to play to and from itself its ideas. If now not even the pre-established *harmony* of the brain and the mind, nor the mutual *accompaniment* of the two, is conceivable, so is their *identity* absolutely impossible; and this is precisely the error from which the above-mentioned Heaven has to keep my friends. The materialist must first set up all that which Reimarus has overthrown; he must petrify in the brain-pap the millions of picture-cabinets of seventy years, and yet again make them movable like *Eidophysica*,* and deal out the shuffled card-images to every second of time; he must see to it that these *animated* dancing images are forced into rank and file. And then, after all, and only then, does his difficulty properly begin; for now — even if we grant him that the images see themselves, the thoughts think themselves, that every imagination darkly mirrors all others, and even the conscious "I," as a monad, does the universe — now (we say) he must first get him a generalissimo who shall command and array this immeasurable, fluctuating host of ideas, a compositor who shall set up the idea-book from an unknown manuscript, and, when dreams, fevers, passions, have shaken all the letter-cases into *pi*, shall rearrange all the letters alphabetically. This ruling unity and power — without which the *symmetry of the microcosm* is as inexplicable as that of the *macrocosm*, that of *the ideal world* as that of the *actual* — is precisely what we call a spirit. To be sure, by this unknown power neither the origin nor the succession of ideas is *mediated* or explained, but, assuming only the known force of matter, motion, all that is not only incredible, but absolutely impossible; and Leibnitz can more easily explain motion by dark imaginings, than the materialist can

* The sensuous images of the ancient Greek philosophers. — Tr.

imaginings by motions. In the former case motion is only semblance, and exists only in the second contemplating being, but in the latter the representation would be show and would exist in the second — *representing* substance.

I have often quarrelled with men of the world who make good observations and miserable conclusions, because in case of the least dependence of the soul upon the body — e. g. in old age, intoxication, &c. — they made the one a mere repeating-work of the other; nay, I have even said, no dancing-master was so stupid as to conclude: "Inasmuch as I dance awkwardly in leaden shoes, more nimbly in wooden ones, and best of all in silk ones, I see clearly from this, that the shoes have special springs to communicate rapidity; and as with leaden shoes I can hardly lift my feet, if I were barefoot I could hardly make out a single *Pas*." The soul is the dancing-master, the body the shoe.

We cannot conceive any action either of bodies upon bodies or of monads upon monads; consequently, of the organs upon the conscious being, still less. This we know, that the cohesion and community of goods between soul and body is always the same, or at most greater at the times when others would expect it to be less; for the greatest depth of thought, the holiest emotion, the highest flight of fancy, are precisely what need the waxen wing-work of the body most, as its consequent exhaustion also gives assurance; the more incorporeal the object of the ideas is, so much the more corporeal hand-and-draught-services are necessary to the holding of it fast, and at most the periods of stupid sensuality, of spiritual enervation, of blear imbecility, are the ones with which we must make coincide the periods of liberation from the chains of the body. Even the moral power with which we trample down wanton, upshooting bodily impulses works with bodily crows and tools; and the soul in this case merely summons the brain against the stomach. — Add to this, that the limits and hindrances to such fettering and unfettering are as little to be assigned as the causes of the same. Still less can the bonds of the soul, as some think, grow looser and longer in dream. Sleep is the rest of the nerves, not of the whole body. The involuntary muscles, the stomach, the heart, keep on working therein, not much less than when one lies down awake. Only the nerves and the brain, i. e. thinking and perceiving, are suspended. Hence slumber refreshes men while riding and driving, who therefore rest nothing but the nerves. Hence weak-nerved patients, whom all rest wearies, are refreshed by dreamless sleep. By the way, without the theory of *disorganization* which assumes negative and positive nervous electricity, the phenomena of sleep are inexplicable; — e. g. it is inexplicable in that case, why opium, wine, manipulation, animality, childhood, plethora, nourishing food, perfumes, on the one hand, are precisely what promote sleep; while, on the other hand, torture, exhaustion, old age, temperance, pressure on the brain, winter, loss of blood, fear, grief, phlegm, fat, spiritual enervation, also provoke it. —— At most in deep sleep, when the nerve-body rests, could we suppose the soul loosed from earthly chains; in dream, on the contrary, it should rather be supposed the more closely fastened, because dreaming, as well as deep thinking, which also locks the gates of the five senses as well, is surely no sleeping. Hence dreams wear out the nerves, to the inner overstrainings of which they add outer impressions. Hence morning lends both the brain and our dreams equal animation. Hence the sleeping animal — except the effeminate tame dog — has no unhealthy dreams. Hence even Aristotle assigns unusual dreams as forerunners of the sick-nurse. Hence — I have now dreamed enough, and the reader has slept enough. —

## 37. DOG-POST-DAY.

The Amoroso at Court. — Preliminary Recesses of Marriage. — Defence of Courtly Back-bending.

N the morning after that great night Victor took leave of this consecrated burial-ground of his fairest days with unconcealed tears. Often he looked back on these ruins of his Palmyra, till nothing of them was left standing except the mountain-ridge as a fire-proof wall. "When I come back hither four weeks hence," thought he, "it will only be to see the death-angel lay my Emanuel on the altar and under the sacrificial knife." He bethought himself how dearly he paid for this feast of tabernacles by the death of a friend;* and how the latter, without such compensation, suffered just as great a loss. For he felt that the frightful word "scoundrel" had now come in as an eternal wall of rock between their sundered souls. — He called to mind, indeed, and right gladly, what there was to acquit his late friend, particularly his being hounded on by Matthieu and his listening when *he* swore eternal love to Clotilda; nay, he even suspected that the Evangelist had perhaps let poor Flamin see far in the background peculiar motives (these suggested by the Apothecary) for a love, by whose object the favor of the Prince was to be secured, — but his *feelings* incessantly

* Flamin. — Tr.

repeated to him: "He still ought not to have *believed* it! — ah, hadst thou only," said he with emotion, at the sight of the city, "pierced me with balls or with other terms of contempt, that I might have easily forgiven thee! — But that thou shouldst have done it with just this ever-gnawing venomous sound!" — He is right; the injury of honor is not therefore the less, because the other inflicts it from full conviction of right. — For the conviction is precisely the offence; and the honor of a friend is something so great, that a doubt of it should hardly dare to arise except by its own confession. But thus do separations easily grow out of little concealments, as from March *clouds* July *tempests.* Only a perfected noble soul can forbear to try any longer the tried friend, — can believe when the enemies of the friend deny, — can blush as at an impure thought, when a dumb, flying suspicion soils the gracious image, — and when at last the doubts are no more to be conquered, can still banish them for a long time from one's actions, willing rather to fall into an economical improvidence than into the heavy sin against the Holy Spirit in man. This firm confidence is easier to deserve than to have.

In the noisy foundery and mill of the city he felt as if in a dreary forest. Accustomed as he was to tender souls, the city ones appeared to him all so thorny and unpolished; for love had, like tragedy, purified his passions in exciting them. All hung over so ruinous and moss-grown as if on the verge of a collapse, whereas the clean mirror-walls of Maienthal rose firm and radiant. For love is the only thing which fills the heart of man to the brim, although with a nectar-foam that soon sinks again; it alone composes a poem of some thousand minutes without the rattling repetitions of the letter R, as the Dominican Cardone* executed a poem upon it quite as long under the name *L' R — sbandita*† without a single R, — hence, like crabs, it is finest in the months without an R in their name.

The first thing he had to do in Flachsenfingen was to write to Clotilda. For as the Evangelist Matthieu would now in all probability go out into all the world and preach the gospel of the pistol-duel between the two friends to all people, there was nothing else to do for the sacred reputation of his beloved than to transform her into a betrothed by a publicly declared engagement. Flamin's newly kindled passion could not be considered at all in comparison with Clotilda's justification. The exclamation, "Thou art my brother," which the convulsions of anguish had wrung from Clotilda, had of course been incomprehensible to Flamin, and had fallen unheeded on his ear; but for the listening Mat it had become a grand text and *dictum probans* of his doctrinal system respecting their being brother and sister. — In the letter, therefore, Victor besought his friend for a tacit assent to his suit; he left it to her, by his silence, to guess the most disinterested motives of his prayer.

He appeared now on the war-theatre of souls, of which one seldom catches an exact map, the court; — to his heart, filled with paradises, even the apartments seemed like glass cases of a stuffed aviary, which one strews with powder-brass, conchs, and flowers, and the live articles of the rooms like dried birds stuffed with wood or arsenic;

* D'Israeli, in his "Curiosities of Literature" (Art. *Literary Follies*), ascribes this to one Gregorio Leti, who, he says, presented a discourse to the Academy of the Humorists at Rome, throughout which he had purposely omitted the letter R, and he entitled it, *The exiled R.*" — Tr.

† The R disbanded. — Tr.

through the snakes wire was drawn, as through the tails of great beasts, and the tree-runners on the throne stood on wire. —— So very much had he become through the Whitsuntide festival the antipode of us who in colder blood easily remark what is sublime and noble about a court. — The newest news he heard there was that the Prince in company with the Princess was to take a journey to the mineral springs of St. Luna, he to cure his gouty feet, she to cure her eyes. Victor was really not quite tolerant, when he thought to himself, "If you will not fare any better, then, for all I care, go to the D——." The Paullinum was to him a slaughter-house, and every antechamber a chamber of torture; the Prince treated him not with courtly courtesy, but with coldness, which pained him so much the more as it proved that he had loved him, — the Princess more proudly, — only Matthieu, who loved best to talk with people who mortally hated him, had a face full of sunshine. From him and from his sister and some unknown persons he had to take and worry down some light snake-poison of persiflage about his duel, which the stomach indeed digests, like other snake-poison, but which injected into wounds dissolves the blood of life. —— Does not even my correspondent fall into a fury and send his fury to me through his *Capsarius*,* the Pomeranian dog, saying: "Let any one keep cool, if he can, who is warm, that is to say in love, and whom death has not yet made cold, let him keep cool, I say, before the stinging smiles of a court-sisterhood at his sensitive love, especially before those higher ladies who are Goddesses, and on whose Cyprian altar always (as with the Scythians) a stranger is sacrificed, and to

* A name given by the Romans to the slave who carried the children's school-books after them. — Tr.

whom (as the Gauls believed of their Gods) malefactors, *roués*, Orleanses, are the most acceptable offerings! — Or, even if he can dispose of that, let him composedly hear himself mocked for his love by an Evangelist who invents and dresses up on the subject the following maxims: *La décence ajoute aux plaisirs de l'indécence: la vertue est le sel de l'amour; mais n'en prenez pas trop. — J'aime dans les femmes les accés de colère, de douleur, de joie, de peur: il y a toujours dans leur sang bouillant quelque chose qui est favorable aux hommes. — C'est là où la finesse demeure courte, qu'il faut de l'enthousiasme. — Les femmes s'étonnent rarement d'être crues, foibles; c'est du contraire qu'elles s'étonnent un peu. — L'amour pardonne toujours à l'amour, rarement à la raison.** — Blessed are the adversaries [sighs Knef] who are at liberty to cudgel one another."

The Evangelist threw a corrosive drop on the nerves of Victor's heart, when, despite his knowledge of Flamin's noble extraction, he twitted him with this, that like a modern French Equilibrist of Freedom, he could not marry indeed a citizen, but yet could — fight with one. And it went through his soul to see the friend who had been stolen from him so sorely impoverished in friends, that this Matthieu was the last scion and support of the line, who did not even before Victor take the trouble in the higher circles to assume and continue playing the part of a friend of Flamin. A good man has his sensi-

* "Decency adds to the pleasures of indecency; virtue is the salt of love; but don't take too much of it. — I love in woman bursts of anger, of grief, of joy, of fear; there is always in their boiling blood something which is favorable to men. — It is where *finesse* falls short, that enthusiasm is needed. — Women are rarely astonished at being thought weak; it is at the contrary that they are somewhat astonished. — Love always pardons love, rarely reason." — Tr.

tive heart screwed, as it were, into a flattening press, when he is obliged to stand before people (as Victor here is before so many) who hate and insult him, — in the beginning he is cheerful and cool, and is glad that he cares nothing about it, — but he unconsciously arms himself with more and more contempt, by way of opposing something to the insult, — at last the growth of the contempt announces itself by the disagreeable feeling of love going out and hatred coming in, and the bitter aqua-fortis seizes and devours its own vessel, the heart. — Then the pain becomes so great, that he lets the old human love, which was the warm element of his soul, run again in streams into his bosom. With Victor something else was added to the embittering elements, — his previous softening; one is never colder than after great warmth, just as water, after boiling, assumes a greater coldness than it had before. Love, intoxication, and sometimes the inspiration drunk from the sight of nature, make us too kind towards our favorites, and too hard upon our antipodes. Now when Victor in this bitter mood looked on at a card-table, and delivered to himself internal lectures upon the whole assembly, *lectures on heads*,* in which, instead of heads of pasteboard, he availed himself of thicker ones: then the recollection of the still, humane tolerance wherewith Clotilda had accommodated herself to these very people out of love to her parents, made the whole ice-panoply which had formed around his heart, as round a flower, melt down, and his warmed heart said with the first joy it had known to-day: "Why then do I hate these full as much tormented as tormenting shapes so bitterly? Are they here only on my account? Have

* Such was the title Stevens gave his satirical college-lectures on pasteboard heads, which half London ran after.

not they also their conscious being? Must they not drag with them this defective, afflicted self through all Eternity? Is not each of them still loved by some soul or other? Why shall I then see in them only matter for detestation, and draw acid from every look, every tone? — No, *I will love men merely because they are men.*" — Yes, indeed! friendship may desire merits, but philanthropy only the human form. Hence it is precisely that we have all such a cold changeable love of man, because we confound the *worth* of men with their *claim*, and will not love anything about them, but virtues.

Our Victor felt as light as after a tempest; the bitterest thing which insults can do to us is, that they compel us to hate. On the other hand, he felt now how impure our resistance to evil, which we give out for virtue, is, and how disagreeable it is even to a noble soul to combat enemies without bearing malice against them; for this is still harder than blessing and protecting them without loving them.

Thus some weeks elapsed during his enforced landings at the hostile court, — for the request of his father ruled his heart, — and vain hopes of Clotilda's decision, and tearful retrospective yearnings toward the suspended days of love and the *desolated* days of friendship. Clotilda's silence, however, was precisely an assent to his coming; still he superfluously announced to her by a second letter the day of the same. For the rest, to him, thus bound to the throne as to a whipping-post, thus hurled out from all the objects of his love, thus fixed upon nothing but a far-off thundering future, in which his Emanuel after fourteen days sinks into the earth and his Clotilda into a thousand sorrows, the present grew close and sultry. Around him whirled an unripe tempest, and, as at the equinoxes, the clouds hung immovably about him as a great thick mass, and the secret laboring in the high element had not yet decided whether it was to run together in tear-drops or break up into blue.

At last he went to St. Luna . . . in sooth only sadly blest! O could he glance at the Luna footpath or at the Parsonage, which covered the stages of buried friendship, without turning away his overflowing eye, without thinking how much vainer is the loving than the life of men, how fate employs precisely the warmest hearts for the destruction of the best (just as one uses only *burning-lenses* for the calcining of *precious stones*), and how many a silent breast is nothing but the sunken coffin of a beloved and faded image? — It is a nameless feeling to wish to love a friend for memory's sake, and be obliged to shun him from honor. Victor *wished* he *could* forgive his infatuated darling; but in vain: the arsenical word which pains me in his name remained still, in spite of all sweetening juices with which he swathed it, lying undissolved and corroding and deadly in his soul. Good Flamin! a stranger could love thee, I, for example; but the friend of thy youth, no more.

Victor strode along tremblingly before the picture-gallery and music-hall of his mirrored and echoed childhood, the parsonage, likewise before the scouring Apollonia, to whom he gladly gave a deeper greeting than his rank allowed, and before old Mops, who mixed himself up in no family feuds, but cordially invited him with his tail. — Not his pride kept him back from visiting the (assumed) parents of his adversary, but the anxious apprehension that the good people would perhaps worry themselves to death before him in an embarrassing conflict between politeness, between old love and new resentment. But he resolved by a letter to the noble-souled Parson's wife to satisfy his love and her sensibility.

Then he came into the presence of his beloved! — I remarked day-before-day-before-yesterday, while reading the German-French history, where, as is well known, the crowned name Clotilda also reigns, by the redoubled beatings of my heart, how I should feel then, when I came actually to see this Clotilda, whom for three quarters of a year I have praised; for that Knef, and the dog too, are no knaves, and that the whole history has not merely transpired, but is still transpiring, I see by a hundred traits which no fancy can well invent. If the biographer should get sight of the heroine, there would arise nothing but a new volume and a new — hero, who would be — myself. . . . .

She was sick; that evening had pounced like a vulture upon her heart, and had not yet drawn out its bloody claws. Her soul seemed only the angel that guards the earthly casing of a saint, from which the soul has fled. The Chamberlain met the Court Physician, as if he knew nothing of any duelling. What mothers generally do, that the father did; he forgave every one who was in high station and who wanted his daughter. The proposal which Victor at last made to him surprised him only because he had hitherto thought the latter postponed it merely on account of uncertainty respecting Clotilda's inheritance and relations in life. His answer consisted in infinite pleasure, infinite honor, &c., and other infinities; for with him all was one; hence, too, Platner asserts with justice that it is in fact only the finite of which man cannot conceive.* Le Baut would have

* Lacon says: "As to time without an end and space without a limit, these are two things that finite beings cannot clearly compre-

handed over his daughter, even if he had not wished to; he could not refuse anything to one's face, not even a daughter. Moreover, no one could come and sue for Clotilda who would not have fitted into some one of his projects (the four chambers of his brain were full of them up to the ceiling). Naturally, therefore, a son-in-law was what he now most wished, since his daughter might actually die without his having yet used her for a leaping-pole and lever of his body, — and because, secondly, the duel-talk preyed upon his heart; not as if he had not by healthy *vermiform* * motions digested the *hardest* things, but because, like cultivated men without honor, he loved to appear on occasion of slight insults with alarm-cannon and fire-drums, in order to steal the right, in the case of complete but productive cases of dishonor, pierced with veins of silver, to lie there still as a mouse. The only thing which looked unpleasant to the Chamberlain, but which he immediately got over by the fact of giving his word (regarding his daughter) to the Court Physician, was, that he had previously given the selfsame word (secretly) to our Mat. As his Lordship, who was soon to return, could harm him and help him more than the minister could, he gladly broke his old word, for the sake of keeping his newest; for not only his *last will*, but *every* will, man can change as he will, and if he is a man of his word, he will be fond of making entirely opposite promises, in order to oblige himself to keep one of them. If the lying conduct of the Chamberlain, after such excuses, still needs one, he has this in his favor, that he

hend. But . . . there are two things much more incomprehensible, . . . time that *has* an end and space that *has* a limit. For whatever limits these two things must be itself unlimited, and I am at a loss to conceive where it can exist except in space and time." — Tr.

* Peristaltic. — Tr.

certainly hoped Clotilda, when *he* had given his Yes, would answer No, and dare and — suffer instead of him. At least he held out this hope before his angry wife, and referred her to Clotilda's former No, which had laid upon our Victor such heavy hours, and to her unchangeableness. I wish one could have afterward petrified or cast his face in plaster in the state into which it fell upon being informed of Clotilda's Yes. What could the stepmother, the Chamberlain's lady, who was always the esquire and ally of the Evangelist, do in the matter further than to make a friendly face and the remark, that "no one was harder to manage than a spouse whom everybody managed"?

The formalities of the betrothal itself awaited the return of the Lord, and other circumstances. Let me not say anything of the love of this couple, exalted as it had been by so many sorrows. When, to love, the love of man also is actually wedded (a thing which many a one will not understand at all); — when in the breath of love all other charms of the heart become more beautiful, all fine feelings still finer, every flame for the sublime still higher, as in oxygen gas every spark becomes a lightning-flash, and every glowworm a flame; — when the eyes of the two lovers seldom meet, but their thoughts often; — when Victor almost dreads to retain a heart to which he has cost so much, so many dark days, so many anxieties and almost a brother; — and when Clotilda divines this delicate shrinking and rewards *him* for *her* sufferings; — then is it impossible to convey to many persons a sketch of such an ethereal flame, to say nothing of its colors; for the *few* it is unnecessary.

In every new relation into which a beloved object

enters, love begins again at the beginning and with new flames; e. g. when we meet her in a strange house,— or among new persons,—or as a traveller,—or as a hostess,—or as a flower-gardener,—or as a dancer,— or (which has the greatest effect) as a betrothed. This was Victor's case; for from the hour when the wish of inclination is exalted into the command of duty, and when the dear soul delivers herself and all her hopes, and the reins of her whole future, into the beloved hands, there must in every good man's heart be a voice calling: "Now she has no longer any one on earth but thee,—now let her be holy to thee; O, now spare and guard and reward the dear soul who believes in thee!" —Victor was inexpressibly moved by this relation through the incidental circumstance that this very Clotilda, this firm, proud ball-queen and queen of heaven, who with so many energies and so much independence went her way over the snares of men and under their laurel-wreaths, was now by the betrothal giving her Declaration of Independence with a gentle smile into Victor's hands, and wished now nothing more than to love and to be loved; for this sweet condescension of so lofty a form Victor knew no sacrifice, no wound, no gift, which would have seemed to him great enough to repay her.—Thus should one love; and every new right and sacrifice which chills the common man, makes the good one warmer and more tender.

Although Victor by the rights of his new relationship found a more domestic and comfortable life with his parents-in-law; nevertheless it pained him that he was daily obliged to see the ever-memorable parsonage-people in their garden, and yet that the iron fence of the previous duel and the present betrothal shut him off from their hearts. For the same reason must he also renounce the Britons and their standing club. Le Baut however thought it an act of prudence: "for it was known on good authority, that they were Jacobins, and Frenchmen in disguise." —

But Clotilda's soul could no longer bear the deep sorrow which she felt to be weighing on her friend, the Parson's wife; she invited her by a note to a friendly walk. They met on the observatory; and Victor saw, with the deepest emotion, how Clotilda immediately took the hand of her oldest friend, and never, for the whole way, let it go from hers.

Clotilda came back with a countenance illumined with joy, and with eyes which had wept much, and with heavenly features in which shone an unnamable, not so much more ardent as more tender, love. Not for some time could she sufficiently command her emotions to communicate to Victor *something* of the interview: for I think I can detect that it was not *all*. The Parson's wife — Clotilda related — received her with a look full of crushing sorrows, but neither with coldness nor suspicion. At first neither could do anything but weep, and they spoke not a word; Clotilda was still more overcome, and her tears still continued to flow, when she began to relate her betrothal. She laid the hand of her friend upon her heart, and said: "Now is our friendship severely tried. I still believe in yours, — believe in mine! — O only this once, dear friend, stand firm! Heavy secrets, over which I have no right and to which I have only in a small degree the key, bring us all so near to these dreadful misunderstandings. Only this time rely upon it firmly, that you and I are changing *our relation* to each other as little as our characters." — Here the

Parson's wife beheld her with a great look in which the old love for Victor still gleamed on, and then embraced her all at once with dry eyes and said: "Yes, I rely upon you, do you what you will, and though I should at last be the only soul left." — The last addition would at another time have offended Clotilda; ah, it could not do so now; O, she was glad to have something to forgive!

After the narration she told her friend, that, in case the invisibleness and the silence of his Lordship lasted much longer, she should perhaps, rather than wait, undertake the toilsome journey to London to her and Flamin's mother, in order to persuade the latter, as the solution of all these dangerous riddles, to come to Germany. — Ah, could Victor's self-sacrificing heart make an objection to the sacrifices of others? — No! his woe was redoubled, but also his respect and love.

In this situation of things there came to Clotilda a short letter from Emanuel.

* * * * *

"Last evening my Julius came to me with a basket full of garden-earth and begged me for flower-pots and for hyacinths, because, he said, he was bringing earth for both. He had fetched the soil for his flowers from the hill of thy Giulia. — — I drew his white- and red-blooming face, which resembles the pink with the red point, to my breast and said, 'Ah, who tends the flowers of man, when he has passed away?' And I meant *him* too with his tender bloom, into which may sorrow never fling its heavy rain-drops! — O Victor and Clotilda, when the lilies of the earth benumb me and put me into the last slumber, then adopt ye my blind Julius, and let this soul full of love be guarded by your loving souls!

"Clotilda! I now beg or wish something of you, which you perhaps can hardly grant. Ah, come on the *longest day* to Maienthal, thou fair soul! Cannot thy heart bear it? Didst thou not accompany thy Giulia even to the *blind gate* of the grave and there see her soul soar up and her body fall to the earth? O, if thou and thy friend, in the last hour, when life folds up its flashing peacock-mirrors and lets them sink heavy and colorless into the grave, could stay by me, as the two first angels of the future world! — For at the moment when the whole earth like a shell breaks off from the heart, the naked heart clings faster to hearts and would fain warm itself against death, and when all bonds of earth tear away, the flower-chains of love bloom on. O Clotilda! how heavenly to close my life in the presence of thy Elysian form! I should already be hovering around thee unfettered on the wings of eternity, to look upon thee, and if I could not wipe away thy tears with the ethereal hand, I would console thy heavy heart with a strange rapture! Ay, if man were blinded in the forecourt of the second world, still thy form would remain as an after-shining sun-image before my closed eyes! — O Clotilda, if thou shouldst come! Ah, probably thou wilt not come; and only the Eternal, who numbers the hours of the second life, knows when I shall see thee again, on the second earth, and how great are there the pains of longing. And so then farewell, and move on, lofty soul, in thy path beneath the clouds, — when I behold thy friend, thou wilt touchingly stand before me, — and when I die on his heart, I shall pray for thee, and say to God: Give her to me again, when on her head the flower-wreath of earth is great enough — or the crown of thorns too great! — Clotilda, never change, and then I shall not ask Destiny: How long will she smile down below there, how long will she weep there? Never change!

"EMANUEL."

The two fell softly on each other's hearts and were silent over their thoughts; Emanuel's love glorified theirs, and Victor had too great a respect for his friend and his beloved to console the latter. He did not once ask her, how she answered Emanuel's prayer; he knew that she must refuse it, because otherwise her heart would break beside the loved one.

When at last he parted from her and from St. Luna, and she was compelled to reflect that in a few days he would go to Maienthal, — and when in his eyes and hers tears stood which indicated more than *one* sorrow, and which not man dries away but death or God, — then Victor during the farewell looked upon her with the mute question, "Shall I say nothing to our beloved?" — Clotilda's soul remained most erect under burdens, and she never appeared greater than through tears, as the stars in a heaven full of rain come out brighter and larger; she looked up to heaven as if asking, "Couldst thou, all-gracious One, crush us so deeply?" — then she weighed with oppressed heart the heavy grief, — then she found it too great for utterance — and too great for endurance, — and she no longer believed it, and said ambiguously, with wet eyes and with ambiguous smile, "No, Victor, we shall surely all meet again!"

Victor went off not long before the two crowned bathing-guests arrived with a considerable retinue. — I remark it with quite as little resentment as Victor felt on the occasion, that Agatha, notwithstanding the maternal example, broke off entirely, first with Victor, i. e. with the Antipode and Anti-Christ of her beloved brother; secondly and still more with Clotilda.

It may be stated, that I suppressed the foregoing letter of Emanuel in the first edition, for the simple reason — for I had it in my hands early enough, as well as many other documents of this history, which nevertheless (for reasons) will never be published — that I feared it would be affecting; a susceptible soul finds, as it is, too many sorrows in this volume! — But for that very reason we will not leave out what there was, in the first edition, of the comic, and accordingly I proceed.

We readers will, with Victor, take leave of the Chamberlain, who, with his half upright eyebrows, — they incline to each other at the bridge of the nose in the form of the mathematical sign of the root,* — parts from us with true, obliging courteousness. I know, when we are gone, he will let us find justice, and will make too much out of us; for he never calumniates either from malice or from levity, and whom he calumniates, him he has a serious intention to destroy, because he would rather make one unhappy than paint him black. — When I saw him bend down so to us, I executed in thought a half-satire upon him, whereof the true and serious purport may be this: that men are actually created for the purpose of making themselves as crooked as the *spiritus asper* † is. I do not exactly build much upon this, that geometers have written: If the Gods assumed a form, it must be the most perfect, that of a circle; I might,

* That part of the nose happens also to be called its root in German. — Tr.

† The rough breathing (in Greek) which has a crooked shape, thus: ( ‘ ). — Tr.

to be sure, draw this conclusion from that, that a crooked back is at least an approximation to the divine form, because it is an arc of a circle, — but I do not care to; for the physical is child's play on this subject, and only of consequence in so far as it partly indicates the crooking and creeping of the soul, and partly (e. g. by the narrowing of the chest) promotes it. Even at court they would dispense with the external bending, if they could be sure that the inner and nobler crook of the disposition were there, without the sign; for as, according to Kant, the subjection and casting down of our self-conceit is a requirement of the purer and the Christian morality: accordingly one who has absolutely no moral excellences must with his self-consciousness thereof stoop still lower than to lowliness, which even the virtuous has; he must sink to that which I call a noble crawling. I confess I do not despise the practice which the little rules of breeding insure herein, and which besides undertakes to be nothing but virtue in trifles, the rules, namely, that one shall bow when one contradicts, — when one praises, — when one receives an insult, — when one offers one, — when one bows another down, — when one would just precisely play the Devil. But it is well that such a virtue of crooking has its own places of exercise, and does not depend on chance. At court a man with straight body and spirit would be cast out as dead, in the court sense, like a crab with a straight tail, which only a dead one carries. If formerly hermits chose lowly cells, in order not to stand upright, a man of the world does not need this; lofty banquet-halls, temples of pleasure, dancing-halls, press him down so much the lower, the higher they are themselves. — It were bad, if this so important virtue of bending downward presupposed a special strength of mind or body, which no one, indeed, can bestow on himself; but exactly the reverse is the case; it will have only weakness, which with horses is not so, for they can no longer let down the tail when its sinews are cut. If the Pharisees carried lead in their caps in order to make it easier for them to stoop,* the lead which one brings into the world with him, and which lies in the head, renders perhaps still greater services. Hence it is a fine arrangement, that great souls, for which, as for tall statures, stooping is disagreeable, fortunately (but for their punishment) never come to anything, whereas mediocre ones, who make nothing of it, flourish and put forth a goodly crown: thus have I often seen in the baking of bread, that every moderate loaf in the oven rose and arched beautifully, but the big one remained sitting there flat and miserable. — But we should be subjects for pity, if a virtue which constitutes the worth of the civilian, the virtue of becoming not merely like children, but like fœtuses, which double themselves up in the mother's body, — if this could only prosper in the highest place, as one must almost suppose, since the courtier *after* the fall goes upright again on his estate, — whereas the serpent *before* the fall and during the temptation did not creep. — But in all civil relations educational institutions for *crooklings* are provided; everywhere there stretches out in the air now a spiritual and now a secular arm, which gives us the regular crook, and still higher are the longest of all set, which reach over whole nations. The scholar himself bends over his writing-desk under

* The Pharisees did it, — like certain Jews, who also always walked bent, and so were called *crooklings*, — in order to leave a little room for God who fills the whole earth. — *Ancient and Modern Judaism*, Vol. II. p. 47.

the birth of introductions and courtly dedications and opinions. By the mere hoariness of old age the body as well as the spirit ripens to a bony humpback, and the lower clergy, because they are always looking downward into the grave, work themselves into the crooked posture. — I conclude with the consolation that bending does not *exclude* inflation, but *includes* it; just as the circle, of which one is a section, runs innumerable times around the swollen surface of the sphere. . . . .

I would truly have written over this "Extra-leaf" that title as a heading, — so that the reader might have skipped it, — had I not wished that he should read it, by way of diverting himself, and of sharing more easily with my Victor his dismal hours. For every stroke of the clock is a death-bell sounding out a dead march for the wreck of his fairer hours.

The very evening he entered into Flachsenfingen, stories quite as ugly as probable came to his ears; Mat had told the Apothecary a good deal; but this time I give in to his reports.

That is to say, the Parson, so soon as he heard of the betrothal, had set out for the city in order to frustrate murderous deeds and duels on the part of his son. As during his dressing the whole of his travelling uniform did not lie at the very instant before his eyes, he threw off to his family light red-crayon-drawings of the bloody scenes and bloody scaffolds, upon which, he said, he reckoned, as he probably, on account of the detention in dressing, should arrive too late. The shrunk boot which Appel had dried a little at the fire could not be got on to the foot, — Eymann gasped, — pulled, — "It is possible," said he, "that they are at this very moment letting fly at each other"; — at last he let his arms fall back powerless, and sat calmly and firmly bolt upright, and waited silently for them to fire at him and question him. When nothing came, he said with fury: "Whatever Satan it may be that has got into my house, and has made my boots shrink up so, (I would undertake to get my foot into a leather queue, through a needle's eye, but not into one of them,) he has the murder of my child upon his soul. — Is there then no child of misery about here, that will just polish my heel for me with a little soft soap?" — While they were forcing in his foot, he saw Appel still busily ironing away at his shirt-bosom: "Enough, Appel! very good!" — said he, — "I really shall not unbutton myself." She glided away lightly on the flat, which was, as it were, the skate under her hand. "Daughter, thy father wants his shirt. The life of thy own brother is put in jeopardy by thee, — it is just as if thou wert giving him the finishing stroke!" She glided nimbly only once more on her hand-skate over the whole, and then handed it to him with pleasure.

On the way the chaplain sketched to himself a safe and sound plan of proceeding in the business. He would in the beginning make no disclosure of the engagement to Flamin, — then he was going to read to him only the penitential text upon the Maienthal duel, — then to extort from him the *Urphede* or solemn oath to keep quiet, — and only at the very last to come out with the report. While he was thinking over the plan and the danger, he ran himself into a hotter and hotter sweat of anxiety. Just as he had once, by a long drawing out of consequences, driven himself and a patient who had a slight buzzing in the ears to such a pitch, that they both expected the next minute apoplexy and paralysis of half one side: so, in the present instance, by a picturesque treatment of the details of an *imaginary* duel he at last removed from himself so thoroughly all doubts about one's having already *transpired* that he passed in through the city gate with the firm conviction that the Regency-Councillor was lying either in chains or on the bier. "Thank God that I see thee without wounds and without chains," was the expression that escaped from him on his entrance; and he had almost spoiled his whole business plan, or at least reversed it. Flamin understood him to refer to the first duel. Eymann could so much the more easily follow out the management of the case and phlebotomical table of rules which he had laid down, and, so to speak, fight a duel with the duel. The silent son had nothing to oppose to him — but light beer. While he was getting it, the Parson had pulled at the knobs of all the canes to see whether there were no sword-canes. A pistol-like tinder-box at a distance was a suspicious object to him. A double-barrelled gun on the wall near by, with its — stock aimed at him, took away much of his courage. Flamin excused his taciturnity on the ground of legal *plethora* and over-freighting of the brain, and pointed to the pile of criminal documents before him. When he was called upon to give him an extemporaneous abstract of them, and when of course the war-cries *prison, blood-guiltiness, avenging sword,* whizzed like a hissing rain of bullets round Eymann's ears; then did the agony which he aggravated by the more rapid *douche* of the pale ale expand itself so mightily within him that the double-barrelled gun had to be hung up in the chamber: "I get nothing by it," said he, "if it goes off and bursts, and the lock flies into my face, or if the stock actually kills me." Now he began in a compound fit of emotion and intoxication to weep and to exhort:

that a man ought to think on the fifth petition in the Lord's prayer, — that a country clergyman could with ill-grace preach to his spiritual fold reconciliation, if he had a son in the city, who during the sermon was fighting a duel, — and that Flamin must never say he was his son, if he either got or gave the fatal shot in a duel. — Nothing so easily drew the storm-wind of Flamin's anger out of its cavern, as a doleful voice and long religious edicts. "For God's sake," cried Flamin, "let that be enough now, — God shall punish me, I will be lost to all eternity, I swear to you, if I ever touch *him* even." This oath which escaped him was magnificent marsh-mallow-paste and soft ice-cream for the heated court-chaplain, who from forgetfulness of his order of business now adopted the opinion that the betrothal was already full well known to the Regency-Councillor. "Thinkest thou not, son," said he joyfully, "that such an oath refreshes and comforts an anxious father like the latter rain, especially as, since *her* betrothal to him, I have had absolutely nothing better to look for than murder and assassination? Am I right or not?" — Flamin flung up by a single question the cover from this murderous armed spectre of his heart, — and now he heard his father no more; pale, full of convulsions, he sat there in silence, — the back of the chair cracked under his pressure, — he twisted and tied his watch-chain round his fingers, and tore it off and mashed the remnant again round the bruised finger and crushed it to pieces, — in his glassy eyes stood two heavy, rigid, cold drops, — his heart shrank up empty and spiritless before an approaching and frightful *death-chill*, which, when a friendship is murdered in a bosom, always precedes the burning wrath thereby excited. — Ah, who of us does not pity the unhappy, forsaken soul? — Eymann went away deceived, and took this calm for mere calm, and the broken and choked voice for emotion.

And in this bloody state he was found by Matthieu, who had just come to announce to the Regency-Councillor, as if with twenty-four blowing postilions (from a note of the wife of the Chamberlain), Victor's victory over the whole of them. This fellow now first transformed the iceberg into a volcano, and made Flamin in his pent-up fury feel as if he could shatter to pieces one quarter of the world against another.

Victor heard nothing now for some days. Flamin locked himself up. Matthieu visited him often, but not the house of the Apothecary. The crowned pair arrived at last at the baths of St. Luna.

Thus all remained till the morning when Victor took leave of the Apothecary to go to Maienthal before the curtain of a heavy scene. Here the Apothecary could not deny himself the pleasure of depriving the Court-Physician of his, by imparting to him the (probably false) intelligence, that the Page had challenged the Chamberlain on account of his breach of promise with regard to Clotilda. Little or no importance is to be attached to the report, for the reason, if for no other, that the Apothecary wanted only to cough out his own praise and disguise it in the shape of a commendation of Victor, that the latter had known how, with such infinite finesse, to carry out *his* recent hints of undermining the Evangelist. The hints were, as will be recollected, the two propositions of becoming the lover of the Princess and the husband of Clotilda, in order to gain the Prince, and thus, as a swine does a rattlesnake, to swallow Mat with impunity. One must forgive the soul of Victor, gnawed by a worm's-nest of afflictions, for blazing up and attacking Zeusel with an eye full of the profoundest contempt, "I know not who would deserve to listen to such propositions, — unless it is he who can make them."

My correspondent leaves off abruptly and sadly with the words: "Late in the evening, Victor arrived with swollen eyes at Maienthal, to see whether on the next day his noblest-teacher and greatest friend would wither away." — — We can all conceive what must be the embrace of a loved one a few paces from his grave. The friend who threatens us with his death takes a painful hold of our soul, even if we doubt it. We can all imagine the wet eye which Victor must have cast on the still blooming scene of his withered rose-feast. — What consoles him is the improbability of the predicted death, since Emanuel is as well as usual, and since suicide is still more impossible with this pious spirit, who long since compared the suicide to the lobster, who cannot draw out the claw which he himself in his stupidity has jammed and crushed with its mate, but snaps it off. — May the reader bring with him to the description of the longest day,* which I am to make all alone under the exalting stillness of night, a heart like that of the East Indian, which like old temples is dumb and dark, but vast and full of holy images!

* Thus did Emanuel always name St. John's day, though not with perfect astronomical accuracy.

## 38. DOG-POST DAY.

THE SUBLIME HOUR BEFORE MIDNIGHT. — THE BLISSFUL AFTER-MIDNIGHT. — THE SOFT EVENING.

O-DAY I present Emanuel's last day (which now lies cooled off and extinguished among the days of eternity) with pale outlines to the fantasies of men. My hand trembles and my eye burns before the scenes which in funeral veils glide around me and lift their veils so near to me. — — I shut myself up to-night, — I hear nothing but my thoughts, — I see nothing but the night-suns which move across the heavens, — I forget the weaknesses and the stains of my heart, that I may get the courage to lift up my head as if I were good, as if I dwelt on the height where around the great man like constellations lie only God, Eternity, and Virtue. But I say to them who are better, — to the silent great heart, which *increases* its obligations in *fulfilling* them, and which satisfies itself *as its conscience grows* only with daily increasing merits, — to the lofty men who have warmly pressed the hand of death, who can calmly ask him, when he walks round on morning-meadows, " Seekest thou me to-day?"— to the panting soul which cools itself under the *cypress-tree*, — to the men with tears, with dreams, with wings, — to all these I say, " Kinsmen of my Emanuel, your brother stretches out his hand after you through the shortest night; grasp it, he would fain bid you farewell!"

THE SUBLIME HOUR BEFORE MIDNIGHT.

Victor rose sadly from his dreams, in which he had seen nothing but graves and funeral piles for his friend; but he gathered secret hopes at the morning-greeting, as he saw him step forth into his alleged death-morning without fever, without oppression, without change. His only concern was about the impression which the disappointed hope of departure would make upon the heart of the beloved friend, already half torn from the earthly soil and laid bare from earthly environment. The latter, on the contrary, still held fast to his dreams, to which even his nightly ones gave nourishment; and he looked yearningly into the starless blue, and calculated the long road to the twelfth night-hour, when out of heaven should peer forth the stars, and death with that dark, immense mantle of his, in which he bears us through his cold realm. His heart lay in a sweet siesta, which proceeded partly from bodily exhaustion and from the beauty of the day. His inner calm, never so great and magical as in souls in which whirlwinds and hurricanes have swept to and fro, overspread his whole being with a bliss of yearning which in other eyes than his would have melted in tear-drops.

O Rest! thou soft word! — autumnal bloom of Eden! Moonlight of the spirit! Rest of the soul, when wilt thou hold our head, that it may be still, and our heart, that it may cease beating? Ah, ere the one grows pale and the other stiff, thou comest often and goest often, and only down below with sleep and with death thou abidest, whereas above, men with the greatest wings, like birds of paradise, are whirled about most of all by the storms!

The tranquillity with which Emanuel played out the star-part of life, even to the last catch-word, — with which he packed up everything — set all to rights — gave all directions — took leave of all, — stirred up tears and tempests together in his tormented friend. His heart had been, indeed, dragged till it was sore over a stony road, but its inflammations were now softly cooled off by the thought of death; yet he could not — though with the greatest incredulity about Emanuel's death — endure to hear it, when Emanuel committed to him at a distance the blind Julius, from whom this death was concealed, with the low-spoken words, "Hold him dear as I do, protect, provide for the poor child, till thou canst deliver him over to Lord Horion." His trembling hands could hardly take from him a packet to that lord, which the friend handed to him with tender eyes and with the words, "When these seals are opened, then my oaths have ceased and thou wilt learn all." For his tender conscience allowed him to conceal only the *import*, not the *existence* of secrets. — It will not astonish us, as Victor's veins received one wound after another, that, in order not to increase their bleeding by agitations, he begged the flute-player not to play to-day; music would, on this day, have had too much power over his dissolved heart.

The morning they spent in farewell-visits to old paths, bowers, and heights; but Emanuel performed not here the sharp, passionate climax-part of the fifth act; he broke not forth, upon an earth where death grazes, into any unphilosophical outcry because he should not see the flowers plucked and the grain cut, nor the green fruit grow yellow; but with a higher rapture, which beyond the earthy spring promised itself still fairer ones, he took his leave of every flower, went through every leafy winding and shadowy night-piece, drew out of every mirroring pond his transfigured form lying as it were in the earth, and showed a more affectionate attentiveness to nature, now that he hoped to-night to come nearer to Him who created it. He sought and Victor shunned every occasion to speak of all this. "Only not for the last time!" said the latter. "Not?" said Emanuel. — "Does not everything happen only once and for the last time? — Do not Autumn and Time, as well as Death, separate us from all? — Does not all part from us, even if we do not part from it? — Time is nothing but a death with softer, thinner sickles; every minute is the autumn of the past one, and the *second* world will be the spring of a *third*. —— Ah, when I one day retire again from the flowery surface of a second, and when on the heavenly death-day I see the twilight of the memory of two lives, —— O in the future lies a groundwork for infinite bliss as well as woe, why does man shrink with awe only before this?" — Victor disputed the immortality of memory. "Without memory," said Emanuel, "there is no life, only existence, no years, only seconds, — no *I*, only representations of it. — A being breaks up into as many million beings as it has thoughts, — memory is merely consciousness of present existence." * — Even the Poet philosophizes at least for poetry and against philosophy. — Victor thought: "Thou good man! to myself, not to thee, I made these objections."

It was towards noon; the sky was clear, but sultry;

* See Dr. Thomas Brown's Mental Philosophy on the subject of consciousness. — Tr.

the flowers announced by their shutting up the gathering of the electric fires; all meadows were altars of incense, and fragrances went forth as prophets of the storm-clouds. With the *physical* stormy material there accumulated in Victor a corresponding *moral* element; — he reflected that often a hot day ended the life of consumptive patients; — he confounded at times the *bitterness* of parting with its *probability;* for man, deceived by the *aerial perspective* of fear, fancies a shape of terror so much the *nearer*, the *larger* it is; he wept at the very thought that he might weep; but nevertheless reason would have held the upperhand of the feelings, had not the following occurrence benumbed both.

In Maienthal there dwelt a madman whom they called by no other name than that of the crazy skeleton. For three reasons he was called so: first, because he was an anatomical preparation of leanness; secondly, because he carried round the fixed idea, that Death was after him and wanted to seize and abduct him by the left hand, which he therefore concealed; thirdly, because he gave out that he could see when any one was going to die soon by the look of the face, which in that case was already overspread with the indentations and abscesses of corruption. In Moritz's experimental psychology * a similar man is described, who is also said to be able to detect the forerunners of death and its triturating hand on faces which appear to others smooth and ruddy, whereas he sees them seamed with the lunar caustic of corruption. — This skeleton it was, which, on the night of the fourth Whitsuntide day, when Clotilda was in the churchyard, cried out, Death! I am already buried.† — Victor and Eman-

* In the second part of the second volume.

† Page 266. — Tr.

uel went home during the striking of the twelfth hour, and on their way passed a hill, whereon the skeleton sat agitated; the left hand, at which Death grasped, buried itself deep into the opposite arm-pit: "Brrr!" it said, shaking its head at Emanuel, "he has thee, but not me! Nothing but mould is hanging on thee! The eyes are gone! Brr!"

The words of the insane are, to a man who listens at the gate of the invisible world, more memorable than those of the wise man, just as he listens more attentively to sleepers than to the waking, to the sick than to the well. Victor's blood stiffened under the ice-cold clutch at his warm life. The crazy skeleton ran off, shielding the left hand with the right. Victor took his friend's left, looked up at the warm sun, and sought to conceal and to warm himself and could say nothing. Down near the margin of the deep-blue heaven little clouds smoked up, the germs of an evening tempest; and in the sultry air nothing but vermin flew abroad.

Emanuel was more quiet and almost troubled, but it was not the anxiety of fear, but that uneasiness of expectation with which we always look upon the folds and flutterings of the curtain of great scenes. The stinging sun kept the couple at home. To Emanuel, oppressed by the sultry atmosphere, the last afternoon was almost too long. But his friend saw all the time hanging in this atmospheric vault a mouldering countenance, which seemed to work its way into the beloved fresh one, and he continually heard the crazy skeleton repeating in his ear, "His eyes are out!"

In the sultry stillness, when the sun dug and charged the mining pits of the thunder, and when the two friends ventured before the ears of the blind Julius to speak only with looks of to-day's future, towards four o'clock a fanning evening-breeze came up, which refreshed all drooping wings and heads. Emanuel let in these cool waves, which ran lullingly and comfortingly over the bent flowers at the window, and flowed down along the wavering folds of the curtains, and strayed and plashed through the fragrant foliage of the room. Then came an infinite stillness, a dissolving bliss, an inexpressible yearning into Emanuel's heart. The joys of his childhood, the features of his mother, the images of Indian fields, all beloved, mouldering forms, the whole gliding reflection of his youth's morning, flowed along glimmeringly before him; — a melancholy longing for his native land, for his dead friends, distended his bosom with sweet, distressful emotions. That evergreen palm-grove of youthful memory he laid as a cooling herb around his own and Horion's brows, and brought over the whole first circle of his existence out of the Indian Eden into this narrow housing before the two latest objects of his affection. But as he thus heaped up the ashes of the Phœnixes of joy on the altar of the evening-sun, — as he thus at his exodus looked back over all the Elysian fields of his life as they lay behind each other, — as the whole of earth and life, overspread with morning dew and morning redness, transformed themselves before him into the glimmering playground of humanity; — then was he unable to master any longer his emotion and his melted heart, and in a blissful agitation, in a trembling gratitude to the Eternal, he begged the blind youth to take his flute and let the *Song of Ecstasy*, which he always had played for himself on the morning of the new year and of his birthday, sound after him as an echo of his dying life.

Julius took the flute. Horion went out under a loud-rustling tree and looked into the setting sun. Emanuel placed himself at the breezy window opposite the purple stream of the evening light, and the song of rapture began and flowed in streams into his heart and round the sinking sun.

And as the tones of the spheres seemed to well out from the sun, which in the evening redness, like a swan dissolved in melodies, died of rapture before God in gold-haze and dew of joy, — and as all the flowers wherewith the Eternal goodness covers our heart, and all the blissful fields through which its gentle hand conducts uncertain man, flew by before Emanuel like angels, — and as he saw the future heavens, into which the way of life leads, drawing nearer, — and as he saw these infinite arms cover all wounded hearts, stretch over all millenniums, bear all worlds and yet even him too, him, puny son of earth; — O then was it impossible for him longer to restrain his full heart; it burst with gratitude, and from his eyes again fell the first tear-drops after long, long years. These holy drops he wiped not away; in them the evening-red ran to a blazing sea; the flute died away; Victor found his eyes still glistening; Emanuel said, "O see, I weep for joy at the thought of my Maker!" — — Then were there between these exalted men, on this holy spot, no more words, — death had lost his form, — a sublime sorrow deadened the pangs of separation, — the sun, over which the earth had rolled, touched with his erect beams the heavens and the night and the bottom of the clouds, — the earth glimmered magically like a dream-landscape, and yet it was easy to quit it, for the other dream-landscapes covered the sky.

The earths of night (the planets) had already come out, the suns of night (the fixed stars) had already come forth after them, the moon had already enveloped itself in the southeast storm: when Emanuel saw that it was time to end the scenes of the valley and go up to his Tabor, to give Death the wing-casing of his soul. Hesitating, he begged Victor to go forward a little, that he might not see his parting with the blind one, and haply betray himself by sympathy; for Victor had represented to the blind one the journey into the other world as only one upon this earth. He stationed himself unhappily out before the hushed sultry fields through which once had passed the rivers of paradise of his love, on which he had once at Clotilda's side seen fairer evenings; on the earth was the stillness of death, as in a church by night, only a leaden cloud, bent down toward the earth, blustered round the heavens, and Death seemed to go from cloud to cloud and array them for battle.

At last he heard Julius weeping. Emanuel came flying out, but in his eyes stood heavier drops than his former ones. And as the forsaken blind one turned away his dark head from his friends in the house-door-way, either because he knew not which way they had gone or would listen to know, then was Victor barely able, for inward sadness, to call back to the bowed form, which dwelt in a double night, that he would return after twelve o'clock.

In the bald evening greeting, "Good night, a pleasant sleep," which Emanuel gave and received, there was more stuff for tears than in whole elegies and farewell-speeches; so true it is that words are only the inscriptions upon our hour,* and the ripieno†-voices of the scoring of our key-notes.

* I. e. On the dial-plate of our inner life. — Tr.

† Complementary parts in music. — Tr.

So soon as Emanuel came out before the night heavens, before the hurricane chained thereto and before his death-mountain, angels lifted up again his softened soul, — he saw death descend from heaven and set up the liberty-tree on his grave, — he saw the friendly stars draw nearer, and they were the heavenly eyes of his friends and of all blessed beings. Victor dared not disturb his poetic hopes by any reasons; much rather was he himself from hour to hour drawn deeper into the belief of his death; at least he feared that to-day's storm of rapture might rend asunder the frail dwelling of this fair heart and of its sighs, and that death would creep about the noble soul till by its very wings, as it rose in its ecstasy, he could pluck it away from life, as children go round and round the butterfly till at last it lifts its wings folded on one another into their predatory fingers.

Emanuel delayed by circuitous paths the ascent of the mountain, in order to raise his broken friend, whose eyes were no longer dry, from one sun to the other, so that in that high position he might look down from the midst of lights upon this shadowy earth and hardly notice the corpse of his friend on account of its littleness. "Yes, this is the reason," said he, "why the earth is every day darkened, like the cages of birds, that we may in the dark more easily catch the higher melodies. — Thoughts which the day makes a dark smoke and vapor stand round about us in the night as flames and lights, as the column which floats over Vesuvius appears a pillar of cloud by day and is a pillar of fire by night." Victor perceived the design, namely, of consoling him, and became the more disconsolate and continued silent.

They did not go up on the side of the mountain to the weeping-birch, but over its slowly ascending ridge. They overlooked the theatre of night, over which the moon and the storm were coming up under a veil; Emanuel stopped and said: "O look up and see the eternally sparkling morning-meadows which lie around the throne of the Eternal! Had never a star shone out of heaven, only then would man lay himself down with anguish in his last sleep, on a dark earth built over like a burial vault without an opening." Before eyes which were fastened on suns, flashing glowworms trailed by, and a bat whizzed after a gray night-butterfly, — three St. John's day fires, lighted by superstition, brought three distant hills out of night, — all life slept under its leaf, under its twig, nearer to its mother, and in the dreams that were strewed about lay storms, — fishes tumbled up like corpses on the surface of the water as forerunners of the thunder.

Suddenly Emanuel began, with an ill-fitting, not sufficiently controlled voice: "Verily we should stand more composedly beside the genius who lets fall the last sands of slumber on the eyes of our loves, if they did not afterward sleep out their last sleep in church vaults, in churchyards, but upon meadows, under the open heavens, or as mummies in chambers. . . . . Now then, my beloved," they heard already the waving of the weeping-birch, "control thy fantasy; thou wilt see near the birch-tree my resting-pit open; I have for four weeks sown and clothed it with flowers which are now mostly in bloom, — thou wilt lay me thus to-morrow, without any *other* preparation, in my night-dress among the flowers, — and cover it up to-morrow, — but do not, thou good man, give my little flower-piece such hard names as other men do, — to-morrow, I say; to-day go immediately home to *thy* Julius, when I . . . ." (*am dead*, he would have said, but could not find for emotion the soft paraphrase). —

Ah! Horion with a sigh tore his agonized eyes out from the cold open grotto of his beloved, and could not look down to its blooming flowers. He sobbed aloud and looked out through tears faintly into Emanuel's face, to see whether he was living or dying. Two glowworms crossed one another in glimmering curves above the grave, they settled down beside it, and were extinguished, for their light ceases with their motion.

The thunder now struck into Victor's wounds with its first clap, — a dissolving lightning covered the Eastern horizon, and the flame ran over the Alpine ridges, — the lightning-rod on the powder-house glowed, its alarm-bells rang, the ignes-fatui played about the tower, and in mid-air a hovering luminous point moved fearfully towards it.

In Maienthal eleven o'clock was called, — at twelve Emanuel believed he should be gone hence. At last Emanuel, unmanned himself by another's sorrow, fell upon his friend and said: "What hast thou further to say to me, my beloved, my inexpressibly dear friend? — My hours are fled, — our farewell approaches, — say thine, and then disturb not my dying. Be still, when death climbs the mountain, and send no lamentations after me, when he takes me up. — What hast thou more to say to me, my eternally beloved?" — "Nothing more, thou angel of heaven! nor can I," said Victor with bleeding and exhausted heart, and laid his oppressed head with streams of tears on Emanuel's shoulder.

"Now then break off thy heart from mine, and farewell, — be happy, be good, be great. I have loved thee very much, I shall love thee once more and then forever. Good, faithful one, — mortal like me, immortal like me!"

The storm-bells tolled more violently, — the hovering luminous point advanced upon the powder-house, — all the covered cloud-volcanoes bellowed side by side and flung their flames together, and the thunders passed like alarm-bells between them, — the two friends lay in each other's arms, close, mute, gasping, clasping, trembling before the last word.

"O speak once more, my Horion, and take leave of thy friend, — only say to me, Rest well! and leave the dying."

Horion said, "Rest well!" and left him. His tears ceased and his sighs were hushed. The thunder came to a fearful pause. Nature was mutely ordering her chaos in the tempest. Not a flash gleamed through the funeral pile in heaven. Only the funeral tolling of the alarm-bells on the lightning-rod continued to speak, and the luminous point to creep onward.

Under the wide stillness lay sleep, dreams, and a friend's inconsolable heart.

In this stillness of eternity Emanuel went up without any other hand in his to the high gate which soars away in black darkness above time.

Silence is the speech of the world of spirits, the starry heaven its nunnery-grating, — but behind this nunnery-grating appeared now no spirit, not even God.

The moment was coming when man looks upon his body and then on his individual self, and then shudders. — The *I* stands alone beside its shadow, — a foam-globe of being trembles, snaps, and collapses, and one hears the bubble vanish and *is* one himself.

Emanuel peered into Eternity, it looked like a long night.

He looked round him to see whether he cast a shadow, — a shadow casts no shadow.

Ah! a mute lays man in the cradle, a mute stretches him out in the grave. — When he has a joy, it looks as if a sleeper smiled, — when he weeps and wails, it looks like weeping in one's sleep. — We all look up to heaven and pray for solace; but overhead in the endless blue there is no voice for our heart, — nothing appears, nothing consoles us, nothing answers us. —

And so we die. . . . .

— O All-gracious One! we die more happily; only the poor Emanuel wrestled in the silent darkness with fierce thoughts which for so long a time he had not seen, and which clutched at his paling countenance. But these masks flee away, when a friendly fraternal face appears before thee and embraces thee. — Horion raised himself up and warmed again his bowed friend by a mute farewell. A storm-wind precipitated itself out of the clear west into the dumb, laboring hell, and chased out all the lightnings and all the thunders. Lo, at that moment the bright moon flew out from the backward-drifted mass of cloud like an angel of peace into the unstained blue, — *then in the light Emanuel stood distinguished from his shadow*, — then did the moon illuminate a rainbow of pale color grains, which in the Southeast (the gate to the East Indies) penetrated through the dark water-columns, and arched itself over the Alps, — then Emanuel saw again, as previously, the Jacob's ladder leaning against the earthly night, — then came rapture without measure, and he cried with outspread arms: "Ah, yonder in the *East*, in the East, over the road to my *native land*, there glows the arch of triumph, there opens the gate of glory, there the dying march through." . . .

And as just then it struck twelve o'clock, he spread out his hand ecstatically towards heaven, which was blue above the mountains, and toward the moon, which reposed serenely beside the tempest, and cried, breaking into blissful tears, "Thanks, Eternal One, for my first life, for all my joys, for this fair earth." —

The flute tones of Julius floated around Maienthal, and he looked down upon the earth.

"And be thou ever blest, thou good earth, thou good mother-land, bloom, ye fields of Hindostan, farewell, thou glowing Maienthal, with thy flowers and with thy people, — and ye brothers, all of you, after a long smile, come and blissfully follow me. Now, O Eternal One, take me up, and console the *two* survivors."

The death angels stood on all the clouds, and drew their glittering swords out of the nights, — one thunder clapped after another, as if one prison-door of this earthly life after another were flung open.

The terrible luminous point had crept out of mid-air into the powder-house.

The death-hour had already passed, and yet life had not.

Emanuel trembled with yearning and apprehension, because he felt as yet no sign of dying, — moved his hands as if he would give them to some one, — stared into the lightnings as if he would draw them upon him. . . .

"Death! seize me," he cried, beside himself, — "ye dead friends! O father! O mother! tear my heart away, take me, — I cannot — cannot live any longer." — —

At that moment a blazing, rattling globe flew up into the tempest, and the powder-house shot itself to pieces like an undermined hell. — The explosion threw the flaming Emanuel pale into his flowery grave; the whole thundering east trembled; the moon and the rainbow were darkened. . . . .

### THE BLISSFUL AFTER-MIDNIGHT.

Victor, cast headlong, senseless, at last bestirred his arm and felt therewith the cold face, on which to-day the crazy skeleton had read this night beforehand, and which projected above the grave, turned toward heaven. He threw himself upon it and pressed his face to the pale one. Before his tears had forced their way through the hard grief, the clouds carried back their fire-buckets and their funeral torches, and transparent foam-fleeces softly overflowed the moon and settled down at last over the whole valley and over the still couple in a thousand warm drops, which so easily remind man of his own tears. The blowing up of the powder-house by one of the three Englishmen had broken up the naval engagement of the burning clouds.

The dismembered tempest had drifted about in little clouds and stood above the midnight-red in the northeast, when the cold numbness of the shock still held the two men fastened together; at last a hot hand glided down from above between their faces, and a timid voice asked, "Are you asleep?"

"O Julius," said Horion, "come down unto the grave, thy Emanuel is dead." . . . .

I care not to count the dismal minutes that let two wretched beings lie bound by the thorn-girdle of anguish to a pallid one. But brighter moments came, which first drove every smallest cloud out of the sky and wiped clean the tarnished moon, and then opened the hot eyes before the cleansed and cooled silvery night.

"Ah, he has perhaps only fainted," said Victor after a long while. They raised themselves up with a sigh. Wearily they drew their beloved out of the grave. They would fain carry him down to his dwelling, in order there to bring back again from its *solstice* this fair soul, as the St. John's sun would return from his. With the slight energies which grief had still spared them, and with the little light which still entered into two wet eyes, they struggled along with the crippled angel, while two laboring shadows beside them frightfully carried a third in the glimmer, from the mountain down into the meadows. Here Victor went alone into the village, in order, perhaps, to provide a more cheerful carriage than a hearse. The blind one stayed himself by a birch-tree, Emanuel slept like the other flowers, and upon them, before the moon. . . . But suddenly Julius heard the dead man speak and graze him as he passed through the grass; and, pursued by terror, he fled. . . . .

— Genius of dreams! thou that walkest through the nebulous sleep of mortals and bringest up before the lonely soul imprisoned in a corpse the happy islands of childhood! O thou that therein restorest to our mouldered friends the bloom of the cheek and showest to our poor frenzied heart past heavens and reflections of Eden and undulating lawns, on clouds! — Magic Genius! enter into this holy night before a man who is not asleep, and turn thy crape-covered glass to my open eye, that I may see therein, and paint, the Elysian world of light which struggles with our earthly shadow, as a pale Luna, in the double eclipse! * — —

The enraptured voice of the dead man cried: "Hail to thee, thou still Elysium! O thou glimmering land of rest! receive the new shade. Ah, how softly thou glowest, — how softly thou breathest, — how softly thou reposest!" . . . .

* The sun when eclipsed by the moon is beheld by us in a crape-covered [or smoked] glass.

Emanuel's eyes had opened; but in his brain burned the Elysian delirious idea that he had died and waked up in the second world. O thou over-blest! and indeed a glittering Eden did encircle thee, — ah, this glow, this breath, this fragrance, this repose, was too beautiful for an earth. The moon weaved over with silver threads, as with flying summer-gossamer, the green of night, — from leaf to leaf, from trees to trees stretched the sparkling veil of the illuminated rain, — over all waters floated glimmering banks of vapor, — a gentle fanning threw jewels from the twigs into the silver streams, — the trees and the mountains rose like giants into the night, — the everlasting sky stood over the falling sparks, over the fleeting fragrances, over the playing leaves, it alone unchangeable, with fixed suns, with the eternal world-studded vault, great, cool, radiant and blue. — Never did a valley so glimmer, so exhale, so whisper, so enchant before. . . . .

Emanuel embraced the sparkling soil and cried out from a burning breast, subdued and stammering with rapture: "Ah, is it true, then? do I really hold thee, my native land? — Ay, in such fields of rest wounds are healed, tears are stilled, no sighs demanded, no sins committed, here in sooth the little human heart dissolves for overfulness of rapture and creates itself anew to dissolve again. . . . . Thus have I long since imagined thee, blessed, magical, dazzling land, that borderest on my earth. . . . . O dear earth! where mayest thou be?"

He lifted his intoxicated eye to the star-bedewed heaven, and saw the low-sunken moon hanging faint and yellow in the south; this he took for the earth, from which he supposed death had borne him into this Elysium. Here his voice dissolved into emotion at the beloved earliest garden of his life, and he addressed the earth flying overhead above the stars:—

"Globe of tears! Dwelling of dreams! Land full of shadows and spots! — Ah, on thy broad shadowy spots * the good children of men will be at this moment trembling and sinking! . . . A ring of clouds † encircles thee, and they see not Elysium. . . . . Ah, how silently thou bearest through the still, blessed heavens thy battle-cry — thy storms — thy graves; thy enveloping atmosphere shuts in like a coffin all the voices of wailing round about thee, and thou glidest with thy bowed and enshrouded ones only as a pale, still ball away above Elysium! . . .

"Ah, ye precious ones, my Horion! my Julius! Ye are still up yonder in the tempest, ye cover up my corpse, ye look weeping towards Heaven and cannot see Elysium. . . . . O that you were already through the wet cloud of life! — but perhaps ye have already been long sleeping and waking, perhaps time goes otherwise on earth than in eternity. — Ah! that you might come down into the still pastures!" He saw in the magically magnifying glimmer two forms walking. "Oh, who is it?" he cried, flying to meet them. "O father! O mother! Are you here?" — But when he came nearer, he sank into four other arms, and stammered, "Blessed, blessed are we now, my Horion! my Julius!" — At last he said: "Where are my parents and my brothers and Clotilda and the three Brahmins? know they not that their Dahore is in Elysium?"

Victor beheld disconsolately the delirious ecstasy of his beloved, and said neither yes nor no. The latter

* The seas of our earth look in the distance like the spots of the moon.

† The halo round the moon.

gazed with a heavenly smile and a stream of love into the face of Julius, and said, "Look on me, thou couldst never see me on the earth." — "Thou knowest well that I am blind, my Emanuel," said the blind one. Here the frenzied man, turning away his quivering eyes suddenly and with a sigh to the moon, fled from his friends, saying to himself in a low voice: "The two forms are only shadowy dreams from the earth, — I will not look upon them, so that they may melt away. — So then the shadowy and dreamy woe of earth reaches over even into Eden. Haply I am still in a dream of death, for the region round about me looks like the landscapes in my life-dreams, — or is this only the fore-court of heaven, as I do not find my parents?" . . . . He looked toward the lofty stars: "Where do I now stand below you? New heavens lie on new heavens. — — Ah, does one yearn then even here?"

He sighed and wondered that he sighed. He leaned down on the pearl-glistening hill of flowers, with his back to the beloved shadows and his eyes towards the kindling dawn, and groped and dreamed, — but at last the coolness of morning overspread the seeking, dazzled, burning eyes, which to-day had fallen now upon shapes of terror, now into seas of ecstasy, with gentle slumber and with corresponding dreams. . . . . "Rest softly, thou weary man!" said his friend; but the sleeper glowed with the horizon, and the old delusion played on within him again. . . . .

A dream and the morning laid for him the groundwork of a still higher Elysium.

He dreamed God would descend from a throne of suns, and in the form of an invisible, infinite zephyr's breath move over Elysium.

The first morning of summer heaped around him the bridal finery of the earth, — it lined the fields with pearl-banks of dew, and flung over the burrowing brooks the gold tinsel and spangles of the descending flush of morn, and hung upon the bushes the bracelets of burning drops. — But not until it had cloven open all the flowers, — sent out all the birds, quivering with gladness through the radiant heavens, — hid singing voices in all tree-tops, — not till it had sunk the faded moon behind the earth, and set up the sun like a god's throne over wreaths of clouds just burst into bloom, and over all gardens and around all woods had hung intertwined rainbows of dew, — and not till the blissful one stammered in his dreaming, "All-gracious One, All-gracious One, appear in the Elysium!" — not till then did the slowly flowing morning wind awaken him and usher him into the thousand-voiced jubilant choirs of creation, and set him to reeling blindly in the ringing, blazing Elysium. — — —

And lo! at this moment, a vast, boundless breath, cool, stirring, whispering, overflowed the whole enkindled Paradise, and the little flowers bowed themselves down silently, and the green ears soughing undulated together, and the stately trees trembled and murmured, — but only the great breast of man drank in in streams the infinite breath, and Emanuel's heart dissolved, ere it could say, "This is Thyself, All-loving One!"

— Thou, that readest me here, deny not God, when thou steppest out into the morning or under the starry heavens, or when thou art good or when thou art happy! —

— But, unhappy Emanuel!

Thou beheldest five sporting black butterflies, and thoughtest the fair creatures blessed Psyches. — Thou heardest behind thy hill a hewing into the earth, as if men were making a grave. — Thou lookedst upon thy good blind darling, and yet saidst, "Shadow! retire. . . . . Tremble before God, who just passed by, and vanish!" — But thou saidst, before that, something else which I to-day do not disclose. —

— My heart trembles before the coming line! —

Howling with pain, grinning with exultant fury, the crazy skeleton sprang forth from behind the hill into the blessed plain, bearing in its right hand a bloody hand that had been hewed off, and shook from the left stump, from which its madness had hacked it off, trickling fountain-curves of blood, and pressed to itself with the right arm a spade, designed for the burying of the hand, and screamed with a grin of exultation and agony: "Death grabbed me by it, but I snapped it off, — and when he sees the grave of the fist, he will be so stupid as to think it is I lying there . . . Ah, thou there! Lay thyself, prithee, to bed in the coffin; he has bored out thy eyes and clogged thy maw with mould. . . . . Brr!"

"O All-gracious One, thou hast damned me!" stammered Emanuel; the driven blood broke from his crushed lung, and the disconsolate one staggered and sank dying on the blood-stained flowers of his lost heaven. . . . .

Thus does one day rob another of its heaven, and ere bereaved man enters yonder into the last paradise, he has lost too many here below! — Ah, we bear into every spring-air of this life and into the ether of the second a breast yawning with wounds; and it must first be closed, before it can fill itself! . . .

### THE SOFT EVENING.

Towards noon he opened his weary eyes, but only to let them fall into the grave, which death had opened beside him during his sleep. However, one madman had been the God of Medicine to the other; his dream of Elysium was dreamed out, shortly before it seemed about to be fulfilled, and he was rational again. Victor saw by all signs, that toward sundown at least death with his fruit-gatherer would pluck this white fruit from its stem; but he saw it more calmly than yesterday. As he had already rehearsed the part of disconsolateness, the instruments of grief sawed no fissure into his heart, but only moved bloodily to and fro in the old one. Whoever after years deposits for the second time in the coffin one who has been once awakened therein, scarcely mourns with so much intensity as the first time.

With what altered eyes did Emanuel awake in the evening hour, when he yesterday had shed the first tears for joy! His soul, like the mourning tree of Goa,* let fall by day the nightly load of blossoms; to his chilled head the earth turned no longer the meadow-side of poesy, but the light side of cold reason. He confessed now that he had nourished into fulness of blood the nobler parts of his inner man at the expense of the lower, — that his hope of death had been too great as well as his poetic wing-feathers, — that he had contemplated the earth not from the earth, but too much from Jupiter, seen from whose observatory it must needs dwindle to a fiery spark, and that he had therefore lost the earth without getting Jupiter instead. Vainly did Victor oppose him with the true proposition, that the higher man, as the painters do with water-colors, always begins his life-piece with the *background* and with the *sky*, which the painters in oil and inferior men make last; his answer was the complaint that he unfortunately had

* The Upas-tree. — Tr.

not completed his picture so far as the foreground. At last he reproached himself with having made too much ado about so slight a separation as death was, at least for him who goes, since the other separations on the earth were after all *longer*, more *bitter* and *two-sided.*

They came in this way upon the subject of *recognitions* on the other side of this stage of being. Victor said, he could not decry, as many a philosopher had done, conjectures reaching out beyond the earth; for after all we *must* guess about what was beyond this world, whether we asserted or denied. "Without the continuance of memory," said he, "the continuance of my conscious self is no more than that of my knowledge of another's, i. e. nothing at all; so soon as I forget my present self, then surely might any other one instead of me be immortal. Nor does the destruction of my memory follow from its earthly dependence on my body; for this dependence all the spiritual powers have in common with it, and in that case the destruction of the others would follow from this dependence; and what then would be left for immortality?" — Emanuel said: the thought of recognition, however much it presupposed of the sensuous, was so sweet and transporting, that, if men could make themselves *sure* of it, no one would be willing to tarry here an hour, particularly if one painted out to himself the heavenly thought of finding all great and noble men at once. "I have often," said he, "pictured out the future recollection after the analogy of the present, and always had to leave off for rapture when I thought to myself how in that remembrance the earth would shrink up to a dim morning-meadow, and our life to a far-removed day illumined with moonlight. — Oh, if we now dissolve at the image even of a few years of childhood, how tenderly will the image of *all* childish years one day look upon us!"—Victor waived off these deathly raptures, and after saying, by way of transition, "*one* connection, at all events, this world must have with the second," he came upon something else, which had struck him so much among the incidents of this night. . . . .

. . . . .

. . . . .

I still throw a veil to-day over what Victor asked and what Emanuel disclosed; the new perspective would draw away our eyes too long from the great patient.

The blind one held in one steady and agonized grasp his hot hand, in order not to lose the beloved father; and when Emanuel had for a long time been laying soft consolation concerning his death, like cool leaves around the inflamed temples, he still said nothing except, in a tone of fervent supplication, "Ah, father, if I had only seen thee, only once!"—

Emanuel seemed to be composed; but he deceived himself; his present indifference to the earth was in fact more piercing than that in the night, which was merely a different enjoyment of life mixed with the magic drinks of fantasy. With his remorse for his poetic suicide there seemed almost to mingle joy at its consequences. Hence he said, with a look of touching certainty: "To-day towards evening he should certainly go, and no longer torment his two last and best friends with these delayings of his departure. The genius of the world would forgive him his last fault, and not let their *to-day's* separation from him, which for him was too long, be followed by any second one yonder."

The longer he spoke, so much the more did the old blooming Eden re-enter into his languid soul.—Now he made a singular, heart-rending request to his friends. As, notoriously, the sense of hearing remains longest with the dying, when all other senses have already closed to earth, Emanuel said to Victor: "So soon as thou seest that a change is about to come over me, then give thy Julius the flute, and thou! play me then the old *song of rapture*, that I may die upon the tones, as I have already often wished, and continue to play on some minutes after the end."

He began now to reflect how beautifully tones would glide around his last thoughts, like the song of birds around the setting sun; and in his extinguished spirit the old sparks flew up again: "Ah, I shall go hence blissfully, — O my soul could even to-night lay upon this earthly soil a super-earthly adornment, and take it for Eden: ah then, at length, when the soil is fairer and the soul is greater : . . ."

He swooned away again, but the pulse still beat faintly. — And here, in this brooding state, it was that he received from the earth as a last gift the awfully-sweet dream, into which the body infused the feelings of its sickliness, and which, after his resuscitation, he related with a new after-dreaming. It is the last soft triad of our body with our expiring soul, that the former, even in its dissolution (as we know by fainting persons and those apparently dead under the water, &c.), communicates to the latter sweet plays and dreams. —

EMANUEL'S DREAM, THAT ALL SOULS WERE ANNIHILATED BY ONE BLISS.

He reposed in a glorified form in a transparent, dark, and yet colored tulip-cup, which rocked him to and fro, because a gentle earthquake made the tulip-bower sway on its bowed shaft. The flower stood in a magnetic sea, which attracted the blest one more and more strongly; at last he was drawn so far out, that he weighed it down, and fell as a pearl of dew out of the drooping chalice. . . .

What a colored world! A fleecy throng of ethereal forms like his stood hovering over a broad island, about which played a circular balustrade of great flowers in full blow, — above, in mid-heaven, over the island, flew evening suns behind evening suns, — farther in, beside them ran white moons, — near the horizon, stars traced their circles, — and as often as a sun or a moon flew downward, they gazed with a heavenly look as of angels' eyes through the great flowers along the shore. The suns were divided from the moons by rainbows, and all the stars ran between two rainbows, and embroidered with silver the variegated ring of the heavenly sphere. One above another rose gay clouds, in which burned a kernel of gold, of silver, of precious stones, — from butterflies' wings clouds of dust were shed, which like flying colors mantled the ground, and out of the cloud flashed rushing floods of light, which were all intertwined in one another. . . . .

And in this din of colors a sweet voice went round, saying everywhere, *Die more sweetly of light.*

But the souls were only dazzled, and did not yet die.

Then evening winds and morning winds and noonday winds conspiring fell upon the meadow and wafted down the bright-blue and gold-green clouds, which had arisen out of flower-fragrance, and unfolded the ring of flowers on the horizon, and bore the sweet perfume to the hearts of the blest. The cloud of blossoms swallowed them into itself, the heart was baptized into the dark scents as into a feeling from the deepest depths of childhood, and, overwhelmed with the hot steam of flowers, would fain drop asunder therein. — Now the unknown voice drew nearer, and softly whispered, *Die more sweetly of fragrance.*

But the souls only grew giddy, and did not yet die.

Far in the depths of Eternity out of the south rose and fell, as in a curve, a single tone, — a second rose in the east, — a third in the west, — at last from the distance the whole heaven sounded, and the tones streamed over the island, and seized upon the softened souls. . . . When the tones were upon the island, all beings wept for bliss and longing. . . . . Then on a sudden the suns ran still faster, then the tones flew still higher, and, ascending spirally, lost themselves in a keen, endless height, — ah, then all the wounds of men opened again, and warmed softly with the trickling blood every breast, which died in its melancholy, — ah then, indeed, all came flying before us that we had loved here, all that we had lost here, every precious hour, every lamented pasture, every beloved being, every tear and every wish. — — And when the highest tones were hushed and pierced again, and were still longer mute and pierced more deeply; then harmonica-bells trembled beneath human beings who stood upon them, so that the piercing hum agitated to pieces every trembler. — And a lofty form, around which a little dark cloud floated, came up in a white veil and said melodiously, *Die more sweetly of tones.*

Ah! they would have died and died gladly of the sadness of melody, if every heart had held the heart for which it languished on its breast; but every one still wept on lonesomely without his beloved.

At last the form threw off the white veil, and the *Angel of the end* stood before men. The little cloud that floated round him was *Time*, — so soon as he should grasp the little cloud, he would crush it, and time and men would be annihilated.

When the Angel of the end had unveiled himself, he smiled on men with indescribable affection, in order to dissolve their hearts with bliss and with smiles. And a soft light fell from his eyes upon all the shapes, and every one saw standing before him the soul he most loved, — and when they gazed upon each other with a dying look for love and sent a languid smile after the angel, he grasped at the little cloud which was near him, — but he could not reach it.

Suddenly each one saw once more beside him his own self, — the second *I* trembled transparently beside the first, and the two smiled consumingly on each other and exalted each other, — the heart which trembled in man hung once more, tremblingly, in the second self, and saw itself dying therein. —

O then was every one constrained to fly from himself to his beloved, and, seized with dread and love, to twine his arms round other beings who were dear to him. — And the angel of the end opened his arms wide, and clasped the whole human race together in one embrace. — Then the whole meadow glimmers, breathes fragrance, rings with music, — then the suns stop, but the island itself whirls around the suns, — the two sundered selves run into each other, — the loving souls fall on each other like snow-flakes, — the flakes become cloud, — the cloud melts into a dark tear. —

The great tear of bliss, made out of us all, swims more transparent and yet more transparent in Eternity. —

At last the Angel of the end said softly, *They have died most sweetly of their beloved.* —

And he crushed weeping the little cloud of time.—

* * * * *

The fever images of death, with which every sleep, even the last, begins, gleamed in Emanuel's eyes. His spirit hung swaying in his loose nerves, breathed upon by soft airs; for he was already in that dissolving nervous ecstasy of the fainting, the child-bearing, the exhausted by bleeding, the dying. But his emptied breast rose the more lightly, his departing spirit drew out thinner the thread of life.

Victor would have enjoyed the comfort of the dull numbness, wherewith pains heaped one upon another crush us down, had he not been obliged every minute to tell these pains, i. e. all the preparations of death, to the poor blind youth. Ah, the blind one feared perhaps that he might call after this teacher too late with the song of rapture.

Evening came. Emanuel grew stiller and his eye more rigid, and it seemed to see the fantasies of his busy brain in the apartment, until the gold strip of the far-sinking sun, which a looking-glass directed towards him, darted like a lightning-flash through his world of dream. Softly, but with altered voice, he said, "Into the sun!"—They understood him, and moved his bed and his head toward the evening-rain of the setting sun, to which he had of old so often unfolded his susceptible heart. Victor started, when he saw that his eyes stood, undazzled and immovable, open to the sun.

There was a sublime stillness round three discomposed beings; only a breath of evening wind fluttered among the linden-leaves of the apartment, and a bee hovered about the linden-blossoms; but out of doors away from the theatre of distress a blissful evening reposed on the pastures red with sunlight, among joyous, fluttering, singing, intoxicated creatures.

Emanuel gazed silently into the sun, which sunk lower toward the earth ; he clutched not at the bed-clothes like others, but flung his arms aloft as if for a flight or an embrace. Victor took his beloved hands, but they hung down into his without a pressure. And when the sun, like a blazing world on the day of judgment, sank down in a last upshooting glow : then the silent one still hung with cold eyes on the vacant place of the sun, and remarked not the setting ; and Victor saw suddenly shifting flashes of the scythe of death pass yellow across the undistorted face. — Then, deeply troubled, he handed the flute to Julius, and said in a broken voice, "Play the song of rapture, he is dying now." —

And Julius, with streaming, darkened eyes, compressed his sobbing breath into the flute and raised his sighs to heavenly tones, that he might muffle and benumb the parting soul, during the tearing away of its earthly roots, with the after-echoes of the first world, with the preluding echoes of the second.

And as, during the song, a blissful smile at an unknown dream glorified the face that was growing cold, — and when only a quiver of the hand pressed the hand of the disconsolate friend, and only a quiver winked with the eyelid and farther down opened the pale lips and passed away, and when the evening redness overspread the pale form, — lo, then death, cold to the earth and our lamentations, iron, erect, and dumb, stalked through the fair evening under the linden blossoms to the enwrapped soul in the tranquillized corpse and transferred the veiled soul with immeasurable arms from the earth through unknown worlds into Thy eternal, warm, fatherly hand which has created us, — into the Elysium for which Thou hast formed us, — among the kindred of our hearts, — into the land of rest, of virtue, and of light. . . . .

Julius stopped for sorrow, and Victor said, "Play on the song of rapture, he has only just died." — During the tones Victor shut to the eyes of his beloved, and said with a heart above the earth, "Now close yourselves, — the spirit is above the earth, to which you gave light, — thou pale, hallowed form, thou hallowed heart, the angel within thee is gone out and thou fallest back into the earth." — And here he embraced once more the cold, empty wrappage, and pressed the heart, which beat no more, knew him no longer, to his hot bosom; for the flute-tones tore his pale wounds too widely open. — Oh, it is well that when man in grim woe stiffens to solid ice, no tones are with him: the tender tones would lick all the sad blood out of his transpierced bosom, and man would die of his agonies, because he would be able to express his agonies. . . . .

— Here let my curtain fall before all these scenes of death, before Emanuel's grave and Horion's grief! — Thou and I, my reader, will now go forth from another's death-chamber, to look into nearer ones where we ourselves lie prostrate or where our dearest have lain. We will in those chambers behold our death-bed, but let not our eye sink; — the flame of love and of virtue blazes upward above the corruptions, — around the death-bed we see a bier as a couch of rest on which all burdens are laid down, and the broken heart also, — around the death-bed we see a great, unknown form, who breaks off from the *image* of God the earthly *frame*. — But if the heart is made great beside our own resting-place, it becomes tender beside another's. — If thou, my reader, and if I now, with this deeply moved soul, look into the chambers where we received the perpetual wounds of earth, then will the pale forms which therein raise their dead men's eyes once more to meet us, agitate and wound us too sorely. — Ah, that may you well do, too, ye loved mutes, — what have we then left to give you, but a tear which pains us, a sigh which oppresses our hearts? Ah, if the mourning-crape on our faces is torn as soon as the funeral veil on yours, — if the marble gravestone with your name must be turned over above your corpses, in order to cover a new one with its new name, — O, if we so easily forget all the eternal love, the eternal remembrance, which we promised you in your last hour, — ah, then, indeed, in these tumultuous days of life a still hour like this is holy and beautiful, in which we lay our ear as it were close to the sunken graves, and, from the depth of the earth, although every day more darkly, hear the voices that we know call up: "Forget us not, — forget me not, my son — my friend — my beloved, forget me not!"

No, and we will not forget you! And, if it makes us ever so sad, still let each one of us at this moment summon the most precious forms before him out of their resting-places, and behold the wasted features, the reopened eyes full of love, which were so long closed, and contemplate full long the dear, uncovered face, till the old remembrances of the fair days of their love break the heart and he can weep no more.

## 39. DOG-POST-DAY.

GREAT DISCLOSURE. — NEW SEPARATIONS.

I WILL now disclose what in the former chapter I concealed. — When Emanuel on that Elysian morning of the delirium had said to Julius, "Shadow! hence!" he went on: "Conjure not up with thy juggling the blind *Son* of my Horion [Lord Horion] who takes me still for his father, — fear before God, who has just passed by, and vanish!" — And turning to Victor he said: "Shadow! if thou knowest not who thou art, and knowest not thy father Eymann, then descend to the earth again and into the shadow which my Victor casts there." — — And when Victor the next day recalled the dying man to these words, he asked distressfully: "Ah, did I not say it in a delusion, when I dreamed I was in the land beyond earthly oaths?" and he turned mutely his affrighted face to the wall. . . . .

He has, then, in the illusion of having passed through death, spoken it out, that Julius is the son of his Lordship, and Victor the son of Pastor Eymann. . . . . But what a bright illumination does not this full moon give to our whole history, on which hitherto only a moon-sickle has shone! —

I confess, in the very first chapter it struck me singularly that Victor should be a physician; now it is explained; for the medical doctor's hat was the best Montgolfier * and Fortunatus's wishing-cap for a citizen-legate of his Lordship, in order thereby the more easily to hover round the throne and work upon the frail January; then, too, Victor, after his future devalvation,† and after the loss of the feather-hat, could best gather into the medical one his daily bread as a citizen, — his Lordship saw. This was *one* reason why the latter gave him out as his son. Another is, Victor was best fitted to play the part with the prince by his humor, cleverness, good nature, &c., to which was added as a further recommendation the resemblance he bore in everything, except age, to the fifth and up to this time still lost son, whom January so loved. As, now, a physician in ordinary was to be the favorite, his Lordship could not take any one of the princely sons for his purpose, because they must be jurists, in order to fit into their future offices. — His own son Julius he could not use, because he was blind, — by the way! his Lordship was also blind once, and thus adds his example to the cases of blindness inherited from father to son, — but even independently of the blindness he could not possibly, by reason of his disinterested delicacy, let his son reap the advantages of princely favor while he withheld from them January's own sons themselves.

Thou good man without hope! when I compare now thy poetic education of the blind youth with thy cold principles, — when I consider how thou — dead to lyric joys, hardened to the tears of enthusiasm — nevertheless causest the dark soul of thy Julius curtained with eyelids to be filled by his teacher with poetic flower-pieces, with dew-clouds of sensibility, and with the nebu-

* *Balloon* (inventor of the). — Tr.

† Depreciation (of money). — Tr.

lous star of the second life, — then does it enhance quite as much my sorrow as my esteem, that thou findest nothing on the earth which thou canst press to thy starved-out heart, and that thou raisest thine eye withered on empty tear-ducts coldly to heaven, and even there findest nothing but a void waste of blue! —

This painful observation Victor made still sooner than myself. — But to the story! The past portion of it sent a thousand thorns through his heart. We no longer recognize now our once joyous Sebastian, — he has lost four beings, as if to pay off therewith the four days of Whitsuntide: Emanuel has vanished, Flamin has become an enemy, his Lordship a stranger, and Clotilda — a stranger. For he said to himself: "Now, when she is removed so far above me, I will not cost the sufferer, from whom I have already taken so much, absolutely everything, absolutely her father's love and her position, — I will not insist upon the love which, in her ignorance of my connections, she has bestowed upon me. — No, I will cheerfully tear away my soul from the most precious one amidst a thousand wounds of my breast, and then lay myself down and bleed to death." *Now* this determination was easy for him; for after the death of a friend we love to take a new load of misery on our breast; *that* shall crush it, for we *will* die.

Yet destiny had still left two loved ones in his arms; his Julius and his mother. In the former he loves so many sweet associations; even this was one, namely, that one always loves him with whom one has been confounded; and he would fain fulfil the place of father with him as his Lordship had done with *him*, in order not so much to requite as to emulate that noble man. And still more ardently did his soul embrace the excellent wife of the Pastor, to whom his heart had already hitherto beat responsive with the soft warmth of a son. Ah, how would it have comforted in its longing his childlike breast, from which one hitherto his father was thrust away, to be clasped to a maternal heart, and to hear from a mother the words, "Good son, why comest thou to me so unhappy and so late?" But he dared not, because in that case he would have broken the oath to leave Flamin's extraction under the cover of mystery.

He shut himself up four days with the blind one in the house of death; — he saw no one, — did not visit the mourning convent, where from all fair eyes flowed similar tears, — renounced the fragrant park and the blue sky, — and let the flowerage of the departed one fade after him. — He consoled the forsaken blind one, and all day long they rested in each other's embrace, and pictured to each other weeping their teacher and his teachings and the radiant hours of their childhood. At last, on the fourth day, he conducted the blind one forever out of the beautiful Maienthal, — the evening-bell sent after them from afar the knell of a whole coffined life, — Julius wept aloud, — but Victor had only a moist eye, and consoled not himself, but the blind one; for his soul was now otherwise than one would guess; his soul was exalted above this eventide-life: his departed one, like a genius, held it high up above the clouds and above the plays of our little time. Victor stood on the high mountain, where one stands on the burial-day of a friend; at the foot of the mountain stretched far away the dead sea of the abyss,* and drained an expanded, trembling cloud which reared itself on the sea, — and on the cloud

* Allusions to cloud filled with pictured lands and islands which one sees at morning on looking down from Mount Ætna.

were painted gay cities, and swaying landscapes hung therein, and the little tribes of people with red cheeks ran over the landscapes of vapor, — and all, people and cities, dropped down like tears into the absorbing sea, — — only down below along the horizon in the dusky cloud was a lighted rim like morning glow ; for a sun rises behind the twilight, and then the cloud has passed away, and a new green continent lies stretching into the immensity. — —

He would have gone on the whole night, but something frightful in the next village, which is called Upper-Maienthal, arrested him. He recognized in the coach-house of the inn, by its coat of arms, the carriage of the Chamberlain. He set the blind one down on a stone bench at the door, where he could listen to the rustle of unloading hay. Victor, in answer to his question in the house, got the intelligence : "There were two ladies overhead, one of them they did not know (he immediately discovered, however, by the first sketch of her attire, the wife of the Parson), — the other had often passed that way ; it was the daughter of the Chief Chamberlain, and had on full mourning, because her father some days before had been shot dead in a duel with the Regency-Councillor Flamin, and the two were travelling, as these people said, to England.

He screamed in vain, half choking in blood and agony, "It is impossible, — with the page Von Schleunes, you mean." But nevertheless it was so, — Flamin was in prison, — Matthieu out of the country, — Le Baut already under the ground . . . . But demand not now the history of this murder ! — Victor slowly drew out the watch of the happy Bee-father, and stared rigidly at the index of joyous hours, which, for want of winding up, had stopped some days since; something within him counselled the wild and desperate thought to hurl it against the stone floor and smash it to pieces. But three lute-breaths of the flute, with which the blind youth conjured before his benumbed soul a fairer, warmer past, dissolved his congealing heart into a wet eye, and he lifted it up overflowing, and only said, "Forgive me for it, All-gracious One, — ah, I will gladly do nothing but weep." — When the pangs of grief are too heart-rending within us, then something in us gnashes against fate, and the heart infuriate clenches itself like a fist, as it were, for resistance, — but this strength is blasphemy. O, it is more comely towards thee, All-gracious One, to let the crushed and broken heart melt away and become a tear, and to love and be silent until one dies!

The familiar tones of the flute penetrated into Clotilda's thick rain-cloud of grief, — she staggered to the window, — she saw the blind one, — but she went slowly back and wrapped her heart deeper in the cold cloud, — for now she knew all; the blind one was the messenger of death, come to tell that her great friend had left the earth and the disconsolate ones behind him. "My teacher, too, is dead," she said to her companion; and when Victor sent up a request for an interview, she could only nod her head speechlessly. — Then she begged the Parson's wife to step into another chamber, because the sight of Victor, for many reasons, must be oppressive to her. Victor ascended the staircase as if to a scaffold on which fate was to pluck out his heart, namely, the good Clotilda, from whom, as well by her journey as by his purpose of resigning her, he was to-day being separated. When he opened the door and beheld the afflicted maiden leaning pale and weary against the wall; and as both with hands hanging down looked into each other's eyes red with weeping, and trembled in the sombre interval between the sight of each other and the first word, as in the fearful pause between the fire of a great gun and the arrival of the ball, and when at last Clotilda asked in a low voice, "It is all true?" and he said, "All!" — then she slowly laid her beautiful head round to the wall again, and repeated, in one continuous utterance, but in a low, wailing tone, with the soft, muffled funeral tones of exhausted anguish, the words, "Ah! my good teacher; my never to be forgotten friend! — Ah, thou great spirit! thou fair, heavenly soul, why hast thou gone so soon after my Giulia! — — O, dearest friend, be not angry, I could wish now only to be, where my father is, in the still grave." — — Victor began eagerly the question, "Has Flamin —" but he could not add, "killed him"; for she lifted up her head and looked upon him with a swelling, a laboring, unspeakable sorrow, and that sorrow was her *yes*. — —

Exhausted with the bleeding of tears and convulsed amidst remembrances, which, like brain-borers, touched the soul, she was on the point, at last, of sinking down by the wall; but Victor sustained her with inexpressible compassion, and held her upright on his breast and said, "Come, innocent angel, come to my heart, and weep thyself dry thereon, — we are unhappy, but innocent. — O, take thy rest, thou tormented head, rest softly under my tears." — — But always in the height of woe a mountain-air began to flutter around him; it seemed to him as if an iron lever lifted up the broken-in skull, as if vital air streamed in through the pierced, inwardly mouldering breast; the reason why he felt so was that the life of men became little to him, death great, and earth dust.

"Sleep, harassed one," — he said to Clotilda, who leaned languidly upon him, — "sleep away the woe, — life is a sleep, an oppressed, sultry sleep; vampyres sit upon it, rain and wind fall upon us sleepers, and we vainly clutch at waking. — — O, life is a long, long sigh before the going out of the breath. — But alas that the wretched meteor should be permitted so to torment just this good soul, just thyself!" — "Ah," said Clotilda, "if only the so sad flute would cease! My heart is ready to fly to pieces for agony!" But her friend cruelly tore open again all the springs of her tears and poured his into hers, and depicted to her the past: "Four weeks ago it was otherwise; then the flute-tones passed over a fairer region; through the happy plaints of the nightingale they found their way into our hearts, which were then so joyous. — On the first Whitsuntide-day I found thee, when the nightingale throbbed, — on the second, I sank down before thee for rapture and reverence, when the rain glistened round about us, — on the third, at the evening fountain a broad heaven rose, and I saw a single angel stand sparkling and smiling therein. — — Our three days were dreams of fair flowers, for dreams of flowers signify sorrow." — He had hitherto hardened his soft soul against this cruel picture, but when he had actually, with oppressed voice, added, "At that time our Emanuel was still living, and visited at evening his open grave . . ." then must his heart needs burst, and all his tears gushed out over the deeply buried sword-blade like bloody drops, and he said, straining her more passionately to himself: "O, come, we will weep without measure: we will not console ourselves. We shall not be much longer together: O, I could now tear myself to pieces with sorrow. — Exalted Dahore! look upon this dying one and her tears over thee, and requite her mourning, and give the weary soul at length repose, and thy peace, and all that is wanting to man."

The two souls sank, entwined together, into a single tear, and the stillness of mourning hallowed the moment, — and let me not with my oppressed breath say any more of this.

— As if awaking, she drew her head from his heart and with an enervated smile took his hand; for notwithstanding all unhappy events she loved him inexpressibly, and was even now on the way to Maienthal for the very purpose of seeing him once more, — and she said, "I am going to England to my mother, to find his Lordship, and to beg him to come sooner and act as intercessor, and end the sorrows of others and my own." — Her pause, which her look filled out, disclosed to him as much as it concealed from the unhappy wife of the Parson, who could hear a good deal in the adjoining chamber; — what she suppressed was, that she would urge upon his Lordship the expediting of the disclosure that Flamin was the son of the Prince. Besides, this journey withdrew her eyes from so many images of grief, as well as her ears from so many a discordant tone of mockery. To be sure, the design of taking motion on the coach-cushion and on shipboard as a tincture of iron, had only been her pretext at court, where polite untruths are not merely forgiven, but even required.

Victor promised her, under a dark presentiment of his strength and disinterestedness, — for the unhappy makes sacrifices more freely and easily than the happy, — that "he would care for him like a *sister*." — Their eyes exchanged confessions of their secrets, and, for that *very* reason, of their love, and Clotilda overflowed with tearful love, first on account of the journey (because to her sex a journey by reason of its rarity is something of consequence) ; secondly, on account of sorrow, for love makes a woman's heart in full mourning warmer than one in half-mourning, as burning lenses heat black-colored things more powerfully than white.

And this very day, when she looked into his eyes with so much renewed love, he was to be torn from her! He spared her, it is true, the revelation of his birth and his eternal separation, in order not to lay upon her lacerated heart new loads of sorrow; but he would fain wholly gather, in this last minute of his fair love, this gleaning and this after-bloom of his life. Ah, he would fain look upon her as never before, — he would press her hand intensely as he had never before done, — he would say a farewell to her like a dying man. — — For it is all — his innermost being cried unceasingly — for the last, last time! — Only he would not kiss her: a shrinking reverence, the thought of having played out the part of the lover, forbade him to make a selfish use of her ignorance. But when he was about to direct towards her the last look of love, — then did fate thrust all the sharpened weapons, which had hitherto been driven into his nerves, once more into the bleeding openings, just as they replace in the wounds of murdered men the old instruments, to see whether they are the same, — — ah, they *were* the same, — the chamber was darkened as if by an extinguisher, — the tones of the flute were stifled in the internal din, — he must needs look upon her and yet could not for the water in his eyes, — he must look upon her with a long, retentive look, because he wanted to impress her beautiful face as a shadow-image of the shadowy Eden forever upon his soul. — At last he succeeded; amidst a thousand woes he seized with an intense look her tear-bedewed face, through which virtue pulsed like a heart, and shadowed it out in his desolate soul even to every line, to every drop. — So much of her he took away with him, — no more; he left her everything, his heart and his joy. — Ah, tender Clotilda! if thou hadst guessed it! — The sobbing of *his* mother hurried him to the adjoining chamber; he flung open the door, cried in a crushed voice to his mother, whose face was averted: "Dearest! by the Almighty, your *son* is no murderer and no reprobate," — and compressed the hand she gave him behind her back with a wild intensity of grasp.

Look not now, my friends, at the dismal moment when for the last time he takes Clotilda's hand, and severs his heart from hers, and yet only says, "A happy journey, Clotilda, a peaceful life, Clotilda, joy be with thee, Clotilda!"

— And at a distance from the village he fell on his knees beside the blind one, with a mute prayer for the mourning heart which he had now lost for the last time. —

Not until four o'clock in the morning did he arrive with the blind one, without weariness, without tears, and without thoughts, at Flachsenfingen.

## 40. DOG-POST-DAY.

THE MURDEROUS DUEL. — APOLOGY FOR THE DUEL. — PRISONS REGARDED AS TEMPLES. — JOB'S-WAILS OF THE PARSON. — LEGENDS OF MY BIOGRAPHICAL PAST. — POTATO-PLANTING.

S I am on the point of entering upon the fortieth day with the observation, "The history of the duel is still full of regular ciphers, and is a true unfigured thorough-bass," — a piece of the forty-third comes to hand and figures the bass and puts the vowel-points to the Hebrew consonants. To this young forerunning* of the forty-third chapter one is indebted for the fact that I can relate the shooting-history with better spirits.

It will not be guessed who boiled up the most furiously at Clotilda's engagement, — namely, the Evangelist. He was vexed with the bold faithlessness of the Chamberlain, whose courtliness he had hitherto managed by coarseness, and so much the more because a human mixture of imbecility and flattery like Le Baut exasperates us unspeakably, when it passes over from flatteries to insults. Still more was he who set on Flamin himself set on by the widow of the Chamberlain, who stirred into his elementary fire soft oil and some matches; she hated Clotilda because she was loved, and our hero because he did

* A term taken from wine-making, meaning the unpressed wine, the first runnings. — TR.

not, like the Evangelist, set the step-mother above the step-daughter. A woman who has gone to the death for a man, i. e. into a short sleep (which is death to the good), namely, into a swoon, — as this very widow did in the Eighth Post-Day, — must be expected of course to hate this man, if he will not let himself be loved. The Evangelist, who had hitherto taken the love of Victor and Clotilda only for the accidental gallantry of a moment, and who had also looked upon the flying attachment to his sister Joachime as nothing more serious, was devilishly mad at the mis-shot in the first case, and at the royal shot in the second; and he determined to avenge himself and his sister, whom he loved more than his father, on both.

Joachime was additionally and bitterly enraged with Victor, because she believed herself and her love to have been hitherto abused as a mere cloak for his love to Clotilda. I have stated above that Matthieu, after the Eymann visit, made his to Flamin. When the Councillor had disclosed to him the interview with the Parson and his decisory oath, Mat formed his resolution and threw much upon the Chamberlain: " This fellow was a small sharper and a great courtier, — he had perhaps had more to do than the lover had with Clotilda's excursion to the baths of Maienthal, — he, and not so much Victor, sought to make out of his daughter a lark's net for the Prince's heart and a *gradus ad Parnassum* of the Court." Flamin was right down glad that his vengeance had got another object besides him with whom he had sworn to his father not to quarrel. Meanwhile he did not conceal from the Councillor (to be impartial) that the Apothecary proclaimed everywhere, from exasperation against Sebastian, that the latter had gotten the plan of this marriage as a stepping-stone to promotion entirely from him, from Zeusel. Flamin, in such bone-fractures of the breast, always resorted at once to the chalybeate (steel-cure) of the sword, the lead-water of bullets, and the cautery of the sabre; and as the duel with Victor, one of noble extraction, had spoiled him, he would also in the first heat have proposed it to the three-buttoned* fellow, when Mat ridiculed the incompetent plebeian. Flamin cursed in vain fury his defect of ancestry, which hindered him from letting himself be shot by one ancestrally endowed; nay, he would have been capable — as he kindled quickly and yet cooled slowly — for a mere verbal insult from a nobleman (as one actually did on a certain occasion) — of becoming a soldier, then an officer and a nobleman, merely for the sake of afterward summoning the canonical and challengeable defamer before the muzzle of his pistol.

But the faithful Matthieu, — whose spotted soul turned a different side to every one, like the sun, which, according to Ferguson, on account of its spots, revolves on its axis, so as to give all the planets equal light, — he understood the business; he said, he would in his own name challenge the Chamberlain, and in fact to a masked duel, and then Flamin in the disguise could take his part, while he himself stood by under the name of the third Englishman, and the two others as seconds.

Flamin was overmastered by rapidity; but now again there was a want of something, which is still more indispensable than nobility to a game of fighting, — namely, of a good, legitimate offence. Matthieu, to be sure, was ready with pleasure to offer one to the man which should adequately justify a duel; but the man with the Chamberlain's master-key was one who, there was every reason

* Chamberlains wear, as a decoration, three gold buttons over the right pocket-lappet. — Tr.

to fear, would forgive it, — and there would be nobody to shoot. — Most fortunately the Evangelist remembered, that he himself had already received one from him, which he knew how profitably and honestly to bring to bear upon the case: "Le Baut had, indeed, *three* years before, as good as promised him his daughter; and however indifferent this perjury was in itself, still, as a pretext for the chastisement of a greater fault, it retained its full value." . . . Thus on a smutty tongue does truth take the form of a lie, provided the lie cannot dress itself in that of truth. And Flamin did not dream that his alleged groomsman was no other than the veritable Sabine robber of his bride.

I am concerned lest it should be thought that Matthieu imputes to a Chamberlain, especially one with whom making and keeping a promise were the most distant cousins, less full-power of lying than to a Court-Page, and that he forgets how, in general, one gets over the stream of the court and of life as over any natural one, not in a direct line, but in a diagonal and oblique manner. But the rascal *despises* the rascal still more than he *hates* the good man. Besides, he acted thus not merely from passion, but from calculation: if Flamin were killed, then he must needs receive from Agnola, who now was becoming more and more the Princess of the Prince, and for whom naturally an after-bloom of January's and his Lordship's former sowings was a hedge of thorns, the honest man's fee and fairing, and a higher place on the merit-roll of the court; — furthermore, his Lordship in that case could no longer trundle through the gate and bring word, "Your Grace's son is to be had and is alive." — If the Chamberlain fell, then, too, the result was not to be despised; this former boarder and *protégé** of the princely crown was, after all, gone to the Devil, and his Lordship would have at least to be ashamed to think that by his silence he had entangled the Regency-Councillor in a deadly relation with a man to whom he had, at all events, publicly to pay the veneration of a son. Matthieu could not lose, — besides, he could disguise or disclose his knowledge of Flamin's extraction, as the case might require.

As there was nothing to prevent the Englishmen's being seconds, Flamin said, Yes; but Le Baut said, No, when he received Mat's manifesto and war-articles; he was frightened to death almost at the very death-prescription without the ingredient of the bullet. I shall never so belittle a courtier, as to allege that he declines such a potato-war from virtue or from faint-heartedness, — such men tremble certainly not at death, but merely at a disgrace, — but this latter, which Le Baut feared at the hands of the Prince and Minister, was precisely what deterred him. He therefore, on fine paper and with fine turns of expression, which outsparkled the black sand, represented to Mat their former friendship, and dehortations from this glaring "ordeal,"† and declared himself besides entirely willing to do everything which his honor — would be offended at, in case he only were not obliged by this sham-fight to violate the laws of the duel. But he was, — Matthieu wrote back, he would pledge himself for the secrecy as well as for the silence of the seconds, and he made the additional proposal to him, that they should insinuate into each other dragon-‡ and pitch-balls in the night and in

* *Preciste* in the original: one nominated to a benefice in virtue of the right of first petition. — Tr.

† Original: "Gotzsurthel," — properly *Gottesurtheil*. — Tr.

‡ The dragon was an old-fashioned war-machine. — Tr.

masks; "for the rest he remained in future his friend as ever, and would visit him, for only honor demanded of him this step." . . . . And of the Chamberlain too; — for these men swallow only great offences, but no little ones, just as those bitten by mad dogs can get down solids, but no liquids, — and herewith in my eyes is a courtier like Le Baut sufficiently excused, if he makes believe he were an honest man, or as if he were very different from those who pawn their honor for the whole year, and — as in the case of imperial pledges or living pledges of love — never redeem the pawn.

All was fixed for the very evening when Victor sorrowfully entered into Maienthal, — the theatre of war was between St. Luna and the city.

## EXTRA-LEAF IN DEFENCE OF THE DUEL.

IN my opinion the state favors duelling in order to set limits to the increase of the nobility, as Titus for that very reason made the Jews challenge each other. As in chanceries they still continue to make nobles, but no burghers, — as, besides, a burgher must always be used and demolished for the purpose, before the Imperial Chancery can set up a nobleman on his building-ground, — as standing armies and coronations increase simultaneously, and consequently the manufacture of nobles too; the state would accordingly possess too many, certainly, rather than too few noblemen (as is not the case, however), were not a mutual shooting or stabbing of each other allowed them. In reference to the petty princes who are made in the chancery-bakehouse, nothing more were to be wished than that at the same time subjects also — say one or two herds, with every prince — should fall off from the potter's-wheel; just as, in fact, I know no reason, either, why the Imperial Chancery will make poets only, when it might certainly quite as well scrape off from its saltpetrè wall historians, publicists, biographers, reviewers. — Let it not be objected to me, that at court they seldom shoot each other; here Nature herself has in another way set beneficial bounds to the increase of courtiers. Somewhat as with marmots, of whose depopulation Bechstein finds a wise design in the fact, that, though they generally assert their own with a malicious rabidity, nevertheless they do not reckon their brood *as* their own, but willingly let it go. Even Dr. Fenk may possibly be nearer right, who takes their part and says, he grants they are of no use to the weightier members of the state, the teaching class, the peasantry, &c., but of much, however, to the lesser, unprofitable members, the mass-attendants of the stomach and of luxury, the mistresses, the lackey-department, &c., and that an impartial person must compare them with the stinging nettles, on which, while they are of little use to men and large animals, most of the insects get their living.

*End of this Apologetic Extra-Leaf.*

Flamin's soul worked itself off all day in images of revenge. In such a boiling of the blood, moral skin-moles became to him bone-black,* the typographical mistakes of the state appeared to him as grammatical blunders, the *peccata splendida* of the regency-college as black vices. To-day, too, he saw the Prince always before his eyes, whom in the clubs of the twins and still more in relation to Clotilda he mortally hated. He despised the load of life, and in this heat, wherein all materials of

* Color of burnt bones. — Tr.

his inner being were melted into one flood, the inner lava sought an outbreak in some foolhardy venture. His to-day's exasperation was, after all, a daughter of virtue; but the daughter grew over the mother's head. The three twins, who, although not with the tongue, yet with the head, were as wild as he, kindled absolutely the whole vaporous atmosphere of his full soul.

At length, when night came, the two seconds and Flamin and Matthieu disguised as the third Englishman rode out to the shooting-ground.. Flamin contended furiously with his prancing, smoking steed. By and by a gray nag brought along in curvets the Chamberlain. Mutely they measure off the murdering and shooting distance, and exchange pistols. Flamin, as insulted party, first lets fly like a storm against the other; and, on his snorting steed, and in the trembling of rage, he shoots his ball away over his adversary's — life. The Chamberlain fired intentionally and openly far aside from his antagonist, because the fall of the (supposed) Matthieu would have killed at the same time his whole prosperity at court. Matthieu, with all his slyness, too precipitate and too full of energy, foaming already amidst the very preparations for the fight, and still more exasperated at the frustration of both his alternatives, and too proud to let himself be shamed before the Englishmen by receiving his life as a present under another's name and from so contemptible an adversary, thrust down his own mask and Flamin's too, and rode coldly up to the Chamberlain and said, by way of humiliating him with the disclosure of his ignoble opponent, "You have been under a mistake about rank, — but now let us exchange shots." . . . Le Baut stuttered, confused and offended; but Matthieu backed his horse — stopped — screamed — shot with petrified arm, and hit, and snuffed out the bald life of poor Le Baut. . . . Quick as lightning he said to all, "To Count O.'s!" and — with the conviction of an early and easy forgiveness on the part of the princely couple and of the widow — trotted off over the limits towards Kussewitz.

Flamin became an iceberg, — then a volcano, — then a wild-fire, — then he grasped the hands of the Britons, and said: "I, only I, have killed this man. My friend would have had no quarrel with him; but, as he has sinned for me, it is my duty to suffer for him. — I will die: I shall give myself up to the judges as the murderer, that I may be executed, — and you must back my asseveration." — But he disclosed to them now a much higher motive for his bold lie: "If I die," said he, more and more glowingly, "they will have to let me say at the place of execution what I will. Then will I throw flames among the people, which shall turn the throne to ashes. I will say, 'Lo! here beside the sword of justice I am as firm and cheerful as you; and yet I have sent only one good-for-nothing fellow out of the world. You could catch and confine bloodsuckers, wolves, and serpents, and a lamb-vulture at once; — you could reap a life full of freedom, or a death full of fame. Are then the thousand staring eyes around me all blind with the cataract, the arms all palsied, that none will see and hurl away the long bloodsucker that crawls over you all, and whose tail is cut off, so that the court and the boards in turn suck from it behind? Lo! I too was once part and parcel of all that, and saw how they flay you, — and how the messieurs of the court go about in your skins. Take one look into the city; are yours the palaces or the dog-kennels? The long pleasure-gardens in which they walk, or the stony fields in which you must work yourselves to death? You toil, indeed; but you have nothing, you are nothing, you become nothing, — on the contrary the lazy, dead Chamberlain there beside me'" . . . No one smiled; but he came to himself. The three twins, to whom the body and time and the throne were a fire-proof wall, or a stove-screen against their self-devouring blaze of freedom, vowed to him tied tongues, steadfast hearts, and active hands; yet were they silently resolved, *after* the flashing speech, to rescue him with their blood, and to reveal his innocence. One consequence of this dithyrambic of freedom was, that Cato the Elder, the day after, blew up in the storm the powder-house at Maienthal, which was the only powder-magazine in the country (magazines of corn they had not so many), as he rode towards Kussewitz to join Matthieu.

Now they carried the lie into the village, that Flamin had availed himself of Matthieu's disguise, and in a similar one had attacked the Chamberlain, whom, for want of ancestors, he could not shoot in duel, and blown out with a pistol his lamp of life. The Regency-Councillor was, upon a slight, specious flight, arrested, and placed as a statue of a god alone in that temple, which, like the old temples, was without windows or furniture, and which the gods inhabiting them furnish, as Diogenes did his tub, with inscriptions, and which the common man calls merely a prison. — — — I will, however, first and foremost, call this and the following words an

## EXTRA-LEAF.

THE chapel or vestry of such a temple is further called a dog's hole or dungeon. The priests and fellows of this pagoda are the gaolers and constables.

In fact, the times are no more when the great folk were indifferent to truths; now they rather seek out a man who has uttered weighty ones, and hunt after him, and (with more justice than the Tyrians did their god Hercules) make him fast in the aforesaid temples with chains and iron *postillons d'amour*, that he may there on this insulating-stool (*Isolatorio*) the better concentrate and accumulate his electric fire and light. When once such a Mercury is so fixed, and has for a sufficient length of time had, in common with the fixed stars, beside light, immobility also, then they can finally, if more has been made out of him by this process, get him even up to the tripod, — as they call the gallows, — for a *hanging* seal of truth, where he can shrink up into a regular, dried, natural specimen, because he may not otherwise be stuck as a useful example into the *herbarium vivum* of the philosophic martyrology. Such a hanging is a more dignified and profitable imitation of the crucifixion of Christ, than I have seen in ever so many Catholic Churches on Good Friday, and in fact not a whit less forcible than that which Michael Angelo, according to the tradition, arranged, who crucified *re verâ* the man who sat, or rather hung, to him for the Crucified. Hence in Catholic countries, beside the *bloodless* masses, there are sundry *bloody* ones; for such a quasi Christ, who is raised by a little hemp, not into the third heaven, but still into the tremulous heaven * (*cœlum trepidationis*), must — and for that reason they slay him — render to his doctrines by his death the service which the higher death of the Cross once rendered. And verily the dead

* The old astronomers inserted between the fixed stars and the planets a tremulous heaven, in order to have something on which to charge the slight anomalies of the latter bodies.

still preach; — to die for the truth is a death not for one's country, but for the world; — the truth, like the Medicean Venus, is handed over in thirty fragments to posterity; but posterity will fit them together again to form a goddess, — and thy temple, eternal Truth, which now stands half under the earth, undermined by the burials of thy martyrs, will at last rear itself above the earth, and stand, made of iron, with every pillar in a precious grave!

*End.*

Cato rode after Matthieu, who had fled to Kussewitz, and laid before him, with French eloquence, Flamin's plan to die, and their own to save him. Mat approved all, but he believed nothing of it; he still staid over the limits. Yet he begged for himself the favor, not to take it ill of him, if he should requite Flamin's noble sacrifice with something which would be against their plan, but beyond their hopes. Would he perhaps mention to the Prince that *his son* lay in prison?

In three minutes the readers and I will go into the apothecary's shop to our hero, when we have waited only to be first informed that, as the riderless, bloody nag of the Chamberlain and the three twins with the lying Job's tidings of the murder came up to the window of the parsonage, the Court Chaplain was lathered and half shaved. He had therefore to sit still, and only say slowly under the razor: "O sorrow above all sorrows! — pray shave quicker, dear Mr. Surgeon, — wife, howl for me!" He waved his hand loosely in his suppressed agony, in order not to shake his arm and chin: "For God's sake, can't you scrape more speedily? — You have a poor Job under the razor, — it is my last beard, — they will march me and my household off to prison. — Thou unnatural child, thy father may be decapitated for thy sake, you Cain, you!" He ran to every window: "God have mercy on us! the whole parish has by this time got wind of it. — Dost thou see, wife, what a Satan we have together brought up and borne: it is thy fault. — What is the fellow listening there for? Shear off to your customers, Mr. Shearer, and don't go to blackening your spiritual shepherd anywhere, nor spread the news about." — — At this moment came the gentle Clotilda, downcast and with her handkerchief in her hand, because she guessed what the heart of a disconsolate mother needed; namely, two loving arms as a band around the shattered breast, and a thousand balsam-drops of another's tears upon the splintered and swelling heart. She went up to the mother with open arms, and enfolded her therein with speechless weeping. The whimsical Parson fell at her feet and cried: "Mercy, mercy! none of us knew a word about it. I only heard of the murder just now while in the hands of the barber. I lament only for your sainted father and his relicts. — Who could have said ten years ago, good lady, that I should have raised a scamp that would shoot down my master and patron? I am a ruined man, and my wife too. I can no longer now for shame be *Senior Consistorii.*— I can send off no christening paper and present to his Highness, even though my wife should be taken in labor on the spot. — And if they behead my son, it will bring down my gray hairs with sorrow to the grave." — When Clotilda, without smiling, assured him, on her sacred word, that there was an infallible way of rescue, — by which she meant Flamin's princely extraction, — then the Chaplain looked on her with sparkling eyes and dumfounded mien, and kept calling her half aloud at intervals, "Angel of heaven! — Angel of God! — Archangel!" — But the two female friends retired eagerly into a cabinet; and here Clotilda poured the first vulnerary water into the widely rent soul of the mother, by asseverating and pledging the intervention of a redeeming mystery, and concerting with her on that account the journey to London. — This withdrawal was partly also wrung from her by her false position with the Chamberlain's lady, whose last windlass-maker, together with all the levers of her sunken fortune, had now been buried with her husband; and who, as she threw all the blame upon Clotilda's conduct, sought still more to afflict this mourning spirit by an intentional exaggeration of her own mourning. As Lady Le Baut, for the rest, liked nothing so much as prayer-books and free-thinkers, she now compensated for the latter with the former.

Some of my readers will already have darted on before me, and have peered into Victor's balcony to find his grief hidden within four walls; — frightfully stands the solitude before him, unfolding to him a great black picture, with two fresh graves. In one great grave lies lost friendship; in the other, lost hope. Ah! he wishes the third, in which he might also lose himself. He had the sublime mood of *Hamlet*. The darkened Julius appeared to him like a galvanically quivering dead man. He wholly avoided the court; for his self-regard was far too considerate and proud to keep up a fleeting pomp with a stolen nobility, and the surreptitious privileges of a lord's son. Moreover, a slight chilblain was raised on his heart by the thought that his Lordship, according to the degenerate way of all statesmen and state-machinists, of managing men only as bodies, not as spirits; only as caryatides, not as tenants of the state-edifice; in short, merely as dancing-girls of Golconda,* who have their limbs yoked and tied together as a beast of burden to a single rider, — that his Lordship, I say, this otherwise exalted soul, had misused even his Victor too much as the tool of his virtue. But he forgave the man for it, whom, after all, he had nothing to reproach with, except that he had only the kindnesses of a father, without his rights.

As Victor no longer paid court to any one, naturally the Apothecary cared no more to pay it to him. The former smiled at that, and thought: "So should every good courtier act, and, like a clever ferryman, always leave that side of his boat which is *sinking*, and step over to the other." Zeusel stepped over to the favored Watering-place-doctor, Culpepper, to whose judgment they ascribed January's recovery, which was the effect of summer; and he prostrated himself to lick with his little snaky tongue the feet whose heels he had formerly stung with his poisonous bite. But churls never forgive; Culpepper despised the "ninety-nine per cent fellow," † and the "ninety-nine per cent fellow" again despised my court-physician, although, from fear, — as the Prince from love of ease, — he ventured not either to browbeat him or to turn him out of his house.

Poor Victor! the unhappy needs activity, as the happy needs repose; and yet thou wast compelled to look, with bound limbs, into the future, as into an approaching, distending storm. — Thou couldst neither suppress nor guide

* Nine dancing-women are strung together to make an elephant for the king. One makes the trunk; four, the legs; four, the body. History of all Travels, Vol. X.

† An old German name affixed to apothecaries, in allusion to the alleged profits on their drugs. — Tr.

nor hasten it, and hadst not even the comfort of forging weapons for sorrow, and, like Samson, to express and — extinguish the convulsion of agony by shakings down of the pillars! — He could not even do anything for the imprisoned darling, whom he had plunged into a still greater anguish; for Flamin's sufferings brought back again into his bosom *friendship* for him, though disguised in the domino of *philanthropy*. He must wait to see; but he could not guess whether his Lordship was coming or was living, — neither of which suppositions, in consequence of his silence and of the non-appearance of the fifth princely son, had much in its favor. — At last he came to be afraid of sleep, especially the afternoon nap; for slumber lays, to be sure, its summer night over our present as over a future. It draws two eyelids like the first bandage over the wounds of man, and with a little dream covers over a battle-field; but when it departs again with its mantle, then do the *hungry* pangs pounce so much the more fiercely upon the naked man, amidst stings he starts up out of the more tranquil dream, and reason must begin over again the suspended cure, the forgotten consolation. — And yet — thou good Destiny! — thou didst still show our Victor a streak of evening-redness in his broad night-heaven; it was the hope of perhaps receiving from Clotilda, whom his heart no longer dared call his own, a letter from London. . . .

I was going to close this chapter, first with the intelligence that the chapters come in, in ever-widening comprehensiveness of periods and lessenings of size, — which betokens the end of the story, — and afterward with the request that readers will not take it ill, if the personages therein play and speculate more and more romantically; misfortune makes romantic, not the biographer.

But I by no means conclude, — even on account of the last request, — but rather prefer to freshen a little in the mind of the reader the image of the old, joyous Victor, of whom he will hardly any longer be able to conceive. It is an uncommonly fortunate incident that the dog, on the third Dog-Post-Day, handed in one or two facts, which I at the time entirely omitted. For that reason I can now unexpectedly state them. It must certainly give me and the reader the greatest pleasure, when my picture — which was even at that time quite finished — is hung up here on this page.

The hiatus of the third chapter, wherein I paint Victor's arrival at the parsonage from Göttingen, reads, when filled out, thus : —

"The Chaplain had the peculiarity of many people, that, in the midst of the choir of joys and visits, he thought on his most trifling employments; e. g., on the wedding day, of his mole-traps. To-day, in the servants' room, — while his Lordship was communicating his secret instruction to the Court-Physician, — he was cutting in halves seed-potatoes. There were few to whom he could intrust the cutting up of this fruit, because he knew how seldom a man possesses sufficient stereometry of the eye to split a potato into two equal conic sections or hemispheres. He would sooner have passed the seed-time than have divided a germinal globe into unequal sections; and he said, 'All I want is order.' — It may throw a shade over my hero, if it comes out, — and certainly it must through the press, — and especially if it reaches the ears of Nuremberg patricians and people in offices and *membra* of the supreme court, that Victor in the afternoon marched in state behind the Chaplain and Appel over the vegetable garden, and there executed what they call in some provinces planting potatoes. They gave him the credit, that he incorporated the subterranean bread-fruit in the ground at quite as symmetrical distances as the chaplain; in fact, both looked sharply after the rectitude of the potato-row, and their eyes were the parallel rulers of the beds. The Chaplain had already beforehand looked after and helped on the plough behind a dioptric rule or alidade, in order that the field about which I and the judicial *membra* are now standing might be cut up into equal prisms or beds. When at evening both came home with great gravity and little waistcoats, the whole house loved him so that they could have eaten him; and the Parson's wife asked him what he would have done in his waistcoat, if the Chamberlain's lady had met him; would he have made a bow or an apology, or done nothing?

"'O thou dear Germany!' (he cried and smote his hands together,) 'shall not then the whole country make a joke, except as the court decrees?' (Here Victor looked at the old, deaf coachman Zeusel; for every humorous effusion he regularly addressed to him who least understood it. I will here, however, have it addressed to the patricians and *membra*.) 'Is there, then, my dear man, nothing in the country but gallowses and carpenters and officers of justice, so that, I mean, the former cannot touch an axe, unless the latter have struck the first blow with it? Will you, then, get all follies, like fashions, from above downward, as a wind always roars in the upper regions of the atmosphere before it whistles down below at our windows? — And where, then, is there an imperial recess or a vicariate conclusion which forbids a German of the empire to play the fool? I hope, Zeusel, a time is yet to come when you and I and every one will have sense enough to have his own, and his own private folly, begotten of his flesh and blood, as Autodidact in all folly and wisdom. — O men, poor creatures! catch, I pray, at the wing and tail feathers of joy amidst the forced marches of your days! O ye poor creatures! will no good friend, then, scribble an imperial folio, and prove to you that, like the Devil in the Apocalypse, you have but a short time? Ah! enjoyment promises so little, — hope performs so little, — the mowing and planting days of joy stand in the Berlin Almanac so few in number, — if, now, you were absolutely so stupid as to put away and lay up whole hours and olympiads full of pleasure, like preserves in your cellar, in order, the Devil knows when, to come upon them as fifty or sixty entire pickled and salted years — — I say, if you did not press out on the cluster of every hour the berry of each moment at least with some lemon-squeezers — — — what would come of it at last? . . . nothing but the moral to my first and last fable, which I once made in the presence of a Hanoverian.' . . .

"I wish the reader wanted it; for it runs thus: '*The Stupid Marmot* is the title. The said marmot was once led by the full crop of a pigeon, the contents of which he was eating, to the prize question, whether it would not be better, if, instead of single grains of corn, he should rather bring in pigeons with whole corn magazines in their throats. He did so. On a long summer day, he arrested half a flock of pigeons with full crops. He slit open not a single crop, however, but, though hungry, saved all up for evening and morning: first, in order to catch a goodly lot of pigeons; secondly, to feast on the batch of corn thoroughly softened in the evening. At last, when evening came, he ripped open the crops of his tithe-officers, six, nine, all, — not a grain was any longer there; the prisoners had already digested all themselves, and the marmot had been as stupid as a miser.' "

So far the Third and the Fortieth Dog-Post-Days. — Poor Victor!

Postscript. — The history stops now in the month of August, and the historian in the fore part of October, — only a month lies between the two.

## 41. DOG-POST-DAY.

LETTER. — TWO NEW INCISIONS OF FATE. — HIS LORDSHIP'S CONFESSION OF FAITH.

NE must excuse a man, who, like horses, increases his speed as night and home draw near, from a tenth intercalary day; at the end of a life and of a book, man makes few digressions.

I have already said, that nothing presses the spiritual and spinal marrow out of a man more than when his misfortune allows him no action; fate still held our Victor fast with one hand, in order to beat him sore with the other, when in these weeks of sorrow the water-wheel of time filled up *two* new lachrymatories out of the hearts of men, and emptied them into eternity. First came the dismal tidings, like a funeral knell, to Victor's ear, that the sometime friend of his youth, Flamin, was about to expiate a step which, but for the falling out with him, he never would have taken, with his death. Some days after the canicular holidays, — precisely when, a year previous, the poor prisoner had entered on his new office with so many philanthropic hopes, — that rumor came forth like a pestilential cloud out of the session-chambers. Victor flew, incredulous and yet trembling, to the Apothecary, in order to get, by inquiry, a refutation. The latter candidly unfolded before him — for the very reason that he despised and wanted to shame the Court-Physician — all the *rapport*-lists of the court and the reports of the *cercles*, and recited to him so much as this out of them: it was not otherwise. Victor heard, what he already presupposed, that the Prince had on now the leading-strings or curb-bit of his own wife, and that she came nearer to him in consequence of Clotilda's withdrawal, and, with her *ear*-* and *ring*-finger, moved the bridle, threaded through the *nose*-ring, as if she were in fact nothing less than his — mistress; which is a new and mournful example, how easily in these times a fine married lady steals the privileges of a concubine. Zeusel found it natural, "that she, as the friend of the Minister, who, as well as his son Matthieu, had been the friend of the Chamberlain, should seek to avenge the death of the latter upon Flamin, and that the Minister, in order the better to get his hand into the handle of the Parcæ's scissors, and cut in twain the thread of the Regency-Councillor's life, himself ordained and maintained the continued absence of his son, that the latter might not in any way protect the unhappy favorite." In all this there was not a true word, — Victor knew better; but so much the worse. O, does not everything betray that Matthieu has drawn the Princess, by hints respecting Flamin's birth, into his faithless interests, in order, like magicians, to destroy at a distance, and by few characters? Would the mere fear of the stigma of the challenge hold him so long beyond the limits of the country? — Add to this, that the sun of princely favor brooded more and more warmly over the ministerial frog-spawn. It is true, — and Victor did not deny it, — one might ex-

* The little finger. The German name is kept for the sake of the allusion. — Tr.

pect of the Princess that she would in time overturn with her foot the Matthieu's- or Jacob's-ladder on which she climbed the princely heart, (whereas she had previously reached only January's *hand,*) just as the marten lets the drowsy eagle snatch him up into the air, and only up aloft begins to hack at him, and keeps doing it till the bearer falls and dies; but by this time, I think, her steadfast gratitude toward Schleunes is abundantly excused with honest men by the fact, that still more remains to be gotten of the uncompleted *gift.* An old lawgiver ordained a punishment for every case of *ingratitude;* in my opinion, every one falls into the same fault as he, if one censures and punishes every instance of gratitude, since often the most selfish at court may have his good reasons for it.*

Victor went sadly into his chamber, and looked on Flamin's picture, and said: "O, may it not be the will of Heaven, poor fellow, that it should be no longer possible to save thee." Victor could never, three days after an offence, any longer avenge himself. "I forgive every one," he used to say, "only not friends and maidens, because I am too fond of both." But what helping hand, what twig, could he reach down into prison to the sinking Flamin? — All he could do was to go to the Prince with a naked prayer for his pardon. Thousands of generous acts remain undone, because one is not entirely certain that they will produce their legitimate fruits. But Victor went nevertheless; he had made for himself the golden rule, *to act for another even when the result is not a matter of certain hope.* For if we chose first to wait for that certainty, sacrifices would be quite as rare as they were devoid of merit.

* All this is neatly summed up in the witty Frenchman's saying, "Gratitude is a keen sense of favors *to come.*" — Tr.

He went to the Prince, for the first time after so long an interval, — with the disadvantage against him of terminating a long absence with a petition, — spoke with the fire of a recluse in behalf of his Flamin, — besought the Prince for the postponement of his fate till his Lordship should return, — received the decision, "Your honored father and I must simply leave it in the hands of justice," — and was coldly and proudly dismissed.

Now precisely it was, on the 5th of September of this year, when a great eclipse of the sun made the soul as well as the earth sad and gloomy, that the water-wheel of time had filled the first lachrymatory vessel in his breast; it rolled over farther, and the second overflowed. Clotilda's letter arrived on the 22d of September, at the beginning of autumn.

"Dear Friend: —

"Your honored father was still in London at the beginning of February, and had much *French* correspondence; then he went off to Germany, and since that my mother knows nothing of his movements. May Destiny watch over his important life! Upon three oaths,* which his absence makes inviolable, hang many tears, many hearts, and, O God! a human life. — I enclose a leaf from your honored father, which he wrote at my mother's, and which contains a philosophy that makes my spirit and my prospects more and more sad. Ah, although you once said, neither the fear nor the hopes of man hit their mark, but always something else; still I have the mournful right to believe my apprehensions and all the dreams of anxiety, as

* These oaths of silence, as is well known, his Lordship had required of Victor, Clotilda, and her mother, with all that tragic circumstance which takes so strong a hold especially on female hearts.

I have hitherto been mistaken in nothing but in hope.— How insatiable is man!—But even though all should come true, and I should become too unhappy, still I should say, how could I now be too unhappy, had I not once been too happy?——

"You will readily forgive me, if I am silent about London, and about the impression which it might make on so *distrait* a heart as mine. The active stir of freedom, and the glitter of luxury and of commerce, simply oppress a sorrowing soul, and do not make one more cheerful who was not cheerful before. Be happy, beloved native city, my heart said, be long and greatly happy, as I was in thee in my youth!—But then I love rather to hasten with my mother to her country-seat, where once three good children * so joyously bloomed, and there I am inexpressibly softened, and then I fancy myself happier here than among the happy. I only fancy it, I may well say: for when I contemplate there all the playthings of those good children, their task-books and their little clothes; when I seat myself under three cherry-trees planted close together, which they in play had set out in the child's garden, which was too narrow for them; and then when I think how on this stage they exercised and built up their hearts for a happier life than they have won, for a higher virtue than their relations allowed them, and for better society than they have found,—then am I sorely distressed, and then I feel as if I must weep and could say, I too was born in England, and was educated in Maienthal by Emanuel.

"Ah, I cannot hide the feelings of my heart, when I write the name of that great soul.—He was often on a mountain here, where lies a ruined church, and where he

* Victor, Julius, Flamin.

climbed a column that was still standing, in order to lift his eye to the stars, above which he now dwells. — I was just on the point of writing to you now what my mother told me of his departure; but it makes me too sad, and I will tell it to you orally. I visit this mountain very often, because one can look down on the whole plain eastward: here is the old tree, still hanging with its roots and twigs down into the quarry, which lies full of broken temple columns. Emanuel often at evening took thither the child whom he loved most,* and who, when *he* prayed on the column, with one arm wound round the tree, looked out and leaned out, longing and singing, over the broad landscape, and, without knowing it, wept in sweet distress at his own tones, and at the distant fields, and at the pale morning-red which gleamed back from the red of evening. Once, when the teacher asked the child, 'Why art thou so still, and leavest off singing?' — the answer was, 'Ah, I long for the morning-red. I should like to lie in it and go through it, and look over into the bright lands behind there.' — I often seat myself under that tree, and lean my head against it, and silently follow with my eye the stretch of distance even to the horizon, which stands before Germany; and no one disturbs my weeping or my still prayer.

"I was there to-day for the last time; for to-morrow we go with my mother, without whom my orphan heart can no longer live, back to Germany, to the best friend of

"The truest friend,

"CL."

O thou good soul! — —

How hard, after this, sounds the singular leaf of his

* She well knows that it was Victor.

Lordship, which seems to be no letter, but a cold apology for his future conduct.

"Life is a petty, empty game. If my many years have not refuted me, then a refutation by my few remaining ones is neither necessary nor possible. A single unhappy man outweighs all drunken ones. For us insignificant things, insignificant things are good enough; for sleepers, dreams. Therefore, neither in us nor out of us is there anything worthy of wonder. The sun near to is a ball of earth; an earthly globe is merely the more frequent repetition of an earthly clod. — What is not sublime in itself and for itself can no more be made so by repetition than the flea by the microscope; at most, smaller. Why should the tempest be sublimer than an electric experiment, a rainbow greater than a soap-bubble? If I resolve a great Swiss landscape into its constituent parts, I get fir-needles, icicles, grasses, drops, and gravel. — Time resolves itself into moments, peoples into individuals, genius into thoughts, immensity into points; there is nothing great. — A trigonometrical proposition, often thought over, becomes a tautological one; an oft-read conceit, stale; an old truth, indifferent. — Again I assert, what becomes great by steps remains little. If the poetic power, which paints either *images* or *passions*, is not already admirable in the invention of the most commonplace image, then it is nowhere so. Every one can, like the poet, put himself into the place of another, at least in some degree. — I hate inspiration, because it is raised as well by liquors as by fancies, and because, during and after it, one is most inclined to *intolerance* and *sensual pleasure*. — The greatness of a sublime deed consists not in the execution, which amounts to mere corporeal pitiablenesses, going and staying; not in the simple resolve, because the opposite one, e. g., that of murdering, requires just as much energy as that of dying; not in its rarity, because we all are conscious in ourselves of the same capacity for the act, but have not the motive; — not in any of these, but in our boasting. — We hold our very last error for truth, and only the last but one as none at all; our to-day as holy, and every future moment as the crown and heaven of its predecessors. In old age, after so many labors, after so many appeasings, the spirit has the same thirst, the same torment. As in a higher eye everything is diminished, a spirit or a world, in order to be great, should be so even before a so-called Divine eye; but then the one or the other would have to be greater than God, for one never admires his own image. — In my youth, I composed a tragedy, and put all the above principles into the mouth of my hero, and made him, shortly before he plunged the dagger into his own heart, add these further words: But perhaps death *is* sublime; for I do not comprehend it. And so, then, will I lead aside the columns of blood which leap up out of the heart and so sportively keep up the human head and the human individuality at such an elevation, as a fountain bears the hollow ball balanced on its flickering stream, — this fountain will I draw off with the dagger, so that the *I* may be precipitated. — I shuddered at this character at the time; but afterward, I reflected upon it, and it became my own!" —

* * * * *

Frightful man! Thy blood-stream and the *I* on the top of it have perhaps already collapsed, or will soon fall through. — And precisely this dark presentiment is also in the hearts of Victor and Clotilda — — O that thou, thou other bowed man, whom I dare not name here before the public, mightest guess that I mean thee, that thou, just as well as the unhappy Lord, art eating away thy own self like blood-sucking corpses, and that, in the *starry night* of life, thou still bearest a deadly *mist* of thine own around thee! O the spectacle of a magnanimous heart, which merely through ideas makes itself helpless, and which lies inaccessible and benumbed in its arbor of philosophical poison-trees, often dyes our days black! — Believe not that his Lordship is anywhere right! How can he find anything to be small, without holding it over against something great? Without reverence there could be no contempt; without the feeling of disinterestedness, no perception of selfishness; without greatness, no littleness. When thou canst explain the tears of the adagio by the vibration of the strings, or by the blood-globules and threefold skins of a beautiful face thy regard for the same; then and as well canst thou think to justify thy rapture for the *spiritual* in Nature by means of its corporeal filaments, which are nothing but the *flute-pieces* and flat and sharp valves of the unplayed harmony. The sublime resides only in thoughts, whether those of the Eternal One, who expresses them by letters made of worlds, or those of man, who reads them and spells them out! —

I postpone the refutation of his Lordship to another book, although this, too, is a refutation. —

## 42. DOG-POST-DAY.

SELF-SACRIFICE. — FAREWELL ADDRESSES TO THE EARTH. — MEMENTO MORI. — WALK. — HEART OF WAX.

HERE is a sorrow which lays itself with a great sucker-sting to the heart and thirstily drains its tears, — the whole heart runs and gushes and spasmodically contracts its innermost fibres, in order to become a stream of tears, and does not feel the wrench of grief under the deadly-sweet effusion. . . . Such a deadly-sweet pang our Victor felt at Clotilda's letter.

But deadly bitter was that of his Lordship. "O this tormented and worn-out spirit," he exclaimed, "longed, indeed, even on the Isle of Unión, for the repose of the dead; — ah! it has surely fled already from the sweltry earth, which seemed to it so small and oppressive." If this were so, then all the oaths, on whose remission Flamin's life hung, were made eternal, and he was lost. If it was not so, then was there at least no hope of his return, since Emanuel's death and confession, Flamin's imprisonment, and all the previous occurrences, all of which his Lordship might learn, had wiped out his whole finely delineated plan. Now a voice cried aloud in Victor's soul, "Save the brother of thy beloved!" — Yes, a way to do it was at hand; — but it was perjury. If, namely he committed that crime by disclosing to the Prince who Flamin was, then he was rescued. But his conscience said, "No! — The downfall of a virtue is a greater evil than the downfall of a man, — only death, but not sin, must be; — shall it cost me still more to break my word, than it has hitherto cost me to keep it?"

It is well known that on the day of this year's equinox, when he had received the two London leaves, there was a cold storm of snow and rain, from which the summer afterward seemed to bloom out a second time. — Victor went on in his pondering. He called up before him once more, with all its moments, that great day on the Isle of Union, and found that he had absolutely sworn to his Lordship forever to be silent, except an hour before his own death. We may still remember that he had at the time reserved this very condition, because he had once sworn to Flamin to throw himself down with him from the observatory, if they should be obliged to part as enemies; and because now, when Clotilda's sisterly relation was announced to him, he feared beforehand it might come to that separation and suicide. In that case, he would at least reserve to himself the liberty, only an hour before his death, of saying to his friend that he was innocent, and that Flamin's beloved was only a — sister.

"So then, an hour before my death, I may disclose all? — O God! — Yes! — — Yes! — I will die, that so I may speak!" he cried, enkindled, throbbing, fluttering, exalted above life. — The tempest hurled the torrents of heaven and the powdered glaciers against the windows, and the day sank gloomily in the whelming flood. . . . "O," said our friend, "how I long to escape out of this black storm of life, — into the still, bright ether, — to the steadfast, immovable breast of death, which does not disturb sleep. . . ."

If he disclosed to the Prince that Flamin was his own son, then was the latter delivered, and he needed only an hour after that to — destroy himself.

And that would he gladly do; for what had he left on earth except — recollections? O, too many recollections, too few hopes! — Who would be grieved at his fall? — the loved one, who, after all, resigns him, — or her brother, whom he saves and flies from, — or his good lord, who perhaps rests already in the earth, — or his Emanuel, whose loving arms are already crumbling to dust? — "Yes, him only will my dying affect," said he, "for he will long for his faithful scholar, he will on some sun open his arms and look down along the way to the earth, and I shall come up with a great wound on my breast, and my streaming heart will lie naked on the wound. — O Emanuel, despise me not, I shall cry; I was truly unhappy, after thou hadst died; receive me and heal the wound!"

— "Seest thou my father?" said the blind Julius, and his face approached a smile of rapture. Victor started and said, "I talk with him, but I do not see him." — But this checked his exaltation. He had been hitherto the paraclete and nurse of the poor blind charge; he could not leave him, he must needs put off the *retreating-shot* of life till the arrival of Clotilda, that she might protect the helpless one. Ah, the good night-walker and night-sitter (in the proper sense) had at first every day prayed Victor to operate upon his eye, and give him back the light, before his dear father should crumble to pieces, that he might see once more, only once more, the fair countenance not yet undermined by worms; yes, he would at least touch blindly the cold mask, — this he had in the beginning implored; but in a few weeks he had drawn his arms away from under the dead man, and folded them entirely (like a true child) with all his caressing love around Victor, who *always* stayed at home with him. And in the night they reached out to each other their warm hands out of their adjoining beds, and thus linked together went into the evening-lands of dreams. To the childlike blind one, even the continuous din of the city turmoil, which his village had wanted, had been a comfort. . . .

Victor, therefore, waited first for the arrival of Clotilda; — ah! he would have done it even without reference to the blind youth. — Must he not see once more his good mother, hear once more the voice of his never-to-be-forgotten beloved? — For the rest, I cannot disguise the fact, that not merely the salvation of Flamin, but a real disgust at life, guided his hand in his death-sentence. The verdict of murderous disgust had, for its grounds of decision, the sunset of Emanuel, — Victor's oft-recurring night-thoughts upon this our lucubration of life, — his entire revolution of his social relations, — the corresponding past or future example of his Lordship, — his panting for a deed full of energy, — and, most of all, the death-chill about his forlorn and naked bosom, which once was covered by so many warm hearts. One can do without love and friendship only so long as one has not yet enjoyed them; — but to lose them, and that without hope, *this* one cannot do without dying. Upon his conscience he played off the optical deception and stage-trick of asking it whether he might not draw his friend out of the water at the hazard of his life; whether he might not leap from the plank, which could hold only one, into the waves, in order to make his death the purchase-money of another's life. — Two singular ideas sweetened for him his deadly purpose more than all.

The first was, that on his death-day (after the disclosure to the Prince) he could repair to Flamin's prison, and grasp his hand, and boldly say: "Come out, — to-day I die for thee, that I may prove to thee that Clotilda was thy sister, and I thy friend. — I quench the black word, which can only be forgiven on the death-day, with my innocent blood, and death folds me again to thy arms. — O, I do it gladly, so that I may only love thee once more right heartily, and say to thee, My good, precious, never-to-be-forgotten youthful friend!" — Then would he fall upon his neck with a thousand tears, and forgive him all; for *in the neighborhood of death, and after a great deed,* man can and may forgive man everything, everything.

Every tenderer soul will easily divine the second thought that sweetened that of death. — It was this, that he could go once more to his beloved and think, though not say, before her, "I fall for thee." For he now felt, after all, that the resolve of a parting for life was too hard, and only that of doing so by death was easy. — O right easy and sweet it is, he felt, to close the wet eye in the presence of the loved one, then to see nothing more on the earth; but with the high flames of the heart, and with the dear image pressed to the bosom, like the encoffined mother with the dead darling, to step blindfold to the brink of this world, and throw one's self headlong into the still, deep, dark, cold sea of the dead. . . . "Thou art," he often said, "painted on my conscious being, and nothing can sever thy image from my heart; both must, as in Italy the wall and the picture upon it, be transported together." — And as now there was no longer any need to care for his body, he could call forth, of his own accord, the tears which agitated him. He wanted really to offer something of his life to Clotilda: therefore he rehearsed, for some days in succession, the part of the bloodiest farewell scene, even to exhaustion, and made pen-and-ink sketches of his sorrow, and said to himself, when thereby headaches and heart-beatings came upon him, "I can thus at least suffer something for *her*, though *she* knows nothing of it."

Here is one such mournful leaf.

"O thou angel! Were it not that it would affect thee too sadly, I would go to thee, and before thy eyes fill my heart with tears, with images of the fairer time, with the bitterest sorrows, until it broke and sank, — or I would slay myself in thy presence. Ah! it were sweet to pierce my heart with lead, as it leaned on thy bosom, and to let my blood and life flow out on thy breast. — But, O God! no, no! Smiling will I go to thee, good soul, when thou comest back again, as if it were merely for joy at thy return, — only the pink with the red drop will I beg of thee, that my heart, adorned with it, may moulder under the last flower of life. I will, indeed, bleed so near thee, heavenly murderess, as the corpse does before its murderess, but yet only inwardly; and every drop of blood will fall merely from one thought to another. — Then, at last, will I be silent for a long time, and go, and that forever, only saying this and no more: 'Think of me, beloved, but be happier than heretofore.' —— Whither then will I go, after an hour? I shall take the dumb, dreary road to the poisonous Buo-upas-tree,* to where death stands

* This poison-tree stands in a bald waste, because it kills everything around it; and the malefactor journeys alone to its poison, but he seldom returns. [This has been ascertained to be fabulous. There is a poisonous valley encircled by banks emitting a fatal carbonic-acid gas, but no tree grows there, and the upas grows in the woods among other trees without harming them. — Tr.]

solitary, and there die all alone, all alone. —— The dead are mutes, they have bells, and in the blue a mute will hover, and toll the death-bell. . . . O Clotilda, Clotilda! then our love on earth is over!"

Dost thou, reader, still recognize the voice which, in his inner being, always, amidst the weeping of music, rang in the cadence of verse? Here it rings again. — But his hurricane of resolve soon gave place to gentler deeds and hours, just as the equinoctial storm of autumn dissolved into still after-summer days. The thought, "In a few weeks thou wilt fly to the land beyond the grave," made him a *free-born* creature and an angel. He forgave everybody, even the Evangelist. He filled his little sphere with virtues as with an after-bloom of life, and devoted his short hours, not to sweet fantasies, but to needy patients. He denied himself every expenditure, in order to leave to Julius his paternal property unimpaired. He was neither vain nor proud. He spoke frankly about and against the state; — for what is there to fear so near to the storm- and weather-shed of the coffin-lid? — But for the very reason that he felt only love for what is good, and no passions and no cowardice in his inner man, therefore he resisted *gently* and *quietly;* for when once man is convinced for himself that he has laid up courage for a day of need, he no longer seeks to make a show of it before others. The thought of death used to incline him to humorous follies, but now only to good actions. He was so happy, men and scenes around him appeared to him in the mild, soothing evening-light, wherein he always beheld both in the *sicknesses* of his childhood. It seemed as if he wanted (and he succeeded in it) to bribe his conscience by this piety to a legible indorsement of his autographic sentence of death. To him, as to the departed

Emanuel, men appeared as children, the light of earth as evening-light, everything seemed softer, everything a little smaller; he had no anxiety or hankering; the earth was his moon; now for the first time he understood the soul of his Dahore. . . .

— And thou, my reader, dost thou not feel that thou, too, so near to the cloister-gate of death, wouldst improve just so? But thou and I are in fact already standing before it. Is not our death as certain as Victor's, although the certainty ranges through a longer interval? O, if every one only had a fixed belief that after fifty years, on an appointed day, Nature would lead him to her place of execution, he would be a different man; but we all banish the image of death out of our souls, as the Silesians on Lætare-Sunday cast it out of the cities. The thought and the expectation of death improve us as much as the certainty and the choice of it.

And now the fair, blue after-summer days of this year's October floated on tender butterfly-wings of spider-webs across the heavens. Victor said to himself, "Fair earthly heaven, I will take one more walk beneath thee! Good mother-land, I will look out upon thee once more, with thy woods and mountains, and fix thy image in the immortal soul, ere thy yellow green grows over my heart, and strikes its roots therein. I will see thee, St. Luna of my childhood, and you, my fair Whitsuntide paths, and thee, thou blessed Maienthal, and thee, thou good old Bee-father,* and will give back to thee thy watch that counts the hours of joy — — and then I shall have lived long enough."

He asked himself, "Am I, then, ripe for the granary of the churchyard? — But then is any man ripe? Is he

* Lind in Kussewitz.

not in his ninetieth year still incomplete as in his twentieth?" — Yes, indeed! Death takes off children and Patagonians; man is summer fruit, which Heaven must pluck before it matures. The other world is no uniform alley and orangery, but the tree-nursery of our present seed-nursery.

Before Victor left the blind one, with tears and kisses, he sent for poor Marie the evening previous to come to the cabinet, and commended to her (as well as to the Italian servant) the care of the dependent youth. But his design was to give and announce beforehand to the crushed and powerless soul the hope of some hundred florins; for so much he could already expect as inheritance from his well-circumstanced father, Eymann. The selfishness of this humiliated creature, which would have made others cold, was precisely what moved his innermost being. Long since he had said, "One should not have compassion on any man who thought philosophically or loftily, least of all on a learned man, — with such a one the wasp-stings of fate hardly went through the stocking, — on the contrary, with the poor vulgar soul he suffered and wept infinitely, which knew nothing greater than the goods of earth, and which, without principles, without consolation, pale, helpless, convulsed, and rigid, sank at the sight of the ruin of its goods." — It therefore only redoubled his pity when this Marie in wild gratitude passed in his presence from abrupt utterances of thanks, ejaculations, gushes of joy, to kissing of the coat, silly laughing, and kneeling.

When he went the next morning, — first to St. Luna, — and passed along before the convent of Mary, where once the adopted daughter of the Italian Tostato would have offered a sixth finger, Marie was just coming out of a limb-shop,* where she had bought two wax hearts. Victor drew out from her by long and ingenious questioning that she was going to hang one of them, which represented hers, on the holy Mary, because hers no longer pained her so much nor was so much oppressed as it had been the week before. — As to the second, she would not for a long time let anything out; at last she confessed: it was Victor's own, which she was going to offer to the Holy Mother of God, because she thought it must pain him also right sorely, as he looked so pale and sighed so often. —— "Give it to me, love," he said, too deeply moved, "*I will offer my heart myself.*"

"Ay," he repeated out under the still heaven, "the heart behind the wall of the breast will I offer, — that, too, is of wax, — and to mother Earth will I give it, that it may heal, — heal." . . .

Let him weep freely, my friends, now that he beholds smiling the still, pale earth, even up to its hazy mountains. — For softness of sensibility loves to ally itself with petrifying processes and the art† of Passau against the calamities of fate. Let him weep freely, as he looks upon this flowerless earth, spinning itself, as it were, into the silk of the fugitive summer, and feels as if he must fall down and kiss the cold meadow as a mother, and say, "Bloom again sooner than I; thou hast given me enough of joys and flowers!" — The silent dissolution of nature, on whose corpse the full-blooming daisy stood as if it were a death-garland, softly unnerved his powers by this loosening friction, — he was exhausted and stilled, — nature

* Around numbers of chapels (see Schlötzer's Correspondence, Part III. Vol. XVIII. 45) stand warehouses of wax limbs and animals, which they buy as ear-rings and bracelets for the saints, in order that the originals may be healed.

† Of making one's self invulnerable. — Tr.

reposed around him and he in it, — the exhaustion overflowed almost into a sweet, tickling faintness, — the tear-gland swelled and pressed no more before it ran over; but its water trickled down like dew out of flowers, easily and without stopping, as the blood flowed through his breast.

He saw now St. Luna lying before him, but, as it were, withdrawn from him in a moonlight. He passed not through, in order not to see the wax statue, whose funeral sermon he had delivered, and for which he also possessed a heart of wax; but he went round along the outskirts. "Grow ever broader and more bustling, fair spot: never may an enemy beleaguer thee around!" He said no more. For as he passed by the church-yard he thought, "Have not all these, then, also taken leave of the place; and am I the only one who does it?" — The mere backward glance at the slated roof of the parsonage kindled one more lightning flash of pain at the thought of a *mother's* tears for his death; but he soon whispered to himself the consolation, that the maternal heart of the parson's wife, never weaned from Flamin, would cure its sorrow for the victim by its joy over the rescued favorite.

He went now towards Maienthal, and carefully kept away his dreaming thoughts from its exalted places, in order (at evening on the arrival) to enjoy so much the more — sorrow. But now his conscious soul spun itself into a new ideal web. He thought over the pleasure of sinking without any sick nights into the earth, bright and erect, not prostrate, but upright like the giant Cænæus,* — he felt himself shielded against all disasters of life, and purged from the fear perpetually gnawing on in every

* The Centaurs could not prostrate him with trees, but had to press him, as he stood erect, into the earth. Orph. Argonaut. 168.

heart, — all this, and the joy of having fulfilled his duties and controlled his impulses, and the lights of the blue day standing as if in flower-dust, so cleared his turbid life-stream, that at last he could have wished (had not his determination forbidden it) to play longer in the bright stream. . . . So great does contempt of death render the beauty of life, — so sure is every one, who in *cold blood* renounces life, of being able to endure it, — so sound is the advice of Rousseau, before death to undertake a good deed, because one can then do without dying. . . . — As Victor thought thus, Fate stepped before him and asked him sternly, "Wilt thou die?" — He answered, "Yes!" — as, just before sundown, he beheld again in Upper Maienthal Clotilda's carriage, which he had seen there at its starting upon the journey. Now the death-cloud fell upon the landscape. He hurried by, — at the window he saw his mother and the lady, the mother of Flamin, — his inner being was in a tumult, — his eyes glowed, but remained dry, — for he was choosing among the instruments of death. — Why did he go, so late, in the dark, with a stormy soul, which obscured all sweet dreams, to Maienthal? — He would go to Emanuel's grave; not to mourn there, not to dream there, but to seek for himself a hollow there, namely, the last. His impetuous grief had sketched a picture of his dying, and he had approved the sketch; namely, so soon as fate had decided the necessity of his death by the disappearance of his father and by the peril of Flamin, he meant to scoop out his grave near the weeping birch, lay himself down in it, kill himself therein, and then let the blind Julius, who could not know nor see anything of it, fling the earth over him, and so, veiled, unknown, nameless, flee out of life to the side of his mouldering Emanuel. . . .

Black funeral processions of ravens flew slowly like a cloud through the sunless heavens, and settled down like a cloud into the woods, — the half-moon hung above the earth, — a strange, little shadow, as big as a heart, ran fearfully beside him. He looked up: it was the shadow of a slowly hovering hawk; he rushed through Maienthal; he saw not the leafless garden nor Dahore's closed house, but ran through the chestnut alley toward the weeping birch. —

But under the chestnuts, at the place where Flamin would have killed him, he saw Clotilda's withered pink, with the bloody drop in its chalice, lying on the ground. . . . And as a lark, the last songstress of Nature, still quivered over the garden, and called with too ardent tones after all the spring-times of life, and pierced the heart with an infinite, deathly yearning, then did my Victor look up and weep aloud; and when, up on the grave, he had wiped away the great, dark tears, there stood — Clotilda before him.

One thrill ran through him, and he was dumb. . . . She hardly recognized the paled form, and asked, trembling, "Is it you? Do we see each other again?" — His soul was torn asunder, and he said, but in another sense, "We see each other again." She was in the bloom of health, having been restored by the journey. But there was blood on her handkerchief, — it was the blood which Emanuel's bosom had shed during the duel in the alley. He stared inquiringly at the blood. She pointed to the grave, and veiled her weeping eyes. — With the question, "Has your honored father come?" the good soul sought gently to lead him aside; but she led him to his grave, — his eye sought wildly the place for the last cool grotto of life, — she had never seen her gentle lover thus, and would fain soothe his soul by quiet remembrances of Emanuel, — she filled out the chasm in her letter, and related how quietly and composedly the dead man went from England, and previously at his departure lowered down into an extraordinarily deep hollow of the fallen temple all his East-Indian flowers, three pictures, written palm-leaves, and collections of loved ashes. . . .

Victor was beside himself, — he supported himself by his hand on the dew-cold, wet, yellow grave, — he wept in one steady stream, and could no longer see his beloved, — he threw himself upon her quivering lips, and gave her the farewell-kiss of death. He could venture to kiss her; for there is no rank among the dead. He felt her streaming tears, and a cruel longing seized him to provoke these tears forth; but he could only not speak. He choked her words with kisses and his own with grief. At last he was able to say, "Farewell!" She extricated herself with terror, and looked on him with greater tears, and said, "What is it with *you?* You break my heart!"— He said, "Only mine must break!" and hurriedly drew out the heart of wax, and crushed it to pieces on the grave, and said, "I offer my heart to thee, Emanuel; I offer thee my heart." And when Clotilda had fled with alarm, he could only call after her, with exhausted tones, "Farewell! farewell!"

## 43. DOG-POST-DAY.

MATTHIEU'S FOUR WHITSUNTIDE DAYS AND JUBILEE.

T is a stroke of art in me to write down true scenes of villany in the higher classes in French first, and then interpret them into the vernacular, as Boileau composed his insipid verses originally in prose. — As I attach great importance to the Forty-Third Dog-Post-Day, — because therein the noble Mat seeks to save his Flamin even at the sacrifice of his virtue and of Lord Horion, — accordingly I meditate to translate it so faithfully into German out of the French, in which I have written it, that my French author himself shall bestow on me his approbation.

Hardly had Matthieu heard that Clotilda's and Flamin's mother had come from London, when this Reineke marched out of his fox-kennel to Flachsenfingen, because he would not let any one take from him the honor of releasing Flamin. He seldom, despite his fieriness, anticipated opportunity; but he watched and only helped things on here or there; as in a romance, so in life, a thousand light trivialities, brought together at last, hook into each other firmly, and a good Mat twists at last out of scattered cobweb-meshes of accident a regular — silk noose for his fellow-man. — He boldly contrived to get himself a secret audience with the Prince, "because he would rather go to meet his punishment (on account of the challenge to the duel) than. let certain weighty things remain in silence any longer." *Weighty* and *dangerous* had long since been kindred terms with January, but now were absolutely identical, because the Princess entertained him every morning with a few strophes out of the penitential psalm and owl's song about sedition, Ankerstrœms,* and propagandists. She and Schleunes blew upon *one* horn, — at least, they blew one melody from it.

Matthieu entered and produced the great weighty matter, — the bold petition for Flamin's life. January pronounced an equally bold "No!" for man is quite as indignant at him who drives him into a groundless fear, as at him who drives him into a well-grounded one. Matthieu coldly repeated his request: "I simply beg your Highness not to suppose that I should ever hold mere friendship as an adequate apology for such a bold petition, — the duty of a subject is my excuse." — January, who was annoyed at the uncourteous retraction, broke it off: "The guilty cannot petition for the guilty." — "Most gracious sir," said the Evangelist, who sought to drive him into fear and fury at once, "in any other times than ours it would be quite as punishable to guess or to predict certain things as to decree them; but in ours, these three things are easier. Against the day when the Regency-Councillor should lose his life, a plan is arranged, which certain persons have formed for the salvation of his life at the expense of their own." — The Prince — enraged at a boldness which ordinarily resides not within the *snow-line* †

* Ankerstrœm was a Swedish regicide, born 1759, and executed, for killing Gustavus III., in 1792. — Tr.

† The name given to a certain elevation above the sea, determined by Bouger, at which the mountains in all zones are covered with snow.

of courts, but only at the democratic equator — said, with the death-sentence which Mat had long since wanted to get into his face: "I shall have you required to tell to-morrow the names of the wretches who propose to sacrifice their lives for the sake of turning the course of justice." . . . Here the page fell down before him, and said quickly: "My name is the first; it is now my duty to be unhappy. My friend has killed no one, but I did it; he is not the son of a priest, but the first-born son of the murdered Mr. Le Baut." . . .

Since pier-mirrors first existed, never was such a dumfounded, distracted visage seen in them as to-day. January dismissed him, in order to collect himself.

We will now in the antechamber say three words about the absent one. A shrewd thinker once said to me, that he had once said to a great connoisseur of the world, "The fault of the great was never to trust themselves in anything, and hence they were led by every one"; and that the connoisseur answered, he had hit it. — January had a grudge against Mat, and that merely on account of his satirical and sensual face, — but not anywise on account of his vices. I take for granted that the reader will certainly have seen courts enough — on the stage, where the higher classes get their notions of country people, and we ours of them — to know what one hates there — — not vicious persons, not even virtuous ones, but both of these one really loves there (precisely as they do violinists, mechanics, Wetzlar attorneys, intendants) whenever they have need of them. — —

The page appeared again. January had allayed the sweet paternal ebullition at the news, since he had heretofore given up all his children for lost. He desired now the proof that Flamin was the (nominal) son of the Chamberlain. About the duel he gave himself not the least concern. The proof was easy for the upright soul to produce. The soul appealed directly to the mother, who had this very moment arrived from London, having come to save her son, and to the sister herself. The soul had again the antecedent proposition to prove that both had knowledge of the matter: — Matthieu appealed to the letter of the mother which he had some years before read to the blind lord with the borrowed voice of Clotilda, and to the sister's exclamation during the duel in Maienthal Park, "It is my brother," — and finally he adduced one more domestic witness in the case, the after-summer, which would now soon appear, and would retouch the maternal mark of the apple, which Le Baut's son bore on his shoulder.

Matthieu had too much veneration for his Prince and master to call the sovereign of the son the son's father. He now closed by saying, "He knew not for what reasons Lord Horion had hitherto concealed Flamin's extraction; but whatever they might have been, all excuses his Lordship had were also his own excuses for having himself kept silence so long, — and so much the more, as the proof of this descent must be more difficult for him than for his Lordship. — Only now, by the arrival of the mother, the *facility* of the proof was made as great as the *necessity* of it. — All that he could do as a family friend of the Chamberlain had been to become Flamin's confidant in order to be his protector."

Thereby the Prince was necessarily brought back to the subject of the duel, which he in the beginning, after a few hints, had let drop. It was his way of business to break off soon from an affair of importance to him, to talk quite as long about other things, then to bring that matter forward again, and so pack the important matter away under quite as big layers of unimportant matters, as the booksellers slip contraband books in sheets under white or other paper. Then, too, Flamin's innocence of the murder was now of more consequence to January; he therefore naturally inquired why he had exposed his friend as a victim even to the show of a duel.

Matthieu said it would be a long story, and it was a bold step to entreat so much attention on the part of his Highness. He began with reporting what — the Dog-Post-Days have hitherto reported. He lied very little. He intimated that, in order to *break off* Flamin's love for his unknown sister Clotilda, — at least he wanted to *increase* it, — he had tried to make him jealous, but had not been able to set him at variance with any one except the lover; nay, it had not even helped matters at all that he had let him be himself an ear-witness of the very pardonable infidelity of Clotilda, but that his friend had at the very last manifested a rage at his sister's betrothal, which he had been able to appease in no other way than by the illusion of a disguised duel with the father. For in order to prevent a second fight between father and son, he had himself undertaken it, but unhappily with too disastrous an effect.

So far the noble Mat. The true circumstances, which are familiar to us, I suppress. January, who was now favorably inclined toward the Evangelist for the removal of a fear into which he himself had thrown him, put to him the natural question, why Flamin took upon himself the murder. — Matthieu: "I fled at once, and it was not in my power to prevent his untruth, which I could not have looked for; but it was in my power to refute it." — January: "Go on in your frankness; it is your vindication; do not evade!" — Matthieu, with a freer mien: "What I had to say I have already said in the beginning, for the sake of saving him; and now he is saved." — January went back in thought, could not comprehend, and begged, "Make yourself a little more clear." — Matthieu, with the designed look of a man who prepares silverings-over of his story: "From magnanimity he would have died for him (Mat) who had sinned for him, did not his friends come to the rescue." January shook his head incredulously. "For," the other continued, "as he knows not his high *rank*, he more readily adopted certain *French* principles, which would have *alleviated* for him his death quite as much as certain Englishmen would have made use of them with the people to prevent it." As a proof, by the way, he adduced the blowing-up of the powder-house.

January saw with astonishment a light glide into a dark cavern, and saw far into the cavern.

One wrongs the excellent Evangelist, if one thinks it satisfies him merely to have saved his friend. His good heart was also bent upon setting up for his Lordship a monumental column, and of laying him under the column as its corner-stone. He gladly (as in "Hamlet") quartered in the play another play, and raised two theatre-curtains. We will seat ourselves in the first box. His previous conduct toward the Regency-Councillor shows plainly enough how far he was capable of carrying a true friendship without offending other friends, e. g. the Princess; for to the latter the finding again of the lost son of the Prince was no remarkable disadvantage, since the son was presented at once as master of a Jacobin lodge and rebel against his step-father and father both, and since his Lordship was so terrible a loser in the matter besides.

But inasmuch as Matthieu had nothing to reproach himself with in the case, except his excess of philanthropy, he sought to counteract this extreme by an opposite one, of malice, because Bacon writes: "Exaggerations are best cured by their opposites." Neither, according to his too ardent notions of friendship, could he be a genuine friend of his Lordship's, since, according to Montaigne, one can have only *one* true friend, as well as only one lover; and his Lordship already exhibited one such in the person of January.

Allow me in three words to be short and agreeable. If the Arabs have two hundred names for the snake, they should certainly add the two hundred and first, — that of Courtier. — Indulge me further in saying, that a man of influence and tone, by a capital crime, — a so-called *debt of blood*,* — flourishes full as well as a whole state does upon more pitiful ones in the matter of money. —

January was now prepared to believe anything that explained the foregoing singular things. A lie which unties a knot is more credible to us than one which ties one. Matthieu went on: "He had attended all the republican *concerts spirituels*, in order to take measures against Flamin's catching the contagion; and he did not carry to an extreme friendship for the three Englishmen and the Lord's son (Victor), if he looked upon them and him more as tools of some other concealed hand, than as themselves workers on a plan. — This was confirmed by the misuse hitherto made of the innocent Flamin." — By way of excusing Victor, he said, — in doing which, he all along named him the Court-Physician, so that January, in his present mood, was more likely to think of a court-poisoner

* *Blutschuld*, — forfeiture of life (*Schuld* meaning both *debt* and *guilt*). — Tr.

than anything else, — by way, then, of setting *him* in a favorable light, he said that individual was a mere lover of pleasure, and only carried out obediently what his father had sketched out for him, — that Victor had disguised himself as an Italian to watch the Princess, and afterward to report to the Lord, at whose behest he probably did it, in a secret interview on an island. — As Italian, he had handed the Princess a watch, in which he had covertly pasted a slip of paper, wherein he had forgotten the higher rank to flatter his own.

The Prince, who loved his spouse with greater jealousy than his betrothed, swept the floor with heavy strokes of the turkey-cock's wing, and pulled out the point of his nose to an unusual length, and proudly inquired how he knew that. — Matthieu replied calmly, "From Victor himself; for the Princess herself knew nothing of it." . . .

The reader owes it to me, that he knows better about a thousand things. — Agnola certainly knew the contents of the watch very well; nay, I even imagine, that, when the enraged Joachime informed her of Victor's direct confession of his *concepit*, she had allowed Mat or Joachime to trace the present recipe, according to which the bridegroom here has to swallow Sebastian's *billet-doux*.

— "On the contrary," he continued, "she had long after presented his sister the watch, together with the billet. — Joachime had taken it out in Victor's presence, and he had thought fit to confess to her freely that very thing, which neither she nor he himself had, out of respect, yet disclosed to the Princess. — Meanwhile his sister had *thereupon* given him the slip, — *whereupon* he had made advances to Clotilda, perhaps according to a paternal instruction to bring the brother into nearer relations. — But in every instance he mixed up with the paternal schemes of ambition his own of pleasure, and was well disposed, just as the Englishmen were, whom he held to be Frenchmen in disguise."

The Prince, during the whole exhibition of these pretty snake-preparations, concealed his fear behind anger; Matthieu, who saw both *mask* and *face*, had hitherto cut all according to the former, and made the apparent want of fear the cloak of his boldness in exciting it. — And so he went from the Prince into a sort of indefinite, mock arrest for the murder; but January began to examine *persons and papers.*

Before reporting the result, let me gladly confess that Mat, the noble, knows how to lie well enough, and all the more, that he puts in truth as lath-work to his mortar of falsehood. As in the Polish rock-salt mines, the good liar always, in the undermining, leaves so many truths standing for pillars as may be necessary to prevent the breaking-in of the arch. In fact, every lie is a happy sign that there is still truth in the world; for, without this, no lie would be believed, and therefore none attempted. Bankruptcies give pleasure to the honest man, as new evidences of the unexhausted religious fund of other men's honesty, which must be extant, if it is to be deceived. So long as treaties of war and peace are disgracefully broken, so long is there still hope enough left, and so long courts will not want for genuine honesty; for every breach of a contract presupposes that one has been made, — and that is what no one could be any longer, if not one were any longer observed. It is with lies as with false teeth, which the gold thread cannot fasten, except to a couple of genuine ones still remaining.

January began the mint-probation days of Matthew's Gospel.

1. The Parson was summoned to confess, in the presence of the supreme authority of the state, what meetings he had suffered in the priestly house. The poor man turned over the leaves of Œmler's Pastoral Theology, to find out how a parson has to behave who is going to be hanged. Without a murmur he now laid his neck upon the block and under the axe for lesser and moderate mishaps, for the Rat-King, who went like a whirlwind through his dwelling, for the garter which, while he walked, gradually slipped down over his knee-pan, and exchanged the *anxiety* of the happy for the *agony* of the unhappy. At the audience he said, he had, at church and elsewhere, inveighed against the clubs as much as any one, and had bought Girtanner* for the purpose. To the question, whether Flamin was his son, he replied sadly, he hoped his wife had never violated his and her marriage vows. — When he got back to his house, in order not to be in agony for fear of arrest, he took a bundle of old manuscript sermons with him into a quarry, and learned them there by heart for three or four Sundays to come.

2. On the same day the Minister Von Schleunes (out of complacency to the Princess) paid a visit at Le Baut's house, and communicated to the lady and Clotilda the current rumors about Flamin's birth. Both ladies had to believe that Victor must have disclosed the secret to the Prince, in order to save his unhappy friend. How could they have helped imitating him, when the iron

* Died in 1800. He was a famous and forcible writer against the French Revolution and the Jacobin clubs, from which latter he drew on himself extreme odium. He wrote "Historical Sketches and Political Observations on the French Revolution," in seventeen volumes. — Tr.

pear* of the oath was taken from the tongue and out of the mouth, and since one may violate a vow of secrecy when one would otherwise have to violate truth, and the tender souls rejoiced now so heartily at the opening of the door of the year of Jubilee into the prison of their darling? — In one word, the Minister brought back nothing but confirmations of the hypotheses of his son.

3. On the same day, the merchant Tostato was examined by Count O. respecting his shop-partner, and Victor by the confessor respecting the author of the pastoral or bucolic letter in the watch, and then heard. Here, too, Matthieu, as was to be expected, had the truth entirely on his side. Victor was now too proud, too good, too resigned, to conceal anything.

4. All the tallies of sins in Kussewitz and everywhere fitted into each other; even from Victor's former mediatorial office, which he once discharged with the Prince for Agnola, from his little indiscretions, from his satires, from his dressing up the juvenile soldiery in breeches, from his journey with the Prince, there was now spelled out nothing but draughts and ground-strokes of a sketched plan of battle against the throne. In fact it was necessary, January was obliged, the more spy-glasses he directed at this meteorological phenomenon of lies, to behold it only so much the greater.

I have forgotten the Princess, who made believe that she was very much offended and wholly ignorant in the matter of the billet, and could hardly be contented with the punishment, that the hero of the Dog-Post-Days should be forbidden the court. — The court! *thee*, good Victor! thee, — who wilt soon forbid thyself the *earth!*

January easily overlooked *past* offences, but he strictly

* A piece of iron that made speaking impossible. — Tr.

punished *future* ones. And since, moreover, Mat, like a rattlesnake, rattled so terribly, not to give warning, but, as more recent naturalists have found in the case of the real rattlesnake, for the sake of making the victim stiff and fearful: accordingly his Lordship was tumbled down so out of January's heart over all the steps of the throne, that it could not have helped him at all, even if he had immediately stept forth out of the air. Flamin was found without his help. — To the house of the three Englishmen permission was sent to take passage for their island, when they pleased. They sent back word, they needed only *one* day to reach their island, and waited only for their travelling companion. By the island, however, they meant the *Isle of Union*, — and by the travelling companion the fettered Flamin, whom they wanted to persuade to go along with them.

I am pleased that my Victor was forbidden the court. Dismissal from court is generally a favor, — (now a deliverance from court-services may well deserve that name,) — which is not always bestowed on the worthiest, but often on a devil like Louvois,* as well as on an apostle like Tessin.† But does it not amount to taking away from an eminent favor, an order *pour le mérite*, all its value, when one tosses it to knaves, whereas it ought to be laid up as the greatest and last reward, as a premium and pike-bearer's reward, ‡ as an ovation, for the most honest, candid, and oldest man at court?

* Prime Minister to Louis XIV. in the most brilliant part of his reign; — arrogant, cruel, inflexible; — had the chief hand in revoking the Edict of Nantes. — Madame de Maintenon overthrew him. — Tr.

† Tessin was an excellent Swedish count, born in 1695. — Tr.

‡ Lit. "Spiessfolgedank." So, too, citizens who act as a military guard are called "Spiessbürger." — Tr.

In the next chapter one may hold himself prepared for an uproar, the like of which is heard in few German chapters; the alarm-cannons of the court-party, the knocking down of scaffoldings and upsetting of chairs, in getting from the criminal court, I shall be able to hear even over on my island. The black-haired and black-hearted court-page, when he is discharged from arrest, with his ironical mien and his peculiar *low* voice, — the ripiěno-voice of his most malicious scorn, as it is with others that of the most exalted enthusiasm, — will stalk round everywhere and say, he wishes his Lordship would appear, he has hitherto labored in his matters to the best of his ability. At court one sometimes becomes sublime by an eminent wickedness,* as, according to Burke, no smell is sublime except the most stinking of all, and no taste except the bitterest. And just so every one easily conceals there his compassionate interest in the falling favorite, like the wise father, who, at the *fall* of a child, disguises his compassionate face under a comic one.

On the 21st of October, Matthieu is set at large, and is at liberty to go to Flamin, — he has begged the favor for himself, — to announce to him his freedom and promotion at once. . . . In a few days the incidents, and my protocol of them, might run out of the hour-glass of one and the same time, if the dog should come regularly; but he comes when he will.

* "By merit raised to that bad eminence." — Tr.

## 44. DOG-POST-DAY.

BROTHERLY LOVE. — FRIENDLY LOVE. — MATERNAL LOVE. — LOVE.

THE Dog is here, but not his Lordship, — the noise is small, but not the joy, — all is prepared for, and yet unexpected, — vice maintains the battle-field, but virtue the Elysian fields. — In short, it is very foolish, but very fine.

I think this is the last chapter of the book. I look upon the Post-Dog — my Pomeranian messenger,* whose tail is his official pike — with real emotion, and it vexes me to think that he, too, has fallen in Adam, and has eaten a bone under the forbidden tree; for in Paradise the first canine parents shone like diamonds, and one could see through them, as Böhme asserts. — For this very reason, as the Mining Superintendent will soon have written himself out, let it be forgiven him that, in this chapter of love, he is more ardent and agreeable than ever, and in fact writes now as if he were possessed.

In the beginning, the heavenly chariot is still drawn by mourning steeds. . . . It was very early, on the 21st of October, 1793, when the court-page ran into Fla-

* At the University of Paris they still keep up the *messenger from Pomerania*, who annually set out for Pomerania, &c. to fetch the Paris students letters from their parents.

min's block-house out of his own, and announced to that brother, doing penance there, the whole budget, — his release, — his relation to Clotilda as brother and sister, — his affiliation into the princely house, — his ascending career, and at the same time the amnesty of the murderer and messenger, namely, his own. O how did joy kindle his stagnant veins at Matthieu's acquittal and intercession, and at his elevation of rank! For Flamin mounted the higher station as an eminence whence he might send out farther his benefits and plans; Victor, on the contrary, had rejoiced at his bankruptcy of rank, because he craved stillness, as Flamin did tumult. The former was more desirous to amend himself; the latter, to improve others. Flamin thrust the live crew overboard, and nailed the Bucentaur of state full of galley-slaves, in order to propel it more swiftly against the winds. But Victor allowed himself to make only *one* corpse by way of lightening the privateer, — namely, his own. He said to himself, "If I can only always sacredly maintain the courage *to sacrifice myself, then I need no greater;* for a greater sacrifices after all stolen goods. — Fate can sacrifice centuries and islands to benefit millennia and continents; * but man, nothing but himself."

Exultingly Flamin hastened with his savior to St. Luna, to embrace gratefully and apologetically the true sister in the untrue mistress. — Ah! as the high observatory rose upon his sight, with pain and bleeding did the covering fall from them like scales, which had hitherto

* And even there only with reference to immortality and compensation. We feel no injustice when one being becomes a plantation-negro, another an angel of the sun; but their creation begins their claims, and the Eternal cannot, without injustice, purchase even with the sufferings of the minutest creature the joys of all better ones, if it is not made good again to the sufferer.

obscured the innocence of his best friend, Victor! "Ah, how will he hate me! O that I had trusted him more!" he sighed, and nothing any longer gladdened him; for the grief of a good man who has been unjust, even under the notion of the fullest justice, nothing can console, nothing but many, many sacrifices. He stole, sighing, not to his new mother, but sank softly on the unoffended heart of the three true twins. The honest souls all welcomed the Evangelist as a friend in need; and this gayly-colored spider crawled round with his unclean spider-warts over all these noble growths of an open love. The spider heard everything, even the agreement that the Englishmen should take the injunction to go off to their island literally, and seclude themselves in the English island of his Lordship, until such time as Flamin and her Ladyship were ready to embark with them all for their greater island, — the workshop of freedom, the classic soil of erect men.

The same morning the Chaplain betook himself to his quarry, and lay at anchor there, because he knew as yet nothing of the latest news. There in the open air, all day long, he sat away his agony, and at night he came home again. He conversed there with no one but his own body, — as many commune with their souls, so do others with their bodies, — and looked from time to time, not at Nature, but at his water, in order — as its want of color, according to physiology, betokens sorrow — to ascertain from it whether he was pining away very much or not with grief; although his *protomedicus* will answer for him, that he shall not have mistaken *urinam chyli* or *sanguinis* for *urinam potûs*. As the physicians assert that sighs are beneficial, to quicken the pulse and lighten the lungs, — accordingly a prince can benefit whole countries at once, by compelling them to sigh, —

Eymann, therefore, prescribed to himself a definite number of sighs, which he had daily to draw for the benefit of his lungs.

The same morning went my Lady to the wife of the Parson to tell her that Flamin was an innocent man, but not her son; and Clotilda went with her to take the hands of the two daughters and say to them, "You have another brother"; for Victor had still concealed his extraction. "O God!" said the Parson's wife, now becoming impoverished, and clasped Flamin's mother and sister to her pining maternal bosom, which, with hot sighs, yearned for a son, — "where, then, is my child? — Bring me my true son! — Ah, I had a presentiment that the duel would certainly cost me a child! He regains all, but I lose all. — O you are a mother, and I am a mother, help me!" — Clotilda looked upon her, weeping with a desire to give consolation; but the Lady said, "Your son lives, and is happy too; but more I cannot say!"

And the same morning, this son, our Victor, was *not* happy. It seemed to him, at the report of Flamin's discharge and of Matthieu's officiousness, as if he heard the hissing and the bullet-like whistle of the swooping hawk, that hitherto in motionless poise, as if with nailed pinion, had hung high in the blue above his prey. — Think not too hardly of the Doctor, that he mourned the lost opportunity of freeing his friend out of the narrow prison, and himself out of the wide one of life. For he has lost too much and is too lonely; men appear to him as people in the Polish rock-salt mines, who grope round with a light bound to their heads, which they call "I," encircled with the unenjoyable glitter of the salt, clad in white and with red fillets,* as if they were bandages. — The speech of his

* The white flesh of the human body and the red veins of blood. — Tr.

acquaintances, like that of the Chinese, is monosyllabic. — He must live to see the mortifying day when January and the city will set down against him the lowliness of his rank as a fraud. — Before every eye he stands in a different light, or shade rather. Matthieu regards him as coarse; January, as intriguing; the women, as trifling, — just as Emanuel regarded him as pious, and Clotilda as too ardent; for every one hears in a full-toned, harmonious man only his own echo. What heart could henceforth induce him — his own could not — to hold an oar any longer in the slave-ship of life? O, one could do it, a warm and mighty one, — his mother's! "Only once plunge out of this world," said his conscience, "then will thy mother, in the fulness of love, die after thee, and appear before thee in the next world with so many tears, with all her hot wounds, and say, 'Son, this sorrow is thy work!'" — He obeyed, and perceived that, if it is noble to die for a mistress, it is still nobler to live for a mother.

He therefore determined this very evening — in the evening, so that night might place its screen before certain weather-wasting ruins of better times, before certain gliding *night-corpses* of memory — to go to St. Luna, to call to his mother, and to refresh her sick and weary heart with at least *one* flower of joy, and say to her, — as no oath any longer bound him, — "Now for the second time thou givest me life!" How sweet was the thought to him! — A single good purpose makes up and airs the sharp sick-bed of a shattered life.

But at evening, you good, oppressed souls, in the evening — not of life, but — of the 21st of October, all will be lighter and fresher to you, and the ball of your fortune will revolve from the stormy to the sunny side.

At evening, Victor arrived at St. Luna, and ensconced

himself in the arbor of the parsonage garden, where he had given Clotilda the first tears of love. — The parsonage, the hall, the observatory, the two gardens, lay around him like dilapidated knightly castles, from which all joys and inmates have long since departed! — All so autumnally still, so stationary around him, — the bees sat mute on the sill of the hive beside the executed drones, — even the moon and a little cloud stood fast beside each other, — the wax mummy stood with rigid face turned round toward the still chamber! — At last the Parson's wife came through the garden, on her way to the hall. He knew how exceedingly she must needs love him again, now that his fidelity to the jealous Flamin had come to light. O, she looked so weary and sickly, so red with weeping, and exhausted with bleeding, and prematurely old! It grieved him, that he must say first an indifferent word, in order to call her into the arbor. When she entered, he raised himself up, and bowed low, and laid himself, as if he would expire, on the dear bosom, within which was a world full of sighs and a heart full of love, and said: "O mother, I am thy son! — accept me; thy son has nothing, loves nothing more on the whole wide earth, nothing more but thee. — O dear mother, I have lost much before finding thee. — Why dost thou look on me thus? — If thou despisest me, then give me thy blessing, and let me flee. . . . Oh! and besides it was only for thy sake that I chose to live any longer." — She looked upon him, bending backward, with a moist eye, full of inexpressible tenderness and sorrow, and said: "Is it true, then? O God! if you were my son! — Ah, good child! — I have long loved thee as a mother. — But deceive me not, my heart is so sore!" — The son gave his oath . . . . and here let the curtain slowly sink on the maternal embrace, and when it has wholly covered son and mother, then let a good child look back into his own soul, and say, here dwells everything that thou canst not describe!

And now, at evening, the Chaplain was stealing home from the field and through the garden, and cried out, as he came to meet his new son: "Ah! Herr Hofmedicus, I am falling away abominably. I look really and manifestly like an *Ecce Homo* and feverish patient. I am doomed. — I am destined to make a *souffre-douleur*, a *persona miserabilis*, a Patripassian." * — When Victor had reported to him, "It is all over, the Regency-Councillor is liberated and innocent," Eymann looked steadfastly up at the observatory, and said, "Verily there sits the Councillor up there, peeping over," and was on the point of going up to him; but Victor gently held him back, and said tenderly, "I am your son," and disclosed to him all. — "What? — you? — thou? — the son of such an eminent Lord, my son? — I to have begotten my Herr Godfather? — That is unheard of, one brother to be another's godson. — I have two Sebastians in my house at once." — He got sight of the Parsoness, and began a quarrel, — which was always with him a sign of joy. — "So, wife! thou hast known this all day, and let me sit out there in the quarry, on the anxious seat, in the midst of grief, tolling away till night at the poor-sinners'-bell? Couldst thou not have let the bellows-blower come out to notify me? That was very ill done, — the wife sits at home and drinks bitters, into which are thrown whole casks of sugar and dishes of comfits, — and the man keeps himself in stone-quarries, and swills

* Name given to the believers in the dogma of the *Father's* suffering on the cross. — Tr.

down steadily his bitter extracts out of an emetic-cup." — She never answered a word.

Now, for the first time, Victor learned from his mother that it was only for his friend (Matthieu), and for his country, Flamin had meant to die; that he repented his unjust jealousy, and bewailed the friendship he had trifled away; and that she had sent for him for the very reason that she might conduct him to the arms of his true mother, and before the face of an afflicted sister. It had been this morning a human weakness, that the frozen limb of friendship, his heart, had been a little more cold and unfeeling towards Flamin, when he heard of his deliverance from imprisonment, — but it was now, at evening, the part of human kindness, that Flamin's great resolve to die restored, like a chilblain ointment, to his stiff heart warmth and motion. His inner being stirred itself mightily, welled up, overflowed his crushed resentment, and the image of the youthful friend rose up and said: "Victor, give thy hand again to thy school-friend, — O, he has suffered so much, and acted so nobly!" Tears shot from his quivering eyes, as he resolved to ascend the observatory, and say to his old favorite, "Let it be forgotten, — come, we will go together to thy sister." He went alone up to the tower, intending to present him to the lady afterward. The Parson's wife flew off some minutes before Victor started, to inform and bring his two sisters, and send for the blind Julius to be conducted from the city, that no link might be missing in the golden necklace of love.

What a Jacob's ladder, on which every minute is a higher round, is set up this night on the swinging earth, whereon good beings climb up one after another! —

Down on the lowest step of the throne of reconciliation was Victor's heart laboring mightily in the hot blood through which it struggled. Flamin saw him slowly coming up, but he came not to meet him; because he was uncertain whether Victor came angry or forgiving. When the latter at last reached the top, Flamin, ashamed, supported his averted face in the branches; for he could not look his so sorely abused darling in the eye, till he knew that he had forgiven him. They maintained an awful silence beside each other, under the rippling linden-top, — they could not wholly guess each other's feelings, and that made the silence more gloomy, and the reconciliation doubtful. At last, Flamin, breathing intensely, and with his face buried in the foliage, reached out to him a trembling hand. When Victor saw the trembling of this dumb hand imploring reconciliation, boiling tears dropped through his heart and dissolved it asunder, and only from sadness and loving forbearance he delayed taking the lowly hand; but at this moment Flamin turned round (under the influence of a false suspicion), proud, blushing, full of tears and full of love, and said: "I beg thy forgiveness with all my heart for having been a devil to thee, an angel; but then if thou dost not grant it to me, I hurl myself down, that only the devil may get me!" — Singular! this extortion of forgiveness contracted a little Victor's open soul; but still he embraced the friendly wildling, and said with the mild voice of tranquil love: "From the bottom of my soul have I to-day forgiven thee; but loved thee I ever and always have, and in a few weeks would have died for thee, to save thy life." — Now their souls approached each other without reserve, and disclosed their lives, — — and when both had told all, and Victor had unfolded to him, that he had been substituted in his place, and was the son of the bereaved mother, then would Flamin have died for remorse, and only pressed his face more closely for shame into Victor's bosom, — and their newly wedded souls celebrated their silver wedding on the nuptial altar of the watch-tower, under the bridal torch of the moon; and their bliss was equalled by nothing but their friendship.

They wandered in the tender intoxication slowly into Le Baut's garden, and the stream of rapture grew deeper and deeper; but suddenly ice-cold waves, as from the river Styx, terrified the softly warmed Victor, when he came to the mournful bower, where, exactly a year ago to-day, on the 21st of October, — to-day then is Clotilda's birth-day, — he had torn her image out of his distracted heart, and where he now arrived again, perhaps again to tear it out from the old scars. For the lowering of his rank had made him a little — prouder, and his love for Clotilda more shy. To tell the truth, he could not himself fully believe that his inferior extraction had been unknown to her; he rather inferred the opposite, from the interest which his Lordship had let her take in his letters, and all secrets, — from her struggle in the beginning against her germinating love, and from the slight haughtiness towards him on the first day, — from her praise of misalliances, — from her favoring of Giulia's love for Julius, whom she knew to be his Lordship's son, — from her ready assent to the betrothal, which certainly otherwise her father, after the recognition, would no longer have granted, — and from other signs which one will more easily gather up for himself on the second reading of this work. As was said, this hope, that she had all along known who he was, refuted certain objections of his delicacy and of his spirit of renunciation, and bloomed out still higher to-day, among so many joys and pleasant incidents.—Ah! if he had been devoid of all hope, then he would certainly, in the midst of the circle of so many blessed ones, have been obliged to fall as the last victim!—But that something in man, which always prefigures to him a great loss as so probable, and a great gain as so improbable, united with melancholy remembrances, now tormented his soul.

He therefore begged Flamin to leave him alone for a while in the bower, and to hasten alone (as the Parson's wife was already in the garden) to the friendly arms of the newly-found sister and mother, and added that he would presently follow him. When Flamin was gone, Victor began to tremble more and more at the thought of the agitation of Clotilda, which would perhaps get the mastery of her at the intelligence of his pedigree; and it oppressed him sorely when he thought that for all in the garden sorrow had been removed from the black-hung mourning-chamber of earth, only for him haply not.—

But at that moment came his mother, beaming with the reflection of new raptures, and before questioning him first wiped his eyes. Her new raptures proceeded from this, that Clotilda, when she had related his descent, had fallen on her neck and begged her forgiveness for so long a concealment of the so long continued robbery of a child,—and that she had reminded the mother of a promise which had been given during the walk after the betrothal and was now redeemed. Much had escaped the mother,—and, I fear, the reader,—and Clotilda only glided hastily and blushingly over the matter; but had she not there said to her, "We change not our *relation*"? namely, that of a sister by marriage.—The Parson's wife concluded her report with the entreaty of her Ladyship, that she would bring her new son to her as speedily as possible.

Victor could say nothing, for tearful rapture, except, "Have not then my good Agatha and the blind one yet arrived?" — And both stood — behind him; and he concealed the overmeasure of his bliss under the caressings of the sister and the friend; his capacious cup of sorrow was truly poured full of tears of joy.

As, in the accompanying circle of three loving souls, he entered upon the fair road to the dear united ones, they all came to meet him with radiant features, — with swimming glances, — with remembrances from which the sting had been extracted, or rather which had been turned into joys; for from the crushed flowers of gladness on the road of life a sweet perfume is wafted over to the present hour, as marching armies often send out from heaths the fragrance of trampled plants. Her Ladyship was conducted by her two children, and said, with an obliging smile: "I present to you here my beloved children; continue towards them the friendship which you have hitherto shown them." — Her son Flamin, heedless of decorum, flew to him and flung himself upon his neck. Clotilda bowed lower than she would have done before a Prince, and in her eye swam the question of melancholy love, "Art thou still unhappy? Have I still thy heart? Why is thy eye moistened? why is thy voice broken?" — Victor replied with quite as much tenderness as dignity, as he turned to the Lady, "You could not on a fairer day find again your son than on the birthday of your daughter." . . .

Of *that*, in the previous whirlwinds, no one had thought. What a chaos of gladness! What a hearty, loving confusion of tongues on the part of congratulating improvisators! What affecting eye-thanks from Clotilda for such an obliging remembrance!

They went in ecstasy through the cool garden to the hall. O, when sisterly love, filial love, maternal love, love of lovers, and friendship burn side by side on the altars, then does it make a good man feel glad that the human heart is so noble, and preserves the material for so many flames, and that we feel love and warmth only when we dispense them out of ourselves, just as our blood never appears to us warm, until it flows, outside of our veins, in the open air. — O love! how happy are we that thou, when contemplated by a second soul, regeneratest and redoublest thyself, — that warm hearts attract and create warm ones, as suns do planets, the greater the lesser, and God, all, — and that even the dark planet is only a lesser, veiled, monœcian * sun! . . . All these souls stood to-day high on their Alp, and saw — as on a natural one — the *rainbow* of human fortune hanging as a great completed *magic circle* between the earth and the sun. — In the hall the Lady begged her daughter to go alone into the dark Jew's-harp chamber; she wanted to give her her birthday present. Clotilda's eye bade her friend, as she left him, with a second expression of thanks for his soul, a tender farewell.

After her departure, the Lady gave him a sign to stay with her behind the rest, — then he gladly fell on his knee before Clotilda's mother, who had not yet been asked her consent to his love, with the words, "If you do not guess my prayer, I have not the courage to begin it." She raised him up and said, "Prayers that are made so silently are quite as silently fulfilled; but rather come now and see what present I make to my daughter." — He

* A botanical term, meaning literally *in one house*, and designating Linnæus's twenty-first class of plants, of which the male and female (or barren and bearing) grow on one stock. — Tr.

must first, however, for a long time, moisten and kiss the hand which is about to offer him the lime-blossom honey of a whole life.

The two proceeded now, in this evening sent over out of the millennial kingdom, to the dark chamber of the daughter. Why did tears flow from Clotilda's eyes for rapture, even before her mother spoke? — Because she could already guess everything. The mother conducted the lover to his beloved, and said to the bride: "Take here thy birthday present. Few mothers are rich enough to give such a one; but then few daughters good enough to receive such a one." — The bridal pair were brought to their knees before her by the weight of overwhelming bliss and great, dumb gratitude, and took respectively the two beneficent hands of the mother; but she gently drew them out of theirs, and laid those of the loving ones in each other, and slipped away with the whisper, "I will bring our guests hither!" — —

— O ye two good souls, kneeling beside each, blest at last! how unhappy must a man be who, without a tear of joy, or how happy one who, without a tear of longing, can see you now fall speechless and weeping into each other's arms, — after so many painful partings, at last linked together, — after so many exhaustive bleedings, at last healed, — after thousands and thousands of sighs, yet at last blest, — and inexpressibly blest by innocence of heart and peace of soul and God! — No, I cannot to-day take my wet eyes away from you, — I cannot to-day behold and sketch the other good souls, — but I lay my eyes, with the *two* tears which belong to the happy and the unhappy man, softly and steadfastly on my two still lovers in the dusky chamber, where once the breath of the harmonica tones wafted their two souls together like gold- and silver-leaves. — O, as my book now ends, and my beloved vanish from me, — withdraw thyself, dim Holy of Holies, with thy two angels, — send back a long echo, when thou fliest upward with thy melodious souls, as swans in the night glide with flute-tones through the heavens. — — But, alas! does not the Holy of Holies already stand far away and high above me, and hang as a little silver cloud on the horizon of dream? — O these good souls, this good Victor, this good Emanuel, this good Clotilda, all these vernal dreams have gone up, and my heart looks up sorrowfully and calls after them without hope, "Dreams of spring, when will ye return?"

O why should I do it, were it not that the friends whom we firmly grasp by the hand are also dreams that soar upward? But the convulsive, prostrate, moaning heart on the gravestone does not call after these, "Dreams of spring-time, when will ye return?" — —

## SUPPLEMENT TO THE 44TH DOG-POST-DAY.

### Nothing.

AS this supplement to a little Post-Day was too small, I kept waiting for the dog and for new biographical pipe-clay and dough. — Since, however, the *post-aux-chiens* still delays, I will just score down the few cat-tones which I left out of the concert of love in the former chapter. It is nothing but vexatious stuff that I have still to supply here, and just these creaking tones may topple down again a new avalanche and institute new mischief. It is simply stupid that in this way the book is done, and yet not done, since the dog of a — dog is quite unexpectedly out of the way, like snuff.

The step-mother, the Chamberlain's lady, who has been long since banished the country by the biographical conjurer of spirits and bodies out of these leaves, had, on the advent of her Ladyship, from a very natural antipathy, marched off to a little country-seat. Speed on; besides, thou art not my Amancebada! * — Matthieu had, in the former chapter, conformably to his old audacity, stayed awhile among none but antagonists of his dark nature, and was sitting in the hall as the happy procession marched in from the garden. He knew not yet that the courtier Victor was in reality nothing but a mere, flat parson's son. At first he continued to carry on the antique joke of his declaration of love to Agatha, and set the Parson up to compliments and addresses of thanks for the services which he had rendered all to-day. But when he found there was too much indifference to his cold malice, he took away from his contempt its ambiguity. In fact, his heart was sincere, and rather made itself out more malicious, than more virtuous, than it was; he hated a dissimulation, whereby many a courtling easily gives himself that look of the virtuous man, which is best to be explained by Lavater's observation, that the angry person transfers to his own face the looks of the one whom he hates.

At last, Matthieu guessed the secrets, and the Parson ratified his guess. Such a water for his saw-mill, on which he cut men straight for his throne-scaffolding, had never before flowed in upon him. — If he represents to the Prince this falsehood, this new, terrible, abominable fraud, which his Lordship has played upon him, then — he concludes — must January go beside himself with amazement at Lord Horion's lies and at Matthieu's

* A Spanish word, equivalent to *Inamorata* (or sweetheart). — Tr.

truths. — Now, he held it for his duty to smile, indeed, but no more with malicious pleasure, like Mat, but with a regular contemptuousness, as a court-vassal should; he felt, too, how much beneath his dignity it was to let himself any longer be twisted into this citizenly quodlibet, without at least making a fool of it. He went accordingly, — for the sake of throwing out the news from his seed-apron into good ground, — after a short but sincere congratulation upon the marriage, the very same night back to the court, — — — and the Devil, following him as attendant blackamoor, decorously brought up the rear.

I wish the villain would never step into my biographical writing-chamber and *casa santa* again; he is conscious of so many immoral resources, that, in the feeling of strength they impart to him, he actually plays with sins, and always ventures upon several more than he needs; just as, e. g., in the Maienthal alley, out of mere wantonness, he enticed Victor and Clotilda into his neighborhood with the voice of the nightingale, although Flamin might have overheard both without that Philomelic machinery. In this view, I could absolutely almost wish that the Post-Dog would not come again; I have too much reason to fear that Matthieu may bring new frog-spawn and new mother-of-vinegar to January's warmth, that it may hatch out new, sharp, poisonous misery; for he will certainly report in the highest quarters, that the three Englishmen are hiding themselves in the island as in a catacomb, — that Flamin is associated with them, — that Victor has hitherto deceived a Prince, whose subject he is, — to say nothing of still other things, which the ministerial spy and Chamberlainess von Le Baut communicates, and his father, who is so much of an anti-clubbist, paints black, — which the former draws and the latter colors. And when I consider that in this biography a little misfortune has always been the egg-shell and the white-of-the-egg of a great one, — I am very much inclined to believe that the expression of the Parson on the 21st of October contained more wit than truth: "That they were all at present, instead of the bread of tears, cutting into the bride's cake of joy." . . . Ye good people! in which may now, at this moment, your bosoms be rising and falling, — in the soft, thin ether of gladness, or in the stormy vapor of agony?

## SUPPLEMENT TO THE SUPPLEMENT.

WHILE the first edition has been getting out of print, I have learned some very interesting additional circumstances for the second. Julius hugged his Victor in the garden right heartily, and said: "I am very glad to be here again, — I have been so alone all day, and not heard a human being, — thy Italian domestic has absolutely run away." In Victor's bosom, this unaccountable absconding of a faithful and contented servant raised, if not a storm-cloud, yet a dark mist. The quiet Marie had diligently discharged toward the blind one the duties of the fugitive. "I would gladly have given the Italian his letter first," Julius continued, "but here I have it still." Victor looked at it, and found, to his amazement, the address in the handwriting of — his Lordship. The letter was handed to the *blind one* a few minutes after the man's flight, with the request that he would give it to no one but the Italian. Although Flamin and her Ladyship promised to be answerable for the breaking of the seal, still Victor addressed himself reluctantly to this solution of a new charade of his life; for Clotilda was silent in the matter. Here is an authentic copy: —

"You are right. Do not, however, start till to-morrow, but go immediately to Mr. * * *. The place remains 5. But VI are necessary."

*Mr.* might mean *Monsieur* (the fifth son). Further than that there was nothing to be guessed from this flight of clouds of the coming weather by the best weather-prophets. The reader, however, may imagine, merely from his own eager desire to know the significance of these celestial signs, how great must have been that of our hero.

## 45. OR LAST CHAPTER.

KNEF. — THE TOWN OF HOF. — SORREL HORSE. — ROBBERS. — SLEEP. — OATH. — NIGHT JOURNEY. — BUSHES. — END.

 SAY only this much beforehand: in all the time that ink — like currant-wine — has been drawn from quill-tubes, — in all the time that quills have been cut to make instruments of peace, or carbonized to make instruments of war (for the coal used in manufacturing gunpowder is prepared from feathers *), — and still further back, in all that time the singular occurrence has never till now happened which I am now to report to the world. As I said, this is all I say beforehand; the incident is a tolerable one.

Inasmuch as the Post-Dog has, since the forty-fourth chapter, withdrawn his hand, or paw, from this learned work, my plan was to make it out alone, and only append one more and last chapter, — but not this one, — as capstone and swan-song, so that the *opus* might be given at once to the post, the press, and the world. Good reviewers (thought I) I can let wrangle with the Post-Dog and biographical bell-wether as long as they please over the want of a final cadence. . . . It was already getting toward the end of October, and of my Robinsonade on

* *Feder* means, in German, both *feather* and *pen*, as *plume* and *penna*, in French and Latin, mean both *feather* and *quill*. — TR.

the island of St. John's, when the good old Friday of this Robinson, my Dr. Fenk, returned from his long botanical Alpine tour home to Scheerau, but immediately put out to sea again, and landed on my St. John's domain.

We sat down to two or three courses with minced-meat (or ragout) of travelling-anecdotes. At last, I drew his attention — as all literati do — to what I had written, to my latest *opusculum,* what stood before us in a cursed pile as high as a conical orrery: "It has dropped from me," said I, "in an entirely cursory manner, often in the night, just as Voltaire or the pea-hens let fall their eggs on the straw in their sleep. I have taken pleasure in endowing the world with this legacy of four volumes; but the legacy still waits for its last chapter, — without which the labor of the dog (in the noble sense) will be in the bad sense a dog's-work." He read the whole bequest through before my eyes, — which gives an author a foolish, oppressive sensation, — and flung his two arms up and down often during the perusal, and would fain make the author red with extravagant praise. But it did not take; for an author has already bestowed every compliment upon himself beforehand a thousand times, and is at the same time his own flesh-scales, his own flesh-weight, and his own flesh, because, like a virtuous man, he is satisfied with his own approbation.

"The hero of thy Post-Days," said he, "is modelled somewhat after thyself." — "That," I replied, "is for the world and the hero to decide, when they both become acquainted with me; but all authors do so, — their personality is either pictured opposite the title-page, or farther on in the midst of the work, as the painter Rubens and the designer Ramberg in almost all their works bring on a dog."

But now let one imagine with what astonishment I clapped my hands when the Doctor named to me the little country where the whole story transpired: * * * is the little country's real name. "I had only to go thither," he said, "and I could draw the forty-fifth (tail-) chapter from the fountain-head. As he passed through Flachsenfingen, they had only just got to the Fortieth Dog-Post-Day. If I would take my own horses," ("That I will," said I, "I will buy me some this very day,") "I might, perhaps, come up with a distinguished passenger, who, unless all signs deceived him, was his Lordship incarnate." For the sake of a few ounces of asafœtida which Fenk needed on the road, he had even been with Zeusel in his apothecary's shop, upon whom, he said, the number ninety-nine was as legibly imprinted as the number ninety-eight was on the butterfly * (the Catalanta).

No one certainly can blame an author who was crabbing and fishing for his forty-fifth, tail- or train-chapter, for running away as if distracted, — packing up, — tackling up, — jumping in, — starting off, and driving so furiously, as he shot by hotels, country-houses, processions, stars, and nights, that not in * * days, but in * * * days (many a one will actually think I am drawing a long bow †), I sprang, bedusted but unpowdered, into the inn of the *Golden Lion*. The said inn is situated in the town of Hof, which again on its part is situated in something greater; namely, in Voigtland. I am careful not to name either the days of my journey or the gate through which I shot into Hof, in order that I may not reveal to curious knaves and *mouchards* ‡ by my

* In the original, *Nummern-vogel* (numbered bird). As to the 99 [i. e. per cent.] on Zeusel, see page 368. — Tr.

† Literally: *Ich mache Wind.* — Tr.

‡ Spies. — Tr.

route of march the real name of Flachsenfingen. Hof I could name right out without harm, because from there — the moment one is past the gates — one can travel to all points of the compass; and so, too (which is a very good thing), one can arrive there from all places, — from Mönchberg, Kotzan, Gattendorf, Sachsen, Bamberg, Böheim, and from America, and from the Rascally Islands, and from any part of Büsching and Fabri.*

Not far from the Golden Lion (properly in Oat Lane) stood a distinguished Englishman, looking on while his four smoking horses took a medicine of two thirds common saltpetre and one third horse-brimstone against foundering. The stranger — who might have been about as many years old as this book is days — was dressed in black; tall, respectable, rich (to judge by his equipage), and of a manly build. His bright and fixed eye lay kindling like a focus on men, — his face was fine and cold, — on his forehead stood the perpendicular secant as the time-*bar* denoting business, as sign of exclamation at the toil and trouble of life, — faint, horizontal lines were ruled across this time-bar like staves; both sorts of lines were cut into the too high forehead, as if for signs how high the tear-water of affliction had already risen on this brow, on this soul. "I would," thought I, "have painted Lord Horion differently, if this face had appeared to me sooner." Perhaps the reader thinks this was his Lordship himself.

When the Englishman had seen my tiercet of sorrels, he came straight up to me and introduced a project of exchange, and wanted to take my sorrel for a black. He had the fancy of Russians in the higher ranks, of

* Geographical writers. — Tr.

travelling with a regular cento* of differently-colored horses, — as he also had the finer custom of the Neapolitans, to let a free, loose horse prance along beside the carriage. Accordingly, for the sake of the equine quodlibet, he wanted to bid in my miserable sorrel, who, to tell the truth, wore nowhere any hair of his own, except behind on the bob. I told him frankly, — to leave him no suspicion of selfishness or design, — "My three sorrels looked like the three Furies, and represented tolerably well the *three cavities* of anatomy; only the dark sorrel which he wanted was magnificently built, particularly about the head, and I should be sorry to lose him now, when the head was just going to be of use to me." — "So?" said the Briton. — "Of course," said I; "for a horse's head is the best remedy against bed-bugs, and this one must now very soon fall off from the nag, like a ripe plum, — the head I can then put into my bed-straw." The Englishman did not even smile; during the whole bargain he stirred not a finger, not a feature, not a muscle. Not until I myself had said, "If the three Fates only keep on their legs till I have fetched away the forty-fifth chapter on wheels," did it strike me that he had been in a distant manner studying and sounding me more than the sorrel, — and I fell upon the hypothesis, whether he had not misused the whole horse-exchange as a mere cloak and blinder of his suspicious, pumping questions.

Let the reader only just read on! — The Englishman started off with my sorrel muscle-preparation; and I followed some time after with my black, who was as strong, black, and glossy as the old Adam in man.

But I must first tell what I was going to do in Hof, —

* Patchwork, — a term applied also to poems plagiarized from all quarters. — TR.

I was going to dedicate. At first each of these volumes was to be inscribed to a female friend; but I had reason to fear I should rue it, because my wont is to quarrel with a different one — never with all at once — every month. I should like to know in what parallel of latitude the man were to be found who does not fall out with his lady friend a thousand times oftener than with his male one. The biographer must, therefore, of necessity, because he is too changeable, cross the street from the Golden Lion with his four volumes, and enter the house of the only man towards whom he never alters, and who never does himself either, and say to him, "Here, my dear good Christian Otto, I dedicate something to thee again, — four volumes at once. — It were handsome, if thou again wouldst dedicate each to one of thy family, — three are just enough, and thou hast thine own left for thee, too. — I am riding now after the forty-fifth chapter, and thou — cut and clear away meanwhile at the forty-four other beds as much as thou wilt."

And here, my faithful one, must thou absolutely have the last chapter also; and I only add further, "This *Hesperus*, which stands as *morning-star* over my life's fresh morning, thou mayest still look upon when my earthly day is over; then is it a quiet *evening-star* for quiet men, till it also sets behind its hill."

Inasmuch as all letters to me are notoriously delivered in the busy and somewhat surly city of Hof, and as in fact many travellers pass this way, one will readily indulge me with the small space for two observations, which the town itself makes upon the town. The Hofites, namely, all remark and complain that they cannot exactly become accustomed to each other. "We ought all to be able," they say, "to bear with each other very well, and, if only thereby, refute the observation of the great Montesquieu, that trade knits together nations and sunders individuals. Secondly, they all reproach each other, that from year to year they barter for in quantity, and accumulate and store away in green-houses, great cornucopias full of balsam, rose, clover, and lily-seed, and tall boxes full of splendid apple-seeds (particularly of princes' apples, violet apples, Adam's- and virgin-apples, and Dutch ketterlings), — — but that they sow or set out of this seed little or nothing. "In old age," they say, "good fruits and flowers will come apropos to us, if we save a good quantity of seed out of the present ones, and then plant it." — A certain candidate (an academical chum of mine) took occasion from these two observations to make two very good points in an afternoon sermon. In the first part, he showed his Hofites out of the Epistle that they should not torment, but heartily love, each other in this fleeting vapor of life, without reference to the numbers of their houses; and in the second *pars*, he made it plain that they ought in this brief, waning light of life to make from time to time one and another joke. . . .

I had hardly travelled a few hours — days — weeks (for I do not state the truth), and had gone to sleep towards midnight in my carriage as I mounted a hill in a thick forest, when suddenly two hands, which had worked their way in behind through the back window, jammed down a bee-cap* over my head, fastened it hastily round my neck with a padlock, covered and blinded my eyes, and ten or twelve other hands seized, held, and bound my body. The worst thing in such a case is, that one expects to be killed and robbed of his jewel-caskets; but nothing

* A cap worn by those who take up hives, to defend them against stings. — Tr.

can vex and annoy more an author who has not yet finished his book than to take away his life. No man wishes to die in the midst of a plan; and yet every one at every hour of the day bears about with him at once budding, green, half-ripe, and wholly ripe plans. I sought, therefore, to defend my life with such valor — since the forty-fifth chapter and its critics weighed upon my mind — that I — although I say it — could easily have mastered four or five prince-stealers, had there not been half a dozen. I laid down my arms, but occupied the battle-field (namely, the coach-cushion), — and observed, in fact, that they did not want so much to kill the Mining-Superintendent as to blind him. The adventure grew still more romantic, — my own fellow was not tumbled from the throne of his box, — my carriage continued on the road to Flachsenfingen, — two gentlemen seated themselves in beside me, who, to judge by their feminine hands, were persons of rank, — and, strangest of all, a dog began to bark, who, by his barking, must have labored as mass-assistant and fellow-master on this learned work.

We supped and lunched in the open air. Here a surgical order-ribbon was drawn around my naked body, because I had unfortunately, during the quarter-wheelings and manual evolutions of my defence, run my shoulder-blade upon the point of a sword. I could eat very well, inasmuch as the tin canary-cage door of my bee-cap was turned wide open. Good heavens! if the public had seen the author of the Dog-Post-Days shove in his eatables through the open leaves of the leaden gate, he would have died with shame! — During the meal, I called the dog to me by the name, Hofmann! He actually came; I felt all over him, if haply any forty-fifth chapter might be hanging on his neck, — it was bare.

After a long alternation of journeying, — eating, — saying nothing, — sleeping, — days, — nights, — I was at last set down in a sea, and there carried about (or did it come from a narcotic?) till I slept like a rat. What followed — strange as it is — I shall not make known till I have first written out the observation, that, to be sure, great *joy* and great *sorrow* enliven and gratify the nobler propensities within us; but that *hope*, and far more *anxiety*, hatch the whole worm's nest of miserable hankerings, the infusorial spawn of petty ideas, and unravel them and set them to gnawing, — so that in this way the *Devil* and the *Angel* within us contrive to maintain a worse *parity* of their two religions than holds even in Augsburg with two others,* and that each of the two religious parties in man has in pay its own night-watch, censor, innkeeper, gazetteer, just as much as the aforesaid ones in Augsburg. . . .

— I had my eyes still closed, when a whispering, swelled and multiplied into a great murmur by a thousand tree-tops, floated round me; the rushing aerial sea swept through narrow Æolian harps, and raised waves thereon, and the waves rippled over me with melodies, — a high mountain air, flung down from a cloud shooting by overhead, fell like a cooling stream of water on my breast. — I opened my eyes, and thought I was dreaming, because I was without the iron mask. — I was leaning against the fifth column on the upper step of a Grecian temple, whose white floor was encircled by the *summits* of tossing poplars, — and the tops of oaks and chestnuts ran waving only as fruit-hedges and espaliers round the lofty temple, and reached only up to the heart of a man standing within.

* The Lutheran and Reformed: — at the Diet of Augsburg, in 1555. — TR.

"I must surely be acquainted with this luxuriant harvest of tree-tops," said I. — "Lo, weeping birches hang their arms yonder, — out there stems kneel before the thunder which blasted them, — do not nine crape veils and sprayey fountains, in many-colored twigs, flutter through each other? — and the tempests have planted here their conductors as five iron sceptres in the earth. — This is most certainly a dream of the *Island of Reunion*, which has hitherto so often darted rays across the mist of sleep, and with heavenly and winning radiance beamed upon my soul." — —

But it was no dream. I rose from the step, and was about to enter the illuminated Grecian temple, which consisted only of a Grecian roof, of five columns, and the whole earth encamped around it, when eight arms embraced me, and four voices accosted me: "Brother! — we are thy brothers." Before looking upon them, before addressing them, I fell gladly with outspread arms into the midst of three hearts which I knew not, and shed tears upon a fourth, which I knew not, and at last lifted my eyes, not inquiringly, but blissfully, from the unknown hearts to their faces; and while I looked upon them, I heard behind me my beloved Dr. Fenk say: "Thou art the brother of Flamin, and these three Englishmen are thy incarnate brothers." . . . . Joy darted through me convulsively like a pang. — I pressed my lips mutely to those of the four embraced and embracing ones, — but I fell then upon my elder friend, and stammered, "Dear, good Fenk! tell me all! I am distracted and enchanted with things which I still do not comprehend."

Fenk went back with me smiling to the four brothers, and said to them: "See, this is the *monsieur*, your fifth and lost brother of the seven islands,—and your biographer into the bargain. — Now at last he has caught his forty-fifth chapter." — Then turning to me: "Thou seest, of course," said he, "that this is the Isle of Union, — that the three twins here are the sons of the Prince, whom our Lord wanted to bring back. — For thy sake, because thou hast this long time been absent from the seven islands, he has travelled through all market towns, and around all islands of Europe. At last I wrote to him." . . .

"Thou hast certainly, also," I interrupted him, "been my correspondent through the dog." —

"Just go on," said he.

"And *Knef* is *Fenk* spelt backward, — and thou gavest thyself out with Victor for an Italian, who could speak no German, — copiedst off all day his own list of rules for deportment, for his Lordship, and for me too, in fact, in order to be his and my spy." —

"It is so, — and therefore I also wrote to his Lordship," said he, "that thy French name, *Jean Paul*, brought thee under suspicion; and as thou, besides, didst not thyself know thy origin, and, in addition to that, thy foolish bit of life-road, which, as in an English garden, would not reach a mile in a straight direction" — —

"The biographer," said I, "should, in fact, be his own." * —

"It is incomprehensible to me now how it was that I did not happen upon this in the first instance; for thy resemblance to Sebastian, which the fifth son of the Prince should also have, thou hast thyself long since

* And I here with pleasure hold out to the public hope of my own biography, wherewith, when I shall have lived out a few more indispensable chapters of it, I propose to present it under the title, Jean Paul's Acts of the Apostles, or his Actions, Experiences, and Opinions.

remarked, — and thy Stettin box-picture on the shoulder-blade, which these gentlemen here all have about them, and which his Lordship himself beheld day before yesterday, during the bandaging."

"So! so!" said I, "it was for this, then, that your biographer got the falcon's hood, the wound in the back, the fine black steed, and the stranger in Hof was his Lordship?" —

In short, by all this his Lordship had fully convinced himself that I was the one whom he had so long sought; for he had previously long since received Fenk's communication through fifteen hands, inasmuch as it travelled from Hamburg, or rather from the land of the Hadeln, to Ziegenhain in Lower Hesse, then into the Principality of Schwabeck, then into the Duchy of Holzapfel, to Schweinfurt, to Scheer-Scheer, and still back again to * * and to * * *, and finally to Flachsenfingen, where he at last received it; there, in the Isle of Union, he had been concealed a long time, until the communication, the ending of October, which as it were underscored the maternal marks with red ink, and, most of all, the banishing from St. Luna of the three brothers who landed on the island, constrained him to travel off to Scheerau, or rather to Hof in Voigtland. Here, naturally, I was obliged to meet him, according to a concert with the Italian servant (i. e. with Dr. Fenk), on account of which he sent me from my island after the forty-fifth chapter, and whose repetition came to hand in the billet intercepted by the blind one, and now deciphered; and my old face, which he forthwith compared with a younger engraving of the fifth princely son, threw at once in the "Oat-lane" the most ample light upon everything.

So soon as he knew this, he left me to travel on alone,

under my tin bee-cap and Moses's veil, and hurried forward to the Prince just one minute before it was too late. For Matthieu had betrayed all; and they were just on the point of sending to arrest the three twins, on the island where they had taken refuge, and our Victor at his mother's house, wherein he had already forgotten court and nobility for patients and sciences and bride, when his Lordship sent in his name to the Prince. The Prince was afraid of being persuaded by him, as Cæsar was of Cicero. His Lordship — whose soul, indeed, was a *petrographic* * chart of sublime ideas — confounded the measures of the Prince by a more daring and defiant boldness than these measures had reckoned on. He began with the intelligence, that he brought not merely *one* son to the Prince, but all; which last thing he had not promised, for the reason that he could not know how far fate would perhaps leave or lead him. — He forced the Prince to listen to a long and cold discourse, wherein he laid before him the plan of study for the five sons, and their development, history, and destiny; while he seemed to presuppose the proofs of their extraction, he however wove them elaborately into the inferences he drew from it. Thus, e. g., he said, no one had known about the important secret but her Ladyship and Clotilda and Emanuel, whose sacred documents, sealing all with death, he here presented him, together with others for the children; only a certain court-page had, during his blindness, stolen and abused one of five secrets. His Lordship did not pluck to pieces this snare of a soul, because, as he said, it was too insignificant for satisfaction, too black-dyed for punishment, and because he himself be-

* Or *litho*graphic, only *petro* is used designedly with a *moral* reference. — Tr.

sides would soon depart out of these regions forever. In short, with his omnipotence he took such a hold of the Prince, and drew all veils so clean off from the past, that he almost compelled him, instead of condemning or acquitting, merely to deprecate and to exchange accusation and mistrust for gratitude. The single good thing, Lord Horion said in conclusion, which the Page had done, was, that, by his weed-sowing-machines, he had ripened and expedited the great and fair recognition precisely for a monthly period, when the festoon of the five shoulders (the maternal moles) were in full bloom. The Prince, in spite of the other party's iciness, was melted, for his paternal love was enriched with new treasures. Nevertheless, he mixed in with his thanks this delicate reproach against Victor's pretended nobility: "I am full of gratitude for you, although you deprive me too soon of the opportunity of showing it. Hitherto I have rejoiced that I could at least prove to the son how very much indebted, if not grateful, I was to the father. But you know my error." His Lordship — now made more pliant by victory — replied: "I know not whether good intentions and bad circumstances excuse me; but I could regard him only as worthy to be your body physician, whom I acknowledged worthy to be my son." — The Prince embraced him cordially; his Lordship reciprocated it quite as warmly, and said: "On the 31st of October," (that is to-day, and he said it yesterday,) "he would seal his honest sentiments toward the Prince in a manner more decisive than words." — —

Noble man! Thou consumest nothing on the earth beyond thyself, and art a storm-bird, through whose fat a wick of the lamp is threaded, and which is now burned out and carbonized by its own light, — I have a presentiment, as if thy fair soul would soon be on another, *higher Isle of Reunion* than this earthly one!

I write this on the forenoon of the 31st of October, at ten o'clock, on the island.

* * * * *

## EVENING, AT SIX O'CLOCK, IN MAIENTHAL.

WHEREWITH will this book end at last? — with a tear or with an exultation? —

Dr. Fenk, until two o'clock (for not till then would his Lordship arrive), threw the brown or lump-sugar of humor upon our minutes and sorrows; his whimsical red face was the violet sugar-loaf paper of sweetness. My good Victor was with Clotilda in Maienthal. Fenk kept up one continued laugh at me as a dauphin. He makes many similes, he says: "I should not, until the end of a book and of the whole play, get my true title, as they do not print the general title-page of the journals till the last number, — or," he says, "like a pawn at chess, I should not be promoted until the last row to be an officer." It is, however, very well known to me from history, that in France, even under Louis XIV., the present system of equality already existed, though first with reference to princes, whom the king made equal, whether they entered upon life as Mestizoes * or Creoles, or Quatroons † or Quintoons, or as born to the throne. As now one can produce new laws and novellæ ‡ of imperial statute quite as well in Germany as beyond its limits, it might well hap-

* Children of a European and an American Indian. —Tr.

† Children of Terceroons, who again are children of Mulattoes and whites.

‡ Alluding to Justinian's *new* statutes. — Tr.

pen in my lifetime that legitimated princes should be declared competent to the throne, — whereby I of course should come to be ruler. It were well for Flachsenfingen if that should happen, because I will buy me beforehand the best French and Latin works on government, and study the subject in them so well that I cannot fail. I think I may venture to take it upon me to set the poor human race, which is forever living in the *first of April*, and which never gets out of its standing-stool or go-cart, — the only change being the addition of more wheels to the cart, — on its legs again a little by my sceptre. Time was when a nobleman and the horse of an English riding-master were capable of doffing the hat, of firing a pistol, of smoking tobacco, of telling whether there was a damsel in the company, &c.; but now-a-days horse and nobleman have come to be so distinguished from each other by culture, that it is a true honor to be the latter, and that it does not harm my nobility (though I feared it in the beginning) that I have more than common learning. In our days the head-horses of the nobility are no longer harnessed on so far ahead of the citizenly wheel-horses to the chariot of state as they were a hundred years since; hence duty, or at least prudence, dictates (even for a new nobleman like me) that he (or I) should let himself down, and hide the consciousness of his rank (why should not I succeed in that as well as another?) under the grace of an easy and complaisant good-breeding, and in fact take no airs upon himself about any ancestors, except for the *future* ones, of whose collective merits I cannot think greatly enough, because the earth is still mighty young,* and just in petticoats, and, like the Poles, in Polish frock.

* *Blutjung* is the German; a vulgarism, corresponding, perhaps, to the English *bloody*-young. — Tr.

To return: at two o'clock, his Lordship came with his blind son, like Philosophy with Poesy. Beautiful, beautiful youth! innocence has sketched thy cheeks, love thy lips, enthusiasm thy forehead. His Lordship, with his Laudon's* forehead, and with a face more obscured and shaded to-day than in Hof, on which the honeymoon of youth and the passion-weeks of later age threw a confused chiaroscuro, — he came to us to-day almost warmer than usual, although with features expressive of nothing but the feeling that life is an intercalary day, and that he loves only philanthropy, not men. He said, we must do him and the Hof-medicus the pleasure of visiting the latter this very day in Maienthal, and bringing him hither, because he had still to complete here without eyewitnesses all sorts of arrangements for the arrival of the Prince; we must, however, come back again with Victor in the night, because our distinguished father would arrive very early in the morning. The blind one, as blind, could stay where he was. It did not occur to me, that he concealed from the good, darkened Julius, that he was his father, for he said, with double and treble meaning: "As the good creature has once already had to endure the pain of losing a father, we must not a second time expose him to this sorrow." But *this* did strike me, that he begged us to requite him for what he had hitherto sought to do in behalf of Flachsenfingen, by doing *this* ourselves, and assuring him with an oath, that in the public offices which we should

* Gideon Ernest Laudon (Baron) was a great soldier and captain, born in 1716. The Emperor of Austria, under whom he chiefly served, had the following epitaph written for him: "Gideonis Laudoni summi castrorum præfecti, semper strenui, fortis, felicis militis et civis optimi exemplum quod duces militesque imitentur Josephus 11 Aug. in ejus effigie proponi voluit, anno 1783." — Tr.

get, we would fulfil his cosmopolitan wishes, which he delivered to us in writing, at least until such time *as he should see us again.* The Prince had been obliged to give him the same solemn assurance. We looked up at him as at a beclouded comet, and took the oath with sorrow.

We entered on the road to Maienthal. An Englishman related to us that he had seen behind the mourning-thicket — the sleeping chamber of the blind one's mother, his Lordship's beloved, who rests beneath a black marble slab — a second marble set up, which the crape-veils sweeping over it were meant to cover, but could not. O then did each of us look round him with a heavy heart toward the island, as towards an undermined city, ere it is blown to pieces and hurled into the air. — But my longing to behold Victor and Maienthal, that labyrinthine flower-garden of my warmest dreams, drowned the anxious apprehension.

At last we climbed the southern mountain, and the variegated Eden, with its fulness of foliage and with the multitude of its pulsating twigs, grew with a murmur down into the valley. — Up yonder among the boughs lay, like a nightingale's nest, Emanuel's peaceful cottage, in which was now my Victor, — nearer to us rustled the chestnut avenue, and without, overhead, reposed the mowed churchyard. — To me, who had seen all this hitherto only in the dream of fancy, it seemed now again as if dreams were coming on; and the opaque ground became a transparent one, full of shapes created out of vapor, — and I sank full of sadness on the hill. . . . I went down at last as into a promised land, but my whole soul was swathed in a soft funeral veil.

— And my Victor tore away the veil, and pressed his

warm soul to mine, and we melted together into one glowing point. — But I will, by and by, when he comes back from the abbey, once more and still more warmly fall on his breast, and then at length truly tell him my love. . . . O Victor, how gentle thou art, and how harmonious, how ennobled, how beautiful in the tear of joy, how great in thy inspiration! — Ah, love of man, thou that givest to the inner man the Grecian profile, and to his motions lines of beauty, and to his charms bridal ornaments, redouble thy wondrous and healing powers in my hectic breast, when I see fools, or sinners, or uncongenial men, or enemies, or strangers!

Victor, who never made the anxiety of a man still greater, gave us some satisfaction about his Lordship. He went to the convent to Clotilda, to announce our visit to her and the Abbess, — the lateness of the visit he excuses by the necessity of a nightly return. Till he comes back, I suspend my story. My eyes followed him on his way to the betrothed; and his hand, his eye, and his mouth were full of greetings for every one, especially for despised people, for old men, for old widows. The joy of my hero becomes mine. Time is working at the beautiful day, when his heart shall forever melt into one with the betrothed, when, without a remaining link of the sundered flea- and ape-chain of the court, he shall walk freely through nature, be nothing but a man, make nothing but cures, instead of *cour*, love nothing but the whole world, and be too happy to be envied. Then will I, for once, my Bastian, eat with thee at evening in the moonlight, under the steam and the hum of the linden, and seat myself on the bales of freshly unpacked and printed Dog-Post-Days. For the rest, — although I did let my own inner man sit to paint his by, — I am but a wretched, dissolved, wiped-out slate-copy of him, only a very freely paraphrased interpretation of this soul; and I find that a cultivated parson's son is, at bottom, better than an uncultivated prince, and that princes are not, like poets, born, but made.

I hope I have material enough to keep me writing till he comes back. I have, in fact, in this biography, as supernumerary copyist of Nature, all along borrowed from reality, — e. g. for Flamin's character I had in my head a captain of dragoons, — in the case of Emanuel, I thought of a great man dead, a celebrated writer, who, the very day when I with sweet, shuddering entrancement wrote Emanuel's dream of annihilation, went from the earth and half under it, — the goddess Clotilda I compounded of two female angels, and I shall see for myself, in a few minutes, whether I hit them. It is provoking, that in conversations, from the force of habit, I give to the people of this book the names they bear in the Dog-Post-Days; whereas Flamin is properly called * *, and Victor * *, and Clotilda actually * *. It were to be wished — I have not sworn not to do it — that I could, after the death of some moral *blasés* and plague-infected personages of these volumes, or after my own, make known to the world the true names. If I do it, then will learned Europe be initiated into all the reasons, which the political world already knows, that have kept the Mining-Superintendent from letting fall upon some parts of his history (especially upon the court) so much light as he might actually have given; and I am curious to see whether, after the *exposé* of these reasons, the newspaper correspondent A. and the secretary of legation Z. — the two greatest enemies of the Flachsenfingen court, and of me personally — will still assert that I am stupid. Nay,

I am bold enough to appeal publicly here to the * * agent in * * to say whether I have not wholly left out many persons in the history, who had acted a part in it, and who had entered into the actual machinery of my biographical sugar-mill as undershot wheels; nay, more, I even give my pair of adversaries permission to name to the world the personages I have left out, — who have some power to do injury, — if this two-head vulture has the heart to do it. . . .

The good Spitzius Hofmann is now wagging his tail, and leaping up before me. Good, industrious Post-Dog! Jean Paul's biographical Egeria! I will, as an encouraging example, so soon as I have time, flay thee and stuff thee neatly, and fill thee as with a sausage-filling of hay, in order to set thee up in a public library as thine own bust beside other distinguished scholars! — Meusel is a reasonable man, to whom I will apply, in a private and autographic communication, for a seat in his Learned Germany for Spitz. This scholar will not be able, any better than I, to see why such a diligent hod-carrier and compiler and forwarder of learning as my dog is should suffer a more pitiful and colder fate than other learned hod-carriers, merely because he bears a tail, which represents his posterior-toupee. That is all which gives the poor beast an inferior place in the scale of literati.

— I now see Victor escorted with lights through the bowers of the garden. I will only throw out, as hastily as possible, the further statement, that I am sitting in the sacristy of Emanuel, which is latticed with leafless shrubbery. Hurry not so, Sebastian, thou that, in respect to thy previous transformations, resemblest the three or four pseudo-Sebastians in Portugal; hurry not, that I may still simply say to my sister, "Thou beloved ex-sister, thy crazy brother writes himself *von*, but thou hast lost only his breast, not his heart. When I come to Scheerau, I will care for nothing, but weep on thee during the embrace, and finally say, It is no matter. My spirit is thy brother, thy soul is my sister; and so, change not, sisterly heart."

— The good Victor walks hastily. Ah, men whom sorrow has often chilled have neither in their bodily nor moral motions the slow symmetry of prosperous fortune, just as people who wade in the water take great broad strides. — Poor Victor! why dost thou now weep so, that thou absolutely canst not dry thy tears? . . .

* * * * *

## FOUR O'CLOCK IN THE MORNING, IN THE ISLAND OF REUNION.

AH, it is long ago that I asked, "Will this book close with a tear?" — Victor came back at eight o'clock last night with two great immovable tears on the brink of his eyelid, and said: "We will just hasten back somewhat rapidly to the island. Clotilda herself begs us to do so, and to take another time for seeing her." — "A misfortune," I have dreamed, "is just now rearing itself large and high like a sea-serpent, and flinging itself upon human hearts, as that does upon ships, and crushing them under." She had grown every minute more anxious and oppressed, as one becomes in a damp spot over which the lightning darts and hisses. What else did this imply, than that his Lordship had disclosed to his faithful friend things which we feared this night to experience? And we could none of us any longer conceal from ourselves the fear that his weary spirit meant perhaps, like Lycurgus, to stamp the seal of his corpse upon his assurance that we were January's sons, and, moreover, on our oath to be good, and on that of the Prince to obey my brothers, till he should return.

"Weep not so sorely, Victor," said I; "it is not, after all, yet certain." He quietly dried his eyes, and merely said: "We will, then, now go to the island, — it is already nine o'clock."

We went along, far, far aside from the spotted weeping-birch, which threw its torn-off leaves toward the wasted remains of the great man. Victor could not look that way for sorrow; but I looked with a chill trembling where it swayed in the serene night-heavens. Not until after some days, when Victor had become happier, had the dust of Emanuel contracted itself again, as it were, into a pale form, and erected itself out on the burial-green, and opened wide its arms for its old darling, — and Victor moaned and pined, and sought vainly to press the white shadow to his dying breast.

He smiled sadly, as he sought to divert us and himself by the words, "Foolish man ducks like a bird, if calamity only approaches him from afar off." His tears made him a blind man, and Flamin and I were his guides; nevertheless he greeted in his pain a night-express.

I have said nothing (for I cannot) of the *garden of germination*, of the withered scene of faded, leafless days of joy.

Over the stubble and over the chrysalides of night-butterflies (the jugglers of future spring-nights), and over the steadfast, subterranean winter sleep, swept the solitary night-winds. — Ah, man might well think, "Breezes, come ye not hither over graves, over precious, precious graves?" —

I said, "How slender is the pale-green interval of earth between human bodies and human skeletons!"—Victor said, "Ah, Nature has so much repose, and why has our heart so little?"

It was near midnight. The heavens glittered nearer to the earth; the *Swan*, the *Lyre*, *Hercules*,* beamed from where they had gone down through another blue of heaven. Great heaven,—said every heart,—dost thou belong to the human spirit, dost thou one day receive it, or art thou only like the ceiling-picture of a minster, which hides the limiting walls, and opens out with colors the prospect of a heaven which does not exist?—Ah, every Present makes our soul so small, and only a Future makes it so great.

Victor was beside himself, and said again: "Repose! neither joy nor sorrow can give thee, but only hope. Why is not all at rest within us, as around us?"

At that moment the knell of a shot, repeated by all the echoing woods, rang through the silent night,—and the Isle of Union swam up in the night-blue, and its white temple hung over it,—and beside the mourning-thicket, which grew up over the mouldering remains of a youthful heart, nine slender flames, which ran up on the nine crape-veils, shot up toward heaven, as if they were *feux de joie* to a festival of *peace*.

Pale, hurrying, sighing, and silent, we touched the first shore of the island. The water was sucked up dry by the ground. The black Eastern gate had flung itself wide open, and leaned and hid its white painted sun against the trees. Many funeral torches, on white lustres, attached themselves to the Eastern gate, went in through

* The Swan is Giulia; the Lyre of Apollo, Emanuel; Hercules reminded one of his Lordship.

the long green avenue, flickered over ruins, sphinxes, and marble torsos, and ended darkly in the mourning-thicket.

Fluttering music of Æolian harps was permeated at the entrance by long tones. Under the Eastern gateway the blind one rested quietly and played joyously on his flute, — just as a dove flies into the thunder.

He fell joyfully on the neck of his Victor, and said: "It is good that thou comest; a tall, still man has lain a quarter of an hour on my heart, and wept into my hand, and given me a leaf for thee."

Victor snatched the leaf; it read: "You have all sworn to fulfil my requests until such time as you hear my voice again; but uncover not the black marble." — His Lordship had given it to the blind son. Victor cried: "O father! O father! I could not then make thee any requital!" and sank upon the breast of the son. He was about to tear himself away again, but the blind youth hung around him, and smiled with glad unconsciousness into the night. — We hastened into the mourning-thicket, — and, by the dim light of the two funeral torches that were burning down therein, we saw that a second grave had been scooped out there, the fresh earth of which lay near by, — that a black marble covered the hollow, and that the black dress of his Lordship peeped out a little way from the opening, and that in there he had killed himself. — And on his black marble stood, as upon the marble of his beloved, an ashy-pale heart, and below the heart stood in white letters the words:

"IT IS AT REST."

THE END.

# APPENDIX.

## ADDITIONAL NOTES TO "TITAN."

# ADDITIONAL NOTES TO "TITAN."

ELUCTANT to encumber the pages of a romance with more Notes than seemed absolutely necessary, the present translator, in giving to the public his version of Titan, was (he has had reason to think) too chary of helps to the reader. Having, moreover, gained new light himself on some points since that translation was made and printed, he ventures to insert here (having a little spare space) a few explanatory or illustrative (occasionally corrective) Notes, principally to the first volume of Titan, which has generally proved more difficult than the second.

[The translator's reason for giving such Notes here, rather than in a (possible) third edition of Titan, is that a great many more of the buyers of the first editions of that work will also (may it not be presumed?) buy Hesperus than would be likely to see a third edition of Titan; and therefore the present way of furnishing the additional matter seemed to be the fairest to all parties.]

## INTRODUCTORY AND GENERAL NOTE.

IN a note to Vol. II. p. 174, occurs an allusion to certain *Comic Appendices* to Titan. There is a special good reason for recalling the reader's attention to that subject, inasmuch as that appended matter contains, slyly hid away by the waggish J. P., what is generally regarded as an important part of a work. These Comic Appendages contain apparently nothing essentially connected with the story of Titan, but only satirical hits at men and things in connection with the names of persons and places that occur in the work. For the sake, however, of one interesting thing found there (beside the aforesaid Preface), we will simply state that the "COMIC APPENDIX TO TITAN" consists of two (so-called) little volumes, the first of which ends with a "Preface to Titan," and after the second follows, as an "Appendix to the First Comic Appendix of Titan," a "CLAVIS FICHTIANA, SEU LEIBGEBERIANA" (*Key to Fichte, or Leibgeber*, — Leibgeber, alias Siebenkäs, alias Schoppe, being so much a quiz of the philosopher Fichte in the Titan itself).

The "Preface" is as follows: —

## "PREFACE TO TITAN.

"I WRITE it last, in order that it may not be read first. I will here leave the world free again, after I have had it in my service barely 2 hours 33 minutes and 36 seconds longer,* seeing that I have been in *its* service just so many years and months. Let it not begrudge me three words more; that is to say, seven last ones.

"The *first* is my joy in the fact that the readers, like children, have been obliged to eat the bread, which they would not bite at the table, afterward. With a similar stroke of art I shall drive them into my future flogging-cellars. For from this time forth no book of mine will appear without such an Appendix, — unless I send it out *first* and the work itself afterward. — Has not everything on this Anglicized comet-ball

* It is estimated that one can read 60 letters in a second, consequently a moderate octavo page in 16 seconds, therefore an alphabet † in an hour 42 minutes 24 seconds. My book I assume to be one alphabet and a half strong.

† Printer's term for 23 sheets. — TR.

its appendix [or -*dage*], — the Universal German Library the dearest, the Almanac the cheapest? — has not Robespierre his queue, — the comet of 1769, a tail of forty million miles, — the Predicaments,* four Postpredicaments, — and Kant, his Fichte?

"The *second* last word is to beg the reader that he will not quite yet — as I have hardly made a feeble beginning in my deliveries of Titan — draw two or three hundred conclusions therefrom, but wait for the twentieth volume. The *opus* desires to be judged like the moon, which rises bay-colored and swollen and cloudy, and which one needs to allow half a night's time before expecting to find her on her high-climbed pathway pure, white, and radiant. Modern romances easily get themselves into the greatest repute on the appearance of their very first volume, because they take no thought for the next morning (i. e. for the next volume), but enjoy the present; because they have not so much a plan — and thereby, too, the pauses in the same, the episodes, are avoided — as ten thousand plans, which they carry out one after the other; so that the work, when one gets it at length from the bookbinder, then and not till then, produces a good effect and represents a whole; just as the army-worm appears to the vulgar to roll itself along magnificently in a length of twelve ells, although it amounts only to an inch-deep procession of mere gnat-larvæ (*Larvæ tipulæ*). *My* infusorial, on the contrary, is entire, and yet is fed till it grows to a giant-snake, — but that is quite as wonderful.

"*Third* word. In every epic history there lie whole volumes full of morals, more than in a fable; but not otherwise than in actual history, which is not the daughter of moral philosophy, but the mother, of whom every one can beget such a daughter as he pleases. I find in the biographies which the Infinite One writes more poetry, more poetic justice and justification by motives, than in those which the heroes of the former, like poor fools, send to the press. A divine biography is,

* The Ten Predicaments are the various aspects or relations under which things may be considered. — Tr.

besides, not only a little work of art, but also a part of an infinitely great one; and we are all so bound to our paths that one must be able, from the diurnal arc of his life's epicycloid of the 988th power, to calculate the ellipse which humanity describes around the immovable Infinite; in other words, one can (bold as it may sound) from the incidents of his forenoon infer much with regard to the next that will appear in the newspaper.

"*Fourth* last word. They still continue in Jena, Wenigen-Jena, Jena-Priesnitz, and the surrounding localities, to moot the proposition, that a poet must, like a fly, travel along on transparent gauze-wings, and not on any heavily bedizened pinions of the bird of paradise. The reader, they continue without metaphor, cannot at once fly and carry; Pegasus cannot be a packhorse; still less may a poetic pinion like that of the angel alluded to have *eyes*, which at most can belong to the peacock's tail. —— Thereto I lately, while attending Mozart's *Zauberflöte*, came out with the striking answer, namely, the question: 'But the opera, good people? — Must not here, 1st, the genial interworking of all the instruments, as well as, what is quite as great, of all the actors; 2dly, the optical, and, 3dly, the acoustic imitation; then, 4thly, the poetic composition itself; and finally and 5thly, the splendor of the decoration, — be all comprehended and enjoyed at once? A building in the *five* orders of architecture is easier for you than *one* with gorgeous foliaceous ornamentation? The five wise virgins at once leave you wiser than one foolish one? — Say, Jenaite! But no; write on, and a happy journey home to you in this infernal cold!'

"Since one word begets another, and accordingly the *fifth* begets the *sixth*, I give my word with both, that to-day, on which I say my last word and this next, is to me no day of finding a cross, but of taking down from one. Is not to-day Virgil's day, and are not the first volume of this work and the first and last winter months over? — For to-morrow there blooms for me the morn of spring; namely, the first of February, the Sunday eve (*Sonnabend*) of Candlemas. Already must many a freezing German have with me found in February the aurora of spring, at least in the rapid lengthening of the days. Hovers not already in the cold ether out there the first vernal song, the first fluttering lark? Does not the wren climb and glide up along a black bough, dripping in the sunshine, and chirp, warmly gilded with bright rays, his winter-solo? Does not the returning sun re-bind my manuscript books with gilt edges? and has not my neighbor shoved up the slides of his beehives, that the merry bee-tribe may joyously fling themselves forth from the narrow, sultry prisons upon the fresh green, variegated, not with flowers, but with sunbeams, and creep about over it with vigor? — Virgil, whose anniversary is to-day celebrated, on *thy* grave they break now only fictitious laurel-twigs; but on the graves of the seasons ever fresh ones bloom after. —

"To-day shall, after a long satirical ice-month of quarrelling, reconcile me again to the times. Let my last and *seventh* word be, Peace! as He also said it who spake the seven words on a more painful wood than my writing-table is.

"Peace be with the age! — one should often exclaim to himself.* As an annoying day does not put us out in the hopes of our life, so neither should a suffering century deprive us of that hope wherewith we paint the far future. The pyramid of the age seems, like an Egyptian one, to lift itself up, either to a narrow and sharp apex, or into completeness; but when one climbs it, the summit proves to be a roomy level.

"Where a *goal* appears to us divine, there must *the road* also have been so; because *this* was once *that*, and that will become this. Well may we all be nearer to Thee, O Infinite One, than we know: — for Thou only canst know how near we are; and we live *in* Thee, not merely *from* Thee, just as our earth moves in the midst of the atmosphere of the sun's globe,† while it seems only to revolve far off around his light."

* *Cry into himself*, is the German.

† The zodiacal light manifests the dipping of the earth into the sun's atmosphere.

Explanation of Title. — As regards the title of Titan, the translator has been strongly tempted to fall back upon his first idea, that Jean Paul hardly meant, after all, anything more definite by it than to express the magnitude of his aspiration in undertaking the work; and that, as Mr. Longfellow's "Hyperion" hints at a book of the beautiful, so *Titan*, like *Hesperus*, has a corresponding, more moral than mythological reference, and signifies that this was to be the author's Titanic work.

## NOTES TO VOL. I.

Page xi. — By some slip or confusion of memory, the first and second editions were made to say, in the note, that Louisa, one of the four reigning sisters to whom Titan is dedicated, lived in the *Liberation* War. This mistake probably arose from mixing up the French Revolution with Körner's august apostrophes to Louisa as guardian genius of her people in the later war for freedom.

Page 2, line 8. "Wolf's tooth." — The tooth of a wolf or boar, or some other animal, was once used just as we use an ivory handle, or (sometimes) the thumb-nail, to rub down smooth the paper from which ink-marks had been erased. — Line 15. "Burning-glass" means here properly a *concave-mirror* (Brenn-*spiegel* in German, — there being another word, Brenn-*glas*, corresponding to our common burning and magnifying glass). — Line 18. "Cutting *hollow*"; *concave grinding* would seem a more scientific phrase, but the word *hollow* seemed necessary in carrying out the *moral* allusion.

Page 5, line 27. — The reference is probably to *Wilcke*, who broached a new theory about magnetism, that of two fluids. (See art. in Encyc. Britan.)

Page 5, line 31. "When it struck 23 o'clock." — The Italian clocks, though they indicate on the face up to 24, strike only to 12.

The above is a comparative table of German and Italian ways of reckoning time, adapted to the latter half of September. It is taken from Goethe's Italian Tour. He says: "The inner circle denotes our 24 hours, from midnight to midnight, divided into twice 12, as we reckon, and our clocks indicate. The middle circle shows how the Italian clocks strike at the present season (namely, up to 12 twice in 24 hours), but in such a way that it strikes 1 when it strikes 8 with us, and so on. . . . Finally, the outer circle shows how the 24 hours are reckoned in actual life. For example, I hear 7 o'clock striking in the night, and know that midnight is at 5 o'clock; I therefore deduct the latter number from the former and thus have 2 hours after midnight. If I hear 7 in the daytime, as I know that noon is at 5, I have 2 P. M. But if I wish to express the hour according to the fashion of this country, I must know that noon is 17 o'clock; I add the 2, and get 19 o'clock." It must have been, it would seem, then, *in his mind* that Albano would have "counted up the tedious strokes."

Page 6, line 16. "Juno Ludovici." — The fine colossal head known as the *Lodovisi* Juno (so Murray spells it) in the Villa Lodovisi.

Page 9, line 24. — " Kremnitz " is a town in Moravia. The

ducats coined there were of the very finest gold. — Line 24. "More *lightly* on her *left* arm," — *and therefore the old man was not actuated purely by the pious motives which Albano gave him credit for, but by more mercenary ones,* — is the connecting link to be supplied before the next clause.

Page 11, line 12. — "Micromegas," — *little giant.*

Page 19, line 13. — Bouverot, here called the German Gentleman (in German, the *Deutsche Herr*), was in reality a *Teutscher Ordensherr*, or Teutonic Knight. The translator has throughout simply called him the *Gentleman*, merely, however, by a sort of general, parliamentary etiquette, and not, of course, as if the word defined his technical standing. The reader will please bear this in mind.

Page 19, note. — He was also nicknamed *Peter de Mulieribus.* He was a fine painter, but a coarse-grained scapegrace. Was born at Haerlem in 1637. Went to Italy, and from Calvinist became Papist. Was famous for his animals and landscapes. In Italy he fell in love with a woman, and, as he already had a wife, he sent for *her* to come to him, and then caused her to be murdered on the road. He was arrested and sentenced to be hung, but, in the confusion consequent on the breaking out of some war, escaped, and died in 1701.

Page 20. — The translator confesses himself in the dark (with a scholarly German friend also) as to the process which may have been pursued by Don Gaspard with that German debauchee. It may simply be that Gaspard operated on the man by holding out worldly inducements to make him play the saint, and then, by disappointing them, left him to sink back again to his real character.

Page 21, line 7. — The Pasquino was a mutilated statue, so called from a cobbler who had his shop near it, and was always quizzing and caricaturing passers-by. After his death, the statue, which had come to be nearly buried in the ground, was dug up, and people said, "Here is old Pasquin come to life again!" When any one wanted to satirize a public or private enemy, he would affix his lampoon secretly to the Pasquin statue. The statue of Marforio, supposed to be that of a river-god, which, about the end of the sixteenth century, was placed near the Capitol, was made the vehicle of replying to the attacks of Pasquin.

Page 22, line 10. — If any one would see how queerly Jean Paul used his queer knowledge, — what

> " A sea-change
> Into something rare and strange,"

the driest material "suffered" in passing over the ocean of his fantasy, — let him read the article in Bayle's Dictionary on Gaspar Scioppius. Scioppius, a German critic, philologist, and controversialist, equally remarkable for acumen and acrimony, was born in 1576; had a precocious youth; changed from a Protestant to a Catholic, and wrote bitterly against his old friends, and even against the King of England; then became equally bitter against the Jesuits; and, after a life of constant quarrelling with living and dead scholars (for he charged even Cicero with barbarous Latin), "he died," says a biographer, "universally hated and hating," in 1649. One of his opponents called him the "Grammarian Cur." — As Jean Paul makes *his* Schoppe call himself *Titular Librarian*, &c., it may be worth mentioning that the historical Scioppius had the following titles: "Patrician of Rome, Knight of St. Peter, Counsellor to the Emperor, Counsellor to the King of Spain, Counsellor to the Archduke, Count Palatine, and Count de Clara Valle" (Clairvaux).

Page 25, line 21. — *Trembley* led the way in the actual study from life of the Polype tribe, particularly the *hydra.* "Sometimes two polypes will seize on the same worm; and most amusing is it then to witness the struggle that ensues, sometimes resulting in the swallowing of the weaker polype by the stronger, which, however, is soon disgorged with no other loss than his dinner." "If the body be halved in any direction, each half grows into a perfect hydra." "When a polype is introduced by the tail into another body, the two unite and form one individual; and when a head is lopped off, it may safely be engrafted on the body of any other which may chance to want one." "A polype, cut transversely in three parts, requires four or five days in summer, and longer in cold weather, for the middle piece to produce a head and tail, and the tail part to get a body and head." — *English Cyclop.*

Page 26, line 23. — The pigeons spoken of are the common house-pigeons. (In German, *Flug*-taube: pigeons that go in *flocks*, — which misled the translator in the first edition to call them *wild* pigeons.) I am told that Jean Paul is here really picturing his own traits too. For instance, it is said he would not look in at a shop-door in passing, lest he should hold out promises which he was not going to perform.

Page 27, line 22. — "Snow-*ball*." (In German, *Kugel:* globe, — *ball* being the word used where the *snow-ball* of the schoolboys is meant.)

Page 31, line 10. — Gold wedges, — "the *golden wedge* of Ophir." In the first edition the word *Stufen* was rendered *steps.* But it has also a technical meaning of *ore* in masses or strata.

Page 35, line 32. — Otto Guerike, who was born at Magdeburg in 1602, and died in 1686, invented the air-pump and the barometer. The Wetter-männchen was a little man on the top of the clock, for instance, who came out in fair weather and went in in foul; or one in a bottle with a skin cover, who rose and sunk according to the pressure of the atmosphere. (See the *Bubbles of Nassau.*)

Page 38, line 13. — If Gaspard was simply a Knight of the Fleece, Jean Paul would seem to have taken a liberty in decorating him. "The decoration of the *Grand Master* is a chain composed of alternate flints and rays of steel, with the golden fleece fastened in the middle. The *Knights* wear a golden fleece on a red ribbon." — Line 17. Dragons and basilisks are both *amphibia* in the strict sense, only the two dwelling-places of the former are *air* and land, and of the latter *water* and land. The basilisk has a membranous bag on the back of his head which can be filled with air at pleasure, and also a spinal fin along his back, which adapt him to swimming.

Page 43, line 16. — The *flower* on behind the stag is the hunter's name for *tail.*

Page 44, line 11. — " Bed-*tail* " does not mean here, as an English reader might imagine, the foot-board, but the cord hanging down like a bell-rope befere the nose of the sleeper, by which old or feeble persons (in Germany) used to raise themselves out of bed. In the Eighth Dog-Post-Day of *Hesperus,* Victor is represented as raising himself slowly by the bed-tassel out of bed, which he usually left with a spring. One would think it would need mechanical aid to hoist the fevered frame from *under* a German feather-bed.

Page 47, line 25. — The *piping* of Schoppe was simply with his *windpipe;* the *whistle* one is said to *wet* when he drinks.

Page 48, line 14. — " Dissolving " is not quite strong enough. The idea is, that, as ships have their bolts drawn out by the *lodestone* and fall apart, so the senses fall apart as man sinks to slumber.

Page 52, line 24. — *After*-Stimme means, strictly, *mock*-voice.

Page 59, line 10. — " Cellini's History "; i. e. probably Goethe's translation of Benvenuto's Autobiography.

Page 60, line 18. — " Dog-Post-Day " is the title of the chapters of *Hesperus,* a former work of Jean Paul's, which he pretends to have composed on an island in some Indian Ocean, the materials being brought to him by a dog who swam over from the mainland with the basket containing them in his teeth; and the days of the dog's arriving with fresh material were called *Dog-Post-Days.*

Page 61, line 19. — The "*chiffre banal*" is the common cipher.

Page 62, line 15. — " Veimers," — so Jean Paul spells it. " Vehmic (or Fehmic) courts were secret tribunals, established in Germany in the Middle Ages, terrible from the secrecy with which they carried on their proceedings, as well as from their organization and the extent of their authority. The members, who at one time are said to have amounted to not less than one hundred thousand, were bound by a horrible oath to secrecy, and to obey and carry out the laws of the order. These tribunals are said to have originated with Charlemagne; but it was not till the thirteenth century that they reached their greatest prominence. The lawlessness and anarchy which prevailed at that time gave them work to do, and they gathered strength in the performance of it. They were professedly established to support virtue and honor; but there is no doubt they were often perverted to the gratification of private malice and tyranny. Westphalia was the great centre of their jurisdiction, and was hence termed the Red Land." See Wigand's *Fehmgerichte Westphalens*, 1827. A very good popular account of this court may also be found in Markham's History of Germany, Chap. XXI. (Supplement). — Line 17. "Pointeurs." See note to p. 221.

Page 63, line 12. — The author refers here to a process of slipping off the outer coating of the quill by soaking it in boiling water.

Page 64, line 12. "Wooden legs." — *Spindle-shanks* would better express the author's slur. — Line 26. The *cul de Paris* is what is technically called the *bishop* or *bustle*.

Page 76, line 26. — "Flying [i. e. transient] teachers" (*journeymen*).

Page 80, line 32. "Ah, what bliss," &c. — Compare a passage in Faust (p. 58 in Brooks's translation), beginning, "O for a wing," &c.

Page 82, line 17. "Fatal." — This German word is hard to translate here. Perhaps *plaguy* or *confounded* would help give the idea.

Page 84, line 14. — "The *lost* son" means of course the *Prodigal Son*.

Page 86, line 5. "Diabolically possessed," — "des Teufels

auf Bänder." Literally, "the Devil on ribbons"; or, as we should say, *death on ribbons*.

Page 87, line 2. — Jean Paul may well have recalled his own sore experience on the subject of queues. See his biography, as referred to in Carlyle's article on Richter. — In the next paragraph, "the everlasting rogue" is, in German, the *persistent Mæcenas*, — alluding to Albano's lavishing of his patronage on the blind girl. — In the next paragraph, the translator is responsible for the play on the word *monkey;* Jean Paul having simply *Capuchinades*.

Page 92, line 7. — A music-pen is an instrument for ruling five parallel lines at once.

Page 93, line 28. — "Real territion" (or terrification) is explained in a note to Vol. II. p. 1.

Page 95, line 1. — The special kind of *floor* which Jean Paul's fancy calls up is the *threshing*-floor. — Line 7. In regard to the "leather aprons," it may be proper to mention that *miners*, to whom the musicians had been compared on the previous page, wear them *behind*.

Page 98, line 30. — "The new commission"; i. e. the newly appointed tutor, Falterle.

Page 100, line 15. — "Pump-chambers" is a figurative expression here for *top-boots*. — Line 21. The word rendered "chub" may mean *tadpole*.

Page 101, line 23. — A "pike *au four*" (*four* meaning *oven*) is simply a *baked pike*.

Page 102, line 6. — "Shop-keeper" here does not mean the *man* who keeps shop, but an article that *keeps the shop;* i. e. remains on the shelf as unsalable lumber. "Keep" is used in the same sense as when we say one *keeps his bed* or *keeps house* when sick. — "Paste-eels" are minute creatures found on scraping away the paste from under the binding of an old book.

Page 103, line 13. "St. John." — See Mrs. Jameson's Poetry of Legendary Art, Vol. I. p. 168. "St. John had a tame partridge, which he cherished much; and he amused himself with feeding and tending it. A certain huntsman, passing by with his bow and arrows, was astonished to see the great Apostle, so venerable for his age and sanctity, engaged in such an amusement. The Apostle asked him if he always kept his bow bent. He answered, that would be the way to render it useless. 'If,' replied St. John, 'you unbend your bow to prevent its being useless, so do I thus unbend my mind for the same reason.'"

Page 107, line 18. "Wehmeier's." — Jean Paul uses here the old-fashioned double genitive. *Wehmeier's seiner* (Wehmeier's's) like our antiquated *hissen*, which we still sometimes hear from the lips of old people.

Page 111, line 26. — "The history of countries"; i. e. of individual countries, — the beginning, e. g., with that of one's own country as a centre, and going backward.

Page 112, line 25. — *Kanstein* was the founder of a Bible-establishment for the printing and diffusion of the Scriptures.

Page 113, line 9. — *Foundery*, or perhaps a *gallery* of casts.

Page 114, line 12. — His thoughts fell upon the Middlemark. This was one of the three Marches (hence the words Marquis and Marchioness), — Alt-Mark, Neu-Mark, and Mittel-Mark, — in which last Berlin was, and Frederick lived.

Page 114, line 16. — Christoph Scheiner, a German mathematician and astronomer, eminent for being one of the first who discovered spots on the sun (in 1611, a few months after Galileo), was born at Wald, near Mundelheim, in Swabia, in 1575, and died in 1660.

Page 115, line 9. "Partner." — In the German, *Moitistinn*, a somewhat hard word, apparently of Jean Paul's own coining, from the French *moitié*.

Page 123, line 25. — Aldert van Everdingen, a celebrated Dutch painter of wild and rugged landscapes, was born at Alkmaar in 1621, and died in 1675. "Some of his fine *forests* are extremely true and picturesque." — John van Huysum, born at

Amsterdam in 1682, "was the most eminent painter of *flowers* and fruits in the eighteenth century. Every term of panegyric that language can furnish has been lavished, and with justice, on his productions. He seems to have dived into the mysteries of Nature, to represent the loveliest and most brilliant of her creations with all the magic of her own pencil. His *flowers*, however, are more beautiful and true to nature than his fruits."

Page 124, line 33. "Leaves of her heart." — Literally, however, *heart-leaves*, a technical term in botany.

Page 134, line 17. — That is, by this course which he had now adopted, he put himself beyond the reach of those severe censors.

Page 135, line 11. — "Murmuring" is hardly strong enough here to give the force of the *many-meaning* German word *brausend*. "Roaring" would come nearer to it.

Page 136, line 17: —

"'T is better to have loved and lost,
Than never to have loved at all."

TENNYSON.

"O, in this chilly world, too fast
The doubting fiend pursues our youth!
Better be cheated to the last
Than lose the glorious hope of truth!"

FANNY KEMBLE.

Page 141, 2d note. — The meaning seems to be, that strips of gold-foil were hung up to flutter round and frighten the birds, just as our farmers hang up strips of tin for scarecrows.

Page 146, line 3. "She kept," &c. — There is something very obscure here. For the German reads that the old Princess made this comparison "im Wahne der Verschwisterung" (under the illusion or in a fancy of relationship). Now Eleonore knew that this was her son Albano; because, in the letter she wrote to him that day and laid up (see Vol. II. p. 493), she says, "To-day I have seen thee again," &c. May the meaning be, then, that Eleonore tried to imagine by looking at the children that Albano might be a relative of hers? Or had Richter forgotten that Eleonore knew who Albano was, and does the *bonus Homerus dormitat* here?

Page 157, line 33. — The *cane;* more exactly, the *pike.*

Page 159, line 20. — "Adopt" is rather too strong a word. "Take an interest in them" is all the original requires.

Page 164, line 4. — We use the phrase "within four walls" as synonymous with "in a room"; and in this case there would be *three* rooms or *twelve* walls (one of J. P.'s trivial niceties).

Page 168, line 21. — The *fat-eye* (*exophthalmy* it was wrongly rendered in the first editions) means such little *globules* of fat as show themselves, for instance, on the surface of *bouilli*, or marrow boiled down.

Page 169, line 7. — As army-cloth shrinks when wet, so Malt grows thin and falls away under the soaking of his tears.

Page 176, line 2. "It is a sin," &c. — There is a degree of obscurity in this sentence arising from the elliptical and allusive style Jean Paul employs; but the "innocent conditions" seems to mean the extent to which one may safely go in certain pleasures. Surgeons attend at the rack to tell how far torture may be carried without producing death; * but no physician is at hand to tell the poor prince how much he may enjoy without killing himself.

Page 177, line 11. — "Scholar-like"; more properly, *tyro-like.* The Germans hardly have a word corresponding to our *scholar* as meaning a scholarly man. Their *Schüler* means a *learner*, not one who is *learned.*

Page 178, line 7. — "Sprinkled him with rose-vinegar"; i. e. gently rebuked his moral indifference.

Page 178, line 9. — Luigi's father was lying on the coffin-board (or bier); and L. himself was in that state of stupidity, thick-headedness, and brazen-facedness which the proverb describes: "Er hat ein Bret vor dem Kopf."

Page 181, line 28. — "Fire-mounds," or, more exactly, *fire-*

* See Vol. II. p. 74.

*moles;* described in the German works as *feuer-rothe Muttermäler* (fiery-red marks inherited from a mother).

Page 184, line 7. — "Leading-hounds," — or *pointers,* which gives rather more effect to the surprise produced by saying, after the dash, instead of *noses,* — *ears.* — The allusion to *le Cain* of course has a double meaning, referring not only to the actor, but to the wicked and murderous brother.

Page 188, line 12. — "Chap-sager," sap-sago, — derived from two words, meaning *scraped cheese.*

Page 188, line 21. — When children in Germany are set at a little side-table, they are said to "sitzen am Katz-tische." These expressions come from the custom of giving the cat a side-bit while the dinner is going on. — Line 31. The Ephraimite was a coin named after one Ephraim, a Jew, who alloyed the legal coin of the Empire. The counterfeit was readily to be detected by suspending the piece in wine, the acid of which acted upon the spurious element, and turned the metal black.

Page 197, line 2. "TEN PERSECUTIONS." — In allusion, of course, to the number the Christians are estimated to have suffered under the Roman Emperor.

Page 203, line 25. "The gossiping letter." — *Gevatter's-brief* (godfather's letter), a request to her to stand as godmother.

Page 211, line 1. — A *Spanish wall* means a temporary partition put up to make two rooms of one.

Page 213, line 27. — "Sun-path," used here in the astronomical sense and figuratively. "Sweet moon, I thank thee for thy *sunny* beams!" says Pyramus. — In line 12 occurs again that peculiar word *fatal,* which does not bear exactly our sense, but means ugly, disagreeable, &c.

Page 215, line 15. — "He can't count more than five," is a proverb expressing dulness or stupidity.

Page 217, line 17. — "Conditions"; i. e. apprentices, hires.

Page 218, line 3. — "A box of letters"; i. e. a case of type.

Page 219, line 3. — The time of the Indiction among the Romans was that wherein the people were summoned (*indicted*) to pay a certain tribute. — The Romish or Papal Indiction, which is that used in the Pope's bull, begins on the first of January.

Page 221, bottom. (*Faro* is said to derive its name from *Pharaoh*, whose image was formerly on one of the cards.) — " The banker turns up the cards from a complete pack, one by one, laying them first to his right for the bank, and then to his left for the *punter* (or player, so called from the Italian *puntare*), till all the cards are dealt out. The banker wins when the card equal in points to that on which the stake is set turns up on his right hand, but loses when it is dealt to the left."

Page 224, line 13. " A round pearl." — *Zahl-perle* means strictly a pearl that is counted, not weighed.

Page 225, line 31. — The translator was not sure whether the abbreviative H. prefixed to these names meant *Heilige* or *Herrn;* and he chose the former, merely because the author calls them *disciples*.

Page 242, line 11. — *Hirschfeld* (erroneously translated *deer-field*) is a proper name, of a writer quite obsolete now, who lived from 1742 to 1792, and wrote a work on country life. Richter says that Lilar is not like a page out of Hirschfeld (made to order).

Page 243, line 23. — Of the "wild Germander," old Thomas Johnson says in his Historie of Plants, 1633, " The floures be of a gallant blew colour, standing orderlie on the tops of the tender, spriggy spraies."

Page 246, line 3. — Castor and Pollux were brothers of Helen; and, according to one tradition, *all* were born at once, being children of Zeus and Leda. Horace calls them

> "Fratres Helenæ, lucida sidera."
>
> Carm. 1. 3.

Page 248, " 43ª cycle." — It was apparently an oversight

of Jean Paul's, making *two* 43d cycles, and it was left so in all the editions.

Page 252, line 19. "Sad-cloak." — A butterfly called the *Trauermantel*, or *mourning mantle*.

Page 262, line 26. — *Blazing sea* is a bold figure. Perhaps *boiling* would be more appropriate to the outer element, though not to Albano's inner emotion.

Page 267, line 4. — "Voice" means here *vote*.

Page 272, line 22. — There is a trick of language here, which cannot be given in translation, but only in explanation. The idea is that Schoppe was *turning* (or rather twisting) something similar to what the children were making; namely, an imaginary nose. Now in English we have no concise expression for that symbolic art of pressing the thumb to the nose and stretching the fingers into the air with a whirling motion, to convey the idea of having outwitted the person pointed at. The gesture is described very elaborately in one of Marryatt's novels; and Bon Gualtier, in his parody of Locksley Hall, speaks of "coffee-milling care and sorrow, with a nose-adapted thumb."

Page 284, line 7. — "Shut up," literally *crooks up*, as a prisoner is doubled up by fetters.

Page 285, line 9. — The "Charles" referred to is *Charlemagne*. "Sacramentarian" is strictly the English of *Sacramentierer;* but the word Schoppe uses is *Sacramenter*, which may mean one who says *Sacrament!* (a vulgar oath). Or it might be translated here "a poor curse."

Page 286, second note. — Subscription is called in German *prænumeration*, because the subscribers are numbered, or the money counted out, beforehand.

Page 291, line 6. — This does not fully express the ceremony, which consisted in breaking the helmet in pieces, and flinging them in upon the coffin.

Page 298, line 17. — "Awaiting his sword," which he had been obliged to leave behind on entering.

Page 299, line 11. "Paper dragon." — The German name for a child's kite.

Page 301, line 31. Properly rendered, "What will he — you?" — The mechanic, thinking at first he was addressing one of his own class, used the familiar "he," then, recognizing his mistake, he changed it to the more respectful "you."

Page 306, line 9. — "Whipped" is too strong an expression. The meaning is, that, the punishment having been commuted to a mere grazing of the neck with a rod (twig), the penitent had died under the stroke by the effect of imagination; — as is said to have actually occurred in the case of a beadle at a German university, whom the students, after a mock-trial, pretended they were going to execute, and, having laid his head on the block, simply struck it with a sausage, when to their horror he died of pure fright.

Page 312, line 4. — It was not a chocolate *mill*, but a twirling stick to stir chocolate. — Line 8. "Support"; i. e. to lay paper on for writing.

Page 312, line 33. — Richter has, not "Russia," but *Saanen*.

Page 327, line 7. — "Bleeds" *to death*, is the force of the original.

Page 329, line 32. "Just then," &c. — Compare a passage in Richter's "New Year's Night of an Unhappy Man."

Page 335, line 10. — Jordan- or paper-almonds are those of which the shell is scraped to the thinness of paper.

Page 387, line 15. — The "touching ambiguity" spoken of cannot be expressed in the English translation. It lies in the fact that Albano's last three words, *es seines wird*, may mean either "When it becomes his," or "When his is so"; i. e. my heart will be happy when his is so.

Page 390, line 2. — The "English horsetails" are the *Bobtails*.

Page 391, line 2. "Overstrained image." — Rather the *stretched pictures* (as pictures are stretched in framing).

Page 392, line 5. — "Thickness" is a proper name; but

the translator has not been able to learn anything of him, or of the fact here adduced on his authority.

Page 393, line 18. "To dream and *enjoy*." — Instead of *geniessen*, some editions have *genesen*, to *get well.*

Page 405, line 12. — The *Schneider's skin* is the *Schneiderian membrane*, so called from its discoverer, Conrad Victor Schneider, who was born in 1610, was Professor of Medicine and Physician to the Elector, and in 1660 wrote a treatise, "De Catarrhis," in six books, devoted chiefly to an anatomical description of the cavities of the nose.

Page 429, line 14. — The literal meaning of this bold figure is, "It struck epileptically, till they bled, the limbs of the inner man."

Page 436, line 22. — The *time-keeper* means the *metronome.*

Page 465, line 18. — The "seven pleasure-stations" allude to the stations in the Catholic Church, which are a series of pictured scenes in the life of Christ, before which the devotee successively pauses. They correspond here to the "Point of View, No. 1," "Point of View, No. 2," and so on, which one meets in the neighborhood of certain great wonders of Nature, such as Niagara Falls.

Page 469, line 7. "The wain." — Query, *Charles's Wain.*

Page 475, line 24. "The golden splendor of the strings of joy." — One edition has *Der goldene Seiten-* [instead of *Saiten-*] *glanz der Freude,* — "The golden side-glance of joy."

Page 479, line 16. "The fiery rain," &c. — One edition has *Wagen* instead of *Regen,* — the fiery *chariot.*

## NOTES TO VOL. II.

Page 74, line 25. "The laughter-plant." — "The *Illyrium Crow-foot*," says Thomas Johnson, in his "History of Plants," p. 953, "in Greek, may be that kind of crow-foot called *Apium risus*, and γελωτοφυη [laughter-producing]; and this is thought to be that *Gelotophyllis* of which Pliny maketh mention in his 24th Booke, 17th chapter, which being drunke, saith he, with wine and myrrhe, causeth a man to see divers strange sights, and not to cease laughing till he hath drunk Pine-apple kernels with pepper in wine of the Date-tree (I think he would have said untill he be dead), because the nature of laughing Crow-foot is to kill laughing, but without doubt the thing is clean contrary; for it causeth such convulsions, cramps, and wringings of the mouth and jaws, that it hath seemed to some that the parties died laughing, whereas in truth they have died in great torment."

Page 487, line 20. — Hemsterhuis, a Dutch critic and philologist, of remarkable precocity, was born in Groningen in 1685, entered the University at fourteen, and at nineteen became Professor of Mathematics and Philosophy at Amsterdam. He died at Leyden in 1766.

Page 499, line 29. — Saint Alban is said to have been the first martyr for Christianity in Britain. He renounced Paganism in Rome, and suffered martyrdom during the persecutions under Dioclesian. A monastery was built in his memory, and around it grew up the town of St. Alban's.

Page 500, line 1. — Philip the Good, Duke of Burgundy, founded the order of *el toysón de oro*, on occasion of his marriage with the Princess Isabella of Portugal, January 10, 1430.

Page 508, line 4. — Nicholas Jerome Gundling, a learned and in his day noted professor of law and eloquence, was born near Nuremberg, and died in 1729 at Halle, where he had been Rector of the University. He left many works, among them "Otia, or a Collection of Discourses on Physical, Moral, Political, and Historical Topics," in 3 vols., 8vo.

---

Cambridge: Stereotyped and Printed by Welch, Bigelow, & Co.

www.ingramcontent.com/pod-product-compliance
Lightning Source LLC
LaVergne TN
LVHW020923110826
845150LV00004B/749

* 9 7 8 1 4 2 5 5 5 4 8 6 6 *